MOSQUITO MEN

DAVID PRICE's early interest in aviation was inspired by days exploring deserted RAF airfields in his native Cumbria. He has written for many newspapers and magazines on military aviation and is the author of *A Bomber Crew Mystery: The Forgotten Heroes of 388th Bombardment Group* and *The Crew*, the story of an Avro Lancaster crew during the Second World War.

ALSO BY DAVID PRICE

The Crew: The Story of a Lancaster Bomber Crew

*A Bomber Crew Mystery: The Forgotten Heroes
of 388th Bombardment Group*

DAVID PRICE

MOSQUITO MEN

THE ELITE PATHFINDERS OF
627 SQUADRON

HEAD
of ZEUS

An Apollo Book

First published in the UK in 2022 by Head of Zeus
This paperback edition first published in 2023 by Head of Zeus,
part of Bloomsbury Publishing Plc.

9 7 5 3 1 2 4 6 8

A catalogue record for this book is available
from the British Library.

ISBN (PB): 9781800242302
ISBN (E): 9781800242319

Typeset by Adrian McLaughlin
Maps by Jeff Edwards

Printed and bound in Great Britain by
CPI Group (UK) Ltd, Croydon CRO 4YY

MIX
Paper | Supporting
responsible forestry
FSC® C171272

Head of Zeus
5–8 Hardwick Street
London EC1R 4RG

WWW.HEADOFZEUS.COM

*To my father, whose passion for history
is an inspiration*

Contents

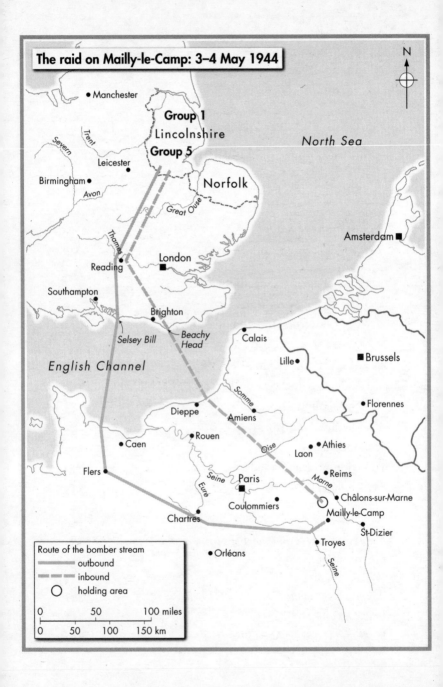

The raid on Mailly-le-Camp: 3–4 May 1944

N

- Manchester

Group 1
Lincolnshire
Group 5

Norfolk

North Sea

Severn

Trent

- Leicester

Birmingham •

Avon

Great Ouse

Thames

- Reading

London ■

Amsterdam ■

Southampton •

Brighton

Selsey Bill

Beachy
Head

English Channel

Calais •

Lille •

■ Brussels

Somme

• Dieppe

Amiens

• Florennes

• Caen

• Rouen

Oise

• Athies

Laon

Flers •

Seine

Eure

Paris ■

Marne

• Reims

Chartres

Coulommiers

Mailly-le-Camp

■ Châlons-sur-Marne

St-Dizier •

• Troyes

Seine

• Orléans

Route of the bomber stream
— outbound
--- inbound
○ holding area

0   50   100 miles
0   50   100   150 km

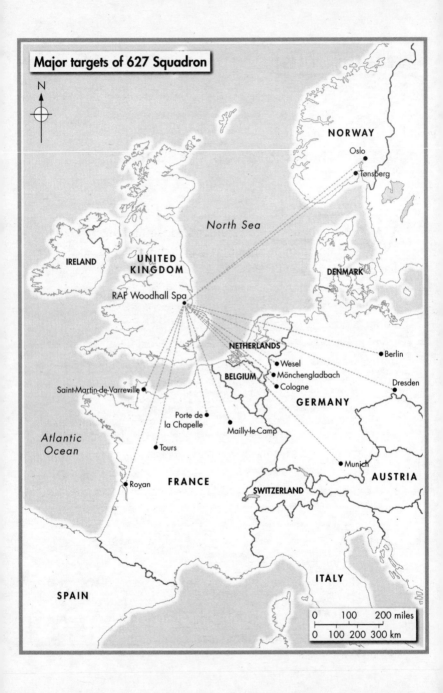

Major targets of 627 Squadron

N

NORWAY
Oslo
Tønsberg

North Sea

IRELAND

UNITED KINGDOM

RAF Woodhall Spa

DENMARK

NETHERLANDS

BELGIUM

Berlin
Wesel
Mönchengladbach
Cologne

Dresden

GERMANY

Saint-Martin-de-Varreville

Porte de la Chapelle
Mailly-le-Camp

Atlantic Ocean

Tours

Munich

AUSTRIA

Royan

FRANCE

SWITZERLAND

SPAIN

ITALY

| 0 | 100 | 200 miles |
| 0 | 100 200 | 300 km |

A Note from the Author

Writing about the de Havilland Mosquito engendered a certain amount of trepidation in me. Previous authors have covered almost every technical specification of this legendary aeroplane, from tyre sizes to the thickness of its wooden composite construction. They have written in detail about its outstanding performance and the many and varied roles it played throughout the Second World War. With so many studious tomes written on this most fascinating of aircraft, was there anything new to say?

As a subject for a storyteller, the Mosquito does not disappoint. Novel in construction and exceptionally fast, it encouraged feats of audacity and courage on the part of its fliers. It is an aircraft that from its earliest development placed new capabilities in the hands of its crew; for the Royal Air Force, it became the first true multi-role combat aircraft. What tends to be missing from the many accounts of the Mosquito are the stories of the men who flew them. Their names and ranks appear, but we learn very little about who these men were and where they came from – or how they came to be flying one of the most advanced aeroplanes of the era.

Some years ago I had the pleasure of welcoming the Commander of the Battle of Britain Memorial Flight to a Veterans' Day at my local air museum. He had just dazzled the crowd with a low pass in a shining blue Mark XIX Spitfire, its Rolls-Royce Griffon engine producing the combination of musical note and growl that drew spectators like a magnet to the runway boundary fence. There was no denying that this most iconic of Second World War aircraft could woo a crowd into a state of misty-eyed romanticism. Later, over a mug of coffee, the Wing Commander confessed that it was the aeroplanes people came to see, and not the pilots. This truth struck a chord with me and, as an aviation enthusiast of many years standing, I realized that I too could be guilty of neglecting that most critical component of any aircraft, housed in the cockpit – its crew. The success of any wartime operation was not solely about the technical prowess of the flying machine, but at heart had to be about the skill and character of the men who controlled it.

It was while carrying out research for my previous book, *The Crew: The Story of a Lancaster Bomber Crew*, that I first came across the fearless young men of 627 Squadron, who were involved in low-level target marking in de Havilland Mosquitos. Apart from an excellent book published by the Squadron Association in 1991, *At First Sight* – a selection of first-hand accounts by the airmen themselves – there has been no comprehensive study of their exploits. This volume, alongside the expanded writings on the 627 that appear on the Squadron Association website, has been invaluable. All of its contributors, bar one, at the time of writing, are no longer with us, but by corresponding with their families I have been able to piece together their experiences of flying with the Squadron. Their family archives provide a treasure trove of previously unseen photographs, diaries and word-of-mouth accounts that deserve to reach a wider audience. The constraints of space mean that the personal stories I tell here represent only a small proportion of the riches contained in these resources, but hopefully enough to allow the reader to enter these men's lives for a short time, and to share a small part of their experience of flying the de Havilland Mosquito.

Over the past thirty years, I have taken every opportunity I could to speak to the remaining eyewitnesses of the air war. To spend time talking to old men about their youth is always rewarding, amusing and poignant – often all in the same sitting. I count it a great privilege to have been able to visit and speak to Ken Oatley – to my knowledge the last surviving airman of the illustrious group who flew with 627 Squadron. His accounts are particularly vivid, his sharp mind recalling wartime events as if they had taken place only yesterday. He is the last among us to have seen their target grow large in the small windscreen of a Mosquito as it dived to place its markers. Ken met – and served with – such men as Guy Gibson and Leonard Cheshire. His period of combat flying was a brief interlude in his one-hundred years of living, yet, as with so many of his compatriots, the experience forged his character for the years ahead.

Investigating the exploits of 627 Squadron requires the writer not only to tell the story of the de Havilland Mosquito itself, but also – in order to set this singular aircraft in its strategic context and explain the necessity of its particular method of flying – to provide some wider background narrative of the bombing war in which it took part. There is, accordingly, some overlap between *Mosquito Men* and my previous book, *The Crew*, but I have – wherever possible – attempted to keep repetition within bounds. The narrative of *The Crew* was built around the lives of seven airmen who flew together in the same heavy bomber; *Mosquito Men* offers more of a tapestry of characters, all of them interconnected by their association with an extraordinary flying machine, but each coming with his own unique story. I make no apology for including extended details of the crews' lives and experiences before they joined 627 Squadron. The character and skills of the men who flew the Mosquito were forged by what they had learned from flying other types of aircraft, so I felt it important for this book to capture that crucial element of their previous experience. It is notable that the men who excelled at 627 Squadron were in the final stages of their operational careers – for many of them, service on the 'Mossie' was their swansong as aircrew.

I am much indebted to the unnamed hundreds of enthusiasts who have striven to build websites to catalogue Second World War operations. The lengths they have gone to and the exactitude with which they have carried out their task can sometimes appear beyond comprehension. Without their collective input it would not have been possible to present even half of the detail contained in this book. Underpinning all research are the records held at the National Archives at Kew. The digitizing of millions of typewritten pages enables authors to explore a subject at an ever-expanding level of detail. I apologize to aviation enthusiasts that I have not been able to cover the career of other Mosquito squadrons in detail, or to spend more time writing about the in-service development of this outstanding aeroplane. Some significant elements of the story of the de Havilland Mosquito are absent from this account, but my focus on just one squadron allowed me only limited space to mention others.

I have no qualms in describing the men of 627 Squadron as 'elite' – their service record bears witness to their extraordinary achievements. For all the attention we give the 'Mosquito Men', however, we must not forget the heavy burden borne by women during this most turbulent of times. For mothers, wives and girlfriends, each day was accompanied by persistent, gnawing worry about the fate of their loved ones – a concern that was certainly not misplaced when it came to those serving with Bomber Command. This was also a time in history when women fulfilled many roles traditionally reserved for men, and thereby changed society irrevocably. Although women were not allowed to fly in combat, their work on the manufacture of the Mosquito – together with the many tasks they carried out on the airfields that operated them – proves that they made an incalculably large contribution to the winning of the air war.

My hope is that this book will serve to strengthen our understanding of 627 Squadron, a unit that is often mentioned in official histories but until now has been largely overlooked in studies of the Second World War. The considerable risks that its fliers took played a significant part in the overall Allied victory; furthermore, their operational experiences led to improvements in the accuracy of weapons, which would aid the development of the deterrents that maintained peace in Europe for many decades.

Prologue

The enormity of a historical event is sometimes hidden behind a single handwritten line. In this case, there is nothing in the hand of the writer that indicates anything is out of the ordinary – the script is steady and confident, simple but effective. The logbook is written with a fountain pen, each line noting the flight of a de Havilland Mosquito from RAF Woodhall Spa in Lincolnshire. At the head of the page, 'FEBRUARY 1945' is written in black ink, as it would be in a personal diary; the well-spaced lines that follow record seven flights on this leaf. There are no expressions of emotion, little detail as to the planning or intention of their mission, only basic functions and outcomes. Flights against the enemy are marked in red with 'OPS' for Operations, double underlined. Each red entry records a raid on a German town whose name would not have been known to the twenty-two-year-old writer before the war – *Karlsruhe, Dortmund, Ems, Ladbergen, Pölitz, Stettin*. After five years of aerial conflict, these places were now etched on the minds of the men who faced and overcame the terrors before them.

Details of the seventh flight of the month appear at the foot of the page:

13.02.45 20.00 Mosquito F F/O Walker Navigator <u>OPS</u> Dresden. Marker 2. Backed up. 14000 Red TI.

The logbook belonged to the 'Navigator' of the above entry – Warrant Officer Kenneth Oatley, son of a baker from Frome in Somerset. He assumed that this raid would be like the many others carried out at the time. Dresden was to be one of their longer flights; it was as far away as Berlin, whose outer limits the advancing Soviet Army was inexorably approaching. The crews of 627 Squadron could sense the end of the war was near, some even daring to make plans for life after the arduous six-year conflict. The maps showing the relentless advance of the Allied armies told them the day of reckoning for Germans and their Nazi masters was drawing close. For weeks through the winter of 1944/45, the positions of the ribbons and pins marking the extent of the advance on the *Daily Express* maps that adorned walls and doors the length and breadth of Britain had hardly moved. Through the hard fighting of the Battle of the Bulge in the west, Bastogne in Belgium had held out and been relieved. Now the Allies were on the move again, rolling up the German army before them as they neared the Rhine. The Soviets had crossed the Oder, and now had their eyes on the ultimate prize: 'The Lair of the Fascist Beast' – Stalin's epithet for Berlin.

That evening Ken Oatley and his pilot 'Jock' Walker listened to the rumble of heavy bombers taking off from the airfields around them. It was around 18.30 hours as the sky filled with noise, hundreds of Rolls-Royce Merlins straining to lift the heavily laden Avro Lancasters into the darkness in a throbbing wave of sound. Oatley and his pilot would wait another hour and a half to take off, but they would still reach Dresden before most of their comrades. When their time came, the flight was unremarkable, with nothing to be seen in the pitch blackness. They flew, seemingly alone, as Oatley plotted their course across the North Sea to occupied Europe. On his lap a piece of plywood was fashioned as a navigator's table with his chart stretched over it. He was content that he had his course plotted correctly as they swept over the invisible towns and villages below. The deafening noise of the engines and the tiny vibrations that pulsed through every part of the Mosquito did not concern them. Their minds had long since tuned into how the aircraft sounded and felt, a sense that would immediately alert them to anything abnormal.

As they approached Dresden, Walker reduced their height from 15,000 feet to 5,000 feet in preparation for the attack. They were aware that they were in clearer air, leaving the thick cloud that could have blocked their view. They had relied on their own calculation thus far and they hoped that they were in the correct position. They checked their watches. At any moment they expected to see the first flares drop over the city from the Pathfinder squadrons. Almost to the second, small balls of piercing light began to appear far above them, shining in an unearthly brilliance of white. A false daylight rose over Dresden, picking out every building and illuminating the empty streets. Domes and spires cast long shadows, acting as guidance to the advancing Mosquito. Three arenas were now clearly visible near the city centre. Jock Walker manoeuvred the Mosquito in over the middle stadium,* lining up for his dive. There was a sound of rushing wind as the bomb bay doors opened and the aircraft slowed perceptibly. Walker's finger hovered over his transmit button as he prepared to radio the 'Tally Ho' announcement that would signify they were the first marking aircraft going in for the attack. A split second later he heard 'Number one, Tally Ho' from the lead Mosquito, who had, as always, pipped him at the post. Walker waited and saw the dazzling red spot of the flare on the ground. Pushing his transmit button, he told the raid controller he believed the marker had dropped 150 yards east of the marking point. It was now his turn to attack. Pushing his joystick down, he radioed 'Number Two, Tally Ho' and watched the oval playing field below him grow larger in his windscreen. The black cross

---

* The Ostragehege stadium.

on his glass lined up with the centre of the green field, which began to loom large. Pressing the bomb toggle, Jock Walker released the target indicator and pulled Mosquito DZ599 out of its plunge.

As the horizon and the taller city buildings appeared above the aircraft's nose, Ken Oatley could see they were heading for the twin spires around the cathedral. It seemed Jock Walker had not seen them and instinctively Ken shouted a 'look out' warning. Deftly, Walker placed the Mosquito in between the two spires* and shot over the cathedral at an altitude of less than two hundred feet before pulling DZ599 into a long orbit around the city.

Nothing seemed to be happening. The intense light of the Pathfinders' flares bathed the city in an ethereal brilliance, but no guns were fired on them, and as yet there was no further activity from above. Feeling strangely alone, they circled the city, waiting for the onslaught to begin, but Dresden was still sleeping. Flying the Mosquito at low level across the quiet streets once again, they checked their marker and saw it glowing brightly from the centre of the stadium. Suddenly, they felt a huge surge of air lift their aircraft, as if an unseen hand had grasped it from above. The percussion hit them like a wave as the first 4,000lb bomb exploded close by. 'Time to get out of here,' Walker observed drily to Oatley as they sped towards the dark border of the city.

We were welcomed warmly at the door of Ken's well-appointed house in Ipswich. 'Come in,' he beckoned, ushering us into the living room and placing us on the couch near his armchair. We had intended to wait for Ken's son Rodger to arrive before

---

* The cathedral has only one spire but the second is on the adjacent *Hausmannsturm*, part of Dresden Castle.

we entered, principally because of concerns over Covid-19. The pandemic had first swept Britain several months earlier, but social distancing measures had been eased of late – and Ken was insistent. The room was just as Ken's wife had left it, each ornament in its place even down to the ashtrays on the coffee table, which remained unused. Trish was with me, taking advantage of the long trip south from our native Cumbria to spend a few days on holiday. Of all the aviation activities she has been subjected to in our long marriage, talking to veterans is probably her favourite – and preferable by far to standing on lonely airfields in blasting winds.

Ken's story is of a wartime which began with a degree of frustration as he trained for Bomber Command, but, through a series of unusual circumstances, failed to fly operationally. One day, lying on his bunk and somewhat disconsolate at his lack of progress within the Royal Air Force, a Scotsman called James Walker walked in and said, 'Are you Ken Oatley?' 'Yes,' Ken said, nodding. 'Come on, you're going to be my navigator on

Ken Oatley, September 2020.

Mosquitos.' With that simple exchange a new partnership was born that would take Ken to twenty-two operations with 627 Squadron. In the way of society in the 1940s, James Walker was always going to be 'Jock' as surely as a Welshman would be called 'Taff' and an Irishman 'Mick'. Ken Oatley nicknamed his pilot 'Mad' Jock Walker in the deepest affection for the man who could close out all distractions and fly into the teeth of the strongest defences without blinking.

As the last surviving ambassador of the crews that flew fearlessly for 627 Squadron, Ken is sharp and witty, capturing the sense that flying the Mosquito was, in comparison to the gruelling life of the heavy bombers, a fairground ride. Their task was to find the target and place markers accurately from a shallow dive, often placing themselves at high risk of ground fire. He recalls that they were rarely fired on; the sight of an aircraft thundering towards the ground seemed to paralyse their German enemies with surprise and disbelief. Ken is modest about his navigational skills, confessing there were times when he didn't know where he was. On one occasion, as they returned at low level from a daylight raid, the white trail of a launching V-2 rocket shot up close to them at the start of its supersonic journey to London. Having relaxed somewhat by this point in their journey, and confident that Jock knew his way home, Ken was later unable to tell the debriefing officer where the encounter with the V-2 had happened. However, since the missiles were launched from mobile sites and therefore difficult to find afterwards, Ken's lapse of concentration was hardly a cause for concern.

Was there fear? 'Of course,' Kens admits. 'I was nervous before every flight.' But the abilities of his pilot and the super-lative aeroplane in which they were flying helped to dissipate his feelings of trepidation. As one of the last surviving aircrew to have attacked Dresden on that fateful night in February 1945, and only the second man 'in', it is inevitable that every researcher asks him the same questions on the morality of the bombing campaign. Ken's response is similar to many who fought in the drawn-out battle that cost so many lives both in the air and on the ground. In war, terrible things happen nearly every day, he asserts. Ken moves closer to the edge of his chair. 'We didn't think about these things. Our concern was getting to the target first and getting our marker down on the spot.' He lifts his hand and brings a pointed finger down firmly on the coffee table in front of him. Behind his glasses, there is a glint in his eye as he is transported back seventy-five years to a time when his squadron competed to fulfil their task to the best of their abilities. He confesses that he and Jock Walker always strove to be first and transmit the 'Tally Ho One' message, but on every occasion were beaten to the prize. After flying over occupied Europe in the dark, their timing was so precise that on at least one occasion the first and second aircraft to reach the target pressed their transmit buttons simultaneously.

In the telling of 627 Squadron's story, we have to wait some time before Ken Oatley appears in our narrative. Although he joined the squadron only eight months after its inception, many of the founding members of the unit had finished their tour and moved on. By the time of his joining, in July 1944, 627 Squadron had come of age; supremely talented and confident in their abilities, they would be part of a generation that propelled the Allies to victory.

There is no doubt that Ken Oatley believes 627 Squadron comprised an outstanding group of men who accomplished much. Their list of battle honours is too long to embroider on a standard, some target names so obscure that they are only notable because they were destroyed by a small number of bombs dropped with supreme accuracy. The fame of 617 Squadron, the 'Dambusters', with whom they shared an air-field, has cast a long shadow over their history. Although not enjoying the adulation of their more famous neighbours, they are correct in their conviction that they were every bit as skilled as the men of the Lancaster Squadron. Like supporting actors, their actions are often close to famous names and events, but partially obscured by legends formed over the decades following. Perhaps now is their time to shine, late in the day but nevertheless glorious in memory.

Ken Oatley in conversation, September 2020.

1

THREE FLIGHTS TO SCANDINAVIA

Ørland airfield, Norway, 2 April 1942

A distant booming sound rang out across the plain. Its echoes rebounded off the range of hills that rose some five miles from the airfield perimeter, before dying away gently over the snow-covered ground.

A plume of dark smoke gave away the source of the noise, at first a wisp, but quickly growing into an angry black column rising hundreds of feet into the still air. On the other side of the airfield, men ran to nearby vehicles donning fire coats and helmets. In the Watch Office, binoculars strained to make out what was happening. There was some confusion – whose aircraft was it? Parts of the airfield were still under construction – why would someone try to land here? The fire burned intensely as vehicles approached the crash site, making fresh tracks in the snow.

A telephone rang in the guardroom; soon a Feldwebel was barking orders to his men, who jumped up from their places by the stove and quickly put on their thick overcoats. They grabbed guns from the racks, each man instinctively knowing which was his. Rifle over the shoulder, steel helmet on, out, into the lorry and off – a drill they had practised dozens of times, but now performed with a new sense of urgency. Their fingers felt around pockets and pouches for ammunition clips as they bumped across the frozen ground, the canvas top of their lorry keeping out little of the early spring chill. In common with soldiers everywhere, their experience of war was long periods of boredom interspersed with moments of extreme tension. As guards, they already knew they were considered less important than first-line infantry, and their fear was being caught unawares, not while aiming their rifles at the enemy, but being surprised in their bunks with thick blankets pulled around their chin. The British had spoiled their Norwegian holiday; instead of withdrawing gracefully as a vanquished army in June 1940, they had chosen to launch small but effective attacks, nibbling at strategic points. In the minds of men who spent many hours staring into the snowy landscape for movement there was a feeling of unease, not helped by the daily drone of lone enemy aircraft high above. They knew they were being watched.

By the time the guards arrived, two strangers in flying kit were being ushered into another lorry and were soon spirited away. Two fighters droned above the unfolding scene. They circled slowly, their grey undersides and black crosses dark against the lighter sky. Men stood a distance back from the burning aeroplane, afraid that bombs might go off. Playing their hoses on the blaze, they closed in, but such was the intensity of the inferno that they initially struggled to bring it under control. As the flames gradually subsided, they could see, as they suspected, that it was not a Luftwaffe aircraft, but a British one. Only the tail section remained unburned and, even for those who possessed good aircraft recognition skills, its shape was an unfamiliar one. It was clear this was one of the new reconnaissance planes seen high above Trondheim – an aircraft that German airmen had been striving to shoot down in recent weeks. Four months ago, one of the planes had been caught off the coast by their fighters after being damaged by flak. The attack was successful, sending the aircraft falling like a leaf into the sea, but nothing further was found of either it or the crew.

Soon there was very little left of the flying machine, no framework or fuselage shape, just an ugly black pile of debris like a bonfire after Walpurgis Night. It was still early afternoon, and for the guards, memories of lunch gave way to the realization that they were going to have to keep watch over the remains of the curious aircraft for some time. Although the darkest winter had given way to the light nights of a Norwegian spring, it was still cold. A steady stream of cars crunched through the snow, bringing officers to the scene, some sightseeing, some taking notes to report back. The word was that Berlin was very interested in their unexpected visitor, believing the aircraft to be a new, fast, twin-engined design that had been making regular high-level trips over the area, probably taking photographs. In these northern latitudes it would be light until midnight, but the chances were they were going to have to stand guard for many hours yet, even through the whole night, short as it was.

The second of April 1942 was the day the Germans had their first real encounter with the de Havilland Mosquito: not as a fleeting dot chased by fighters but as a machine they could at last examine. And they would soon have the opportunity to investigate the components of other Mosquitos, downed in places as far apart as Arctic Norway and North Africa. At first the Mosquito was considered an amusing quirk of British ingenuity, but for the Germans it was soon to become a weapon feared by the common soldier and general alike.

That grey chilly morning, Pilot Officer Ian Hutchinson and his navigator Pilot Officer Basil Allen had settled themselves into the cockpit of Mosquito W4056. It still smelled new, a mixture of paint, canvas and the distinctive combination of woods and adhesive that was unique to the aircraft. Flight checks completed, they pushed the start button on the first Rolls-Royce Merlin engine. It was an operation approached with care; the propellers had to be spun one at a time, on their electric starters, in the hope of producing a near-instantaneous popping sound accompanied by a plume of exhaust fumes. Things did not always proceed as smoothly as that, however, and an ill-primed engine could take a while to get going. On-board power for starting was boosted by additional batteries in a small trailer, a 'trolley accumulator', connected by a power cable to a socket behind the port wing. After starting, the starboard engine would provide sufficient power to start the port engine and the trolley would be disconnected. Flattening the trolley batteries was not only embarrassing, but would serve as a source of amusement and annoyance in equal measure to the ground crew, who called the crews 'Two Trolley Acc Jacks'. Hutchinson completed his scan over the instruments to make sure everything looked as it should before signalling 'chocks away', sending the ground crew scurrying underneath to pull away the triangular plywood blocks on tabs of rope. A little nudge of the throttles was enough to start creeping forward from the dispersals* and soon they were taxiing along the peritrack towards the runway at pace. Hutchinson kicked the rudder pedal a few times, creating a gentle weave as he satisfied himself that the control surfaces were performing as they should. They were the only aircraft moving – not part of a large gaggle of bombers or fighters, as was common in other squadrons. It was in the character of their work as Photo Reconnaissance to remain

---

* Dispersals were semicircles of hard-standing large enough for two bombers; they were located along the peritracks, the connecting 'roads' that surrounded an airfield. It was felt spacing parked aircraft protected them from air attack.

alone. They had no defensive armament to fall back on; their advantage was speed, height and stealth.

Pointing their nose into the robust breeze, they paused for a moment at the threshold of runway 09/27 at RAF Leuchars, near St Andrews in Scotland. Leuchars had only two runways, rather than the interlocking pattern of three that was commonly used at RAF airfields. This was because the winds on the east coast of Scotland were more predictable, providing the all-important headwind for take-offs and landings.* Today was no exception – the breeze was strong and constant from the southwest. A light flashed from the chequerboard-painted control caravan halfway down the runway. 'Go'. With nearly everything else covered in camouflage or drab paint, this was one of the few structures on the airfield that advertised its presence. It was an exposed position for the observers watching several tons of laden bomber hurtle in their direction. Mosquito W4056 was a willing partner that morning, picking up speed quickly as Hutchinson opened the throttles. By the time he reached the caravan the tail was up and the wheels were barely touching the asphalt. The aircraft was not heavily laden; it carried no bomb load, just cameras, and the pilot needed only the lightest of touches to be airborne.

The wheels retracted into the engine nacels, providing a reassuring clunk as W4056 climbed away. Freed from the drag of the undercarriage, Hutchinson rolled the Mosquito gently to port, pulling her into a turn in the direction of the airfield circuit. The North Sea coast appeared under his nose, an uninviting grey mass flecked with white wind-blown wave tops. In quieter times there might have been time for a round of golf at St Andrews, whose famous old course slipped by on the starboard side. Even with the privations of war, the good

---

* The greater air flow of a headwind increases lift, making take-off and landings safer.

gentlemen of the Royal and Ancient Golf Club would not be deterred from playing a round, even managing to bypass the posts and obstacles placed on the fairway to prevent airborne invasion. Such was the enthusiasm for the sport in Scotland that James II banned the game in 1457, as he felt it was taking young men away from archery practice, an activity deemed essential given the need for accomplished bowmen in late medieval armies. RAF Leuchars was a modern bow, shooting arrows towards Norway with speed and accuracy.

In common with most airmen on operations, Hutchinson and Allen had attempted to dispel their anxieties about the dangers that lay ahead by busying themselves for the task in hand. Perhaps if they had known they were enjoying their last precious hours of freedom, they would have savoured the taste of the bacon and eggs with a dab of brown sauce a little longer, relishing the strong brown tea served at breakfast as if it were a fine wine. Theirs was to be a future of watery soup and coarse bread with the occasional salvation of Red Cross parcels to sustain their strength.

As the patterns in the swell grew smaller below, they entered a swirling bank of cloud, clipping the base briefly with the cockpit before being enveloped in deep mist. Hutchinson had plenty of speed by now, and pulled back the stick, feeling his back getting heavier in the seat. They broke through into clear sunshine, the carpet of light cloud tops stretching into the horizon. Easing the rate of climb back gently, they continued to gain altitude as Allen checked his coordinates. They were alone, flying towards the enemy in brilliant daylight, a position their colleagues on other types of aircraft might have found disconcerting. But this was the Mosquito, capable of speeds to match the best fighters the Germans could muster. They flew the outward leg at 15,000 feet, rising to 20,000 feet, before the radar on the Norwegian coast could spot them.

With an additional petrol tank in the bomb bay, they could

make the 1,300-mile round trip to Trondheim in Norway with fuel to spare. Their comrades flying Spitfires with 1 Photographic Reconnaissance Unit (1 PRU) were based further north, at Wick, but they still had to refuel at an outstation at Sumburgh in the Shetland Islands before continuing the hazardous North Sea crossing. For the experienced airman, the de Havilland Mosquito was new, fast and a delight to fly. Its two engines and two crew were regarded as significant advantages over the single-seater Spitfire, which the Mosquito had outpaced in trials in 1941. Only a handful of Mosquitos had been produced to date, and 1 PRU counted it a great privilege to operate these first models. Although exciting to fly, the pilots would soon discover that the Mosquito could bite back, particularly if it lost an engine. Crashes were an ever-present feature of the operational career of the Mosquito; nearly half of all aircraft were lost to mechanical failure or pilot error. Unless it was flown with appropriate care, the Mosquito could become a moody companion. In the event of an engine failure and a ditching, Hutchinson's and Allen's chances of survival were bleak. Search aeroplanes would be sent out, but the challenge of finding their little yellow raft in thousands of square miles of sea would likely be insurmountable.

Ian Hutchinson had been an experienced Spitfire pilot before his transfer to the Mosquito. Joining the Royal Air Force in May 1938, he trained as a pilot and served first on Bristol Blenheims, a two-engined fighter bomber, which in the early months of the war the RAF imagined could be used as a fighter.* Before the weaknesses of this dangerous theory were fully exposed in combat, in March 1940, Hutchinson's 222 Squadron

---

* By June 1940, after heavy losses, the Bristol Blenheim was transferred to night-fighter duties leaving only Coastal Command using them in a daylight role. Nevertheless, of the 2,938 airmen who qualified for the Battle of Britain 'clasp', 800 flew Blenheims.

Pilot Officer Ian Hutchinson.

were re-equipped with Spitfires. The Spitfire, perhaps more than any aircraft, would initiate a love affair with its pilot. It was not just a case of flying a Spitfire – as they climbed into the cockpit, many pilots felt that they were strapping it on. It became part of them, almost instinctively moving in the direction they wished it to. Compared with the slower Blenheim, the Spitfire's power and agility allowed them to become true fighter pilots at a time when the nation's future was hanging by a slender thread. Hutchinson was based at RAF Hornchurch in Essex during the hot summer days of the Battle of Britain. He experienced mixed fortunes in those intense weeks, as day after day Britain faced punishing raids by the Luftwaffe. He shot down three Messerschmitt Me109s and a Heinkel He111, and claimed a further three 'probable' aircraft. His most notable victory was in downing veteran German ace Oberleutnant Eckhardt Priebe on 31 August 1940. Priebe survived this encounter and was later sent to Canada as a prisoner of war.

Hutchinson's achievements were not without personal cost. The day before his victory over Priebe, he had to make a forced landing at Damyns Hall Farm, in the East London suburb of Rainham, after his Spitfire was damaged in combat. Although a little shaken, he was unhurt, and in the furious tempo of the air battle, he flew to gain his revenge next day. A winning aspect of the RAF's performance in the Battle of Britain was that its supply of fighters remained constant and indeed outstripped the numbers of pilots trained to fly them. Each pilot was a precious commodity, but in the life-and-death struggle over Kent, there was no time to rest them. On 14 September Hutchinson made another forced landing at Detling, and, four days later, he was shot down over Canterbury in Spitfire R6772, from which he was forced to bail out. Ian Hutchinson's battle was brought to an abrupt end on 30 September when in action over London he was forced down a further time at Denham. At 1.45pm he was forced to bail out when his fuel tank was hit by machine-gun fire. He was badly burned about the face and hands and was sent to RAF hospital Uxbridge for treatment.

Hutchinson's return to flying was a personal triumph and the fulfilment of a dream that many of those recovering in the hospital beds at Uxbridge were later denied. As a proven pilot with 'kills' and the right to swagger a little in Fighter Command, his Spitfire experience on the PRU would be very welcome. It was a further honour to be able to fly the new Mosquito when it was delivered. Unfortunately, his flight of 2 April 1942 would bring him into contact with one of his old German adversaries who had also cut his teeth in the Battle of Britain.

Most PRU operations, by the nature of their task, had to be carried out in daylight. A Perspex nose accessible through a narrow crawl space at the navigator's feet allowed for observation and bomb aiming, but this was little used for Photographic Reconnaissance. Instead, cameras were fitted into the Mosquito's fuselage and operated by a thumb switch. The crew relied on swiftness and manoeuvrability to get them out of trouble, and with a top speed above 400mph they could theoretically outpace any German fighter. However, nothing could be taken for granted; the crew were mindful that they were still vulnerable at lower operating speeds. Over Norway they would face flak batteries and a determined and experienced fighter force. They knew too that they were not immune from the attentions of a well-positioned fighter – there was little defence against a closing head-on or beam attack.

As Hutchinson and Allen approached the coast of Norway they were entering an area increasingly reinforced with ground defences and Luftwaffe fighter stations. The Norwegian Air Force had possessed only six major airfields before the outbreak of war. The German were now building quickly, and would establish fifty-one airfields during their five-year occupation of Norway. A month earlier the British had raided the Lofoten Islands, some distance to the north of Trondheim, blowing up oil installations, taking prisoners and bringing back more than 300 Norwegians who wished to leave. Taking measures against RAF reconnaissance was a priority for the Germans – the eyes in the sky led to bombs on the ground. Since the German invasion of Norway between April and June 1940 the British had tried to fight back. There was no prospect of invading the country and driving the Wehrmacht out; nevertheless, a policy of short, sharp exchanges was designed to prevent the invaders from relaxing in their newly won lands.

Norway had fallen at the time of the disaster at Dunkirk; for Churchill, Hitler's Nordic adventure was another slap in the face. There was more than national pride at stake in the efforts to prevent the fortification of Scandinavia. What worried the sea-focused British was the new availability of deep-water western ports to the German navy. While the Kriegsmarine lacked the strength to take on the Royal Navy squarely, it had a number of fast, modern fighting ships capable of launching rapid attacks on convoys. Through the winter of 1940–41 the Germans sowed over 100,000 sea mines to control the approaches to Norwegian ports. The mighty 52,600-ton *Tirpitz* arrived in the Norwegian fjords in January 1942, and would present a constant threat to British convoys until 1944. Norway was evidently a prize Hitler intended to retain: in addition to their naval operations, the Germans continued to fortify the country throughout the war. It was this hive of activity that the PRUs were called on to observe.

As Mosquito W4056 approached the craggy Norwegian islands by the Frøya Bank, it was clear the weather was better here than the overcast gloom of Scotland. They could see breaks in the cloud, portholes of detail that gave tantalising glimpses of rocky mountains and the deep blue of the fjords below. Ideally, they liked to stay over 20,000 feet for an operation like this, zig-zagging a course to keep rising fighters at a distance. There was a fair chance that from this altitude they would be able to see trouble coming in the form of black dots against the white sunlit tops of the clouds below. Today, however, Hutchinson had no choice but to take the Mosquito in lower. To get any photographs they would have to fly into the cloud breaks below. The passage over their 'target' would still be rapid, around 325mph, but not fast enough to avoid an ambush by a well-placed enemy.

The attack happened quickly. One moment they seemed to be alone in the sky, and in the next it was apparent that two Messerschmitt BF109s had latched onto them. Cannon and machine-gun shells streaked past them, some ripping through the fragile wood of the Mosquito, creating sharp snapping noises above the roar of the engines. As Allen craned his neck backwards to see, Hutchinson threw the Mosquito into a twisting dive, jinking and shaking the aircraft from side to side. Still the Messerschmitts pressed home. Hutchinson and Allen had the misfortune of running into experienced fighter pilot and rising Luftwaffe star Oberleutnant Herbert Huppertz. At twenty-two years old he was already an Iron Cross holder in recognition of his service in France in 1940. Huppertz had served two periods on the Eastern Front from April to December 1941 and now commanded Luftwaffe fighter wing 9/JG5. His tally of downed aircraft already stood at forty* – and there

---

* Herbert Huppertz is credited with a total of seventy-eight victories, five of which were on D-Day, 6 June 1944, against Allied fighters. He was shot down and killed two days later by an American fighter over Caen.

The adversary, Oberleutnant Herbert Huppertz.

would be no escape for W4056. Huppertz saw one of his gun bursts produce the telltale fine mist of splintered material that showed his shells had struck home. Within seconds the Mosquito had taken shelter in a cloud bank, interrupting the hunt.

Although he had lost the fighters, Hutchinson had been badly hit in the tail; he quickly realized that they had no chance of making the long return journey over the North Sea in a crippled Mosquito. The controls of W4056 were not responding as they should, and now the instincts of an experienced and battle-hardened pilot took hold. In the next few crucial minutes, he had to make life-or-death decisions, a process in which he would have no second chances. Even if he had shaken off the persistent fighters, attempting to bail out was hazardous – all crews were agreed it would be their final option. Losing height rapidly, Hutchinson knew he had to look for somewhere to land while he still had speed and some control. His northerly course out of Trondheimfjord took him over the only flat land he could see ahead. The runways of the Luftwaffe airfield at Ørland stood out clearly in the light snow. Hutchinson and Allen prepared for a crash landing, eyes focusing on a landscape now coming sharply into view as they lost altitude. In such circumstances, trying to land with wheels down on unfamiliar terrain, especially when snow-covered, was too hazardous. The chances of hitting a concealed rut and flipping the aircraft on its back were high. It would be wheels up or nothing. Hutchinson throttled back the engines at the last moment, chose his spot in a clear patch of snow and set W4056 down on its belly. With a roller-coaster of rushing noise, the grounded Mosquito seemed to take a long time to stop, slithering on its curved underside. Once the aircraft had finally come to rest, the crew took stock for the briefest of seconds as an eerie silence descended. It was time to get out – and quickly. The exit door beneath them was possibly blocked, so popping out the hatch in the canopy above was their only option. After releasing their seat straps, they exited quickly, for there was a real risk that the aircraft might catch light at any second. Allen went first, clambering onto his seat and squeezing his way clear. It was a tight fit – a matter of getting his head and shoulders out first before pushing hard to free himself from the frame in the canopy. Hutchinson followed, and both men walked rapidly rearwards to alight from the trailing edge of the wing.

*German troops examine the severed tail section
of Mosquito W4056.*

W4056 was in a sorry state, its once pristine paintwork scuffed and holes punched through the ply and balsa skin in numerous places. The tail, already damaged in the attack, had been torn off in the landing, and sat forlornly a short distance away. The two Merlin engines had stopped, their propellers bent back through the force of the landing. Allen and Hutchinson faced a stark choice: stay here and be captured or run across the flat white landscape and try to evade their enemy. Above them the Me109s were beginning their vulture-like circling. Before thoughts of escape could formulate, another duty was at the forefront of their minds. The Mosquito was a new aeroplane, and they could not allow W4056 to fall into the hands of the Germans. Knowing this, Allen had brought the Very pistol and some flare cartridges with him from the cockpit. Perhaps aware of Hutchinson's experiences of fire, it was Allen who stepped forward and calmly fired a shot into the pool of petrol leaking from the ruptured tanks. The Mosquito was soon engulfed in a roar of flame from the ignited fuel. Standing at a safe distance from the blazing wreck, Hutchinson and Allen watched the German vehicles approach from the other side of the airfield.

Time for a cigarette, perhaps? It would, after all, be a while before they would be able to enjoy a smoke in freedom. Just as the de Havilland Mosquito's flying career was starting, theirs was ending. The abrupt finale of their flight left them feeling forlorn and dishevelled, the flying equipment they wore now useless. Their first encounter with the enemy was, however, an amiable affair. The Luftwaffe officers were elated that they had downed one of the troublesome Mosquitos. Ushering them into a building, an officer spoke to them in perfect English, 'We've been waiting for you for a while. I'm afraid our coffee's cold, but have some schnapps instead.'

Questioned by the Luftwaffe about the nature of their activities with their prized aeroplane, Hutchinson and Allen remained tight-lipped, just as they had been trained to be. After a spell at the *Dulag Luft* near Frankfurt, the Luftwaffe's holding and interrogation centre, the men were eventually transferred to Stalag Luft III, near Sagan (now Żagań) in Lower Silesia.*

What remained of W4056 told the Germans that the new aeroplane relied on what they considered to be old technology. The extent of the fire had destroyed nearly all the aircraft's structural components, so it was clear to them that the Mosquito was built out of lightweight woods. The tail, the only part of W4056 that was relatively unscathed, revealed that the skin was laminated from thin layers of wood and resin. The Rolls-Royce Merlin engines sat as islands amid a blackened mass of destruction. They did not appear to be very different from the Merlins recovered from crashed Spitfires and Hurricanes in France. The cockpit instrumentation, from what they could see, looked similar to that of other British bombers. W4056 lacked any defensive armament, but the Germans assumed – rightly – that the weight of guns would not significantly slow this sleek new adventurer. This was an aircraft that could fly very quickly, indeed potentially faster than any aircraft available to the Luftwaffe at that time.

In April 1942 the Mosquito was a curiosity to the Germans, but over the course of a few short months it would present a threat unlike any other. It was an aircraft the Germans would have liked to have built themselves, although they considered it to be a typically peculiar British invention. In some respects, the Mosquito was an aircraft perfectly in tune with the Nazi strategy of *Blitzkrieg*; it was a *Schnellbomber*,† a fast and

---

* A *Dulag Luft* was a *Durchgangslager der Luftwaffe* ('air force transit camp'). Captured Allied airmen spent time at the *Dulag* before being housed permanently in a *Stalag* (*Stammlager*, or 'main camp').

† The concept of the *Schnellbomber* originated in 1930s Germany, and proposed that light bombers carry no defensive armament but evade fighters by speed and agility. Hitler greatly approved of the idea, instructing the Luftwaffe to concentrate their efforts on such designs.

The burned-out remains of Mosquito W4056,
Ørland, 2 April 1942.

powerful attacker capable of carrying a destructive bomb load. Their initial admiration would quickly turn to apprehension as fear of the capabilities of the Mosquito wormed its way into the psychology of senior German commanders.

The appearance of the Mosquito came at a crucial time for Britain's rearmament for victory. Although the Spitfire and Hurricane had distinguished themselves in the Battle of Britain in the summer of 1940, many other aircraft designed in the 1930s had turned out to be underwhelming in combat conditions, and, more importantly, unable to match designs of their German rivals. The Boulton Paul Defiant, with its rear-mounted gun turret, had limited success in the summer of 1940, but could not compete on equal terms with German fighters in daylight, and was moved to night fighting. The Gloster Gladiator biplane fighter, famed for its plucky resistance in the defence of Malta in June and July 1940, suffered heavy casualties in Norway and Belgium. Perhaps most disappointing in performance was the Fairey Battle light bomber, which suffered substantial losses in the Battle of France. The Vickers Wellington was an outstanding bomber and highly commendable in its modernity; the Blackburn Botha, on the other hand, was declared unfit for combat duties almost immediately after its introduction in June 1940 – but the Air Ministry still managed to have 580 of these underpowered bombers built.

The year 1942 saw the introduction not only of the Mosquito, but also of other, critically important new aircraft such as the Avro Lancaster and later models of the Vickers Supermarine Spitfire. However, the impact of these advances in aeronautical technology would take some time to make itself felt and, in the meantime, Britain was still experiencing significant setbacks.

There had been some solid steps to recovery after the disaster at Dunkirk in May/June 1940: Operation Compass, the successful eviction of the Italian 10th Army from Egypt in the winter of 1940/41 was the first large British military operation of the Western Desert Campaign, and was followed in November/December 1941 by an offensive to relieve the Axis siege of the Libyan port of Tobruk. The entry of America into the war in December 1941 produced a further surge of optimism, but with the turn of the year, events in Europe, North Africa and the Far East showed that the tide of war had yet to turn in the Allies' favour.

The fall of Singapore in February 1942 caused dismay, not least in the corridors of Whitehall. Winston Churchill was particularly affected by the loss, and although he attempted to bolster British public morale with his characteristic stoicism, he believed it to be an unprecedented disaster. In a broadcast the day after the surrender, Churchill attempted to inject some optimism into this bleakest of hours: 'This is one of those moments when it can draw from the heart of misfortune the vital impulses of victory,' he declared. Privately he was much more morose, rebuking himself for not having taken measures to strengthen Singapore's defences that might have averted the defeat.* He grieved the loss of a jewel of empire for months afterwards. On one occasion an aide discovered him in his bathroom wrapped in a towel after one of his frequent baths. Looking disconsolately at the floor, he mumbled, 'I cannot get over Singapore.'

In North Africa, Axis forces under Rommel took Tobruk in June 1942 and drove the British out of Libya in a series of desert battles. The Axis advance into Egypt was halted by a stand at El Alamein in July, but decisive victory in the Western Desert – in the Second Battle of El Alamein – was still some months away. Other than brief raids on Norway, Allied land forces had yet to make their offensive mark in Europe. However, in preparation for a seaborne invasion thought to be possible in 1943, a substantial amphibious raid on the French port of Dieppe was planned for the late summer of 1942. The action on 19 August proved to be a costly mistake, with 3,623 men killed, wounded or taken prisoner from the 6,086 men who landed. The Allies had underestimated the strength of the German defences, failed to provide an adequate naval bombardment beforehand and were hampered by communication errors. A large proportion of the casualties were from Canadian regiments who were pinned down on the beaches and behind the sea wall of the port. While vital lessons were learned, not least in the realization that a lot more preparation would be necessary for the eventual D-Day landings, the Dieppe fiasco was a bitter blow to Allied hopes.

---

* Despite fortifications and a half-mile moat, Singapore had no substantial artillery positions facing north, where it was considered the jungle would prevent an attack. Instead, the guns pointed out to sea.

Under the cloud of seemingly unending unfortunate events, one man could see an opportunity to lift flagging British morale and boost his war strategy. Air Marshal Arthur Harris had taken the helm of RAF Bomber Command in February 1942 and quickly established his vision of area bombing. His unwavering belief that the Royal Air Force could pummel Germany into submission formed the backbone of operational planning for the next three years. Harris was also a man who knew the value of good propaganda, and he possessed a keen eye for morale-boosting raids. If his bombing campaign was to be successful, it would demand unparalleled investment in aircraft and crews, which could only be achieved by wooing politicians and the civil service. The Army was in no position to provide overnight successes, and even the Senior Service, the Royal Navy, could only produce small glimpses of victory. Pursuing German battleships in icy North Atlantic waters (such as the Navy's protracted hunting of the *Bismarck* west of Brest in May 1941) made for dramatic stories, but was hugely costly in time and resources. Harris intended to use Bomber Command to deliver a series of swift and brutally damaging punches to the enemy's heartland – and he also had the luxury of being able to choose his targets.

The de Havilland Mosquito was about to break into this grim and indecisive period of the conflict. Considered by its admirers to be capable of making a telling contribution to the air war, its opponents saw it as a side show – even a distraction from the real business of getting heavily armed bombers over mainland Europe. That any successful bomber could fly without guns went against the prevailing thinking and created a substantial obstacle for the acceptance of the Mosquito. Air Marshal Harris reserved judgement on the Mosquito* but saw

---

* It transpired that while Harris loved the aircraft, he hated the name, and wished to have it omitted from press releases. His view was that a mosquito was irritating but 'did not have a particularly effective sting'.

the opportunity to seize the initiative in a morale-boosting operation to lift the spirit of war-weary Britons. The scene was set for a set-piece raid by Mosquitos that would grab the headlines. Such actions were often dismissed as 'stunts' by the services, operations that gave morale a brief fillip, but had few long-term strategic advantages. At this stage of the air war, the Mosquito remained an unknown quantity; placed in the right hands, however, it was soon to demonstrate that it could achieve results that were much more meaningful than a sensational news headline.

Oslo, 25 September 1942

The building boom that transformed many European cities in the late nineteenth century also swept across Oslo. As steamships and railways brought more and more places within the reach of travellers, capital cities sought to impress foreign dignitaries with the finest architecture their countries had to offer. Oslo wished to display a degree of opulence in the manner of its southern counterparts, but with the population of Norway – at that time the smaller entity of the 'united Kingdoms' of Sweden and Norway – numbering less than two million, it could never compete with London or Paris or Berlin. The architect Henrik Thrap-Meyer began building the Victoria Terrasse in the centre of Oslo in 1884 and spent six years completing the fashionable apartment complex. Featuring ornate stonework and fine slate pitched roofs and domes, it was designed to house those with exquisite tastes and deep pockets. Its imposing proportions and location next to the gardens of the Norwegian Royal Palace were a deliberate attempt to attract high-status residents. Ultimately, the private development could not attract enough clients, and parts of it were taken over by the Norwegian government for offices in

Victoria Terrasse, Oslo.

1913. Had it not been for the Second World War, the Victoria Terrasse might have remained an attractive but relatively anonymous building in Oslo's centre.

After the invasion of Norway, the Victoria Terrasse was occupied by the *Sicherheitspolizei* (SiPo), the Nazi secret police, and the *Sicherheitsdienst* (SD), the intelligence agency of the SS responsible for state security. Often referred to by the Allies as the 'Gestapo', the SD was in fact a sister organization of the latter, which employed the same brutal techniques, and was led by the same chief, Reinhard Heydrich. Norway was to be held not only by an invading army at the point of a gun, but by a network of shadowy and murderous organizations created by the Nazis. The Victoria Terrasse was available by virtue of its governmental status, but its scale also appealed to Nazi tastes for flamboyant displays of authority. While efforts were made to indoctrinate the population in National

Socialist ideology, Norwegians were left in no doubt that they were to be ruled with an iron fist. The building was used as a prisoner interrogation centre, and soon sinister tales of torture and execution within its walls began to circulate. Such was the terrible reputation of Victoria Terrasse that some prisoners chose to throw themselves from its windows to certain death below rather than endure further suffering.

The activities of the SD were brought to the attention of the British by the Norwegian resistance. Although an attack by saboteurs might be effective, destroying the building more comprehensively could only be achieved by aerial bombardment. Up to this point in the war, no one had attempted such a pin-point operation, and to carry it out in the centre of a city would be to put the lives of many civilians at risk. Arguably, the audaciousness of the proposal was unmatched in the brief history of aviation to date. The new Mosquito presented an opportunity for a low-level attack, but could the RAF deliver bombs on a single block within a crowded city? The stakes were high, but other political forces swirled over the proposal; there was the crucial consideration of morale, both that of the Norwegian people and the British, still desperate for some signs of victory.

In the shadow of significant military setbacks, the Royal Air Force were keen to demonstrate that the vast resources allocated to it were not wasted. In April 1942 it had sent a force of its new Avro Lancaster bombers on a daring low-level raid to the Mann diesel works at Augsburg. The daylight raid over such a long distance proved costly in terms of aircraft and crew lost, but in propaganda terms, it was considered a success. The raid leader, Squadron Leader John Nettleton of 44 Squadron, was awarded the Victoria Cross for his efforts, and became a national celebrity. Perhaps the de Havilland Mosquito could similarly lift the spirits of both the British and the Norwegians?

The Nazis realized that in the building of the Third Reich, populations could not be constrained indefinitely by sheer brutality. In Germany itself, they had suppressed opponents of National Socialism by persecution, imprisonment and execution, but they had won over the majority by portraying themselves as true defenders of the Vaterland, as patriotic guardians of German national values, ruthlessly exploiting damaged national pride to gain political advantage. The task of persuasion was more problematic in the countries invaded by Hitler's armies. Nevertheless, in each occupied country the promotion of National Socialism was seen as essential in the long-term conversion of the society to Nazism. In planning an attack on the Victoria Terrasse to coincide with a political rally by the Nazi puppet leader, Vidkun Quisling, there was the opportunity to make a bold statement of resistance. Quisling, whose name was later adopted in several languages as a synonym for a traitor, was a Norwegian army officer who turned to politics in the 1930s. Although parties of the extreme right enjoyed a measure of success in a number of European countries, including Britain, Quisling's Norwegian Nazi party, *Nasjonal Samling* (National Union), failed to win any seats in the Storting, the Norwegian parliament. His elevation to nominal political authority along with other members of his party after the German invasion was wholly the work of the Nazis; Quisling remained an object of hatred and derision for the majority of Norwegians.* His use of rooms in the Royal Palace – next to the Victoria Terrasse – as an office from early 1942 was regarded as a further insult to the Norwegian people. A strike at the heart of his pro-Nazi puppet government would further emphasize the Allies' commitment to Norway.

---

* After the war, justice was swift. Quisling was tried and found guilty on counts of treachery, embezzlement and murder on 10 September 1945 and was executed by firing squad at Akershus Fortress on 24 October 1945.

Nearly six months after Hutchinson and Allen's adventure in Norway, the British public still did not know of the existence of the Mosquito. Although production at Hatfield near St Albans in Hertfordshire increased throughout 1942, the Mosquito was not yet a common sight in Britain's skies. Its presence could hardly escape the attentions of keen young aircraft spotters – local boys whose plane-spotting abilities and knowledge were often greater than that of the Home Guard. Other than provoking flickers of interest around factories and airfields, the Mosquito remained relatively unknown. Perhaps unusually, it had yet to attract the curiosity of the national press – although of course coverage of new developments in military aircraft technology was strictly controlled by the government. Throughout the 1930s, every new aircraft design was trumpeted by the press, which often described a plane's expected speed and range – details which during wartime would remain classified. The growing brinkmanship between Germany and her opponents led to fevered speculation as to the capability of these new aircraft. The unveiling of the Mosquito to the British public came late in the day, but when it finally happened, it was a choreographed entrance to coincide with a daring raid.

In November 1941, the first operational squadrons to receive the Mosquito, other than 1 Photographic Reconnaissance Unit, were 105 and 139 Squadrons based at RAF Horsham St Faith in Norfolk. Twenty-six-year-old Flight Lieutenant George Parry from Essex had joined 105 Squadron just as the new aircraft were arriving. Parry had completed his first tour of operations on the Bristol Blenheim with 110 Squadron and had been instructing at RAF Bicester when a former colleague phoned to find out when the next group of trainees were expected to pass out. During the course of a brief conversation, the caller asked Parry if he would like to return to operations to fly a new aeroplane that the Squadron were about to receive. George was intrigued at the prospect of flying the Mosquito; given he already had a considerable amount of experience on twin-engined aircraft, he hoped the conversion to the new Mosquito would not be too difficult. A test flight at the Royal Aircraft Establishment test centre at Boscombe Down left a very favourable impression on him. The Mosquito handled beautifully; it was clearly in a different league from other aircraft currently available to the RAF.

After training, the fledgling Mosquito squadrons were employed through the spring and summer of 1942 in daylight attacks on strategic industrial and military targets, some at high level, others at low. The Operational Record Books for this period show operations were infrequent, with 105 Squadron making only fourteen sorties during June 1942. Of two aircraft deployed at high level on 1 June to photograph the damage to Cologne after the first 1,000-bomber raid the night before, one failed to return. W4068 was shot down on the sortie and the pilot, Flying Officer Leonard Pearman, and navigator, Flying Officer Richard Scott, had to bale out. Their successful escape from W4068 was no doubt helped by the fact that they were flying above 20,000 feet, an altitude that gave them ample time to squeeze themselves and their parachutes out of the Mosquito's small crew door. It was clear that using the Mosquito at high level over German targets exposed them to the same risks of flak and fighter concentrations experienced by the heavy bomber force.

A month later, on 2 July, a combined low-level attack by 105 and 139 Squadron Mosquitos on the Flensburg U-Boat facility in Schleswig-Holstein resulted in the loss of two of their aircraft out of the five sent. The lead Mosquito, flown by Flight Lieutenant Albert Skelton and lead observer Group Captain John MacDonald, was hit and subsequently abandoned over the North Sea off Pellworm Island. The two men were rescued and became prisoners of war. The serving joint Squadron

Commander, Wing Commander Alan Oakeshott, DFC, and his navigator, Flying Officer Vernon Treherne, DFM, were not so fortunate. Although highly experienced and decorated, they could not escape the guns of a Focke-Wulf FW190 flown by Feldwebel Günther Allmenröder. Their Mosquito fell west of Helgoland at 13.54, just over two hours after their departure from Horsham St Faith. Neither Oakeshott's or Treherne's body was recovered from the crash site. It is likely that both men were entirely consumed by flames, the intensity of the fires that erupted on impact being another of the Mosquito's more unfortunate traits.*

Despite such losses, the rate of attrition did not unduly trouble Bomber Command – indeed, the casualty rate was well within their expectations. The Mosquito was performing well and was proving it could carry an adequate bomb load and still maintain its agility. The stage was set for an opening performance and an introduction to the world's media. Even before the Dieppe raid, plans to attack the Victoria Terrasse were in preparation and Flight Lieutenant George Parry was being considered as a potential leader of the operation. On 3 August 1942 most of 105 Squadron were allowed a thirty-six-hour rest period. Parry's Navigator, George Robson, remembered the rushed scenes as aircrew booked rooms in London hotels and prepared to paint the town red. Robson describes walking into the mess lounge shortly after lunch and finding it all but deserted apart from Parry and a few ground staff. Parry's and Robson's curiosity as to why they had not yet received leave passes was soon answered by a voice over the tannoy: 'Could Flt Lt Parry go to the operations room immediately?'

A short time later Parry found Robson waiting pensively outside the ops room.

* Oakeshott and Treherne are remembered on the Royal Air Force Memorial to the missing at Runnymede.

'It's alright, Robbie, we're going to Sweden.'

'In a Mosquito?' Robson asked incredulously.

'Yes, they are going to paint the roundels out and we go in civilian clothes.'

With little time to lose, they took the train to London to collect civilian passports and receive a briefing at the Air Ministry. They were to fly to Stockholm, still the capital of a neutral country, to collect diplomatic bags containing information on the Russian front. Even as the war encroached on nearly every area of normal life, civilian flights from Scotland to Stockholm continued throughout the war. Flying from RAF Leuchars, the *Stockholmsruten* continued under the pretence of civilian freedoms, but in most cases the flights had a military objective. The route was operated by British Overseas Airways (BOAC), using Lockheed Lodestar passenger aircraft, but as the Germans became more inclined to shoot down these flights, the planes wore camouflage instead of their silver and white pre-war livery. The BOAC badge logo remained painted in black on the nose, and all crew were officially 'civilians'. The flights acquired the nickname 'the ball bearing run', as they also carried supplies of much-needed ball bearings back from Sweden. Despite the subterfuge, German interference in the flights was limited as Swedish diplomats might still choose to use the route to travel to Britain. From late 1942 the service was coordinated from London by the Norwegian government in exile using free Norwegian air force pilots.

Parry and Robson were to imitate the BOAC flightpath in their plain-clothes Mosquito, which would no doubt be observed by German radar. Whether the operators would realize the flight was travelling somewhat faster than normal was unknown, but in the event of Parry and Robson being forced to land on hostile soil, they were ordered to burn the still-secret Mosquito.

The Germans found the borders of Norway impossible to

police. The smuggling of people, material and photographs over the Norwegian–Swedish frontier was commonplace, aided by mountain guides who could draw on a centuries-old tradition of trading with their Nordic neighbour. Facing incursions by land, air and sea, the new German occupying army had little chance of stopping all the holes. Although the Norwegian fishing trade to Scotland was halted by the occupation, a flotilla of small ships known as the 'Shetland Bus' was set up to provide a line of communication between Mainland Shetland and Norway. Operated at great risk by the Norwegian Naval Independent Unit (NNIU), the boats were often crewed by fishermen and had some defensive armament in the form of machine guns concealed under oil barrels.

When Parry and Robson returned from London to Horsham St Faith on the morning of 4 August 1942, they found their Mosquito had had its roundels and RAF codes painted out – not that the disguise did much to conceal the plane's real identity. Nevertheless, once they had changed into civilian clothes (which Robson had to borrow, as he didn't have anything suitable with him), they flew north to RAF Leuchars, near St Andrews. From there they intended to fly to Sweden at 7pm that evening, but Parry found a generator fault on the Mosquito. In a phone conversation with a concerned Air Ministry, he promised to undertake the flight the next day at the same time.

The flight to Sweden was tranquil in the brightness of a northern summer's evening. Their course was straight across the North Sea heading for the Skagerrak, the strait that separated Norway to the north and Denmark to the south. Parry put the Mosquito into the gentlest of turns as they rounded the tip of Denmark, still ensuring they stayed out to sea. Ahead of them the Swedish city of Gothenburg appeared on the eastern side of the Kattegat, the sea area between Sweden's western coast and Denmark's Jutland peninsula.

Even now, with safety but a short distance away, they could be pounced on by German fighters. The coast of Sweden was dotted with hundreds of islands and rocky outcrops. They were intrigued to see Gothenburg harbour criss-crossed with the wakes of ships coming and going, seemingly oblivious to the war. Following the inlet of the harbour they flew directly over the city, past the circular gardens of the large cemetery, the Östra kyrkogården, which was clearly visible even at their altitude. Pressing on, they set course for Stockholm's Bromma Airport on the other side of the country.

They experienced a sense of lightness, almost elation, as they flew over Sweden's mountainous interior and then the largest lake they had ever seen – the Vättern, its waters shining in the northern twilight – to begin the descent into Bromma. For three years they had lived with the constant preoccupation of war, and now they were flying, in ill-fitting suits, over a country at peace. The prospect of being in a country that was not subject to wartime constraints was disorientating, and it had not occurred to them that their arrival might draw attention to their Mosquito and their mission.

Welcomed by the Air Attaché's staff, Parry and Robson were whisked off to a hotel in Stockholm and later to a fine restaurant, where Robson remembered the band striking up 'Annie Laurie' as they arrived. A good meal with an ample quantity of schnapps followed, their hosts eagerly quizzing them for news from England. They were, however, made aware of the presence of German spies, and Robson recalls getting a kick under the table from Parry to warn him not to say much more.

Over breakfast the next day, they had also been introduced to Squadron Leader Brian Paddon, a former prisoner of war who was keen to hitch a ride back to Britain in the bomb bay. It struck Parry and Robson, even in their brief meeting, that Paddon was a remarkable character whose enthusiasm to get back home to Britain seemed boundless. They had to reject his request in favour of their precious documents, but Paddon managed to catch a flight back later the same day. Paddon's story is one of determination and fortitude. Shot down over Abbeville in northern France in June 1940, he had made ten escape attempts from prisoner of war camps, and had been detained within the austere walls of Colditz Castle, near Leipzig. Colditz was reserved for the most troublesome and recalcitrant POWs, and was considered the most secure of any prisoner of war camp. In June 1942, while being held at Stalag XX-A in German-occupied Poland, he escaped from a work party, disguised himself in civilian clothes that had been left for him in a pre-arranged place and travelled on several trains to reach the port of Danzig on the Baltic coast. He stowed away on the Swedish collier SS *Ingolf*, only revealing himself once the ship was at sea, and arrived in neutral Sweden on 18 June. As many as thirty-two POWs managed to escape Colditz and the surrounding area, but Paddon was one of only fifteen of them to achieve a successful 'home run' and make it all the way back to Britain.

After instructions from the Norwegian government in exile not to strafe or bomb the Royal Palace in Oslo, the plan to attack the Victoria Terrasse received its final approval. As Parry was a highly experienced pilot who had already flown the North Sea route, there were obvious advantages in his selection to lead the raid. Before the details of the plan were revealed, three other crews were chosen by Parry and Robson. There was little time for preparation and the group only managed forty-five minutes of practice in formation flying at 100 feet or lower before the operation. Although maritime flying presented far fewer risks of collision than land-based flight, a misty horizon and the lack of focal points posed some tricky challenges for fliers nonetheless. While the formation did not have to be really tight, it was essential that the crews followed their leader and trusted him not to fly them into the sea.

The intensity of a low-level attack on a city centre building in the midst of a political rally was not something the crews had any experience of. Intelligence photographs showed three clear domes to head for on the building, but they knew they would only get one clear run into the target. The briefings identified flak and machine-gun positions, including likely roof-top defences that could direct fire towards them. Speed and surprise were their advantages, so correct positioning and identifying the target were the keys to success. They were briefed that the only fighters capable of catching them were the Focke-Wulf FW190s that operated from Heldra, more than 500 miles away to the east, in the heart of the German Reich. The Mosquitos would carry four 500lb bombs, each with eleven-second-delayed fusing to ensure all the attackers were clear of the target before they detonated. At a height of less than 100 feet, normal fused bombs that exploded on impact would almost certainly destroy any aircraft that released them so low.

On the morning of 24 September 1942, the day before the planned raid, four Mosquitos of 105 Squadron made the 300-mile trip north to RAF Leuchars, on the Fife coast. Parry and Robson led in Mosquito DK296, accompanied by Flight Sergeant Carter and Sergeant Young in DK325, Pilot Officers Bristow and Marshall in DK328 and Pilot Officers Rowland and Reilly in DZ313. Staying below the cloud level, the Mosquitos were moved around in a stiff breeze, bobbing up and down gently as they held together. September was proving to be a cold month, and there was speculation that Europe could be heading for another severe winter like that of 1941–42. Apart from Robson, in the lead with Parry, it was an easy ride for the navigators, who had time to spare to take in the scenery of their east coast journey. The view from the small cockpit of the Mosquito was good for both pilot and navigator. It was possible to see all the upper surfaces of the wings and, by craning one's neck, the vertical stabilizer behind. The training path of navigators generally involved less hospitable aircraft than the Mosquito, and, since most navigators were destined to fly in heavy bombers, they had to get used to navigation tables that were sometimes set back into the fuselage. Owing to the need for a light on the map desk, the navigator's position was cocooned behind a black-out curtain. The Mosquito's cockpit was positively airy in comparison, although at night the navigator would have to work under a light little brighter than a dimmed torch bulb.

Unlike some special operations, there had not been an abundance of time in training for the Oslo raid – the Mosquito crews were already considered experienced in low-level attacks. Neither had there been any rest time; some crews continued to fly operations in the week before the Oslo raid. Parry and Robson had been part of an abortive high-level attack on Berlin on 19 and 22 September, while Bristow and Marshall had flown on a low-level raid to the coke ovens at IJmuiden on the Dutch coast. Despite a seaward approach and the potential for surprise, the three attacking Mosquitos encountered an intense barrage of hostile anti-aircraft fire. Bristow and Marshall were hit, the fuselage of their Mosquito DK337* sustaining 'considerable damage', but they still managed to release their bombs.

The four Mosquitos sat fully fuelled and bombed-up waiting for the crews on the dispersals at RAF Leuchars. From any angle the aircraft looked aggressive, but also sleek and agile – the Mosquito was pleasing to the eye. Walking out to their Mosquitos from the briefing – and a lunch of haddock,

---

* DK337 was repaired and served for a further eleven months before being lost on a raid to Duisburg on 31 August 1943 with her crew Pilot Officer Isfeld and Sergeant Strang.

mashed or boiled potatoes and cabbage with parsley sauce*
– the men carried their parachutes and kit to the air-craft.
The crew door was open, a hatch barely two feet wide with
rounded corners on the lower starboard side of the nose.
A thin tubular ladder reached the short distance upwards
into the cockpit. Mounting the steps, the crews pushed their
parachutes and kit in first, then steadied themselves on the lip
of the door frame before pushing themselves up and squeezing
into their seats. The pilot's seat was set a few inches in front of
the navigator's, making the knee the quickest part of the body
to touch if the pilot wanted to gain the navigator's attention
quickly. The two Merlin engines sat forward of the crew on
either side of the light-green, tubular cockpit frame; only the
nose projected a short distance in front of the large three-
bladed propellers.

By 14.00 hours everyone was close to completing their pre-
flight checks. Engines were started a couple of minutes later,
chocks waved away and, with a little power applied, each
Mosquito left its parking place, blowing the grass behind the
hardstands in furious waves. Little time was wasted in taxiing
out towards the runway. This was to be a long trip for the
little Mosquito; the crews wanted to retain plenty of surplus
fuel for unexpected detours. Parry and Robson led the group;
the plan was that they would take off together rather than
individually, so as to cut down the time spent on forming
up. At 14.13 hours Parry opened his throttles fully until the
Merlins began to sing melodiously. From a creeping start the
Mosquitos kept up with their leader, picking up speed rapidly
down Leuchars's runway as the pilots pressed their rudder
pedals occasionally to keep the rising tail straight.

Parry levelled them out early – they had barely left the
ground as he settled them into their flight altitude of 50

* RAF Leuchars menu for the day, in the RAF Museum, Hendon

feet. Heading into the North Sea, they streaked out by dead reckoning on a line towards the Skagerrak; 'it was like a long straight road,' Parry recalled. It was hoped that by remaining so low they could evade detection by radar until very late in their approach to the target. It was a flying technique that would form the principal defensive strategy for the next five decades through the post-war and Cold War years. As it transpired, the Mosquitos were detected by German radar off the southern coast of Norway. Making landfall near Fredrikstad in southeastern Norway, the formation turned sharply to port to follow the eastern side of Oslofjord. By this point the attackers were clearly visible to ground observers and, by an unlucky quirk of war, the plan had already begun to unravel. With only 50 miles to run into target, this distance could be covered in less than ten minutes – not a lot of time for the enemy to react. However, in a show of strength earlier in the day, four FW190s from Heldra had overflown a gathering of Quisling's *Nasjonal Samling* in Oslo before landing at Fornebu airfield on the banks of Oslofjord. Fortunately for Parry's men, only two of the fighters managed to respond to the attack alarm in time to intercept the incoming Mosquitos.

Approaching the city over the Oslofjord, the four Mosquitos prepared for their attack run line astern of each other. As they made landfall, Parry swept across a low hill as he looked forward to try to identify the pattern of avenues leading to the Royal Palace and the three domes of the Victoria Terrasse which would sit slightly to the left. He didn't notice that he had clipped the light aerial of a police station, and only learned of his narrow escape later. In the streets below people stopped in amazement as the aircraft sped over them. Some had time to run for cover; others, unsure whether this was a Luftwaffe fly-past, stood motionless as the aircraft thundered through the flag-lined streets. Parry picked out the domes of the Victoria Terrasse easily as he swept across Karl

Johans Gate, a broad avenue leading to the Royal Palace. He was aware that red tracer shells were whistling past him, and he assumed these had been fired from light flak batteries mounted on rooftops.* But there was no time to worry about where they came from, for Robson had noticed that Carter and Young in DK325 had been hit. Trailing thick black smoke from their starboard engine, they had broken from the others and turned towards Oslofjord to avoid crashing into buildings. As the tall edifice of the Victoria Terrasse grew ever larger in the cockpit windscreen, Parry released his bombs, as did the other two following Mosquitos. Only when his No.2 and 3 aircraft sped past him did Parry realize that the formation was being attacked by the Fw190s, and that one was on his tail. Swift evasive action was required. Using the valleys ahead to gain an advantage on his pursuer and upping the Mosquito's speed, he pulled away, but not before he was hit by cannon shells.

Roland and Reilly in DZ313, having seen the Focke-Wulf FW190s in time, pulled clear to make their escape, as did Bristow and Marshall in DK328. Carter and Young were not so fortunate, and were killed instantly when their Mosquito crashed into Oslofjord.

The three remaining Mosquitos completed the shorter return leg to Sumburgh on the Shetland Islands, all reporting that they had successfully hit their target. The news from Oslo was far less positive; word came back that as many as eighty civilians had died, many of them occupants of the flats surrounding Victoria Terrasse. Four bombs had hit the building squarely, but three had passed through, punching holes in the walls and exploding in the flats behind. The fourth had failed

---

* Some of the rounds fired slammed into the walls of the Royal Palace. The Nazis later tried to blame the Mosquitos for the damage, which was not possible, owing to their lack of guns.

to explode. More than a dozen bombs failed to detonate and others fell wide of the target over four neighbouring streets, causing extensive damage to apartments and blast injuries to residents and pedestrians. In terms of the amount of damage inflicted on the Victoria Terrasse, the raid had fallen short of expectations, but not because of any lack of skill on the part of the pilots. The principal problem was that planners failed to realize the extent to which a 500lb bomb could skip, a distance lengthened by the eleven-second delay in the fuses. The pilots behind Parry had watched his bombs drop but seemingly maintain their forward momentum to keep pace with the aircraft. Other low-level attacks had been carried out on industrial or military targets, where the damage was assessed by reconnaissance aircraft after the attack without any report from the ground. Damage off-target was always assumed to be the result of a bombing error by the crews.

De Havilland Mosquito DZ313, flown by Pilot Officers Rowland and Reilly of 105 Squadron during the Oslo raid.

The problem identified in the Oslo attack provided important lessons in technique of future low-level bombing attacks, but, given the technology of the time, it was not one that was easy to overcome.

Although the Oslo raid is remembered for its grievous loss of life and counted as a failure, it did lay down some notable markers in the growing reputation of the Mosquito. Although surprised by attacking Focke-Wulf FW190 fighters, the air-craft had proved itself nimble enough to pull away swiftly from its attackers. Further pluses were the speed of the Mosquitos' strike on Oslo and their concomitant ability to catch the enemy off-guard. These were major advantages, which would be demonstrated repeatedly – and to good effect – in the course of the Mosquito's operational career. Another heartening aspect of the attack was that it left an indelible impression on German commanders, who realized that they could be targeted more precisely.

Typically, those in higher command found themselves positioned in relative safety behind front lines. It was a centuries-old tradition, common to all of the world's armed forces, that attacks were launched not against senior officers, but against their subordinates. But advances in modern artillery and its deployment during the First World War brought the previously sheltered positions of commanders well within the range of a well-aimed shell. There were few instances of senior officers being deliberately targeted, however, not least because finding their location was difficult.

The advent of the Mosquito changed this perception irrevocably. For the first time, a weapon that could single out a building in a street hundreds of miles from the front was deployed. The combination of speed and agility in delivering a bomb of 500lbs accurately – ordnance of a substantial size – proved to be a game-changer. The shockwaves felt in Berlin at the deliberate targeting of high-level functionaries of the Nazi state were palpable. Suddenly, no one was safe. In the higher circles of Nazism, already rife with faction and conspiracy, the nervousness surrounding the Mosquito became something of a neurosis. An air raid was always an inconvenience, but the rumour of the imminent arrival of Mosquitos would send officers scurrying into their shelters. In the countries they occupied, the Germans had to deal with the challenge of numerous resistance groups who watched their every move, gathering information and passing on all they knew to the Allies. 'The Butcher of Prague', Reinhard Heydrich, leader of the Gestapo and the SD, was already dead, assassinated in Prague by Czechs trained by Britain's Special Operations Executive (SOE). Senior Nazis could always protect themselves from similar attacks by employing extra bodyguards and taking other precautions. But the idea of a lightning-fast assault from the skies by two men in a wooden aircraft of uncanny speed and manoeuvrability was unnerving indeed. Given that the Mosquito was first deployed over Norway, it is fitting that the Oslo raid became a milestone in building an aura of fear around the aircraft. The skills developed by 105 and 139 Squadrons would also be operationally critical for 627 Squadron when it was formed fourteen months later.

2

THE FLYING SWEETHEARTS

Iraq, 20 October 1934

In the cooling Baghdad evening, a dark shadow appeared from the gathering gloom as a black, twin-engined racing plane slipped down onto the dusty airstrip. It had been a long and gruelling day for Mr and Mrs Jim Mollison as they dodged the seasonal rains over Europe and pressed on into the Mediterranean. They had watched the autumn colours recede as they passed over southern Italy and continued, skirting the rocky coast of Greece on their southeasterly course. Having left England on a cool late October day, they then baked for hours under the cockpit canopy before making landfall on the Syrian coast. Ahead a vast desert spread out before them with more than 500 miles of featureless wilderness. They were thankful for the lush green ribbon of the Euphrates that acted as a steady guide, twisting and turning into the distance. To get lost here would invite disaster and, as tired as they were, they could not afford a lapse in concentration. The sun began to sink behind them, the dusky pinks of the desert fusing into the horizon on their starboard side, the small towns and villages with their brightly painted white walls becoming less frequent. The beauty of the landscape and its atmosphere of profound isolation lifted the pilot's spirits; so far, everything had gone their way. As the landscape darkened beneath them, they knew night would fall quickly. The lights of Baghdad were a welcome sight.

Their arrival in Baghdad allowed only time for a bath, a bite to eat and a quick drink. They knew they were ahead of their nearest competitor by just a small margin, and that the next leg of the greatest air race ever known would mean flying through the night. The route from Baghdad to Karachi, a distance of nearly 1,555 miles, would take them over southern Iraq to Basra to meet the eastern side of the Persian Gulf and then onwards along the line of the Iranian coast towards their destination. Leaving Baghdad, they set course south following the course of the Tigris River below cutting a straight line through its constant meanders using the last glimmers of light. The de Havilland DH.88 Comet was flying well, the two Gipsy Six engines ticking like well-oiled sewing machines; with a cruise speed of over 200mph, they knew they could maintain their lead over their rivals. Since they were going to attempt to fly non-stop to Karachi, they had to make constant calculations of how much fuel they had used. The skill of the long-distance flyer lay not only in their airmanship but in their abilities in mathematics.

After two hours they saw the long ribbon of the Persian Gulf ahead. They were blessed with a strong moon that night, glinting from the water and casting shadows on the rising hills. Navigation would be simpler, as they followed the coast leading down through the Strait of Hormuz and Gulf of Oman. Karachi, in British India, the next stopping point on the race schedule, lay on the coast of the Arabian Sea. In the small hours the heat that had built up in the cockpit through the day had long dissipated, but the Mollisons were seasoned aviators, and used to whatever discomforts might come their way.

Their seats were positioned in-line rather than side by side in the slim fuselage, and although the aircraft had dual controls, only the front seat had a full instrument panel. The combination of aeronautical skill and the trust that Mr and Mrs Mollison had in each other was essential for the successful completion of the flight. After some uncertainty in finding Karachi, at 04.53 hours, de Havilland Comet G-ACSP *Black Magic* settled gently down onto the airstrip at Drigh Road* to the east of the main city. The Mollisons had set a new record for a flight from England to India, but the race was far from over.

The idea for an air race across three continents was the brain-child of Sir Harold Gengoult Smith, Lord Mayor of Melbourne, and was intended to celebrate the centenary of the founding of the city in 1834–35. In the dawn of the golden age of aviation, Smith also wanted to promote air travel, which promised to revolutionize passage to Australia from Europe. The first flights from London to Brisbane did not take place until 1935, and took twelve days and thirty-one stops to accomplish, but excitement about the possibilities of air travel was reaching fever pitch.

Smith found an enthusiastic sponsor in Sir Macpherson Robertson, an Australian who had made his fortune in the confectionery business. His enterprises had introduced chewing gum and candy floss to the continent, and products like Freddo Frog, Old Gold Chocolates and Milk Kisses had established him as the leading sweet maker of his time.[†] Macpherson offered £15,000 in prize money, a considerable sum for the time, for what was the longest air race yet attempted, spanning

---

* Now Jinnah International Airport.
[†] The Macpherson Robertson's company was called MacRobertson, a brand that was eventually bought by Cadbury's in 1967.

sixteen countries. Organizational responsibilities for the 'MacRobertson Air Race', which would begin on 20 October 1934 at the newly inaugurated RAF Mildenhall in Suffolk, in eastern England, were handed to the Royal Aero Club of Great Britain. There would be prizes for the fastest aircraft completing the mammoth journey, but also other categories, with no entrant able to win more than one prize. There was no limit on the size or power of the aeroplane or the number of people it carried; the only stipulation was that no pilot could join the race after its departure from England. Pilots would follow a prescribed route with compulsory check points in Baghdad, at Allahabad in India, in Singapore, and at Darwin and Charleville in Australia.

The race was expected to draw the best pilots from around the world, but one thing rankled with the British – there was currently no domestic aircraft design with a realistic chance of winning. At this, the high noon of the British Empire, it was surely unthinkable for the mother country not to have a competitor capable of holding its own in a globally prestigious air race. Geoffrey de Havilland, founder of the aircraft manufacturing company that bore his name, felt that Britain's reputation was at stake. With his designer Arthur Hagg, he began planning a racing aircraft capable of winning the MacRobertson. The race would be a test of speed, mechanical endurance and long-distance capability – an aircraft that could stay ahead of the others would need a range of 2,000 miles without refuelling. In terms of technology, it was pushing at the boundaries of what was aeronautically possible at that time.

Geoffrey de Havilland was an aviation pioneer who had cut his teeth in the early days of flying. After training at the Crystal Palace School of Engineering (1900–03), he worked in the automotive industry, but his interest in flying became a primary driving force. Without much prior knowledge of aircraft design, he borrowed money from his grandfather and spent two years building his first aircraft – a three-bay biplane with a four-wheeled undercarriage – which he completed after his marriage in 1909. Unfortunately, this first effort was not a success, and on its inaugural flight near Litchfield, in Hampshire, Geoffrey crashed it. Undeterred, he pressed on with a second design, which he flew successfully in 1910; so confident was de Havilland in its abilities that he took his wife Louie and his eight-week-old son Geoffrey for pleasure flights. In form, it was not dissimilar to Orville and Wilbur Wright's designs, a wood and canvas-covered biplane with an open framework that held the engine and pilot's seat. The design impressed his employers at the British Army Balloon Factory* at Farnborough, and they bought the aircraft, giving it the designation 'FE1'. Geoffrey de Havilland, perhaps unwittingly, had forged a highly successful pattern of business in which he received commission for every aircraft that was built, enabling him to stay afloat in an infant industry that posed serious financial challenges for manufacturers. Facing a considerable investment in renting premises and employing a workforce, many budding aeroplane designers fell by the wayside. De Havilland's design abilities matched his passion for flying; in 1912 he joined the Special Reserve of the Royal Flying Corps, but was involved in a bad crash the following year. After joining the Aircraft Manufacturing Company (Airco) in 1914 as chief designer, he was called up when war broke out and saw service flying patrols out of Scotland, but his previous injuries prevented him from serving overseas.

Soon recalled from flying duties, Geoffrey returned to Airco – but still with the arrangement of receiving royalties for each aircraft constructed to his design. During the First World War he became prosperous and, when Airco was sold to British

---

* The Farnborough factory became the Royal Aircraft establishment in 1912.

Geoffrey de Havilland's first design, the Royal Aircraft Factory FE1, 1910.

Small Arms (BSA) in 1918, he decided the time was right to strike out on his own. In 1920 he founded the de Havilland Aircraft Company, building his own aeroplanes at a factory at Stag Lane Aerodrome, Edgware. Public enthusiasm for flying, which had cooled somewhat in the Great War, skyrocketed through the 'Roaring Twenties'. With a growing number of civilian pilots to cater for, de Havilland now came into his own. In 1925 he produced his sixtieth design, the *Moth*, which led to a series of innovative light aircraft in a range that was loved by military and civilian flyers alike. By the early 1930s a flourishing de Havilland Aircraft Company was weathering the global recession and ambitious to stay ahead of the competition – in both Britain and America.

By the time the MacRobertson gauntlet was thrown down, Geoffrey de Havilland was acting as much out of commercial shrewdness as from motives of raw patriotism. He believed that high-profile air racing and aviation challenges would continue to propel the de Havilland brand forward, a pattern of promotion that would later be taken up by car manufacturing companies in Formula 1 racing after the Second World War.

No sporting event could draw the crowds in the same way as a flying display, and although few might be able to afford private flying, the thirst for passenger flight presented a case for huge potential profits.

The design drawn up by de Havilland's designer, Arthur Hagg, for the MacRobertson Air Race would be as superlative as it was expensive. Combining thin, lightweight woods cross-laminated by the latest resin adhesives produced a material of ample strength. Hagg calculated he could build a robust monoplane free from air-disturbing features such as support wires. The wafer-thin wings required greater support than the frame could cope with, but the ingenuity of Hagg's use of woods meant a significant load was carried in the skin and not solely in the frame. The coverings of the wings were thin, interlocking laminated 'planks' set at right angles to one another in a pattern similar to a parquet floor. To maximise the aircraft's aerodynamic qualities, it was necessary to make its undercarriage retractable, which was not a common feature on smaller aeroplanes. This was achieved by a wheel in the cockpit that had to be turned fourteen times by hand. Sanded, painted and polished to an ultra-smooth finish, the *Comet* would be a slippery flying machine.

Even if Geoffrey de Havilland managed to produce the Comet in record time, the main problem he faced was cost. New aircraft designs were extremely expensive, and manufacturers had to achieve a high volume of sales to make a profit. But the racing Comet offered no scope for mass production; its eye-watering price of £10,000 per plane was one that even the most accomplished of racing pilots would find difficult to afford. De Havilland knew that he could not push ahead alone; he would need the agreement of his directors – especially as he was to propose that the de Havilland Company subsidize each racing Comet by as much as 50 per cent, making a price of £5,000 for each customer. Despite respecting de Havilland's business acumen, in January 1934 the Board of Directors agreed to his proposal only with stringent conditions attached. The most difficult to accomplish was that the new aircraft, now named the DH88 Comet, must have a minimum of three orders, and that they should be confirmed before the end of February that year. Perhaps the more cautious members of the board satisfied themselves that in the middle of a global depression, finding three wealthy private buyers would be unlikely. Geoffrey de Havilland swiftly disabused them of such thoughts – before the deadline expired he had secured three buyers. He had actually negotiated five orders, but could build only three aircraft in the tight nine-month timescale. His success was undoubtedly due to his existing strong relationships with members of the air-racing fraternity – de Havilland aircraft had already been used in many record-breaking attempts.

The first to sign for a DH88 Comet was leading hotelier Arthur Edwards, not an aviator himself, but someone who realized the potential publicity surrounding the air race. The aircraft was to be painted bright red with white trim lines and lettering. It was to be named *Grosvenor House*, after the luxurious hotel Edwards had completed in 1929 on the site of the Duke of Westminster's former London home. He chose Charles Scott and Tom Campbell Black as pilots, both experienced long-distance aviators and visionaries of passenger transport. Scott had moved to Australia in the 1920s, where he was instrumental in the formation of Qantas, while Black had helped form Wilson Airways, which operated in Kenya.

Following on Edwards's heels were Jim and Amy Mollison, who decided on a jet-black finish with gold trim for their *Black Magic*. Jim Mollison had already gained a reputation for his record-breaking flights, completing Australia to London in eight days and thirteen hours in August 1931, and England to South Africa in four days and seventeen hours. Mollison also had a reputation as a playboy who enjoyed the fruits of his fame to the fullest. One woman in particular stole his heart – the celebrated aviatrix Amy Johnson, to whom he proposed during an eight-hour flight they made together. Arguably, Amy Johnson's fame outshone Jim's, her rise to popularity sudden and dramatic. Gaining her pilot's 'A' licence in July 1929, she also became the first woman to gain a ground engineer's 'C' licence. With the support of her father and Lord Wakefield, a businessman and philanthropist, Amy purchased a second-hand de Havilland DH60 Gipsy Moth and completed the first solo flight by a woman from England to Australia in May 1930 – less than a year after gaining her 'A' licence. The Gipsy Moth was black, and was named *Jason* after her father's trade-mark, a colour scheme that later inspired *Black Magic*.

Johnson was one of the new generation of post-First World War women who realized that the social order had changed irrevocably. Although work as a professional pilot was still considered to be the place of men, women from all over the globe took up flying as a pastime and began to make their mark in the record books. In the United States Amelia Earhart began her career as a flier in the early 1920s. Jean Batten in New Zealand, Carina Massone Negrone of Italy and Zinaïda Kokorina of Russia were other names in a growing list of female aviation pioneers. Even before the First World War, women were proving they were just as capable of flying aeroplanes as their male counterparts. Johnson's success was emblematic of the emboldening impact of the Representation of the People Act 1928, which gave women equal voting rights with men. Her popularity as a heroine of the sky showed that Britain was now ready to embrace women as sporting icons and celebrities, alongside male footballers, cricketers and athletes.

Jim Mollison's marriage to Amy Johnson in July 1932 inevitably triggered a flurry of newspaper coverage; as well as providing eye-catching headlines, 'The Flying Sweethearts' were an air racing team of great promise. Amy still retained her fierce competitiveness, and would go on to beat some of Jim's records in solo flights in the years following their marriage.* For the MacRobertson, however, they were united as one high-class team; Geoffrey de Havilland had achieved a public relations triumph in persuading them to fly the Comet.

The third DH88 Comet was painted Bentley green, and was bought by the Australian racing driver Bernard Rubin. Unfortunately, he fell ill before the race, and employed Owen Cathcart Jones and Ken Waller as pilots. Other than her civil registration number, G-ACSR, to identify the green Comet, curiously, Rubin did not give his aircraft a name.

Initially, forty-five aircraft were registered to enter the MacRobertson Air Race, but the rigours of cost and technical endurance saw the hopefuls whittled down to twenty by the starting date. Sir Charles Kingsford-Smith – an Australian RFC veteran who had achieved the first trans-Pacific flight from the United States to Australia in 1928 – was offered the option of purchasing one of the DH88 Comets, but turned it down. He believed the air race should be contested on an individual basis between pilots flying the aircraft that were available at the time; it was, he felt, unsporting to compete in a machine designed and manufactured specifically for the race. Instead, he chose a Lockheed Sirius 8A, which he modified for the race. However, the Sirius never made it to the start, as it suffered engine cowling cracks and was withdrawn. Owing to the flexible nature of the MacRobertson's rules of entry, not all aircraft submitted were racing planes, the most notable being a Douglas DC-2 airliner operated by KLM. Named *Uiver* (Stork), the twin-engined all-metal DC-2 would even carry three passengers and mail to Australia. Another interesting entry was a Lockheed Vega,

---

* Jim and Amy Mollison's marriage ended in 1939, partly owing to their pursuit of individual ambitions. Amy then re-adopted her maiden name, Johnson.

a single-engined, high-winged monoplane that had already forged its way onto the racing scene with several victories. It was flown by the Scots pilot Jimmy Woods and an Australian, Don Bennett, who were not destined to have a successful race. Bennett, however, would have a major part to play in the story of the Mosquito and its role in the Pathfinder force.

RAF Mildenhall, 20 October 1934

On a grey, cold autumnal morning, 60,000 spectators turned up before 6am at Mildenhall airfield in Suffolk. Considering that Mildenhall was in a rural location 23 miles northeast of Cambridge, the size of the crowd was even more remarkable. The Mollisons in *Black Magic* were first to leave at 6.30am, even before the pale sun had risen on the horizon. The take-offs were staggered at 45-second intervals, with compulsory stops en route that would release the racers on their onward leg in time separations according to their performance. In order to keep ahead of the pack, the Mollisons decided to limit the number of stops they made, and not to avail themselves of all of the optional refuelling stations. They believed that the other two Comets represented their only true competition. Apart from small differences in engine tuning, each aircraft was virtually identical; the race would therefore be won on the wit and skill of the pilots.

Jim and Amy Mollison's successful flight through to Karachi must have given them great confidence, but they were told that *Grosvenor House* was only thirty minutes behind them. Karachi was an optional stop, with the next compulsory stop ahead at Allahabad. The winds of fortune now shifted, however, the Mollisons twice suffering setbacks as they attempted to take off from Karachi. On the first occasion, the wheels failed to fully retract, which required the attention of mechanics back

Jim and Amy Mollison boarding Black Magic, *20 October 1934.*

on the ground. The problem having been fixed, they managed to take off successfully, only to realize once they were airborne that they had left the Allahabad stage map behind, and would have to return for it. Perhaps an understandable tiredness lay behind the Mollisons' oversight, but whatever its cause, it lost them their lead and – a few hours later – the entire race. With a flight distance of 925 miles, the Comet could fly directly to Allahabad, but the Mollisons made navigation errors, which meant they were forced to land at Jabalpur, 190 miles short – and south – of their intended destination. Had this been one of the optional refuelling locations, there might have been some hope of redeeming their error, but there was no aviation fuel to be found at Jabalpur, and they had to resort to refilling with petrol used for buses. By the time they reached Allahabad, the fuel had caused irreparable damage to *Black Magic*'s engines, and Jim and Amy were forced to retire.

Gleefully taking the lead, Scott and Campbell Black pushed on in the gleaming red *Grosvenor House*, but they faced their own technical problems and had to fly on one engine over the Timor Sea. Repaired at Darwin, they roared on via Charleville, Queensland, to cross the finishing line at Melbourne's Flemington Racecourse like a 'winged crimson bullet' in front of 100,000 thrilled spectators. De Havilland's red wonder had completed the race in seventy hours, fifty-four minutes and eighteen seconds. That a Comet had won was perhaps not too much of a surprise for the entrants, but the aircraft coming in second place certainly raised eyebrows. KLM's DC2, *Uiver*, came in twenty hours later, on 24 October, after completing all twenty-two refuelling stops with its cargo of three passengers and 25,000 letters.

Departure of Black Magic *from Mildenhall.*

The DC-2 had been only eight hours behind at Singapore but became hopelessly lost at night in an electrical storm on the last leg from Charleville to Melbourne. The storm had rendered their navigation instruments useless, and the pilot, Captain Parmentier, made several course changes in an attempt to find a safe landing airfield. There followed one of the most remarkable incidents of the race and arguably aviation history. Farmers in remote areas called their local ABC radio station to report an aircraft overhead. Knowing the air race was taking place, the radio station contacted the race control, who asked sub-editor Clifton Mott to try signalling the aircraft with a flashlight in morse code. The residents of Albury, New South Wales, would attempt to show *Uiver* where to land.

Mott met up with electrical engineer Lyle Ferris and District Postmaster Reg Turner, who knew morse code; all three men went to the town's electrical substation and began signalling A-L-B-U-R-Y by turning the lights of Albury off and on. An appeal on the radio at 12.54am led to eighty cars being driven to the racecourse, where they illuminated the ground with their headlights. Approaching Albury, *Uiver* made several passes of the course, and after dropping parachute flares to further illuminate the ground, landed at 1.17am – only 21 minutes after the late-night radio appeal. The DC-2 landed safely, but subsequently became bogged down in the mud and had to be dug out the next morning before it could get airborne again. Despite this, *Uiver* still finished ahead of its nearest rival.

The third Comet, G-ACSR, ran into engine problems caused by an oil leak at Baghdad. Fortunately, an RAF technician was able to carry out the necessary repairs, and after further attention in Batavia* in the Dutch East Indies the racing-green Comet crossed the finish line in Melbourne in fourth position in 108 hours, 13 minutes, 30 seconds.

The MacRobertson Air Race is considered to be one of the greatest air races of all time. Not only was it thrilling to follow, it showcased the finest aircraft produced to date. It also came at a crossroads in aeroplane development. The days of the enthusiastic amateur who scraped together just enough money to build and fly his own aircraft were over. The aircraft that won races and broke records were now manufactured by

---

* In a notable display of sportsmanship, the technicians helping G-ASCR were KLM employees of the *Uiver* team.

larger commercial companies like de Havilland, Douglas and Lockheed. The MacRobertson had spurred de Havilland to produce an aircraft design that provided the test-bed for wood laminated aircraft, and in the DH88 Comet de Havilland had demonstrated it could produce innovative high-speed designs.

The MacRobertson had also been a triumph for its organizer, Sir Harold Gengoult Smith, as the world's media reported the air race and its climax with breathless excitement. A further significant aspect of the race was the performance of KLM's DC-2, which provided a tantalizing glimpse into the future of travel to Australasia. International flights to Australia would begin in the following year via a link from Singapore to Brisbane using de Havilland 86 Express aircraft operated by Qantas. These connected with others already operating with Imperial Airways from London. The adoption of de Havilland's DH86 model – designed in 1933 – on the Australian route followed their success with the DH88 Comet, but in construction, the DH86 was a more conventional biplane made from wood and

Albury residents pull KLM's Uiver *from the mud,*
24 October 1934.

canvas, and not the pioneering laminates that had swept the Comet to success. In common with the Comet, the DH86 was equipped with Gipsy Six engines – but even with two on each wing,* the journey time from Australia to London was still far slower than the DH88 Comet, taking twelve and a half days.

Technological advances increased the range and capacity of passenger aircraft, broadening the scope of intercontinental travel for business and pleasure. In the military sphere, however, they enabled the creation of faster and more lethal airborne killing machines. In 1935, the year after the triumph of the de Havilland Comet in the MacRobertson, the German Führer Adolf Hitler ordered the reinstatement of his country's air force, the Luftwaffe, in contravention of the 1919 Treaty of Versailles. It is a quirk of aeronautical history that the development of the de Havilland Mosquito – a plane that, alongside its larger cousin, the Avro Lancaster heavy bomber, would do so much to lay Hitler's Reich to waste – owes some small debt to the success of a chocolate novelty named Freddo Frog.

Geoffrey de Havilland's belief in Arthur Hagg's brilliant concepts was not shared by other aircraft manufacturers or by the Air Ministry, which held the purse strings of military development. The idea of laminating woods together was seen as novel, but also as a distraction from the task of inventing new aeroplanes capable of competing with Germany's latest models. In March 1934, even as the DH88 Comet was being designed, Willy Messerschmitt and Robert Lusser began work on their 'Project Number P.1034', a German government contract to produce an all-metal fighter capable of reaching speeds up to 400kmph (250mph). Of the many German aeroplane designs

---

* The later two-engined version, the DH89 Dragon Rapide, proved to be a far more successful design.

of this period, the aircraft later identified as the Messerschmitt BF-109 was seen as the greatest threat to the Royal Air Force. The idea of shifting from timber to metal construction had taken years to be accepted – it seemed as counter-intuitive to aircraft manufacturers as steel-hulled boats had been to wooden ship builders. As with many technological breakthroughs that shaped the Second World War, its foundations had been laid in the Great War.

Döberitz airfield, Berlin, 12 December 1915

Fastening the seat straps, Leutnant Theodor Mallinckrodt eased himself into the round opening of his cockpit. It was a snug fit, the lip covered in a leather bumper to protect against injury. Since the cockpit lacked a windscreen, Mallinckrodt's head and shoulders protruded above the top surface of the fuselage, his goggles the only protection against the slipstream. In common with all flying machines of the time, the aircraft had only sparse instrumentation, but it was sufficient to guide the pilot. The panel in front of him was made from wood and varnished to avoid water saturation; other than this, however, the aeroplane's construction was – unusually – all metal. The joystick, rising from the floor and topped by a rubber grip, was a simple bar that could be pushed and pulled with one hand. The fixed undercarriage was rudimentary, its simple frame supporting two solid wheels; there was no tail wheel, only a skid to land on.

The Junkers J1 was an experimental aircraft; it was also a monoplane, which made the pilot who perched above its broad wings feel even more exposed. On this day, Mallinckrodt was intensely aware of the watching group surrounding his aeroplane, checking his progress and scrutinizing every move he made. Among the men gathered was Professor Hugo Junkers, the owner and designer of the J1. Checking that the fuel tap and magneto switch was 'on', Mallinckrodt signalled for the two-blade propeller to be swung to start the engine. After a couple of attempts the engine spluttered into life, the wind blasting the top of his head and filling his nostrils with the smell of the fumes that blew down from a tall exhaust pipe above the engine. He pulled his goggles down, wiggled the joystick and made one final check that his control surfaces moved correctly before opening the throttle. The engine popped and crackled rather than roared and, once the chocks were pulled away, the J1 edged cautiously forward. The task for the day was not to be overly ambitious, a few taxi runs up and down the airfield followed by some short hops into the air – assuming the J1 would actually fly, of course.

The flight testing began on 12 December 1915 at the Döberitz airfield west of Berlin on a far from perfect flying day. There was a gusting breeze, but considering Mallinckrodt's task was to fly only a short distance, the conditions were regarded as safe enough. Time was also in short supply – it was crucial that the testing of this experimental aircraft did not divert attention from the main task of producing air-craft for *Die Fliegertruppe* – the flying arm of the Imperial German Army. Professor Hugo Junkers' interest in aviation was of long standing, although before the war he had been best known for his work in developing gas stoves, pressure regulators and fan heaters during his time lecturing at Aachen University. He was persuaded that military design work was his patriotic duty, although he was never enthusiastic about war. The Junkers J1 was a private enterprise that Junkers felt was an exciting development in the use of lightweight metal rather than wood and canvas. As early as 1909 Junkers had teamed up with fellow professor Hans Reissner at Aachen to produce the world's first all-metal aeroplane, the *Reissner Canard*, which used thin corrugated iron and first flew in

1912. Advances in another German invention, *Duralumin*, a lightweight aluminium alloy, further fuelled Junkers' belief that the future lay in metal rather than wood. However, owing to problems with Duralumin flaking during metalworking, the J1 used thin 'electric steel' that had been developed for electrical transformers. Even before Mallinckrodt had climbed into the cockpit, detractors of the design had named it the *Blechesel*, the 'Sheet metal donkey'; it was a preposterous waste of time, they said, which went against the principles of flight.

Bumping across the grass at Döberitz, Mallinckrodt gently picked up speed, and after a few taxis, he allowed the tail to lift until the main wheels bounced a few inches above the surface. The pilot was not only testing the J1's aerodynamic properties; he wanted to make sure the wings and fuselage were robust enough to take the weight without cracking. Even in these early days, Germany had an *Inspektorat der Fliegertruppen* ('Inspectorate of flying troops'), one of whose roles was to ascertain whether a design was safe, but every test pilot knew that his life could end abruptly while flying an experimental aeroplane. The J1 had undertaken tests using sandbags in the fuselage at the Junkers factory at Dessau, north of Leipzig, to confirm the strength of the structure before certification. Mallinckrodt eased the J1 into the air, flying at an altitude of 3 metres, in a number of short hops. Any elation he might have felt, however, was cut short on one hop when the wind caught the J1 suddenly and the port wingtip scraped along the ground, bending the wing at the root and making repairs necessary.

The J1 took to the air again in a series of successful tests in January 1916, but after this, its work was done and other designs took over. The J1 was retired and was displayed in the Deutsches Museum in Munich from 1926.* The 'Sheet metal

---

* The J1 was destroyed during an Allied air raid in the Second World War.

donkey' had become a celebrated pioneer, the precursor of the metal monoplanes that would dominate civil and military flying in the years to come.

What Junkers was trying to achieve in the J1 was an aerodynamic design without the encumbrances of the struts and wire that were necessary to give strength to wooden-framed aeroplanes. The key developmental features were increased weight and engine power, which enabled these new all-metal aircraft to overcome the retarding effects of drag. This incremental improvement in engine power in the 1920s and 1930s increased the popularity of Duralumin-based aeroplanes and led to their adoption in Germany and America. Britain was somewhat slower in adopting the all-metal designs, partly owing to the cut in defence spending after the First World War. Companies like Boeing, Fokker, Lockheed and Douglas were fast developing all-metal commercial airliners throughout the 1930s. The growing threat of conflict from the mid-1930s gave new impetus to British designs for warplanes, but companies like Avro, Shorts and Handley Page also worked hard to keep up with their competitors in the civilian market.

Geoffrey de Havilland had recognized how light wood laminates could function as effectively as metal in producing a tough, lightweight skin. He too had wrestled with the challenges of ridding a design of support wires, and in Arthur Hagg's DH88 Comet he had come up with a design that emerged triumphant against metal competitors in the MacRobertson Air Race. But the Comet was seen as a novelty, perhaps just an interesting pause in the inevitable forward march of aluminium-based aircraft. Nevertheless, Arthur Hagg had continued to work on the principles of laminated wood, and in 1936 he designed the DH91 Albatross, a twenty-two-seat civilian airliner that flew for the first time in May the following year. The Albatross operated successfully on the routes from Bristol to Shannon and Lisbon, but only seven were completed, and they were largely ignored by the Air Ministry as having little relevance in the aerial arms race of the late 1930s.

Standing in the House of Commons on 17 March 1936, Sir Phillip Sassoon, Under-Secretary of State for Air, cleared his throat to present the estimated air budget for the year. With so many statements on the defence of the realm having been made in recent months, the attendance in the House could hardly be described as a throng. Sassoon was also at a disadvantage in standing at 3.58pm – a time when some members were already thinking about an end-of-day drink before sauntering off for dinner. Sassoon, however, was an accomplished speaker and amiable socialite who was not unduly perturbed by a lack of audience. He announced that spending would increase for the fifth year running, and that expenditure on the Royal Air Force would rise to £43,500,000. Failing to contribute towards the 'collective defence against aggression,' he stated, could lead to a situation where 'the course of Europe and the world is set once more for a regime of international anarchy. The whole fabric of civilization may well be imperilled.' Although politicians were prone to embroider their speeches to gain the attention of dozing back-benchers, Sassoon's words proved to be chillingly prophetic. No doubt spurred by Germany's direct violation of the Versailles Treaty ten days earlier in re-occupying the Rhineland, Sassoon put forward a budget that would propel Britain's air industry onto a war footing.

On 8 September 1936, three months after the outbreak of the Spanish Civil War, the Air Ministry issued specification P.13/36 for a twin-engined heavy bomber capable of carrying 3,000lbs of bombs at 275mph. Amid the welter of specifications and ideas produced at the time, P.13/36 would stand out as a seminal document in the history of the Royal Air Force, and ultimately, the direction of the war. It led to the development of the Handley Page Halifax and Avro Manchester, a project later converted to the highly successful Lancaster bomber. Geoffrey de Havilland was still intrigued by the use of laminated woods, and he believed an aircraft design incorporating his methods could surpass the performance stipulated by P.13/36, but persuading Whitehall mandarins – as we will see – would be another matter. It was not that the Air Ministry was against using alternative materials to aluminium – they recognized that using a broader range of materials would help supply the burgeoning aircraft industry. Anticipating shortages, the Air Ministry commissioned several designs that relied on older technologies than Duralumin, among them Armstrong Whitworth's Albemarle, which utilized plywood over a light steel framework and was designed as a light bomber. By the time it first flew in 1940, the pace of technological advance had rendered the Albemarle obsolete as a bomber, and most of them saw out the war in transport duties, including towing gliders.

The idea of a fast unarmed bomber was raised in May 1937 by George Volkert, chief designer at Handley Page. He argued it might be possible to create a bomber that could cruise at 300mph – fast enough to outpace the fighters of the time. Although his thinking found favour with some in the Air Ministry, the notion of a bomber whose sole defence against enemy fighters would be its swiftness was felt to be too fragile, given that Germany was itself developing new fighters of increased speed. The First World War had demonstrated that bombers, no matter their speed, needed defensive armament. This thinking had become an article of faith not only in London, but also in Berlin and Washington DC. The Boeing Model 299, first flown by the Americans in October 1935, was soon dubbed the 'Flying Fortress' because it was bristling with machine-gun positions. Boeing had adopted a fashionable term, as the fortress mentality was sweeping European defence thinking. France was building the hugely expensive Maginot

Line, a string of emplacements and forts designed to repel a German attack. In response the Germans built the Siegfried Line, which extended 630 kilometres from the Dutch border at Kleve to the Swiss border at Weil am Rhein. As in the arms race before the First World War, both Germany and the Allied powers were building battleships with large guns. The Flying Fortress, also known more simply as the B-17, followed this pattern of thinking. The bomber would, in theory, be so defensively strong that it could beat off any fighter opposition. By developing a box formation, the Flying Fortresses could cover any angle of attack and bring multiple machine guns onto an attacking enemy.

The Air Ministry was not as optimistic as the Americans, but still preferred their bomber designs to have multiple defensive firing positions. They knew that weight affected bomb load and range, so the prospect of a ten-man crew as on the Flying Fortress did not appeal. Given the prevailing view that only aluminium-built aeroplanes could provide the strength necessary, it was unsurprising that Geoffrey de Havilland's proposal to build a lightweight bomber from wood was met with polite bemusement. De Havilland believed that by further developing the principles used in his DH91 Albatross airliner, he could produce a laminated wood aeroplane that was lightweight but strong. He was excited, too, by the Rolls-Royce Merlin, as it was clear that even more powerful versions of the engine would be developed in future. He believed his idea could produce a bomber capable of flying 1,500 miles with a 4,000lb bomb load at a maximum speed of 260mph. On 7 July 1938 Geoffrey sent a letter to Air Marshal Wilfred Freeman, the Air Council's member for Research and Development, setting out his design concepts. De Havilland's first concept included an upper gun turret, but before the end of the month he had written again to Freeman outlining the thinking for what was to become the Mosquito. By reducing armament he could increase speed even further, beyond 300mph, perhaps heading for 400mph. De Havilland's enthusiasm and powers of persuasion won Freeman over to such an extent that the Air Marshal himself became an enthusiastic advocate.

In early October 1938, Geoffrey de Havilland and his chief engineer, Charles Walker, came to Adastral House in central London for a key meeting with the Air Ministry. On entering the building through an imposing portico on the corner of Kingsway and Aldwych, the two men found themselves in a lavish art deco foyer. Tall etched mirrors stretched the height of the walls, and a large rug covered part of the floor, which was adorned with square and triangular patterns. Decorative wall fittings cast light upward from their gold-leafed bases. As de Havilland and Walker clutched their briefcases, they could be forgiven for believing they had entered a cinema or a Hollywood set. Within a few minutes the men were guided through doors, up flights of stairs and down corridors smelling of wax polish to a large oak-panelled room. In the centre of the room was a fireplace, and above it, on a fielded panel, the crest of the Royal Air Force hung resplendently. De Havilland and Walker took their seats at a broad teak table and, after introductions, presented their case for their laminated wood bomber design. The concept was not new to those sitting at the table, but it was a first chance for the Air Ministry to voice their thoughts formally.

The meeting was perfectly pleasant, but the outcome was not favourable to de Havilland. In the very polite way that British culture dictates, papers were moved around the table, the silver ashtrays in front of them pushed back and forth, reading glasses put on and then removed in thought. In this ballet of etiquette, no one was quick to reject de Havilland's ideas, but as the meeting progressed it became clear to him that the members gathered were not enthusiastic about his proposal. De Havilland was a man to be respected, a personality of some repute and no doubt an important manufacturer with much to contribute to the coming war effort. To soften the blow of the rejection, the meeting asked if de Havilland might be interested in making wings for the Bristol Blenheim? Although commercially attractive, the proposal cut straight across Geoffrey's plans – it was meant to put a stop to his design.

Despite this discouragement, de Havilland pressed on with the design process. Although he had not achieved the funding he wanted, his other business activities allowed work on the laminated wood bomber to continue. By the outbreak of war in September 1939 de Havilland had agreed to use land at Salisbury Hall at London Colney, near St Albans. Owned by the railway magnate Sir Nigel Gresley, Salisbury Hall was a modest property with historic associations; in the seventeenth century Charles II's mistress Nell Gwyn had lived in a cottage nearby, and more recently the house had been owned by Lady Randolph Churchill. Here Ronald Eric Bishop, Arthur Hagg's successor as de Havilland's chief designer, set a team to work on the light bomber now known as the DH98. Salisbury Hall's location, not far from de Havilland's factory and flying field at Hatfield, served two primary purposes. Firstly, the site could be kept relatively secret with newly built hangars painted in drab camouflage colours; secondly, de Havilland was able to demonstrate to the Air Ministry that he was not taking up factory space at Hatfield.

Finally, and not before the project had been dubbed 'Freeman's Folly' within the Air Ministry, an order for fifty bomber reconnaissance aircraft was placed under specification B. 1/40 on 1 March 1940, and work to build the prototype could commence. Even then, opposition to the design continued, and the work was briefly halted in June 1940 in the aftermath of Dunkirk. Lord Beaverbrook, newly appointed as minister for Air Production, told Air Chief Marshal Freeman that work on the DH98 should cease, an instruction Freeman carefully

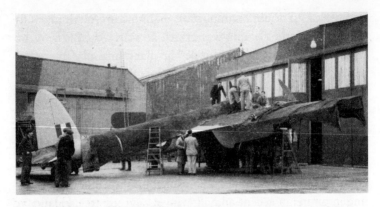

The first de Havilland Mosquito prototype, W4052, is pulled out of its hangar and covered with cloths to camouflage it, 19 November 1940.

ignored, as it was not an official order. Only after de Havilland's General Manager, Leslie Murray, promised Beaverbrook the fifty aircraft by April 1941 did he relent, and the project, now named 'Mosquito', was granted funds to continue.*

The advance from paper to a prototype was carried out quickly, and such were the rigours of early wartime production that only three Mosquito prototypes were built. In an age where test models could range from two to fifty, de Haviland pulled off a masterstroke of engineering on a par with the creation of the Comet racer. Pushed out of the hangar at Salisbury Hall in November 1940, the new Mosquito coded W4052 was quickly covered with cloths to prevent it being spotted from the air. Her bright-yellow colour scheme was conspicuous, and secrecy was paramount. W4052 was dismantled and taken to Hatfield for engine tests and, on 25 November, her first flight with Geoffrey de Havilland Jnr, the eldest of his father's three children, at the controls. The Mosquito immediately impressed with her speed and agility. After some modifications to reduce buffeting, by

---

* Only twenty Mosquitos were delivered in the promised time frame, but the progress from prototype to operational aircraft is no less remarkable.

January 1941 the prototype was obtaining speeds in excess of the Spitfire, and by February it was topping 382mph, closer to the 400mph anticipated by de Havilland many months before.

Even in these earliest of production months the need for secrecy was emphasized on the night of 13 May 1941, when a German agent, Karel Richter, parachuted into a field near Salisbury Hall. Equipped with a radio transmitter, he hid for two days in a nearby wood before setting out on the road to London Colney. A passing lorry driver stopped him to ask directions and was immediately suspicious of the tall man speaking in a foreign accent and carrying a new suitcase. He alerted local police and Richter was quickly arrested. Richter subsequently said that his task was to make contact with another agent, Wulf Schmidt, who had been turned by MI5. Although Richter did not confess to any knowledge of a secret aircraft facility at Salisbury Hall, his proximity to the site was an unnerving coincidence. The Germans seem to have experienced some difficulty in the successful placement of agents into Britain. This may have been partly a result of their policy of recruiting individuals from prisons or concentration camps, who were offered their freedom in exchange for agreeing to serve the Nazi state. Richter had been arrested by the Gestapo after being deported from Sweden for trying to enter the country illegally. Before the war he had served on ocean liners, making frequent transatlantic crossings and by September 1939 he had a girlfriend and son in America. Leaving his ship, he had travelled across Poland and Lithuania to Sweden hoping to make a return to the United States. His lack of training, and possibly nerve, led him to delay his supposed journey to London, but his chances of effectively blending into British society were negligible.*

* After trial at the Old Bailey, Richter was hanged at Wandsworth prison on 10 December 1941, but only after a ferocious struggle with prison warders.

*The prototype DH.98 Mosquito, now marked W4050,
in the field behind Salisbury Hall before its first flight,
25 November 1940.*

In July 1941 the first prototype Mosquito PR1, W4051 (PR for photographic reconnaissance) was delivered to RAF Benson in Oxfordshire for training with No.1 Photographic Reconnaissance Unit (PRU). The first operational sortie of a Mosquito was conducted by 1 PRU on 17 September, flying W4055 via a remote route to photograph Brest and continuing south down the Bay of Biscay to the Franco-Spanish border. Delivery of the first bombers, the Mosquito Mk B. IV, to 105 Squadron based at Horsham St Faith, began on 17 November 1941. However, the completion of the first order for fifty Mosquitos was by now six months late – which did little to boost the reputation of the Mosquito within the Air Ministry. It took 105 Squadron some time to acclimatize to the new Mosquito, but perhaps longer for raid planners to include them in significant operations. Throughout 1942 they carried out low-level raids on industrial targets in Holland and northern Germany. Their activities remained a secret to the British public until Oslo in September, perhaps illustrating the lingering reservations of the Air Ministry in respect of the Mosquito's viability. The Germans, on the other hand, were all too aware of this new fighter bomber, and countered the daylight raids by meeting the incoming Mosquitos with the Focke-Wulf FW190 wherever possible. Despite not inconsiderable losses in these early attacks,* the reputation of the Mosquito built quickly – not least because everyone who flew it was captivated by its outstanding performance.

Geoffrey de Havilland with a DH98 Mosquito, 14 October 1943.

Despite all the hurdles placed in their path, de Haviland had decided that, in both prototype and production stages, they would press ahead with different versions of the Mosquito. Even as the first photo reconnaissance and bomber versions were being assembled, the third prototype, W4052, was being developed as a fighter variant: the F Mk II, with nose-mounted guns instead of an observer's position. The inclusion of four Browning .303 machine guns in the nose and four Hispano 20mm cannon in the lower fuselage produced a fighter with unparalleled punch. Although de Havilland had resisted pressure to fit defensive armament in the form of a rear-firing turret, the inclusion of forward guns was not detrimental to the Mosquito's performance.

---

* 105 Squadron's Roll of Honour shows fifty-one aircrew deaths from the end of May 1942 to April 1943.

The Mark II was an aggressor designed to seek out enemy aircraft – and at a time when the most pressing need was for night fighters.* W4052 first flew on 15 May 1941, only two days after the capture of Karel Richter nearby, and led to the building of the Mosquito NF Mk II (the added letter 'N' stood for 'Night', and the plane was equipped with nose radar) that garnered 176 initial orders from the RAF. Delivery of this second tranche of Mosquitos began in January 1942 to 157 Squadron at RAF Castle Camps in Cambridgeshire. Owing to the need for months of training for crews, the Mosquito did not achieve its first victory as a night fighter until 24 June of that year; but, as with its photo reconnaissance and bombing roles, the Mosquito was proving its mettle.

The shift in identity from 'Freeman's Folly' to the 'Wooden Wonder' was greatly influenced by one man whose vision for the Mosquito was to prove fundamental in its extensive career. In July 1942 Air Marshal Don Bennett took the reins of the newly formed Pathfinder Force (PFF). Hearing of de Havilland's new aircraft, Bennett wasted no time visiting Hatfield to see the aircraft for himself, and in August he acquired the newly equipped 109 Squadron for pathfinding work. In the autumn Bennett took part in his own test flights, having installed the Oboe† navigation device in two Mosquitos of 109 Squadron. At a stroke he demonstrated that the Mosquito would be suitable as a night bomber – and, he believed, a valuable addition to his Pathfinder force. At a meeting Bennett attended at the Air Ministry a few days later, some of the nagging doubts as to the Mosquito's operational viability were aired yet again, with one member reporting the aircraft unsuitable

---

* The period of the 'Blitz' from 7 September 1940 to 11 May 1941 proved a testing time for Britain's night defences and exposed serious shortcomings in night fighter availability.
† A blind bombing system based on a transponder that followed the convergence of two radio signals sent from Britain.

for night operations owing to the glare of the exhausts close to the cockpit.*

'That's strange,' Bennett interjected. 'I've flown it for a few nights this week and had no problems at all.'

It was perhaps this direct intervention by a senior RAF officer that provided decisive advocacy in favour of the Mosquito at an early phase of the aircraft's production. Bennett was one of the first of the RAF Group commanders to grasp the possibilities presented by the aircraft; by his influence, he ensured a steady increase in the numbers ordered. In the hands of Air Marshal Bennett, the Mosquito would prove to be enormously capable, but in time, it became the source of bitter rivalry between RAF bomber groups. The Mosquito's very success led to sharp differences of opinion as to how it should be best used in Pathfinder squadrons within Bomber Command.

---

* This is a curious statement, because by this time 157 Squadron was also successfully operating at night.

3

THE MAN FROM TOOWOOMBA

Fættenfjord, 27 April 1942

Air Vice Marshal Don Bennett, commander of No.8 Group Pathfinders, was well aware that flying a bomber at low level was a dangerous undertaking. On a late April day, only twelve weeks before his rapid promotion and appointment to head the new Pathfinder force, the then Wing Commander Bennett was tightly strapped into the pilot's seat of Handley Page Halifax W1041 heading for Norway. Leading 10 Squadron, his aircraft was one of forty-three bombers sent to hit the German battleship *Tirpitz*, sitting squat in the calm waters of Fættenfjord, one of the eastern branches of the much larger Trondheim Fjord in central Norway. Sheltered by steep hills, the massive 38,000-tonne ship was pulled close to the shore, and her light and dark grey zigzag* painted sides helped her merge into the tree-covered slopes behind. That the Germans had to go to so much effort to hide one of the most powerful battleships of

---

* Zigzag, or Dazzle camouflage, as it is better known, was developed in the First World War to conceal the true outline of a ship.

the era is testament to the relentless hounding of the *Tirpitz* by the British.

Despite the Kriegsmarine being forced to shelter its prize in a distant cage, the *Tirpitz* still posed a significant risk to shipping on the northern convoy routes. Already pressured by U-Boat operations, the Admiralty knew that if this giant were to break free it would take an assembly of some of the most powerful ships of the Royal Navy to stop her. Eleven months earlier, on the night of 26/27 May 1941, her near-identical sister ship, the *Bismarck*, was caught and sunk west of Brest in the North Atlantic after an epic chase by dozens of British warships.* The *Tirpitz* was defended from seaward attack by gun batteries along the sides of the fjords and submarine nets spanning the approaches. It would be a near impossibility for a substantial enough naval force to reach the German battleship's hiding place. The answer seemed to be to attack from the air, but it would be difficult to score a direct hit, and even then, it was likely that any damage inflicted would only temporarily affect its serviceability.

By 27 April 1942 the Royal Air Force had launched nine significant raids on *Tirpitz*, but had recorded no damage. They had chased it from the docks of Wilhelmshaven to Kiel and finally into the deep-water Norwegian fjords, where it had proved difficult to locate the target. Tonight the RAF would send thirty-one Halifaxes and twelve Lancasters into a maelstrom of German defences. The hope was that in the clear moonlight the leviathan could be clearly picked out in its lair and finally dispatched. Wing Commander Bennett knew the attack would be far from straightforward. Even on a light night, the attack

---

* Three days earlier, in the Denmark Strait between Greenland and Iceland, the mighty German battleship had caused a devastating explosion aboard HMS *Hood*, sinking it almost immediately. Of 1,418 men on board HMS *Hood*, only three survived.

The German battleship Tirpitz *anchored close to the trees in Fættenfjord, Norway, April 1942.*

on the warship could not be carried out in formation; the low-level bombers would need to form a queue to avoid each other, thereby presenting the defenders with a line of targets to aim at. The force was to operate in two parts: high-flying bombers would attack the German defensive positions, while Halifaxes from 10 Squadron would roar in at 150 feet and deposit sea mines on the slope above the battleship. It was hoped these would then roll down the hill and fall in the water between the warship and its jetty to explode beneath *Tirpitz*'s armoured belt.*

The first leg of the flight, from RAF Leeming in North Yorkshire, took them to RAF Lossiemouth near Inverness where the aircraft were loaded. There was a grim mood among the aircrew, each hoping they would not be the sacrificial lamb on

---

* The armoured belt was reinforced steel plating installed on the interior of a battleship to protect against shells and torpedoes, but did not extended fully beneath the warship.

a mission that was bound to produce casualties.* The briefing had provided a little comfort. It was not believed that significant defences would be encountered en route into the target. It was an optimistic report, underplaying the risks of encountering fighters in the area or the threat from the intermeshing flak batteries of different calibres likely to be arrayed against them on the fjord's surrounding hills – not to mention the guns of the *Tirpitz* itself and other German warships.

The crew of W1041 had confidence in their captain – Bennett was considered by many to be one of the world's outstanding aviators. Whether flying in marathon air races like the MacRobertson or on long-distance pre-war civilian airline routes, Don Bennett had excelled. If anyone could successfully push home a low-level attack in a large four-engined bomber, it was Bennett. His experience of the events of 27 April 1942 would shape his strategic thinking in a manner that would significantly influence the Allied bombing strategy of the Second World War.

As the fifteen bombers from 10 Squadron took off, they closed up into a stream of dark shapes stretching out across the North Sea. A single blue bulb shone from the tail of each aircraft, pinpricks of light stringing the heavy bombers together. Once they were some way into the journey to Norway, the lights were turned off to prevent them revealing themselves too early to the enemy. The strong moon still enabled the pilots to see each other, the camouflaged upper surfaces of the bombers pale in the blueish light, the Perspex mid and rear turrets glinting. Each aircraft carried seven men, each silently carrying their thoughts, some of which had been committed to paper before they left as a last letter in case they did not return. Unlike the Lancaster, the Halifax had a co-pilot, and Bennett was accompanied by Sergeant Harry Walmsley. Two hundred

* Five bombers were lost that night.

miles from the Norwegian coast they decreased altitude until they could see the rough crests of the waves beneath them. On a long flight such as this – longer even than a raid to Berlin – there was time enough for a sandwich and a nip of hot tea from a flask. Perched in the high cockpit, Bennett could see a dark mass building on the horizon and, before long, he began to glimpse patches of snow on the mountains of Norway through the sea mist.

There could be no hiding the progress of forty heavy bombers once they crossed the Norwegian coast; any element of surprise would be short-lived. The first wave of bombers would drop their bombs from 6,000 feet, and would also try to target searchlight and flak positions before the next wave of low-flying bombers swept in. For 10 Squadron to press home the attack required flying over 30 miles of Trondheim Fjord, an area already well defended with surrounding fighter bases and gun batteries. Each aircraft carried five sea mines* that were to be dropped from 150 feet onto the steeply wooded slope above *Tirpitz*. The concept was as audacious as it was experimental. Speaking after the war, Bennett commented drily that such an operation would be quite possible for a helicopter, but in a four-engined bomber, it was 'to say the least, a little difficult'.

The squadron had tried to complete this operation once before, nearly four weeks previous, on 30 March. It had not gone well. Twenty-two mine-carrying Halifaxes from 10 and 35 Squadrons, with a further twelve Halifaxes from 76 Squadron to undertake high-level bombing, followed a near identical route to Norway, but two of them were lost in grim conditions. With thick cloud and clinging fog down to water level, the remaining force had to abandon the attack. Bennett had not been with them on that occasion, but now clearer

---

* The size of the bomb load was awkward, and the bomb doors did not shut fully.

weather meant that the bombers should be able to find where *Tirpitz* was sheltering.

After skirting the craggy coast they passed through the channel guarded by the large island of Smola before topping the high ground at the neck of Trondheim Fjord. Bennett settled his Halifax 1,000 feet above the water on the approach to the target. The four Rolls-Royce Merlin XXII* engines were being pushed as hard as he dared, straining against the weight of the mines in the bomb bay. In the nose, the bomber aimer was calling out landmarks and heading for Saltøya, the island that served as a navigation point into the mouth of Fættenfjord. In an early form of pathfinding, Bennett's aircraft dropped float flares to guide the force into the target. Ahead they could see the flashes of searchlights flicking across the water waiting for them. As they rounded Saltøya, all hell broke loose. The port side of the fjord lit up with the flashes of guns, tracer shells streaking towards them in a blinding frenzy. The warships on their starboard side also opened fire on them as they approached. *Tirpitz* was obscured behind a smokescreen, but behind it anti-aircraft batteries on the German battleship were also roaring away.

Bennett's first pass was not successful as the bomb aimer did not release his mines owing to the dense acrid smoke. Unable to see *Tirpitz* until the last moment, they whipped over her masts and Bennett put the Halifax into a turn to try again. The manoeuvre was the most hazardous of Bennett's entire RAF career: he flew the aircraft up out of the fjord in order to go round again for a second attempt but was caught in a blizzard of crossfire from either side of the rising slopes. The Halifax was hit by multiple rounds: fire erupted on the wing behind the starboard inner engine, while a hit on the rear gun turret resulted in Flight Lieutenant Herbert How receiving lacerations

---

* Although the Halifax is best associated with the Bristol Hercules engine the Halifax Mk II Series IA used the Rolls-Royce Merlin XXII.

to his face. Despite being in considerable pain, he remained stoically silent throughout the attack. As he struggled to gain height, Bennett realised it would be impossible to return home in his badly damaged aircraft, but he was determined to get his mines as close as he could to the target. Given the precarious state of the fire-damaged Halifax and the need to climb out of the fjord to safety, Bennett knew the mines needed to be jettisoned as soon as possible; by his own confession, he was never sure how close he actually got to *Tirpitz* when they left the bomb bay.

Bennett observed the progress of the fire in the wing with mounting consternation, all too aware that the Halifax might blow up at any time. The time had come to brief the crew to prepare to bail out. The starboard undercarriage suddenly came down with a jolt, which had the effect of increasing the drag to dangerous proportions. Using all his strength to hold the Halifax steady, he pointed the nose roughly in the direction of the Swedish border, but he was aware that time was slipping away from him. The injured Flight Lieutenant How in the rear turret needed to be extracted by other crew members, and it took a few minutes to make sure he was equipped with his parachute.*

Don Bennett recalled, 'I regret to say that one member of the crew became a little melodramatic. He said, "Cheerio, chaps; this is it, we've had it." I told him very peremptorily to shut up and not to be a fool, that we were perfectly all right but that we would have to parachute.'

Shortly afterwards, Bennett gave the order to jump. He ensured that everyone had gone before he left his controls. Despite his attempts to gain enough height, the stricken bomber was only at 200 feet from the ground and, with insufficient altitude for his parachute to open properly, Bennett was

---

* Owing to a lack of space in the turret, parachutes were kept hanging in the rear of the fuselage, directly behind the gun turret.

deposited rapidly into a deep snowdrift. Happily, he emerged unscathed from the impact and soon heard the explosive crunch of W1041 embedding itself in a hillside half a mile away. As the echoes died away Bennett was left in the dark silence to release himself from his parachute, which he then buried in the snow along with his Mae West.* His first instinct was to remain a free man. The knowledge that he was now being hunted brought an intensely uncomfortable feeling – a fear no training had prepared him for.

He was fairly certain that other crew members must be close by. After calling out, he soon found Sergeant Forbes, his radio operator, who was somewhat stunned, but in good spirits. The two men set out on the long trek to the Swedish border, some 50 miles to the east. With the assistance of some obliging Norwegian farmers – who helped them on their way and provided shelter and reindeer soup when they were close to exhaustion – they were able to cross into Sweden three days and three nights later. Bennett was briefly housed in Falun Internment Camp in central Sweden, but was repatriated two weeks later. He had benefited from the attentions of two expatriated Australians, one of whom was married to a Swedish industrialist. Reading of his custody, they gained permission to visit, and using their influence they were able to secure a face-to-face meeting in Stockholm between Bennett and Count Bernadotte, the Swedish Under-Secretary of State. Sergeant Forbes was not so fortunate. He spent over a year as a 'guest' of the Swedish state, and had to wait until the interminably slow wheels of diplomatic process allowed his release. Of the other crew members, Sergeants Warmsley and Colgan also made the long and perilous journey across the Swedish border to internment. Warmsley was repatriated four weeks later, but Colgan, like Forbes, had to wait a year

* The life jacket named after the famously buxom American actress.

before returning to Britain. The remaining three, including the injured How, initially made good progress on their walk, but became lost and, after sheltering in a cabin, were captured by the Germans and became prisoners of war.

The son of a cattle farmer in the lush 'garden city' of Too-woomba, in southern Queensland, Donald Clifford Tyndall Bennett was born into a relatively prosperous family in 1910. He didn't particularly like school, labelling himself as 'somewhat of a loafer'; after a particularly disappointing school report, his father decided it was not worth investing further in his son's education. The youngest of four boys, Don's three siblings all went to university, but his temperament made him the most likely to choose an unconventional path. When the family moved to Brisbane, Don went to work on his father's holding as a *jackeroo*, or farmhand. After a period of working for his father, Bennett's enthusiasm for flying led him to join the Royal Australian Air Force in 1930. After training, in 1931 he volunteered to join the Royal Air Force in Britain.* He trained to fly the Armstrong Whitworth Siskin, Britain's first all-metal fighter, with 29 Squadron at RAF North Weald. The Siskin was far from a delight to fly, and was subject to numerous accidents as pilots tried to control its various handling quirks. On one occasion, the inexperienced Bennett flew his Siskin through freezing cloud, which caused his carburettor to ice up. With the engine faltering, Bennett had to make a forced landing in a small field. The Siskin's undercarriage dug into the soft ground, flipping the aircraft onto its back. Fortunately, Bennett had taken the precaution of tightening his straps and

---

* The RAAF entrants were informed at the outset that, because of budget cuts, they were unlikely to be retained, and that volunteering for the RAF would be the best career choice.

managed to release himself without injury and crawl clear. He noted to himself that he would have been unlikely to have survived if there had been any play on his harness. He escaped serious censure at the court of enquiry, but it was recorded that he and an accompanying aeroplane had flown too far on his outbound leg, making his return journey through turbulent cloud necessary to avoid running out of fuel. Behind the official account, the reality was that both pilots had taken advantage of imprecise orders on their training routine, and had decided to fly further than was wise in the circumstances.

After a year with 29 Squadron, Bennett transferred to 210 Squadron, based at Pembroke Dock in Wales – the beginning of a lifelong love affair with flying boats. With airfields around the world undeveloped for larger passenger-carrying aircraft, it seemed the future might lie in the flying boat, an aircraft that could readily use coastal waters and lakes. The aircraft Bennett flew at Pembroke Dock, the Supermarine Southampton, offered airmen a very different experience from later aircraft designs. At a time when pilots were accustomed to open cockpits, the giant biplane had engines set above the crew with the propellers roaring above them. It was also a large aeroplane for the day, presenting challenges in handling and navigation. Here the hand of history brought Bennett to the attention of Wing Commander Arthur Harris, who had returned from a tour of the Middle East policing colonial tribal disputes and minor wars. Harris's passion and speciality was night flying, and he was brought to 210 Squadron to tighten up their skills. Harris found Bennett to be a highly accomplished airman who made the tasks set before him look simple. He was convinced Bennett was a man to be watched – in the best possible sense. The night-flying skills developed at 210 Squadron had an immediate practical application. Bennett recalls, 'Under Wing Commander Harris we led a very active operational life. We did intensive night flying, which was rare in those days, and carried out fishery protection patrols mainly in the Bristol Channel, dropping flares to identify poachers (mainly French) and then calling in the naval patrol to make an arrest.'

Harris also recognized innate leadership skills in the young Australian, and a desire to test himself through new challenges. It came as no surprise to Harris, when their paths crossed again later, to discover that Bennett had resigned his short-service commission to pursue a career in long-distance civil flying. Bennett was markedly self-assured, somewhat humourless and spoke his mind freely. As a self-made man he was always going to ruffle feathers with a tendency to believe that his way was the best course of action in any circumstance. Coming from a strict Methodist background he neither drank nor swore – which made him less endearing in the eyes of those who believed the bonding of aircrews should involve plenty of both activities. Few could deny his ability to lead men and to those who found a friend in him, he was a loyal and compassionate ally. However, he had a reputation for being aloof and highly focused, attributes that did not make him a popular man in the mess, but perhaps were essential traits for a wartime leader. Arthur Harris said of him that he did not suffer fools gladly, and that his list of fools was 'long and extensive'.

Bennett's next move, after 210 Squadron, was to become an instructor at the RAF seaplane unit at Calshot near Southampton. It was not a posting that energized Bennett particularly, but he was glad to be able to fly frequently. It was already clear that he had the peculiar qualities of a pioneer airman – a restless spirit who was already looking for the next challenge before he had completed the present one. In modern terms, he would be labelled a 'high achiever', but in the days of more rigid social expectations, the path to higher rank was clearly prescribed. If he desired, and as importantly, was deemed fit, to rise through the ranks in the RAF, he had to be prepared to endure monotonous postings to obscure backwaters.

Even in his relatively short time in the RAF he had realized he did not fit into the mould of English gentlemen who seemed to waft their way gracefully to senior command. He was Australian, a curiosity in the pre-war social order of the RAF, and at times treated as an outsider. Most senior officers had served in the First World War and had come to regard Australians as very able, but lacking in respect for doing anything they considered trivial or unimportant – even if it was a direct order. Bennett was not of that mould, but believed in doing things his way – a pattern of thinking that, though not undisciplined, was still likely to bring him into conflict with senior officers. It was clear that Bennett wanted to fly, not to warm a desk and accumulate a healthy pension. Later, during the war, Bennett would crash through the RAF system of ranks, gaining promotion arguably quicker than any airman before or since. His abilities were outstanding, but his elevation caused hostility in the old guard, perhaps fuelled further by Bennett's lack of social grace.

In January 1934, while sitting in the officers' mess at Calshot, he read about the MacRobertson Air Race. He quickly concluded he was not experienced enough to be a pilot, but he could put himself forward as a navigator. Bennett set himself to work tirelessly to gain his First Class Navigator's licence, even getting permission to stay away from dining-in nights* to study. He passed the examination in March. Teaming up with Captain Henry Baird, the 1922 Schneider Cup winner,† the pair received an offer of a Rolls-Royce engine on loan, but the task of building a new aircraft around it was too great. With entries to the MacRobertson closing, Bennett settled

---

* The long-established formal dress dinners were a common feature of all British regiments for centuries.
† Baird won the Schneider Cup race at Golfo Di Napoli in a Supermarine Sea Lion II.

for a partnership with Jimmy Woods, a Scot,* as a navigator. The Australian aviation pioneer Horrie Miller had acquired a second-hand Lockheed Vega for the air race, but realized he was too busy to compete and asked Woods to stand in for him. Perhaps inevitably, preparation of the Vega ran late, since Miller lacked the resources available to the bigger, free-spending teams. As the racers assembled at Mildenhall, Bennett saw the de Havilland Comet racers for the first time; there wasn't time to examine the peculiar bright green, red and black plywood wonders in detail, but it was immediately clear to him that they would be the aircraft to beat. The royalty of the aviation world were arrayed against them: racing pilots

Woods' and Bennett's Lockheed Vega, Puck, Macpherson Air Race 1934.

who were household names, instantly recognizable and loved by the camera lens. Woods fitted into this celebrity set, but Bennett was an unknown.

Taking off at dawn on 20 October 1934, Woods and Bennett enjoyed a good initial leg. They landed the Vega in the dark in Athens, and decided to snatch a few hours of sleep. However,

---

* Woods had moved to New Zealand to fly and later became an Australian citizen.

Air Vice Marshal Don Bennett.

the next day and the next leg proved to be their undoing. As Woods tried to land the Vega at Aleppo in Syria, the undercarriage malfunctioned, flipping the high-wing monoplane onto its back. Bennett was flung from the cockpit and suffered three compressed vertebrae and an injury to his knee. Woods sustained a badly cut head, but despite looking dramatic, the injury proved to be less serious than Bennett's.

After receiving care at a convent, Bennett obtained passage on a ship for home with the help of the air attaché, leaving Woods to await the arrival of funds to repair the Vega. Bennett continued to fly with the RAF during his recuperation, but he was already flirting with the idea of civil aviation. The following year, 1935, he spent some of his weekends flying de Havilland Dragons for Jersey Air as an unpaid hobby. In August of that year Bennett left the Royal Air Force.

By the time war broke out, Bennett was an established transatlantic pilot with BOAC. He was rapidly pressed into service ferrying VIPs and essential items to and from France and Portugal to Britain. In 1940, as an expert in long-distance flying, he was invited to help recruit similarly skilled crews for the Atlantic Ferry Organization, which transported men, materials and much-needed aircraft from factories in the USA and Canada to the United Kingdom.

Bennett's period of flying transatlantic air routes enabled him to build relationships with senior military officers and politicians, and did wonders for his reputation. He rejoined the Royal Air Force in September 1941 as an acting Wing Commander. His first posting was to help set up a navigation school based at RAF Leeming in North Yorkshire, where he sensed a distinct frostiness emanating from his superior, Group Captain Dand. That a young man should rise in rank in such a manner without a collection of medals seemed to irritate Dand beyond all measure. Bennett approached Bomber Command and found them more welcoming. In December of that year he was asked to lead 77 Squadron, operating Whitley bombers. Considered a little under-par by some, the Whitley helped Bennett gain valuable experience in the bomber force; in April 1942 he moved to 10 Squadron, flying the Handley Page Halifax, also at RAF Leeming. Just two weeks later he led the ill-fated attack on *Tirpitz*.

Shortly after Bennett's unplanned holiday in Sweden, he was invited by Air Marshal Harris to lead the formation of the Pathfinder force and promoted initially to Group Captain as a staff officer in July 1942, and acting Air Vice Marshal in December of that year. It had been a meteoric rise for the man from Toowoomba.

The identity of the victim of the first RAF bomb to fall on Berlin has become something of a hardy perennial of the British pub quiz in recent years. The answer generally given – that the bomb killed the only elephant in Berlin Zoo – is, like many random trivia facts, only partially true, but it chimes with the perception that early RAF raids were not only ineffective but inept. Berlin was first bombed by a single French aircraft in June 1940, but it was the night of 24 August 1940 that proved a pivotal point in the history of attacks on the German capital and, ultimately, the bombing war. At the height of the Battle of Britain a Luftwaffe bomber, perhaps a little disorientated at night, dropped a stick of bombs on London. Churchill, mindful of public opinion and the intense pressure placed on the Royal Air Force at this critical moment of the war, could not allow the bombing to go unanswered. He ordered a reprisal attack on Berlin for the next night, 25/26 August, involving eighty-one Vickers Wellingtons and Handley Page Hampdens. It would be a long flight for the crews, particularly those on the Hampden. Even though it had entered service only four years earlier, it was already feeling dated. Nicknamed 'the flying suitcase', its cramped interior made long flights in the freezing atmosphere most uncomfortable.

The raid caught the Germans off guard, for, believing their own propaganda, they had thought it impossible for bombers to break through the cordon of defences surrounding the Reich capital.* Many at their stations that night had never fired a shot other than in training, and when faced with a real raid their coordination with other batteries became ineffective. American reporter William Shirer wrote the next day:

> We had our first big air raid of the war last night. The sirens sounded at twelve twenty a.m. and the all-clear came at three twenty-three a.m. For the first time British bombers came directly over the city, and they dropped bombs. The concentration of anti-aircraft fire was the greatest I've ever witnessed. It provided a magnificent, a terrible sight. And it was strangely ineffective. Not a plane was brought down; not one was even picked up by the searchlights, which flashed back and forth frantically across the skies throughout the night.

* In September 1939, addressing the Luftwaffe, Hermann Göring remarked that no enemy bomber would cross Germany's borders: 'No enemy bomber can reach the Ruhr. If one reaches the Ruhr, my name is not Göring. You may call me Meyer.' His words would come back to haunt him.

Despite finding Berlin, the RAF bombing force were off target, injuring two civilians, destroying a woodshed and the now famed elephant. But it was not the only elephant in Berlin Zoo – they had nine, of which, sadly, only one survived the war. Neither is it possible to conclude that it was killed by the first bomb of the many dropped that night. What made the raid so crucial in history was not the loss of an unfortunate pachyderm, but the reaction of Hitler and his entourage. Characteristically, Hitler was furious, and ordered immediate attacks on London as a reprisal, diverting German bombers away from attacks on Britain's defensive airfields, which were then under intense pressure. It was a strategic error that lost the Luftwaffe the Battle of Britain and, ultimately, allowed Britain to stagger to its feet once more – despite a huge cost in civilian lives during the Blitz.

It is correct to say that Britain's bomber force at this time lacked the technology and training to ensure they could hit their intended target with assurance. Guy Gibson's wartime book *Enemy Coast Ahead** paints an unintentionally alarming picture of early bomber operations: 'Because we had no real navigation equipment, except sextants, which very few navigators knew how to use anyway, we would often stray off track and blunder over some enemy strongpoint and get heartily shot out of the sky for our pains.' Despite glowing after-raid reports that might lead to the belief that a target had been successfully destroyed, it became apparent that the bombers were not only not hitting their target, in some cases they were missing it by miles.

Churchill's chief scientific adviser, the German-born Frederick Lindemann – ennobled in 1941 as Lord Cherwell – instigated research into Bomber Command's performance and equipped more aircraft with cameras to track results. The Butt Report†

---

* Published after the war, in 1946.
† The report's statistical analysis was the work of the civil servant and economist David Bensusan-Butt, former private secretary to Lindemann.

appeared in August 1941 and sent ripples through parliament and Whitehall. It concluded that for every three attacking aircraft that claimed to have bombed a target, only one got within five miles of it. The RAF were stunned by the findings of the report and, facing severe criticism, denied its conclusions. Many have since argued that the data collected over the sample period of research was unrepresentative of Bomber Command as a whole. However, it was clear that radical improvements had to be made to the navigation and targeting skills of the RAF's bombers – and quickly. Progress was already being made in the electronic war; plans were afoot to provide bombers with radio beams, navigational aids and, in time, on-board radar.

One significant strategic move was to focus Bomber Command's efforts away from precision targets at night. The Air Ministry's Area Bombing Directive was released on 14 February 1942, two weeks before the appointment of Air Marshal Arthur Harris to lead Bomber Command. Reinforcing the direction of travel, Lord Cherwell circulated his de-housing report from 30 March 1942, which theorized that destroying workers' homes in Germany's industrial cities could exhaust the Nazi State. However, while recognizing the tenets of bombing accuracy, not all experts agreed with Cherwell's conclusions. Sir Henry Tizard, a highly respected chemist and inventor whose pre-war work leading the Aeronautical Research Committee had led to the development of Britain's Chain Home Radar, believed there was a case for reducing the size of Bomber Command. He advocated that, since so little damage was being done on the ground, the primary benefit of RAF raids was to tie up German resources in defence – and he believed this could be done with fewer aircraft.

The force of these contradicting views led the cabinet to ask Mr Justice Singleton, a High Court Judge, to examine the cases put forward by Cherwell and Tizard. In his report of May 1942 Singleton concluded that the case for area bombing was stronger: 'I doubt whether Germany will stand 12 or 18 months continuous, intensified and increased bombing, affecting, as it must, her war production, her power of resistance, her industries and her will to resist.'

Despite the move away from smaller targets, getting a bomber force to the right area was still a considerable challenge. Of the proposals put forward in 1942, the one that found favour amongst some senior RAF officers, and, more importantly, with the government and Air Ministry, was the creation of a pathfinder force that would arrive before the main body of bombers and mark the target accurately. Air Marshal 'Bomber' Harris opposed the idea, arguing that it would create an elitism in his force that would have a counter-productive effect on morale. He didn't disagree that the RAF had to improve its accuracy dramatically, but he wanted each squadron to contain its own integrated Pathfinders. It was a model the newly arrived US Army Air Force had proposed for its long-range bombers, using the Norden bombsight – in which they had great confidence.* From August 1942 their Boeing B-17 squadrons flew in daylight over Germany, with the most experienced 'lead' crews at the head of the formation to identify the target.

In Harris, the RAF had a plain-speaking, sometimes abrasive advocate who was willing to fight his corner with the tenacity of a rugby union full-back. There were similarities in approach between Arthur Harris and Don Bennett – both men had left a trail of disconsolate colleagues in their wake as they strove to achieve their goals. In Harris's case, he eventually had to bow to pressure, not least because Charles Portal, Chief of the Air Staff, was resolute in his support of the Pathfinder idea.

---

* America was to spend $1.5bn on the Norden bombsight throughout the war. It proved not to be as accurate as promised, not least because it still demanded visual contact with the target in its view-finder – something European weather conditions often precluded.

Navigational equipment like the H2S radar system was becoming available, together with more accurate bombsights based on the American Norden principle, the Mk XIV sight. However, there were not enough H2S sets available to equip the numbers of aircraft necessary for an 'every bomber' approach.

Harris may have lost his battle, but he was determined not to allow his grip of Bomber Command to be undermined. It was suggested that Wing Commander Basil Embry, an experienced staff officer in night operations, should take command of the Pathfinder Force (PFF), but Harris would not hear of it. He had crossed swords with Embry before and argued that his background was too firmly rooted in fighter operations. Among others, Wing Commander Leonard Cheshire had also expressed interest in the job, a proposal never considered seriously by Harris. Instead, in July 1942 he appointed Don Bennett, a man whom he later described as 'the most efficient airman I have ever met' – but one who was not a popular choice within the established staff. Bennett, by way of his route to command, had already established a relationship with high-ranking officials, including Lord Cherwell, who told him to visit at any time to discuss his needs.

With the creation of No. 8 (Pathfinder Force) Group in January 1943, Bennett was free to explore new methods of pathfinding using coordinated illumination techniques to light the target. 'Illuminators' dropped bright parachute flares to turn the night sky above a city into a virtual daylight; target markers would then follow, dropping brightly coloured flares into the streets below to mark the target. In the final phase of pathfinding, supporting squadrons would drop their bombs on the markers to start fires to help identify the target area for the following main force. When cloud cover was too extensive to 'see' the target, navigational aids were used to drop sky markers in the form of parachute flares – or 'Wanganuis', in RAF parlance – to highlight the clouds above the target area with a coloured glow. Despite initial scepticism on the part of fellow Group commanders – and, it must be noted, a desire in some quarters to see Bennett fail – results improved dramatically.

Bennett was still perplexed by the losses his force faced in 1942/43, averaging 5–7 per cent on each raid. Given that each heavy bomber was crewed by seven individuals, this was a human toll in highly trained men that, while sustainable, was far from ideal. He could see the stress etched in the faces of the bomber crews and sensed their weariness at the intensity of the flying. But among the stream of new equipment being offered to him, there was hope for his hard-pressed crews. His acquisition of his first Mosquitos, for 109 Squadron, spurred his imagination. In common with many pilots, Bennett was captivated by the handling, grace and speed of the Mosquito. On 20 December 1942, after extensive test flying, five 109 Squadron aircraft dropped bombs using the Oboe navigation device to find their target – a power station at Lutterade in Holland – and on 31 December dropped target indicators for the first time over Düsseldorf to direct the main bombing force. He built the case for increasing his Mosquito force, proving that at high altitude they matched the performance of his heavier bombers – and in terms of speed to the target, surpassed it by a large margin. Forming the Light Night Striking Force (LNSF) in June 1943, he succeeded in absorbing 105 and 139 Squadrons into No.8 Group, something of a coup, given that both of these squadrons had proved the backbone of early Mosquito operations – including the famed Oslo raid by 105 Squadron. Also in that month, 109 Squadron was re-equipped with the Mosquito B.IX, a more powerful version fitted with Oboe and capable of higher altitude and range.

In many respects, Bennett can be considered the father of the Mosquito in RAF service. Seeing the benefits of the Wooden Wonder rather than its disadvantages, Bennett strove to

The dramatic effect of Wanganuis illuminating Nuremberg,
28 August 1943.

develop new operational techniques for his Mosquitos. These
include increasing the bomb capacity, dropping foil strips
(known as 'window'), to confuse German radar operators and
creating diversionary raids to draw fighters away from the
main target. Flying higher and faster than Avro Lancasters
and Handley Page Halifaxes, the Mosquito could reach its
targets without sustaining as many casualties, and mark just
as effectively from these higher altitudes. Having been more
than satisfied with his Squadron's results, Bennett sought
to obtain more Mosquitos, submitting requests for aircraft
straight from the production line to bolster his squadrons. In
a process of replication, Bennett would establish three flights
before detaching one to become a new squadron.

Bennett attributed his success to his experience, emphasiz-
ing that he was the only senior RAF commander to fight in a

'hot war',* not believing service in the First World War and its aftermath by his peers was sufficient to prepare them for the present conflict. While this assertion was partly true, Bennett allowed himself to believe, mostly based on his tangle with *Tirpitz*, that bomber operations should only be carried out at high altitude. As we shall see, the Mosquito's unparalleled abilities as a low-level strike aeroplane were to prove too extensive to keep within Bennett's constraints.

* A term he used in his 1980 video interview for the RAF Centre for Air and Space Power Studies (CASPS).

4

FRESH FACES

RAF Oakington, 24 November 1943

The deep pulse of Rolls-Royce Merlin engines steadily increased in the grey skies around RAF Oakington, announcing the arrival of 627 Squadron. Ground crew from 7 Squadron's hangar, recognizing the noise was not from their Lancaster bombers, drifted out to see what was happening. Leaning against the large corrugated-sheet doors, they waited for the source of the sound to materialize. One by one, six Mosquitos appeared, each of them a small black dot under the low cloud. As they turned into the final approach, their landing lights pierced the cloud – bright stars announcing the birth of a new squadron. The first Mosquito touched down on the wet runway, producing a cloud of swirling spray, engines chuntering as they were throttled back and the second of the aircraft lined up with the runway for its landing.

The men of 7 Squadron had seen sister squadrons come and go before. As residents of RAF Oakington since October 1940, they considered it to be *their* airfield. By November 1943 they were almost permanent tenants.* This new squadron would share their runway and taxiways, but 627 Squadron would retain their own hangar and living accommodation. As the men sauntered back to work they knew there would be a friendly rivalry with the new arrivals. Both Squadrons – Lancasters as well as Mosquitos – were employed in 8 Group as Pathfinders under Air Vice Marshal Don Bennett, who had no qualms about ruffling feathers in the old order of the RAF. The creation of a special force to identify and mark targets had not been universally welcomed in Bomber Command. Many commanding officers felt it denigrated the skills of their squadrons, who they felt were perfectly capable of finding targets on their own without being shepherded to them.

627 Squadron's first flight from RAF Wyton to RAF Oakington on 24 November 1943 had been a very short hop – a mere 10 miles. The move was the first visible action of an entirely new squadron. Unlike their neighbours, they had no lineage to boast about, save perhaps for the fact that they were created through a division of 139 Squadron, only the second squadron to receive combat versions of the Mosquito. In keeping with the hundreds of new squadrons created during the war, their number was simply picked from a sequential list in Whitehall. If 627 Squadron was to forge a reputation, it would be in the hands of this newly assembled group of men. As part of 139 Squadron they had become part of the Light Night Striking Force (LNSF), which not only performed Pathfinder duties, but also launched diversionary raids to draw German defences away from the night's main target. The announcement of the creation of 627 Squadron came out of the blue one day in the middle of November. As the aircrew were milling around in the crew room at RAF

* 7 Squadron were the only operational squadron to remain on the same airfield throughout the whole of their operational career.

Wyton in Cambridgeshire, mugs of tea and cigarettes in hand, news came that 139's 'C' flight was to detach itself to form part of the new squadron in a matter of days. For the men involved, it meant packing kit and readying themselves, something they had got used to in their RAF careers. Most men in the RAF had very few personal possessions, and all spare clothing and items were packed into a white canvas kit bag with metal eyelets and drawstring around the top. This sausage-like package was easily stowed in trucks and, where necessary, carried around – although it was a burden to lug very far. In keep-

Wing Commander Roy Elliot, 627 Squadron's first commanding officer.

ing with the military ethos of moving men quickly, the kit bag was supplemented with two back packs – imaginatively called 'small' and 'large' – in which more immediate provisions were kept. Nevertheless, the basic supply of clothing issued was spartan: two pairs of trousers, two jackets, two shirts, six collars, three pairs of socks and two pairs of underpants. The men would often buy additional items themselves so that clean items were more readily available, but the average airman still had to fit everything within the bags available to him.

Pathfinders did not occupy a formal rank in the RAF, but were paid a little more and had the right to wear a brass RAF eagle above their battle-dress pocket.* If the new squadron lacked

---

* The badges were removed during operations to avoid questions from German interrogators should they be shot down.

bragging rights, it did not lack experience: many of its crews were made up from seasoned bomber pilots and navigators who had already completed a first 'tour'* – and some of them a second. They were already familiar with flying deep into the night, with all the nagging anxieties that operations brought. To form the Mosquito force, 8 Group circulated an appeal inviting pilots with over 1,000 hours of flying experience to volunteer. This netted a haul of battle-hardened aircrew, many of whom were serving as instructors after their first tour, but still yearned for front-line service.

The man asked to lead this new squadron had not been at RAF Wyton, but was brought in from his command of 83 Squadron on Avro Lancasters. Wing Commander Roy Pryce Elliot typified the qualities valued by Don Bennett; he was a good pilot with admirable breadth of experience, and also a respected leader who understood pathfinding. Born in April 1917, Elliot hailed from Bristol; after attending Bristol Grammar School he found employment as a junior draughts-man at a smelting company in nearby Avonmouth. With the clouds of war approaching, Elliot joined the Royal Air Force in 1937, and by October 1940 was piloting Vickers Wellington bombers with 75 Squadron. It seemed that run-of-the-mill flying did not suit him, however. In December 1940 he volun-teered for 3 Photographic Reconnaissance Squadron (PRU) on Wellingtons based at RAF Oakington – a more exciting but hazardous occupation.

Returning from a raid on Bremen on the night of 17/18 April 1941, Elliot's Wellington had an engine fire on the return leg over the North Sea. It was clear the Bristol Pegasus was severely damaged, and the vibration of the rogue engine eventually led

---

* It was recognized that crews became battle-fatigued. A 'tour' therefore comprised thirty operations not exceeding 200 flying hours before the airman was rested at a training establishment.

to the propeller and spinner assembly shearing off. With the aircraft losing altitude, Elliot had no option but to prepare his crew for ditching. Even in daylight the sea was an immensely hostile place, with wind and wave conditions capable of disintegrating an aircraft on contact. At night, the chances of disaster were greater, but Elliot successfully set the stricken Wellington down, giving his crew enough time to escape. However, their ordeal was only just starting, as only one six-man dinghy was available. That night Elliot was carrying an extra cameraman and a Royal Canadian Air Force scientist, which meant he had two men in the water clinging to the raft. Had the ditching been a few weeks earlier, the men in the water would have succumbed to hyperthermia within minutes, but what little spring warming had happened by mid-April was enough to keep them alive.

With the light rising over an otherwise bleak seascape, the sound of a single Rolls-Royce Merlin engine in the distance filled the men with hope. As a Spitfire swept overhead and turned to begin circling them, they knew rescue was at hand. Above, Pilot Officer Graham Davies of 222 Squadron wondered who must have been aboard the Wellington to warrant the large search effort mounted to find the lost aircraft.* To the immense relief of Elliot and his crew, an admiralty-operated trawler, HMT *River Spey*,† picked them up and landed the bedraggled men at Lowestoft. To their great surprise, they found that Lord Trenchard, a founding member

---

* The search by the Spitfires of 222 Squadron was unusual. Davies, an experienced Battle of Britain pilot, was stationed in East Anglia to undertake fighter sweeps in northern Europe.
† Built by the admiralty in 1918 as an armed trawler, *River Spey* had been sold off for civilian use before being requisitioned in 1939 as a patrol boat and minesweeper. HMT stood for 'His Majesty's Trawler'.

of the Royal Air Force,* was visiting RAF Oakington, and he encouraged their commanding officer to give them seven days' leave. That evening, a student from Selwyn College, Cambridge, recorded in his diary: 'Then we went on to a party with some very lively RAF types from Oakington who were celebrating their rescue from the North Sea yesterday after their Wellington was shot down.'

After his first operational tour had finished in November 1941, Elliot joined the Air & Armament Experimental Establishment (A&AEE) at Boscombe Down, Wiltshire, before decamping to 83 Squadron at RAF Scampton to fly Avro Lancasters in April 1942 on a second tour of operations. Elliot, ever thankful for his sea rescue, named his regular Lancaster, P5669, 'HMT River Spey' in honour of the boat that saved him. Transfer to the Pathfinders in August saw Elliot progress further; in November 1942 he was promoted to Wing Commander. Given command of 83 Squadron, he had already completed sixty-two operations during his flying career. It was this wealth of experience that Bennett liked about Elliot, but he had also heard favourable reports of his leadership style and the appreciation expressed by the men who served under him. Somewhat unconventionally, Elliot had an open style of leadership that allowed information to be passed down to all ranks, creating a culture of inclusion and unity. This approach was not common in the RAF, which still adhered rigidly to the belief that information pertinent to an operation, such as the target and strategy, belonged principally to officers. The RAF had been founded as a separate service as recently as 1918, as an amalgamation of the Royal Flying Corps (RFC) – the air arm of the British Army – and the Royal Naval Air Service

* Not receiving a formal appointment, Trenchard acted as an unofficial Inspector-General for the RAF, visiting deployed squadrons across Europe and North Africa on morale-raising visits.

(RNAS). As a result, the traditions and approach of the RFC's successor organization were similar to those of the Army.

In the traditions of the RAF, certain unwritten rules and conventions sprang up, one of which was to send newly arrived squadrons into action as soon as possible. In the case of 627 Squadron, it would hardly be necessary to break the crews in – they were practised in their job and knew the Mosquito well. Perhaps the most valuable exercise in sending the Squadron out on their very first night would be to ensure everything was prepared for operations from day one. The transport of ground equipment by road could be an arduous task in a short time, but anything forgotten at Wyton could easily be retrieved within a couple of hours.

Even as 627 Squadron made their first landing that day, Bomber Command was in the throes of an all-out effort in a momentous new campaign. The Lancasters of 7 Squadron were being prepared for action, and throughout Cambridgeshire and across numerous airfields in the east of England, the 'heavies' were being fuelled and loaded with bombs for the long trip to 'The Big City': Berlin. Air Marshal Arthur 'Bomber' Harris's assault on Berlin had started only five days earlier. Later called the 'Battle of Berlin', the concerted night attacks lasted from 18 November 1943 to 31 March 1944, and pitted thousands of Allied aircraft against the German defences. Harris hoped that his intense bombing strategy would lead the civilian population to revolt against Hitler and bring the war to an end. As Harris freely admitted in an interview with *Pathé News*, it was a high-stakes – and untested – strategy: 'There's a lot of people saying that bombing can never win a war. Well, my answer is that it has never been tried yet. And we shall see.'

While some targets in occupied Europe could be counted as comparatively easy – a 'milk run', in RAF parlance – Berlin was the antithesis. Harris knew he was poking the hornets' nest, and Hitler's response was to draw his fighters further back to defend the Fatherland. Berlin bristled with anti-aircraft guns, searchlights and early radar stations, where advances in electronic technology controlled the ebb and flow of the action. There was more at stake than damage to a capital city; German national pride, the fuel that had elevated Hitler to power, dictated that the utmost aggression be deployed against the aerial invaders. In retrospect, Harris had failed to grasp how deeply Nazism had embedded itself in the German consciousness, or the cold ruthlessness with which the party put down dissent.

The Battle of Berlin was to become a war of attrition in which Bomber Command paid a heavy price in men and matériel. In the six years of the Second World War the RAF would suffer 7 per cent of its total casualties in the four months of the Berlin attacks: 2,690 men killed and more than 1,000 captured. The impact of this loss of trained airmen and valuable aircraft was compounded by its grievous effect on morale. Speaking after the war, Air Vice Marshal Bennett remarked that, 'The net result was a state of mind amongst crews which automatically reduced the chances of success to negligible proportions. Crews openly admitted that it was useless throwing away crews when there was little chance of success.'

As they entered the hardest winter of their lives, the crews on the front line had little inkling as to the intensity of the battle ahead. For the attack on Berlin on 24 November, three Mosquitos from 627 Squadron would be prepared to support the heavy bombers. Despite their role as night attackers, the aircraft still bore the colour scheme of day operators – dark green and grey camouflage on the uppers and a lighter grey underside, rather than the jet-black finish borne by other bombers. Mosquito crews were less than happy when caught by a searchlight, as the underside of their aircraft would appear white, but the lighter colours added to the feeling of speed and optimism that the de Havilland design so freely exuded. The Perspex nose offered an outstanding view for bomb aiming, which thrilled some navigators. Others were less enthusiastic. The tight crawl space and the exposed feeling in the nose could engender a strange mix of claustrophobia and giddiness. It was, in effect, a tiny room with a glass floor.

Every operational day the crews would be given time to test fly their aircraft to ensure everything worked as it should. Having hauled themselves up the ladder and in through the narrow crew door, they were welcomed by the familiar smell of oil, canvas and that distinctive mix of wood and adhesive. The interior was painted light green, which contrasted the black instrument panels that extended from in front of the pilot to the right wall of the cockpit by the navigator's position. To the uninformed observer, this sea of dials and switches was incomprehensible, but to the crews, each control was a familiar, well-rehearsed part of their lives. In the clear light of day, the location of switches and dials was easy to see and memorize – soon they would be shrouded in darkness. The view from the cockpit was good, allowing the men to see the whole of the upper side of the Mosquito, although the pilot's view straight ahead was limited by the nose when the Mosquito was on the ground. The tubular cockpit frame which held the windscreens was peppered with dozens of small bolts holding the Perspex in place. Every element of this confined working space was designed purely for functionality, with little consideration for the comfort of its human operators. Metal bucket seats allowed the crew to sit on their parachute packs with the back of the chairs sporting only a thin leather-covered cushion. Almost as an afterthought, the pilot's seat had a very small arm rest that folded down.

To each side of the cockpit the engines in their curved cowlings sat only a few feet from the crews – the spinner hubs and curved-end propellers a little ahead of where they sat near the tip of the nose. When running during the day the blur of the blades shimmered their vision on either side – a phenomenon that was almost imperceptible at night. Every inch of the cockpit was refined for the task of the flying machine, and the crew spent little time admiring the view. Pre-flight checks occupied their time, a methodical series of tasks that involved clicking switches and looking at gauges.

The whirring of the starter motors was followed by the jolt and rattle of the Merlin engines starting up. The propellers disappeared into a haze as the engine burst into life, producing a comforting musical note. There were no bombs on board at this point, and the take-off would be sprightly, only a little pressure back on the joystick being required to put the Mosquito into a confident climb. During a test flight was scope to engage in some 'creative flying' of the sort that would be impossible during an operation – clipping the low cloud base with the top of the canopy and turning the aircraft tightly until little wisps of contrail emerged from the wingtips. A few aerobatic manoeuvres away from the airfield proved all was running smoothly and everything tightened down before they returned to practise some swooping dives over the runway.

For the Berlin raid of 24 November, Flying Officers Goodman and Hickox would take Mosquito DZ615, Flight Sergeant Marshallsay and Sergeant Ramshaw D2353 and Flight Sergeant Parlato and Sergeant Thomas DZ442. All had arrived from RAF Wyton earlier that day to form 'A' Flight, and found themselves immediately on operations. The initial task of the Pathfinders was to illuminate the target area with parachute flares. Other Pathfinder aircraft would then identify where the bombs should be placed by dropping coloured phosphorous markers. Their third task was to drop conventional bombs onto the target indicators to provide a focus for the heavy

*Flying Officers Jack 'Benny' Goodman (right) and
John 'Bill' Hickox with Mosquito DZ484 at
RAF Oakington, December 1943.*

bombers that followed, with their much larger payloads.
Armed with four 500lb bombs, 627 Squadron's Mosquitos
had a vital supporting role to play. The bombs they carried
were not special in themselves, but the accuracy with which
they were positioned was key, since it would shape the aiming
of the much larger force behind. By keeping the target area
tight, the Pathfinders could minimize the risk of 'creep-back',
whereby bombs ended up being dropped up to 15 miles away
from where they were supposed to be.

The weather in the late afternoon continued to deteriorate,
with frequent showers becoming more prolonged. An Atlantic
depression was steaming in from the west, and the forecast over
Europe left little to be optimistic about. It was a typical late
autumn day, when darkness and stormy weather never seemed
to be far away. The night before, torrential rain had battered
the bomber force returning from a raid on Berlin, and it had

endured a nail-biting descent through low cloud to find clear air before landing. The majority of the bombers were due to depart their airfields at around 5 o'clock in the evening of the 24th, but word came through that they were to be stood down owing to the unfavourable weather. The raid was scaled back to the three crews of 627 Squadron plus other Mosquitos of 139 Squadron. The intention was for the raid to continue to harry German defences – the offensive against Berlin was designed to be unremitting. The raids of the previous two nights had killed 3,000 and made 275,000 people homeless. Although the horrifying civilian casualties would not be accurately known until after the war, daylight reconnaissance at the time revealed the extent of the damage done.

Flying Officer 'Benny' Goodman and his navigator 'Bill' Hickox* collected their parachutes from the packing building. There was always a smile and a welcome from the parachute packers, normally women of the WAAF who knew the sensitivity of their task. The young men venturing out into the dark winter nights faced a world of uncertainty, and the collection of kit for their flight provided a ritual that could be comforting. Many had their superstitions, and the avoidance of bad omens was key to keeping them in a confident mood. By the time Goodman and the other crews disembarked the bus next to their waiting Mosquitos, they were weighed down by layers of underwear, sheepskin jackets and trousers, life preservers, oxygen masks and tubes. It was very dark, a late autumn night where even the smallest pinprick of light looked bright. Squeezing into their cockpit, they began their pre-flight checks in the glow of the small bulbs with which it was equipped.

A shower rattled the thin Perspex above them as Hickox

---

* 'Benny' after the band leader Benny Goodman, and 'Bill' after cowboy 'Wild Bill Hickok'.

checked his maps on the small fold-down desk in front of him.* Owing to the near impossibility of retrieving anything dropped, navigators 'wore' what they might need using elastic bands around their arms to secure them; pencils were tethered with pieces of string to the board. Space was at a premium in the Mosquito's cockpit. By setting the navigator's seat a little behind the pilot's, a necessity in that it allowed the navigator to clamber down and gain access to the Perspex nose, de Havilland had utilized every spare inch of space. Key to the success of tonight's operation would be the 'Gee' navigation device mounted behind the pilot's seat. Several radio masts in Britain emitted signals which the navigator was able to triangulate onto the target. Despite its potential accuracy, the reliability of the Gee receiver boxes in the Mosquitos could be patchy and, more critically, the Germans blocked the signals wherever they could. Hickox needed to anticipate a journey plotted solely on maps, as there was every chance the Gee signal would be disrupted over the Dutch coast.

Goodman and Hickox were both seasoned airmen, having completed tours on Vickers Wellington bombers and worked as instructors before volunteering for the Pathfinders. Jack Goodman had joined the Royal Air Force Volunteer Reserve in January 1939; after training, he was posted to 37 Squadron from August 1940 on Wellingtons, attacking Hitler's assembled invasion barges in Holland during the Battle of Britain. He was transferred to 99 Squadron, and in the spring of 1941 was based in Egypt flying combat operations during Wavell's retreat through the western desert and in the Battle of Crete.

John Hickox had also completed his tour in the hot sands of North Africa, but not before being shot down in the desert.

---

* 627 Squadron later adopted a fix for the small navigation table in the form of a larger piece of plywood balanced on the navigator's knees, to which his pencil and protractor were attached with a length of string.

Flying from Cairo West airfield on 27 June 1942, his crew had been briefed to attack the Barrani to Matruh road near Benghazi. John had already completed the thirty operations that would bring him to the end of his tour, but he found himself listed on the Ops board two days later – one last trip, he observed. Taking off into the cool of the night in Wellington Z9102, the crew might have hoped for an uneventful flight – bombing missions in North Africa bore little comparison to those over Europe. There would be no intense flak barrages over cities and, they believed, no prowling squadrons of enemy night fighters. Unaware that German aerial defences were strengthening, when an aircraft was spotted stalking them they believed it was an RAF Bristol Beaufighter. They fired two shots from their on-board Very pistol, using the agreed colours of the night to identify themselves. Seconds later, to their consternation, the Wellington was enveloped in the furious clatter of an attack as the unidentified aircraft swept in and raked them with cannon shells, setting fire to the port engine.

Within a matter of minutes, John Hickox found himself parachuting into the pitch blackness of the desert below him. After the noise and commotion of the doomed Wellington, the world became strangely quiet as he swung gently beneath the silk canopy. There wasn't much time for contemplation as the ground suddenly arrived and he landed roughly, but fortunately without injury. Calling out to one another in the darkness, four members of the crew* were soon reunited and, after a short conversation on the position of the stars, began their trek towards where they believed the British lines to be. Stumbling along, they talked about their misadventure and agreed the aircraft that had shot them down must have been

* The pilot, Sergeant V. F. Clayton, and rear gunner, Flight Sergeant M. L. Berg (RNZAF), were both lost, and are remembered on the Alamein Memorial.

a Junkers Ju 88.* They knew they were near the lines when they heard ominous clanking noises; unsure of whose side they were on, they decided to lie low for a time. As the light rose in the desert they found a forward reconnaissance party of British infantry next to their truck drinking tea. For the bedraggled new arrivals, there seemed no better time than this for a cuppa.

Hickox's experiences of his final action in North Africa had not left him by the time he returned home on leave. His sister noticed he had become a chain smoker, and that his hands trembled – a condition that would take some time to improve. When Hickox joined Goodman on the Mosquito, they had both vowed not to get shot down – or at least to take to a parachute. How they were going to ensure they avoided these scenarios was not clear, as the air war had proved there were hundreds of variations of danger lurking for an airman. Their determination was part of an essential survival mentality. In combat, events happened so quickly that there was no time to think, only to act – and choices made in a split second were born out of training, experience and inner motivation.

The flight of 24 November 1943 was no different in many respects from scores of other night flights the crews had made before. Checks completed and engines started, Goodman and Hickox taxied out, leading the other two Mosquitos to the threshold of the runway. The runway lights were briefly switched on for their departure, two lines of gleaming dots stretching into the distance. Beyond this, there was nothing to see, and the climb out through the low cloud would have to be guided entirely by instruments. A green signal light flashed halfway down the runway from the control caravan and Goodman and Hickox were away. There was no question

* The Wellington was shot down by Leutnant Heinz Rökker of 1./NJG at 23.45 hours, flying a Ju 88 C-6. It was his third kill. Rökker survived the war with a total of sixty-four aircraft shot down.

of attempting any kind of formation flying with the other Mosquitos – four minutes were left between their departures. Goodman could see very little through the climb, while Hickox had his head down, keeping an eye on his chart and watching the instruments for any unusual movements. As they broke through the deep band of cloud, the sky was clear, with the faintest sliver of a waning moon. In terms of light, this was the bomber's preference – dark enough to hide them but just light enough to see the dark shadow of another aircraft close to in an emergency. However, even at altitude, winds rocked the little Mosquito, reminding them of the weather front they were flying through. Below them the vast carpet of clouds remained unbroken throughout their journey.

As they closed in on Berlin, and Hickox called out positions and turning points, Goodman was struck by how quiet it was. Naturally, there were no searchlights visible owing to the cloud, but there was also no flak barrage – indeed, no indication from their enemy far below that they had been detected. They were almost upon their intended position above Berlin, and yet there were no fires or glow to be seen under the cloud. They knew the raiding force of Mosquitos was quite light in numbers – perhaps they were the first to arrive? After double-checking their position, Goodman opened the bomb doors and Hickox pressed the bomb drop toggle at 28,000 feet. There was no mistaking that the bombs had left DZ615, as she sailed upwards immediately after losing 2,000lb of weight. All bombers moved upwards and became lighter on the controls when the bomb load was dropped, but with the Mosquito this was particularly pronounced. Later, when the 4,000lb 'Cookie' was introduced, crews compared the upward motion on dropping to a fast elevator.

It was 20.57 hours, and less than two hours since their take-off. Such was the speed of the Mosquito that it had nearly cut the flying time to Berlin in half compared with the heavier

Lancasters and Halifaxes, which toiled their way across the continent at around 240mph. Undoubtedly, DZ615 had been helped by a tail wind for parts of her journey, and the trip home took a little longer. The flight proved to be uneventful, but Goodman recalls landing 'very carefully' back at RAF Oakington, having negotiated 500 feet of thick cloud and heavy rain. The explanation for the quietness of their operation became clear on debriefing. Parlato and Thomas in DZ442 had turned back after fifteen minutes of flight, as their cabin heater had failed. Ten minutes later, Marshallsay and Ramshaw in D2353 also gave up after their Gee set stopped working. Goodman and Hickox were informed that 139 Squadron had also been stood down shortly before departure, which meant that they had been the only Mosquito over Berlin that night – and indeed the only RAF aircraft operating over Europe. The first operational flight of the new squadron was thus a somewhat quiet affair, but nonetheless notable in its singularity.

It would be immediately clear to any observer of the officers' and Sergeants' messes of 627 Squadron that the crews comprised a very diverse group of young men. Not only were their family backgrounds and nationalities disparate, the approach and personality of each was different. From the loud, hard-drinking maverick to the softly spoken church-goer, each had ably demonstrated they were masters of the air. Jack Goodman hailed from Northampton and, in common with thousands, was inspired by the visit of Alan Cobham's Flying Circus to the area in the early 1920s. Cobham brought air travel to the masses with a show that included pleasure flights and dare-devil stunts in a series of tours that covered most of Britain. Goodman recalled the lasting effect of the experience: 'I was thrilled by seeing them tearing around in their flying machines. All this triggered me off,' he would later write. 'I became a voracious reader of every book I could find about flying. A flood of such books reached the libraries in the 1930s recounting the deeds of airmen of World War I – I read these with enormous care.'

Jack Goodman's sister, Pat, remembers him as a polite, well-behaved child, essentially 'upholding the honour of the family'. 'He was a kind person, helpful and popular,' she recalls. When he showed an early interest in music, his parents bought him a harmonium, a choice of instrument no doubt influenced by the family's attendance at Far Cotton Methodist Chapel. Jack had soon mastered the instrument and the need to pedal the bellows while playing. His abilities on the keyboard would come in useful during his RAF career, when he was asked to play the piano for informal sing-alongs.

Jack joined the Boys Brigade at sixteen years old, and became convinced, despite his parents' pacifist leanings,* that war was looming. In autumn 1938, along with thousands of other young hopefuls, he volunteered for the newly formed Air Defence Cadet Corps, with a view to joining the Royal Air Force. Such was his enthusiasm for aviation, he found it unthinkable that he might be called up to serve in the Army in the event of war. He approached his commanding officer, Squadron Leader Roy Brown† – who had flown Sopwith Camels in the First World War – to ask for a recommendation in his application for the Royal Air Force Volunteer Reserve (RAFVR). 'I presented myself to the selection board at the RAFVR at the RAFVR Town Headquarters in Cliftonville, Northampton,' remembers Jack. 'Twenty-five eager souls there that day and only two passed the academic and rigid medical tests.' It was the first day of what would be a thirty-seven-year RAF career.

---

* In 1933 minister Rev. B. J. Coggle was appointed at Far Cotton, a vigorous pacifist and teetotaller who wrote widely in the press and influenced many by his preaching.
† Not to be confused with the pilot of the same name who engaged Baron Manfred von Richthofen in April 1918.

By the time Jack was nineteen, in the autumn of 1940, he was co-pilot of a Wellington bomber with 37 Squadron, engaged in the crucial attacks on Hitler's assembled invasion fleet – the so-called 'Battle of the Barges'. The role carried heavy responsibilities for a young man, and was fraught with danger. On 5 October 1940 he experienced the first of a number of close calls in his operational career.* Launching an attack at 11,000 feet over the docks at Rotterdam, Wellington T2508 was caught by the blast of a flak shell. The loud bang was followed by an immediate roll to starboard and the bomb-laden aircraft went into a spin, leaving the terrified crew trapped in their seats and unable to move. Pilot Officer 'Nobby' Clark fought with the controls, applying the rudder and opening and closing the throttles, but without success. Believing the game was up, Clark shouted, 'Jump, Jump', an order that proved beyond the physical capabilities of most of the crew in the twisting bomber. Jack Goodman unfastened his harness and instead of trying to escape, lunged for his rudder pedals, which seemed to be jammed. Pulling hard, he managed to free them, and Nobby Clark regained control at 6,000 feet. Jettisoning their bombs, they managed to find their way safely home to RAF Newmarket. On landing they found that shell splinters had torn the fabric of the Wellington, and that the nearness of the blast had created misalignments in its control surfaces; it was this that had caused the aircraft to spin so alarmingly – and uncharacteristically.

Eleven days later, on 16 October, Goodman embarked on a mission to attack the *Gneisenau* in dry dock in Kiel. This time he was flying as first pilot – his third such outing. The task of 37 Squadron was to attack the German pocket battleship

---

* Author Max Hastings told Goodman that in seventy-eight operational sorties, he should have died 'five or six times'.

*Vickers Wellington and crew, 99 Squadron, Newmarket,
November 1940; 'Benny' Goodman is second from left.*

in Kiel, with an attack on *Bismarck* in Hamburg* allotted
as a secondary target. Piloting R3224, Goodman opened his
throttles fully for take-off at RAF Feltwell in Norfolk and
watched the speed indicator move reluctantly upwards. The
Wellington was accelerating too slowly and would not 'unstick'
at the point expected, but the co-pilot was unable to identify the
cause of the problem. Despite Goodman succeeding in lifting
the aircraft from the ground just before the end of the runway,
it was clear the bomber would not exceed 90 knots, and he
knew he would need to land as soon as possible. However,
with others taking off behind him, he would have to wait until
the airfield was clear of other aircraft. Goodman climbed at
an agonisingly slow pace, eventually reaching 800 feet. Once

* It appears *Bismarck* had already left Hamburg for sea trials in the Gulf
of Danzig by this date – it is unclear whether this entry in the records
was a mistake in orders or in the squadron diarist's entry.

he had received permission to land, Goodman heaved the sluggish bomber around to line up with the grass strip ahead.* As he sailed over the airfield boundary, he realized he was too high to land, and instinctively closed the throttles. The effect was immediate: the sleepy Wellington fell like a stone, landing so firmly that the undercarriage was forced through the top of the wings. The crew needed little encouragement to leave the stricken bomber. Goodman waited until it was clear that there was no risk of a fire before returning with the Flight Commander to inspect the Wellington. The problem was swiftly identified. The flaps that covered the fuel filler caps on the wing had not been locked down, and had acted as spoilers, disrupting the airflow. The man responsible for this oversight was sentenced to twenty-eight days' detention, but the incident made Goodman more diligent in completing his exterior checks prior to take-off.

Each man selected to fly with 627 Squadron brought his own unique and distinctive story from previous service with Bomber Command. What defined an elite squadron was not the actions it undertook, but the quality of the operational experience of its members; it was this that made success more probable than with an average squadron. In common with many of the pilots of 627 Squadron, Jack Goodman possessed the ability to think quickly and laterally when events demanded it – a gift that could only reveal itself in the heat of combat.

On 18 February 1941 Goodman was flight testing his Wellington with 99 Squadron in the skies over East Anglia, in preparation for a raid that night. When he saw plumes of smoke rising from Newmarket High Street, he realized a lone German raider had dropped bombs on the town. Catching

* RAF Feltwell was still a grass airfield at this time.

sight of what he believed was a Dornier 17,* Goodman quickly swapped seats with his co-pilot, who was sitting in the captain's position, and brought the Wellington around underneath the German attacker. Levelling suddenly on the Dornier's starboard side, the Wellington's rear and front gunners aimed continuous fire at the surprised German bomber. The twin-tailed aircraft swerved and jinked, but took a number of hits to the rear of its cockpit. Pouring smoke, the Dornier eventually lost the Wellington in cloud. Eleven miles away, army gunners claimed to have brought down the attacker, but Goodman was credited with a 'half kill' for his actions.†

In the first few days of 627 Squadron's sojourn at RAF Oakington there was little time for the men to adjust to their new surroundings. Operations continued against Berlin in the weeks that followed their arrival, and raids were also carried out on other targets, including Cologne and Leverkusen. The men's initial impression of their new home was favourable. Construction of RAF Oakington had begun before war broke out, and it included some brick-built barrack blocks alongside the characteristic airfield architecture of draughty wood and steel huts. Some of the new arrivals were therefore able to lodge in accommodation which, although still chilly overall, offered places where one could find a stout cast-iron radiator and rooms that could even be described as warm. But not all could share in the relative opulence of the new airfield – many were housed in the single-storey timber huts hastily thrown up

* A German light bomber sometimes called the *fliegende Bleistift* ('flying pencil'), admired by crews for its handling. It was replaced after 1941 by the heavier and more powerful Dornier 217.
† Records now seem to show that no Dornier was shot down over land that day – despite the army gunners' claims. Luftwaffe records also fail to record a loss, so it would seem that the Newmarket bomber escaped.

to accommodate the wartime expansion of air force personnel. There was little relief from the cold for ground crews, who considered working in the refrigerator-like hangars a luxury compared to the bleak dispersals where most aircraft were kept. These semicircles of concrete, sprouting from the taxiways, could host two Mosquitos; isolated and some distance from the hangars, they were intended to protect the aircraft from air attack. Ground crew pedalling their bicycles to the dispersals in the teeth of a headwind, accompanied by horizontal rain or sleet, could be forgiven for thinking Göring was welcome to any aircraft he could find.

Small olive-green service tents were set up to provide shelter for air crews working in the dispersals; inside the tents, the men would gather round home-made heaters made from an upturned 'Gunk'* lid filled with aviation fuel and equipped with a makeshift wick that produced pungent fumes. Technicians who arrived in the tent, stamping their feet and swearing at the cold, greatly appreciated these unofficial burners, despite their hazardous nature.

Bicycles were much in evidence around RAF airfields, and Oakington was no exception. Most had white stripes painted on the rear mudguard and frame to help identification in the dark. These were heavy machines with few gears, but a determined airman could still get up a good speed. Oakington was an easy bicycle ride from Cambridge, which offered the promise of some relief from the pressures of life on base. RAF Wyton, former home to the men of 627 Squadron, had been close to Huntington, but Cambridge was a larger town and a more promising location for airmen in search of pubs, dances and the company of womankind. The new arrivals at Oakington also explored the taverns in nearby villages, but found supplies of ale to be a little on the short side. A pond at

---

* Gunk was a brand of cleaner and degreaser used on engines.

Long Stanton posed something of a challenge for bicycle-borne pub-goers, particularly as bike lights in black-out-conscious Britain produced little more than a thin strip of illumination. In their quest for a shortcut to the pub, a number of aircrew from RAF Oakington found themselves and their bicycles quite literally in deep water. The local landlord made his feelings explicit when a 'drowned' airman dripped all over his floor.

As operational flying began, the Squadron was still in a state of assembly, with men being posted in from other units, particularly the ground crews. Douglas Garton learned of his promotion to Flight Sergeant while he was in hospital in Ely recovering from a fractured skull after a fall from an incorrectly positioned engine platform. He was particularly annoyed in that he had been called to check an engine by a less experienced fitter, who had failed to ensure the platform was secure enough. During his spell of recuperation, he was visited in hospital by two friends, who told him he was being transferred to 627 Squadron. He arrived at Oakington in late November and, after meeting the Adjutant, navigated his way through a room full of clerks to find a driver to take him over to 'B' Flight. Garton was guided to a knot of greatcoat-wrapped drivers gathered around a coke stove – a scene typical of life in hundreds of airfield huts across Britain during the winter months. One of them, a WAAF, agreed to drive Garton. When he spotted her 'Canada' shoulder flashes, he asked her if she had brought enough dowry over to marry him – a light-hearted query with prophetic overtones. This transpired to be the first meeting of the future Mr and Mrs Garton.

Douglas had trained in carpentry, then worked as an RAF technician before being posted to 83 Squadron at RAF Scampton to work on the Hawker Hind biplane – a light bomber – in August 1938. One of his first major repair jobs was replacing the mainplane of a Hind that had been damaged by a young pilot officer named Guy Gibson. Douglas was also a painter who, when time allowed at Oakington, would adorn the noses of Mosquitos with artwork and insignia. Not all sign-writing was officially sanctioned. Early one morning shortly after their arrival, the men of 627 Squadron discovered that one of their neighbours in 7 Squadron, which flew Lancasters, had written '627 Model Aeroplane Club' in bold letters on their hangar door, a mischievous reference to the Mosquito's construction. Some nights later another sign appeared, this time on the hangar doors of 7 Squadron: 'No.7 Operational Training Unit' – the friendly rivalry satisfied, the brief sign-writing contest ended.

Others were less enthusiastic about being posted to Oakington. Leonard Blake, an engine fitter working on Pegasus engines with Wellington bombers, was well settled into RAF Wymeswold in Leicestershire. As Christmas 1943 approached he and his fellow NCOs were making plans to celebrate at the home of one of their number who lived close by. However, the Royal Air Force had other plans for him. Leonard, who considered himself something of an expert on the Pegasus, a radial engine, was less than pleased to receive an order to transfer to 627 Squadron to work on the Merlin engine, which was very different. His arrival at Oakington on 23 December did not find him in festive mood, and the decorations around the mess hall did little to cheer him. He found the pace of life more urgent than his previous Operational Training Unit, and wryly observed that he had to forget any hope of a 'settling-in' period.

Berlin, 2 December 1943

For the fourth time in a week the cover was pulled from the map in the briefing room to reveal Berlin. Heavy sighs and the restless creaking of the wooden chairs signalled the men's disappointment. News of yet another mission to Berlin never prompted an enthusiastic reaction. On such an arduous and dangerous trip, losses were highly likely, and 627 Squadron would have little time to celebrate having so far kept a clean sheet in operations. A mere eight days after their establishment at Oakington, one of their number would fail to return. In the ceaseless action against Berlin, six Mosquitos were tasked to fly in another all-effort raid, part of a complex pattern of hundreds of bombers heading for the German capital. Briefings for missions involving heavy bomber squadrons, which fielded seven men per crew, could see over 100 men gathered in a single room; 627 Squadron's pre-flight sessions were more intimate affairs, but could still be lengthy. With fewer fliers in attendance, each man had the opportunity to ask questions, but there was less room to hide if the rigours of the day or the monotonous voice of a Met Officer generated drooping eyelids. After thirty minutes on the hard wooden seats, the men would ease their discomfort by perching on the lip of the chair, or by moving from side to side to ease aching extremities.

The route to Berlin was pinned in ribbon to the large map on the wall, but the Mosquito crews were less inclined to follow the prescribed course as exactly as their colleagues in the Lancasters and Halifaxes. It was not the stirrings of a rebellious spirit that prompted this behaviour, but the experience gained over as many as thirty or more previous operations. They might decide to fly at a higher or lower altitude, cut the corner on a jinking route or alter their speed over certain sections, depending on the risk of encountering enemy fighters. The key was getting the job done as requested and returning safely. If these two essentials were completed successfully, there would be little complaint if the plan presented at the briefing was not followed to the letter.

The Gee radio signal was a key element to navigation, but this could be lost because of jamming. The response of the Air Ministry was twofold. First involved an upgrade of the

Gee system to *Gee-H*, which was far more difficult to block and was introduced just as 627 Squadron were formed. The second, and perhaps more dramatic, innovation was a new radar device carried in the Lancasters and Halifaxes called *H2S*, which enabled each aircraft equipped with it to 'see' the ground target. The Mosquitos were not yet fitted with this miracle box of electronics.

As the six crews of 627 Squadron prepared for their operation, RAF Oakington shook with the sound of 7 Squadron taking off. Every serviceable aircraft was being put into the air, nineteen Lancasters, each carrying red/green and yellow target indicators* and 6,000lbs of bomb, including a 4,000lb 'cookie'. The first, JB313, powered down the runway at 16.54 hours carrying eight men – the man over being Pilot Officer Francis Rush,† who was making his first operational flight as a second pilot for the experience. Sixteen minutes later, the final heavily loaded Lancaster lifted off into the early darkness of the winter evening. As the aircraft drifted away, the sky quietened only a little as the deep throbbing of engines merged into a thrumming chorus above. Other airfields to the north and west of Cambridge were discharging their children to Berlin in a massive wave. Fifteen Halifaxes, 18 Mosquitos and 425 Lancasters struck out for the German capital that night.

It was not until nearly two hours later that the Mosquitos were ushered out of their dispersals, the yellow tips of their propellers whirring circles of gold in the ground lights. As the aircraft turned onto the taxiways, the chill blast of air briefly

---

* The sequence and colours used differed on each raid, as the German defenders would attempt to replicate them to draw bombers to false targets.

† Francis William Rush from Hobart, Australia was lost two weeks later on another raid to Berlin, together with five other members of his crew. Hit by flak, their Lancaster, JB656, crashed at Alkmaar, northwest of Amsterdam.

caught the ground crews, who grabbed at their hats to prevent them from blowing off into the inky blackness. Watching their aircraft leave was always a stirring sight, but tinged with melancholy as they wondered whether this would be the last time they would see them. The Mosquitos were lifting off into a much quieter sky. Shortly after the Merlins of the last departing aircraft had sung their way down the runway, the skies above Cambridgeshire at last fell silent – at least for a few hours.

The first mishap for the six Mosquitos came around an hour into their flight. DZ615, which had successfully flown 627's first ever operation, developed a fire in her port engine. The pilot, Squadron Leader Lockhart, and navigator, Flight Lieutenant De Boos, shut it down, re-trimmed the aircraft and turned for home, taking the precaution of dumping their bombs in the sea. This was standard procedure to minimize risk, since the Mosquito was going to attempt to land with only one engine. The crews' maps had circular areas bounded by thick red lines denoting bomb jettison areas. Mosquitos were instructed to avoid these areas, especially at lower altitudes, on nights when a bomber stream was returning to base. The Mosquito could fly adequately on one engine, although the problem was easier to cope with at altitude, where the initial loss of power and the tendency to swing sharply could be countered without too much distress to aeroplane or pilot. DZ615 touched down at Oakington at 20.45, just as Lockhart's 627 colleagues were dropping their bombs over Berlin.

As the Mosquitos approached Berlin they began to see lights in the distance. At first it was an occasional bright white dot suspended like a star on the horizon. Their sky had been empty for many miles, the glow of a quarter moon picking out wisps of cloud, but now more of these intense lights were appearing. The Mosquitos approached the target at around 30,000 feet, a full 10,000 feet higher than most of the bomber force. From this altitude they saw that the white lights were flares dropped from German night fighters to illuminate the bomber stream below them. As anticipated, the fighters were hunting in packs, and tonight there were hundreds of targets for the Luftwaffe pilots to steer towards. The flares were for the benefit of fighters like the Focke-Wulf FW190, powerful single-seater aircraft capable of searing attacks at speed. In a tactic known as *Wilde Sau* ('wild boar'), German radar operators launched free-ranging day fighters into the combat zone, where they relied on flares and ground searchlights to illuminate their targets. Below them and often beneath the level of the oncoming armada of British aircraft, were other night fighters – Junkers Ju 88s or Messerschmitt Me 110s – simultaneously following a tactic known as *Zahme Sau* ('tame boar'). Once they were directed into an area by ground controllers, their onboard radar sets – the Lichtenstein SN2 – could lock on to individual targets. While RAF gunners were watching for higher attacks, the lower fighters would sneak up using the cover of the darkened ground beneath. Positioned underneath a bomber, upward-firing guns could penetrate the bomb bay or fuel tanks of enemy aircraft, causing a massive explosion.

The men of 627 Squadron knew of these dangers, most of them having flown in much heavier aircraft before. They knew the gnawing feeling of uncertainty in trying to maintain a course with prowling fighters about them, sweating as they approached the target and waiting for the bomb aimer to announce, 'bombs gone'. They remembered the rawness of these emotions – the strain and effort of fighting to keep themselves and their six fellow crew members alive. But the experience of flying a Mosquito was very different from the droning progress of the heavy bomber. Here, positioned high above their comrades, they became spectators in a huge grandstand. Buoyed with the confidence that their aircraft was as fast as anything the Germans could muster, they played a game of 'catch me if you can'. Their altitude provided another safety barrier; with so many potential targets below them, why would the Luftwaffe strain another 10,000 feet for a handful of raiders? Here, still some way short of the German capital, they were relatively safe, but in another 20 or 30 miles they would be within the range of dozens of flak guns. Increasingly, gun batteries were radar guided, as were some searchlights. The 'sweet spot' for the German 88mm gun was around 25,000 feet, and the ten-man crew could fire fifteen to twenty rounds per minute. Many batteries operated in groups of four guns, and the rate of fire produced a barrage of fearsome proportions. With each shell exploding at a pre-set altitude, the intention was not to get a direct hit, but to create a cloud of flying shards of metal. Sometimes among the German illuminations a flash of sudden brilliance would appear, as a Lancaster exploded in a ball of fire. On other occasions, the burning aircraft would hang for a while, apparently motionless, before making its slow, arcing descent to earth, like a meteorite. Within this chariot of fire individual stories of immense courage and resourcefulness might be played out, but all too often there would be no survivors to tell the tale.

In the distance the searchlights of Berlin began to appear, their beams penetrating the gaps in the cloud and stretching thousands of feet into the winter sky. From their vantage point, the men of 627 Squadron waited for the next act in the drama to commence. Five minutes away from the target they began to see the illumination flares from Pathfinder Lancasters drop above the city. As the intensity of the parachute flares turned night into day, next to run in would be Pathfinder Lancasters to pick out the target with coloured phosphorous markers. 627's task would be to drop their 500lb bombs on the markers, hopefully within the first couple of minutes of their arriving. The main force would then engage to bomb in a carefully choreographed stream to hit the target with incendiaries and high-explosive bombs. That, at least, was the theory.

Flying Officer Denny and Sergeant Denholm in Mosquito DZ426 were fifteen minutes out from their main target when they developed an engine problem; clearly not over Berlin, but close, they saw three ground markers, two white and one green, and dropped their bombs on what they assumed must have been a secondary target of the raid, before turning for home. At 28,000 feet they had altitude on their side for the slower return journey; they hoped they could maintain sufficient speed and height to make it home. The fact that they had found markers so far out from the intended target was a portent of how the night's raid would unfold. By the time the four remaining Mosquitos reached their target point, the scene was a confusing one. Parts of Berlin were shrouded in cloud, and markers were dispersed over a wide expanse, with at least two major areas of burning fires. As they positioned themselves to drop their bombs, the navigator at the bomb-aiming position in the nose could see the sparking of incendiaries below him, creating a dull white glow in different areas. These were tumbling down too early, before the Pathfinders' target marking had been done correctly. Flak rose in lazy trails upwards, flashing and banging around them like fireworks. The air rumbled, waves of deep sound resonating along the length of their plywood fuselage.

For Flight Sergeant Simpson and Sergeant Walker in DZ479, the night had not gone according to plan from the outset. Even before leaving the English coast, their Gee set had stopped working, giving navigator Peter Walker a lot more work to do. His calculations to target used the forecasted wind direction and speed, but tonight the wind direction was changing rapidly and strengthening from southerly to northerly. Sweeping in from the southwest of Berlin they knew there was no avoiding the belts of flak guns of the protective line defending the capital. At Magdeburg a piece of flak struck their starboard engine, and it began to run roughly. Simpson could see it was failing; the revolutions gauge was dropping fast and, given the risk of fire, he shut it down and feathered the prop.* He decided to press on to the target; they were less than a hundred miles out and, as he needed to drop the bombs, it seemed sensible to hit the target rather than scattering them over the darkened countryside. In hindsight, it was the wrong decision – but it was one made from the best of intentions.

Losing height and speed, DZ479 arrived over Berlin twenty minutes late, and witnessed the confusion over the target. The winds had scattered the raid widely, and the diffused light of fires burning under the clouds produced an eerie flickering. The bombing computer on the Lancasters and Halifaxes relied on wind speed calculations being entered into the dials, but on a night of gusting winds it was difficult to establish precisely what those speeds were. Simpson and Walker dropped their bombs and, relieved to be heading home, turned south to get clear of the city defences before striking westwards. Battered by winds and flying on one engine, their progress was slow. When the other Mosquitos were landing back at Oakington at around 22.45, Simpson and Walker were still over the heart of Germany. As they approached the Ruhr around midnight, a furious anti-aircraft barrage rose and began cracking and exploding about them. They were in all probability the only Allied aircraft in the vicinity, and the German gunners peppered the Mosquito, knocking pieces off and giving Simpson and Walker a very unpleasant time. With fuel running out, they flew on for a further fifty minutes, crossing into France, but they knew their hourglass was draining quickly.

Coming down in the sea on a dark winter's night would be unwise, so Simpson and Walker decided to abandon DZ479 before they reached the coast. They were uncertain exactly where they were, but as their altitude slipped ever

---

* A mechanism in the propeller hub could alter the pitch of the propeller so that it provided less resistance to the air flow.

lower, they agreed it was time to go. Walker unclipped himself and, squatting, pulled on the handle to open the crew door. A blast of icy air pushed him back, roaring into the cockpit and impeding his progress. There was no question of simply dropping out – the hatch was too small for a simple gymnastic leap. Walker dangled his legs outside the aircraft, wriggling hard to get his parachute and Mae West clear of the lip of the opening. It was not uncommon for a pilot to add the weight of his boot at this point to eject a navigator. Walker's departure, when he at last freed himself, was rapid, and deposited him into the rushing slipstream, where he immediately pulled his parachute cord. To his relief the canopy snapped open, but he was swinging wildly – this was nothing like the training jumps from a rig in a hangar, which practised landings rather than control. After a descent that Walker described as 'rough', he became aware of a darkened mass rushing to meet him before crashing into a tree with enough sound to wake a village. He released himself from his harness and, taking refuge for a few minutes on a bough, smoked a cigarette before climbing down and burying his parachute. Apart from a few minor cuts, he was unhurt, though decidedly bedraggled. DZ479 had crashed not far away; he could see the glow of the fire across the fields. There was no sign of Simpson, and it would have been unwise to shout out, knowing the enemy would soon home in on the burning wreck.

Finding a road, he trudged along for the next hour, but frequently had to take shelter in the hedgerows as German cars and motorcycles rushed towards the scene of the crash. With a curfew in place, he knew that any approaching vehicle would not be occupied by friends. In the small hours, Walker decided to knock on the door of a farmhouse. He was taking a risk, but this was not the kind of place in which he imagined German soldiers would be staying. Somewhat shocked by the dishevelled and blood-spattered figure they found outside, the farmer and his wife quickly ushered him in and gave him a pitcher of cider with bread and cheese. He was told that he had landed near the town of Le Bény-Bocage in Normandy. After a short time, with the obvious fear of discovery evident in their faces, Walker's French hosts pointed the way to the coast and he bid farewell to his helpers. He was all too aware of the risks they had taken in showing him the simplest of hospitality.

He walked only a little further in the dark before he came across a parked van. It was now very quiet, and the commotion caused by the crash seemed to have settled down. Walker confesses that the effects of the cider, tiredness and shock were taking their toll, leading him to make an error of judgement. Finding the van open, he decided to sleep in the back for a while, and fell quickly into unconsciousness. It was still gloomy when he awoke, but the slow December dawn was beginning to creep into the lanes and hedgerows of the Bocage. Clambering out, it was only then that he realized the van had German insignia on it. His walk towards the coast was not the best option in trying to evade the Germans – he was heading for the fortified defences of the Atlantic Wall. This belt of concrete blockhouses, gun positions and trenches stretched from the northern tip of Norway to France's southern border with Spain. Built by tens of thousands of slave labourers, many of whom perished in the effort, it was occupied by second-line troops, who were often either very young or rather older than those fielded by front-line infantry battalions. The support and supply lines for the wall stretched inland into the French countryside for some distance. Situated close to the base of the Cotentin Peninsula, Le Bény-Bocage was no isolated rural idyll. Perhaps what saved Walker from detection was that the German workers in the area seemed disinclined to rise early on a chilly December morning.

With light rising quickly, Walker knew his time in the deep hedgerow-lined lanes was becoming increasingly hazardous.

He tried the next farmhouse he came across, and this time was welcomed by a lady who saw to his immediate needs and subsequently accommodated him in her barn for five days. She contacted the resistance, and Walker entered the escape network posing as 'Pierre André', a hairdresser, before being spirited to Switzerland in civilian clothes. Eventually, after several adventures, including a brief spell of imprisonment for trying to leave Switzerland, Walker crossed into France again in September 1944 and met up with American forces from Operation Dragoon (the Allied invasion of southern France), who were moving north. He arrived back at 627 Squadron smartly dressed in a suit and brogues from his Swiss travels. He was later to find that Simpson had also evaded capture, making the loss of DZ479 a little easier to bear.

The disappointing results of the raid of 2 December and the scattering of bombs across Berlin played into the hands of Nazi propaganda, which was always swift to denounce the 'terror flyers' of RAF Bomber Command. This attack and the many others that followed appeared to the civilian population to be entirely indiscriminate. However, despite the inaccuracies of the bombing, two Siemens factories were hit, and a ball bearing plant and railway hubs disrupted. As the pilots had observed, German fighter operations around the city were intense – the Luftwaffe had guessed the location of the raid correctly, and were waiting. Forty heavy bomber crews failed to return, thirty-seven Lancasters and three Halifaxes plus a single Mosquito, DZ479. All of 7 Squadron's twenty Lancasters returned safely. A loss rate of 8.7 per cent of the force was unsustainable, but did not shock Air Marshal Harris and his staff unduly. He had foretold heavy losses, but believed that realizing the aim of destroying Germany's will to fight was worth the cost. The bomber crews were understandably less blasé. Although the 272 RAF men lost on the night of 2 December were spread across many squadrons, the number of casualties remained distressingly high. For most, the feeling remained that it was just a matter of time before their luck ran out. It was not just the sense of impending doom that troubled the men. They also worried that any display of stress-related weakness might be seen as a 'Lack of Moral Fibre'. To have 'LMF' written on their records would mean an immediate removal from squadron – they would effectively disappear as quickly as a man who had failed to return from an operation. Later studies estimated that as many as 6,000 men of Bomber Command suffered some form of psychiatric distress throughout the Second World War, with 2,726 listed as LMF.

Jack 'Benny' Goodman would later write of RAF Oakington that, 'It must not be assumed that Bomber Command crews sat around waiting to get the chop. Nothing could be further from the truth. When stood down we contrived to have an uproarious time. For example, the Station Commander at Oakington, a fierce Group Captain, lived in a suite of rooms at one end of the Officers' Mess. He used to retire to his suite at night and took no notice of the high jinks that took place in the bar.' Whilst most boisterous behaviour was tolerated (and even, it might be said, encouraged), when the inebriated airmen crossed a line, there would be repercussions. After a particularly free night of drinking, some 7 Squadron men decided to deposit an Austin 7 outside the door of the Station Commander, a not inconsiderable feat involving two sharp turns in the corridor. According to Goodman, the next morning 'all hell was let loose', and a party of sober airman struggled to free the car from its resting place. A parade was called for the crews of 7 and 627 Squadrons, and 'the riot act' read, although no attempt was made to track down the culprits – which the aircrews appreciated as evidence of mature leadership.

The formation of 627 Squadron at RAF Oakington had been rapid, as had been the increase in intensity of operations against Berlin, the hardest target of all. Life in the squadron would be a roller-coaster of action and emotion that gave the new arrivals little time to gather their thoughts. The coming months would test them sorely; but for many, they would prove to be the high point of their lives.

5

AGENTS OF THE NIGHT

Ménétréols-sous-Vatan, central France, 1 March 1942

Standing in the lee of a hedge, Stanlislas Mangin and Louis Andlauer shuffled nervously as they listened intently for sound over the darkened fields. Adjusting their berets, they checked the straps of their small rucksacks, running their thumbs underneath to hoist them up on their shoulders. It was not necessary, they were on tightly enough already, but it helped relieve the tension as they waited. Their boots were wet from trudging through the longer grass on the border of the field, each step releasing a fresh, earthy smell into the chilly air. Close by, other shadows moved about, armed men dressed in black mumbling and readying themselves. Others unseen were lurking on the edges of the field, watching the rough tracks that led back to the single-lane road to the village of Ménétréols-sous-Vatan. There was no sign of lights or movement – no one could sneak up on them here. There could be no discovery without betrayal, but it was this constant anxiety that they might be detected that troubled the resistance fighters most. They had left their cars some distance from the main road after driving for several miles without lights.

Now, in the quiet stillness of the countryside, they watched and waited.

The men had chosen their spot carefully. It was south of Ménétréols-sous-Vatan, close to Les Lagnys, barely a hamlet and more of a spaced-out series of farms connected with a spider's web of paths and lanes across the fields. They knew the area well, and in the event of discovery they were confident that by scattering in all directions they could make their escape. It was 1 March 1942, nearly two years since the Germans had occupied the northern part of France, leaving the unoccupied southern half of the country to be administered by a regime based in the spa town of Vichy. But any notion that the collaborationist Vichy government would retain vestiges of independence from the Nazis had long since disappeared. Uncomfortably for the men of the resistance, their enemies now included their fellow countrymen. A rash of arrests and unexplained disappearances was evidence that the dark hand of the Gestapo now extended deep into the Vichy internal security forces. All too often, when dead bodies were found lying in fields or dumped by the sides of roads, there was no public investigation, and it was hard to know who the perpetrators were. Most suspected the Gestapo.

The clouds were slipping gently past a nearly full moon. It seemed hard to believe that this quiet corner of the central French département of the Indre could be thrust into the war, or have any meaningful contribution to make to its outcome. As the minutes passed, the men checked their watches anxiously: was their visitor going to arrive safely? After flying hundreds of miles through the night, would he manage to find this particular field, tucked away amid thousands of hectares of similar-looking farmland? It was past 1am, and the breeze played tricks on them as they listened for the sound of an aircraft. Then, to their north, they heard the distant drone of an engine. Hunched over a radio set on the edge of the field, an operator spoke into his telephone mouthpiece to try to make contact with the pilot. He strained to hear a reply in his headset. The men around him watched him with growing anticipation and, after a few seconds, saw him nod, then raise his hand. 'Oui!' he shouted. The aircraft seemed to be taking a while to get close, the engine noise ebbing and flowing with the passing minutes. They realized the aircraft was changing course, perhaps circling some distance from them. But was it *their* plane or a German decoy hoping to expose their position? This was a risk they would have to take – there could be no delay in lighting the flares to guide the aircraft in. Soon the area was glowing with light from the prescribed 'L' pattern laid out in the field. The engine noise built in intensity, until suddenly Westland Lysander V9248 swept over the hedge at the bottom of the field, its wheels barely clearing the branches, a black bat emerging from the night sky. A piercing light came on from the undercarriage spat,* illuminating the ground and temporarily blinding the watchers.

With a soft groan the Lysander touched down, her engine ticking melodiously as the pilot throttled back. As soon as she had stopped the landing light flicked off again, but this was the most dangerous part of the night. Mangin and Andlauer ran furiously towards the aircraft, and by the time they reached it, the pilot was outside beckoning them to a vertical ladder on the exterior of the fuselage. Whether they climbed or were pushed and shoved into the aircraft they weren't sure, but they found a small space behind the pilot and quickly settled down on the rudimentary bench seat. Instructions were shouted outside as boxes were unloaded, the cockpit hood was slammed to, and the engine rose in tempo. It was now 1.30 hours, and after less than two minutes on the ground, Squadron Leader Guy

---

* The Westland Lysander had a fixed undercarriage with streamlined fairings that partially covered the wheels.

*Wing Commander Guy
Lockhart.*

Lockhart taxied back down the field, kicked the rudder across to make a smart turn and opened the throttle fully. After a series of bumps and lurches, the wheels left the ground, and within seconds the aircraft had cleared the field boundary and flew on at 50 feet into the darkness. Wishing their comrades well, the men on the ground hurriedly collected the booty dropped by the Lysander and walked quickly back to their cars. They heard the aircraft turning north and, as the sound died away, they were left once again with only the whisper of the breeze in the night.

Most aircrew serving with 627 Squadron were born within or shortly after the tumultuous years of the First World War. They were the first generation not to have first-hand memories of the conflict that had swept aside Europe's established political order and so drastically affected their parents' lives. Guy Lockhart was born in Mortlake, in Surrey, in 1916, the year of the Battle of the Somme. In 1920, after the war, with employment prospects plunged into uncertainty, Guy's father took a position in Shanghai as an accountant. The city was becoming the 'Paris of the East, the New York of the West', with a reputation for decadence, glamour and money. Unrestrained foreign investment and immigration had carved out distinct colonial enclaves and, in some instances, created communities where the native Chinese were forbidden unless they were employed by the émigrés.

With his parents' marriage failing, Guy returned to England for his schooling. He attended prep school at Eastbourne, then went on to Sevenoaks School before joining the RAF in 1935. His was a typical path for a young officer in the pre-war RAF, where access to a commission was gained as much by social standing as by examination results. Perhaps Guy's background instilled an independence and resourcefulness that would prove to be an important factor in his wartime service. Granted a short-service commission, Lockhart trained as a pilot at RAF Digby in Lincolnshire in November 1935, and was flying the new Gloster Gladiator biplane by the summer of 1937 at RAF Debden. Lockhart's immediate ambitions in the RAF were cut short by a 'low flying' incident at Stoke-on-Trent's Empire Air Day in 1938, which resulted in a court martial. Spotting a senior officer that he particularly disliked below, he took the opportunity to dive on him, causing his startled victim to throw himself to the ground. With this black mark on his record, Guy resigned his commission shortly afterwards, but was determined to pursue work as a civil aviation pilot.

In 1939 Guy married Judy Potter and, using his contacts in flying instructing, borrowed a Tiger Moth biplane to take the couple to Paris on a brief honeymoon. Chattering excitedly, the wedding party assembled to watch the couple depart from a small airfield in Suffolk. The bride, newly attired with a leather flying cap, jacket and parachute, clambered into the front cockpit and Guy in the rear.* Shooing well-wishers away, a man from the local flying club, cap turned backwards to avoid it blowing away, stepped forward to swing the propeller. After a couple of attempts, the Gipsy Major engine burst into life. Guy taxied out and was careful to perform as neat a take-off as possible as the guests waved and cheered. After coming

* The Tiger Moth had a better all-round view from the aft position, which was the normal position of the pilot, with student pilots sitting in the front.

round flying low to wave goodbye to the wedding guests, the couple set course for Paris. But within a matter of minutes their journey was to be cut short in dramatic – and, it turned out, farcical – fashion. Having been briefed on the drills of flying the Tiger Moth, Judy was alarmed when she heard Guy suddenly shout 'bail out!', a command that she obeyed without question. Jumping from the aeroplane and pulling on the cord of her parachute, she floated down into a ploughed field, where she had a hard landing, breaking her ankle. Instead of enjoying the delights of a stroll across the Pont d'Iéna to the Eiffel Tower, Judy spent her wedding night in Ipswich Hospital, where the full facts of the incident came to light. Guy had been astounded to see his new bride fling herself from the Tiger Moth. It tran-spired that he had shouted, 'I love you' and not 'bail out'.

Having overcome their early communication problems, and with Judy's ankle on the mend, the couple lodged briefly with Judy's parents in a comfortable brick-built semi-detached house in Athelstan Road, Colchester, but the coming of war turned their future plans upside down. Guy had envisaged a career in civil aviation, but when war was declared in September 1939, most passenger flights were discontinued and all private flights without individual flight permits were forbidden. Instead, Lockhart re-enlisted in the RAF, his earlier airborne misdemeanour apparently forgiven at a time of national emer-gency, when experienced pilots were badly needed. This time, however, he chose not to wait to gain access with a commission, and rose through the ranks to become a Sergeant Pilot flying Supermarine Spitfires.

The agility and power of the Spitfire was beyond anything Guy had previously experienced in the robust Gloster Gladiator, but the rigours of war dictated that he was soon thrust into the action. He flew first with 602 Squadron, then, flying with 74 Squadron, he was shot down over France at Herly in the Pas de Calais on 6 July 1941. Judy duly received a heart-chilling 'missing in action' telegram, which left her life in the limbo of uncertainty. Every sighting of a postman or the telegram boy's bicycle filled her with dread as she waited to see if the 'missing presumed dead' communication would come, but, as the weeks stretched out, she consoled herself with the thought that no news might be good news. At last, after months in which she seesawed from mild optimism to desperation, Judy received a communication that informed her that Guy was 'safe and interned' in Spain. However, in the secrecy of wartime, she was told little else.

Guy's daylight mission from RAF Biggin Hill that summer's day had been to escort six Stirling bombers on a raid on Lille. Lockhart was to learn to his cost the same lesson learned by the Luftwaffe during the Battle of Britain – that fighters flying slower to maintain pace with bombers placed themselves at a distinct disadvantage. At 14.30 hours the sky ahead began to fill with the black blotches of flak shells, mushrooms of angry smoke in the clear sky. Within seconds he was hit by flak, which rocked Spitfire W3317 with an ominous cracking sound. Part of the aircraft's wing was blown away, and Guy knew immediately that the fighter would quickly become unflyable. Keeping a grip on the joystick with one hand, he grasped the round knob that operated the catch above him with the other and quickly slid back the canopy. Unclipping himself, he pushed hard on the lip of the cockpit, heaving himself into the headwind to get his feet on the seat. The Spitfire began a hard roll, which he knew would begin the aircraft's death-dive, but Lockhart fell free and instinctively pulled his parachute cord. He knew he had lost altitude rapidly, and had little time to react as the ground soared up to meet him. The impact knocked Guy out and injured him, but after coming to, he came to understand that he was not alone. In his daze he saw people advancing across the field he had landed in, but fortunately none of them were wearing uniforms.

Pilots of 161 Special Duties Squadron pose with a Westland Lysander, Tangmere, 1943.

He was helped to walk and taken into the care of a local man, Norbert Fillerin, who arranged a hiding place in the village of Renty. Fillerin, a Great War veteran who had been held captive by the Germans, was a farmer and beekeeper, and had been active with the resistance movement since 1940.* Guy remained in Renty for some time to regain his health before being handed over to an escape route organized by Louis Nouveau. Guy was the twenty-fifth man Nouveau had helped in his escape network; Louis moved him first to Lille, then began the journey south from safe house to safe house. They reached Marseilles on 10 August and crossed the Pyrenees

---

* Fillerin was betrayed in 1943, arrested, tortured and sent to Buchenwald, then to Flossenbürg and Hradisko camp, where he was liberated by the Soviets on 8 May 1945.

in a small group led by Nouveau's son, Jean-Pierre, only to be arrested and imprisoned by the Spanish for entering the country illegally. However, despite fascist Spain's obvious leanings towards Nazi Germany – not least on account of the help it had given Franco's nationalists in the Civil War – the country was still formally neutral, and the men were released in October to fly home via Gibraltar.

Guy Lockhart's experiences on the ground in France were to prove invaluable, and his next posting brought him into contact with the French resistance once again. By now a pilot of some standing, instead of returning to a fighter squadron, Guy was asked to fly Westland Lysanders with 161 Special Duties Squadron, the chosen unit of the Special Operations Executive (SOE), flying covert missions into occupied France. These highly dangerous operations normally involved the ferrying of agents to and from remote landing sites identified by the French Maquis.* Painted all black, 161 Squadron's Lysanders were modified to have a permanently fixed ladder to access the rear cockpit. This increased drag but made embarking and disembarking agents much quicker. The other key adjustment was the fitting of an internal luggage rack, in the space from which the rear machine gun normally protruded, at the back of the long canopy. The pilot flew alone to allow passengers to occupy the observer's position. Here, in extreme discomfort, up to three people could be crowded in – although most operations carried only two. Throughout the war 161 Squadron would take 293 people to occupied France and bring back 500.

Flights often coincided with bombing raids by other aircraft, so that the lonely Lysanders stood some chance of avoiding detection. Flying deep into the night, Lockhart's journeys could

---

* Rural resistance fighters who often formed and operated along political lines, many of them communist but some loyal to de Gaulle.

take up to eight hours to complete. That first operation, on the night of 1 March 1942, was flown from RAF Tangmere near Chichester across the English Channel to Normandy. Taking off in Lysander V9428 at 20.25 hours, Lockhart made landfall at Cabourg, south of Le Havre, at 9,500 feet and continued south, deep into the interior of France. Although he avoided major towns, Lockhart still risked attracting the attention of the Luftwaffe. His passage across the skies of northern France would have prompted solitary sentries on night watch from Bernay in Normandy to Châteauroux in the Indre to report sightings of a mysterious aircraft. But the farther V9428 pushed south, the harder it was for his enemies to plot his course. Low cloud that night had made finding the landing site difficult, but the maquis had marked the field perfectly with their flares, enabling a smooth landing and departure. Lockhart's mission to Les Lagnys was a textbook operation, but later flights would not be as simple as this first one.

On 31 August 1942 Lockhart successfully landed to deliver a passenger and packages to a landing field near Arbigny in the Ain département of eastern France. But then, as he was taxiing, his Lysander V9597 rolled into a grass-covered ditch, destroying part of the undercarriage. It was an incident that the 161 Squadron's commanding officer would later describe as an 'inexcusable error' on the part of the ground party. Since the aircraft was unflyable, it was agreed that Lockhart would wait for an hour after the departure of the Maquis before setting light to the Lysander. Spirited rapidly south via resistance networks, six days later he was plucked from the beach at Narbonne on the Mediterranean coast by a Polish-crewed felucca named *Seadog*, and taken to Gibraltar. For a second time, Lockhart was flown home to rejoin his combat duties, no doubt hoping that this would not become a habit. He came closest to being shot down on another operation, which had taken him to the landing field at Les Lagnys on 18 November

627 Squadron Mosquitos at RAF Oakington.

1942. On the return leg he strayed into the flak defences around Saint-Malo and spent several anxious minutes trying to evade the searchlights against a cacophony of bursting shells. Shortly afterwards he was attacked by seven Focke-Wulf 190 fighters, but after a period of intense manoeuvres in which his Lysander sustained some damage, he found shelter in cloud – much to the relief of his shaken passengers.

There was no doubt that 1942 had been the most challenging year in Lockhart's life. Not only had he held to an exacting flying programme, he had had to deal with grievous personal loss. His first child, Sauvan, died of meningitis aged only two, just as he was commencing his flying duties with 161 Squadron. By the autumn of 1942, Judy was pregnant again. Already a Squadron Leader and Distinguished Flying Cross (DFC) holder for his previous fighter service, Lockhart was awarded the Distinguished Service Order (DSO) in October 1942. Given the secretive nature of his service with 161 Squadron, the citation feels somewhat cryptic, but the praise for Lockhart's bravery is unambiguous:

> Squadron Leader Lockhart has participated in many operational sorties and the successes gained can be attributed largely to his careful organisation and planning. He has, at all times, displayed courage, skill and fortitude which have been in keeping with the highest traditions of the Royal Air Force.
>
> – *The London Gazette*, 9 October 1942

After the intensity of operations with 161 Squadron, it must have come as a relief to both husband and wife when Guy was 'rested' in the New Year with a new posting in London that did not involve flying duties. In January 1943 he began work at the offices of the secretive Special Operations Executive at 64 Baker Street. In an inevitable reference to Sherlock Holmes, staff were nicknamed 'The Baker Street Irregulars' after the great detective's fictional band of street urchin helpers. Lockhart's role here was to help coordinate air operations into occupied France, drawing on his own first-hand experience of such missions.

The Lockharts' daughter, Tanya, was born in July 1943. Her godfather was none other than Air Vice-Marshal Don Bennett, commander of 8 Group Pathfinders. With family connections this strong, it is unsurprising that in November of that year Lockhart was invited to assist Bennett in his endeavours by joining the Mosquitos of 627 Squadron.

There was no question of Bennett giving Lockhart 'a leg up', as it was clear that Guy's flying experience amply qualified him for pathfinding duties. After his pre-war short-service commission, Lockhart had been denied early war experience by his court martial and subsequent resignation. It may be that Bennett had some sympathy with Lockhart over his premature exit from the RAF, and that, in retrospect, he viewed the effective discarding of such a talented a pilot as a mistake. Given the Lockharts' tragic loss, Bennett's enlistment of the twenty-five-year-old for his force seemed a natural way forward, placing a young and talented flier where Bennett could keep an eye on him.

Cologne, 29 November 1943

There was little in Squadron Leader Guy Lockhart's flying career that was simple and uncomplicated. Arguably, he flew on the edge of reason, yet time and again he escaped where lesser airmen would have perished. His first operation with 627 Squadron from RAF Oakington followed this daring pattern, and was not as peaceful as his navigator might have hoped for. The afternoon briefing seemed straightforward enough; there were only ten men at the folding wooden tables that day. It was early days for the new squadron, but there was an air of confidence in the room, and light-hearted banter as the crews adjourned, carrying their maps and notes to get their flying kit together.

Five Mosquitos were to attack Cologne at 28,000 feet in a nuisance raid designed to keep the defenders awake. Raids by the heavier bombers had been cancelled, as the weather at lower levels was poor and the prospect of a strong moon above cloud level made flying hazardous for the slower aircraft. Twelve months ago, Lockhart had used the pale blue light of a full moon to pick out field shapes and woods as he looked for his landing site at 1,000 feet over France. Now, more than 5 miles up in the frozen stratosphere, he would be lucky to pick out the shape of a forest far below.

During the day, 360 American B-17 'Flying Fortresses' had attacked Bremen to the north. They had intended to hit the shipyards, but the force struggled to find the target, only

104 aircraft succeeding in dropping their bombs. Cloud had extended to 29,000 feet, and the assembling bomb groups found it hard to locate one another; with covering American fighters reaching the extent of their range, some groups decided to turn back. Despite the failure of so many of the bombers to reach the target, the fighter force had given the defending Luftwaffe force a severe mauling: as many as thirty-six German aircraft were destroyed.

Lockhart's Mosquito, DZ616, and the other four 627 Mosquitos were spectacularly fast compared to the lumbering Lysander. They took off from RAF Oakington at 17.55 hours and were over Cologne just over an hour later.* As they climbed they could see the telltale vapour trails forming behind them from the hot exhausts, signposts to their location streaking across the starlit sky. En route to the target they had jinked repeatedly to keep the defenders guessing, but with only twenty-one Mosquitos from Bomber Command out that night, the German radar controllers were not misled into believing this light force posed a serious threat. It was still early in the evening, and they were waiting to see if a stronger force would appear. At Guy Lockhart's elbow that night was Australian navigator William de Boos, who had had many hours of night flying under his belt and was 627 Squadron's Navigation Officer.

As the Mosquitos approached Cologne there were still no searchlights – it was no accident, the defenders were giving nothing away. Pilot Officer Wilmott flying D2353 and Flight Sergeant Parlato in DZ442 both dropped their bombs at 19.00 hours and reported that the searchlights only flicked on after they had done so. It seems likely that the defenders waited until they heard the percussion of the bombs before they acted. Lockhart, who made his run two minutes later and released

---

* The speed on the outbound flight seems to suggest a strong tail-wind, with the return leg taking 30 minutes longer.

his bombs, received the full force of the now aroused German defences. The flak barrage was intense, and was probably an unwelcome reminder of his hazardous flight over Saint-Malo.

Suddenly, light flooded the cockpit, and for Lockhart and de Boos it was as if the whole world was watching. These weren't the pleasant beams that swing about on the cinema screen before a Twentieth Century Fox film, but a frightening portent of disaster. De Boos was still

William de Boos prior to joining the Royal Air Force.

returning from the Perspex observation position, wriggling his way through the crawl space underneath the instrument panel, when they were illuminated. He had barely uttered the words 'bombs gone' before the blinding light from below lit up the cockpit. Already feeling Lockhart reacting, he flung himself back in his seat and fastened his straps. As Lockhart tossed the Mosquito about to try to break free of the clinging beams of the German searchlights, de Boos locked one arm behind the pilot's seat and gripped hard to the base of his seat with the other. Lockhart now took the Mosquito into a steep dive, the pitch of the engines changing as they sped up, racing to keep up with the pressure on the propellers. The Australian's breathing grew heavy; as the Mosquito reached the bottom of the dive it felt as if someone had dumped a sack of potatoes on his chest. Even in the midst of what was a stomach-churning ride, de Boos instinctively spun his head around when he could to watch for the glint of a German fighter in the fine fog of the beams, but thankfully none appeared. Still they dived and twisted, hanging in their straps one second, pushed deep into their seats the next. Glaring bursts of flak detonated disconcertingly close to them, the force of the explosions shaking the thin wood of the Mosquito's skin.

In an instant it was dark again, as they plunged clear of the searchlights. Flying at full power, the Mosquito levelled out as they pounded clear of Cologne city centre at more than 400mph. They could still hear the flak booming behind them. Gradually their eyes adjusted to the gloom, and the gentle orange lights above the instrument panel emerged once again. Even with his oxygen mask on, de Boos could smell the sweetness of cordite fumes around them. Pulling his mask forward a little he sniffed the air for smoke, but there was no sign of fire. The engine temperatures were normal, and DZ616 sailed on as if nothing had happened. There was time for the two men to talk a little about their ride of terror, scattered profanities expressing their relief at a lucky escape. Having checked the state of their fuel, Lockhart followed de Boos's course direction for home. They landed safely at RAF Oakington with the sound of a gentle skid as the tyres touched down at 20.35 hours – a flight of two hours and forty minutes.

What precisely was said on the crew's return to Oakington is probably far from what appeared in the Operational Record Book. Lockhart's debriefing entry on the matter is short and to the point:

S/Ls (searchlights) active and A/C coned for 3/4 minutes on leaving target.

To be held in searchlights for so long was a nightmare for any pilot. As many airmen could testify, illumination as lengthy as that endured by Lockhart and de Boos often ended in disaster. Although some lights were manually controlled, the Germans used a master beam which was radar aided. This 'blue light of death' was the most feared by the crews, as once it alighted on its target, others would quickly swing in to 'cone' the aircraft. At high altitude, sudden twisting and turning in a 'corkscrew' motion could throw a pursuing fighter, of course, but such movements were insufficient to evade the broad beams of the probing searchlights. Diving clear was the best means of escape, but was hazardous in itself, with rising flak shells seeking to find their target. For Lockhart's and de Boos's comrades, there was one advantage to Mosquito DZ616 being picked out like a shining dot; they were able to slip in unseen and bomb their target.

Happily, everyone had arrived back safely. But Lockhart and de Boos were not the only crew to have had an eventful night. Flying Officers Denny and Holdway in DZ479 had returned a few minutes earlier after their hydraulics became unserviceable, preventing them from opening the bomb bay doors. This meant they had not been able to drop their four 500lb bombs, which were still in the bomb bay when they landed. Their return and subsequent landing was thus carried out gingerly. They knew the stories of 'hung-up' bombs dislodging themselves on touchdown and blowing the aircraft and its occupants into tiny pieces. Denny had to adopt a gentle flying style, but it didn't stop both crew feeling each rib and bump in the asphalt as they rolled out. They were glad to squeeze out of the hatch that night and hand the problem over to the ground crew.

In the rich pattern of experience that led men to 627 Squadron, the career of Flight Lieutenant William de Boos was not atypical. He had already completed his first tour on Vickers Wellingtons serving with 37 Squadron on raids over Italy and North Africa. It was with some relief that he had taken up his next position at 27 Operational Training Unit (27 OTU) in

Derbyshire. As a Squadron Navigational Officer, de Boos was tasked with supervising night-flying training at RAF Church Broughton, a satellite airfield to RAF Lichfield, but before long, he confessed to finding life there 'monotonous'. He was still on the Wellington bomber, an aircraft he knew intimately, and despite the enthusiasm of the crews he flew with, the day-to-day task of flying nowhere in particular bored him.

However, danger lurked in unexpected places on 27 OTU, and in common with many training establishments, the catalogue of accidents and losses was extensive. Flight Sergeant Len Watson was a fellow Australian who served alongside de Boos as an instructor. He had trained in Canada before a spell of operational flying in the Middle East, completing forty missions with 458 Squadron Wellingtons in the arid heat of El Shullufa in Egypt. At twenty-four years old he was considered an 'old man' who had already walked the path his students aspired to. He had a glint in his eye and a gentle smile that suggested that despite the war, there was still fun to be had, but he was not a carouser. Writing to his father at home in Casino, Queensland, he said that he received great comfort from reading his Bible. He assured him, 'the knowledge that the truth sustains us sees us through: ahead shines a light of peace to come'.* He had already walked away safely from an accident in his own training in November 1941 when his Wellington swung on landing and deposited itself into the grass at the side of the runway. Other than bending the aeroplane a little, there were no crew injuries, and the incident only proved the adage, 'a good landing is one you walk away from'.

On the afternoon of 20 March 1943, Wellington X3547 took off from RAF Lichfield for a gun camera exercise and did not return. Len Watson was supervising the crew of seven

---

* Tragedy stalked the family: James and Lena Watson would lose three sons serving in Bomber Command before the war's end.

others with their regular pilot, Sergeant Douglas Williams, when the aircraft struck a barrage balloon cable at Crewe in Cheshire at 15.19 hours. X3547 was flying low at 1,000 feet, and the collision sent the stricken Wellington diving to the ground within seconds. Members of 949 Balloon Squadron were powerless to save anyone as the aircraft erupted in a giant fireball.

The official report suggested X3547 was off-course and probably lost. It was not uncommon for flights of this sort to depart from their declared route, but it is not known why the Wellington was close to Crewe on that day. Perhaps what should have been of more concern to the Command Accident Investigator was that just six minutes earlier an Airspeed Oxford had also crashed, killing its four crew in similar circumstances. The barrage balloons were deployed to defend the Rolls-Royce works at Crewe, but with a growing number of training establishments and aircraft in the area, there seemed little that could be done other than warning crews to keep clear.

For William de Boos the clock was ticking. 27 OTU had already lost eleven aircraft in 1943 and the toll of instructors killed suggested that if he stayed too long, he too could be among their number. It was not that he was afraid, but like many instructors he was of the opinion that if he was to die, it would be more worthwhile for it to happen on operations.

In August 1943 de Boos volunteered to fly Mosquitos, and on being accepted had written to his mother in Australia, saying, 'I was envied very much by everyone at the OTU; because flying "Mossies" was considered to be one of the sweetest jobs in the Air Force.' On 2 December – three days after the tangle with searchlights over Cologne – Lockhart and de Boos had the fire in the engine of DZ615 that forced their return from Berlin. They flew again to Berlin the next day, this time successfully, despite the failure of the Gee navigation system. But the de Boos–Lockhart partnership did not last beyond these three operations. De Boos's role in the squadron was to move around the crews providing a steadying hand where needed. Of the men who had newly joined 627 Squadron, Lockhart was the least experienced in bombing, but this was a lack that could be compensated for by flying with a good navigator. Into de Boos's place stepped Flight Lieutenant Ernie Saunders, a talkative south Londoner with a passion for cycling. He and Lockhart were from different social backgrounds, but squeezed together in the cockpit they formed that essential bond of pilot and navigator.

Berlin, 16 December 1943

It had been one of those dreary December days when it never seemed to get fully light around the aerodromes of Lincolnshire. Further south, in Cambridgeshire, the weather was a little clearer, with some breaks in the cloud, but at RAF Oakington the air hung heavy with moisture. With the afternoon light fading fast, the heavy bombers took advantage of the final glimmer of daylight to begin their long journey to Berlin. Free at last of the clouds, a sliver of the low sun touched the rim of the horizon before the ghostly dots of the mass of bombers disappeared into the blackness. Climbing to 20,000 feet, the crews braced themselves for yet another dangerous flight, the constant knot of anxiety kept carefully concealed as they went about their duties.

An hour later, at 17.40 hours, five Mosquitos from 627 Squadron took off, knowing they would overtake their comrades and reach Berlin with the leading Pathfinders. Flight Sergeants Parlato and Thomas in DZ426 turned back after thirty minutes, their Mosquito unable to climb to the desired altitude. The others continued upwards, reaching their cruising height of 28,000 feet. The blackness was now so complete that when the instrument lights were turned off for fear of attracting the attention of German night fighters, it was impossible for pilot and navigator to see their hands in front of their faces. With no outside reference points, the risk of disorientation was high, and crews could not keep their lighting completely extinguished for long. Nevertheless, light was kept to a minimum, and navigators had to strain to see their charts. Unlike Lockhart's lonely night-time forays into deserted skies in the Lysander, tonight the sky was filled with hundreds of bombers, but each was invisible to the other. Collisions were commonplace, particularly on the final turn into target, when the bomber crews were distracted by finding the aiming point ahead. The precise figures for those lost in such crashes are impossible to estimate, but the testimonies of those experiencing near misses at this point suggests a high attrition rate.

627 Squadron once again had the advantage of elevation over the main force. Although the Mosquitos had taken off within a couple of minutes of each other, they were clearly enough separated by time and altitude to make a collision between other members of the Squadron unlikely. Pilot Officers Willmott and Hughes in DZ353 began their run into Berlin first. For a number of miles the sky had been interrupted by man-made light, their first inkling that they were approaching the city. Flares dropped by German fighters above the path of the incoming bomber force produced intense balls of light to the north of Berlin. As Hughes made his way to his bombing position in the nose, the lack of searchlights bore testimony to the complete cloud cover over the city. Timing their run carefully, they dropped their load of white marking flares at 19.48 hours to illuminate the clouds below. It was not the most accurate method of marking but, given the conditions, it was the best they could do. As they swung into a wide orbit, other green and red markers cascaded down, affirming their

marking point. Flight Lieutenants Grey and Boyle in Mosquito DZ616 backed up the marking with their flares, but the flak was, in their words, 'considerable'.

In the thunderstorm of lights and noise, their solitary darkened flight to the target was briefly forgotten. Below the clouds, the flashing of hundreds of bombs lit the atmosphere as the main force began to arrive. With no further flares or bombs, the Mosquitos turned for home, skirting the southern part of the city. Grey and Boyle reported seeing a 15-mile corridor of German flares hanging above the arriving bomber force to the north. The hunters were out – intent on bringing down as many bombers as they could. Having no armament, the Mosquitos could do nothing but observe the drama below them. Soon they would be out of reach of the flak and fanning out across the Low Countries to head into the relative safety of the North Sea.

The first indications that the weather was changing crept in as they began their descent. Wisps of cloud gave way to patches of dense fog. The windscreens of their Mosquitos ran with moisture, and as they made landfall, they sensed the weather was worsening. Seeking to break free of the cloud near RAF Oakington, they were perturbed to find a lack of clear air, but rather a clinging mist. It was a relief to see the runway flare path, dimly visible through the murk. As they turned on their landing light, its diffused beam flickered in the gathering fog, and they were grateful to make a successful landing. By 22.00 hours they were enjoying a mug of tea at debriefing, but the Lancasters still had nearly two hours before their return.

Conditions were deteriorating by the minute over all the bomber airfields. Normally, if such adverse weather was forecast, the raid would have been cancelled, but the speed of the change had caught everyone on the wrong foot. The flak and fighters of Berlin had already hacked down twenty-five

Lancasters that night, killing 148 crew. Others returned home badly damaged, but the whole force faced intense problems dealing with the dense fog that had enveloped their home stations. A number of airfields had fog dispersal equipment, Fog Investigation and Dispersal Operation (FIDO), a series of pipes carrying fuel nozzles along the edge of the runway. Once lit, the plumes of flame provided enough heat and light to burn the fog off. However, there were too few airfields equipped with FIDO, and they proved difficult to find.* RAF Gravely was operating FIDO only seven miles from RAF Bourn in Cambridgeshire,† but 97 Squadron were still attempting to land at Bourn. Ground crews were perplexed to find that even when a returning Lancaster was directly overhead with its lights on at low level, it was hardly visible. As the Lancasters desperately tried to feel their way down through the thick mist, two major crashes took place not far from the runways. RAF Bourn was suffering its darkest day of the war.

In addition to the losses sustained over Germany, a further thirty-one Lancasters crashed or were abandoned that night, bringing the death toll to above 300 men.‡ RAF Oakington had not escaped the carnage; although the small number of 627 Squadron sent out that night had returned unscathed, of the nineteen Lancasters that departed from 7 Squadron, many had diverted to other stations, and three had failed to return. The night had been nothing short of a disaster for Bomber Command, prompting Winston Churchill to write to Air Marshal Harris, 'I am not pressing you to fight the weather as well as the Germans, never forget that.'

---

* FIDO was expensive to operate, burning up to 100,000 gallons of fuel per hour.
† RAF Bourn and RAF Oakington, the home of 627 Squadron, were 3 miles apart.
‡ 'Black Thursday' is remembered as a sombre day in the history of the Pathfinders.

As Christmas came, leave was short in preparation for continuing the relentless assault on German cities in the New Year. Such was the performance of the Mosquito that its crews felt more confident about their chances of survival in the 'wooden wonder' than they had when they were flying with the heavy bomber force. Yet they still knew the risks they faced were considerable, not least because of the unyielding pace of operations. And many airmen were also still trying to overcome some of the stress they had experienced in their previous tours of operation. The fear did not feel as raw as it had in their early days in Bomber Command, but steps still had to be taken to ensure it was kept under control. Camaraderie, smoking and copious amounts of alcohol were the favoured methods. Whatever their subconscious awareness of the dangers they courted, it is probably true to say that these young men chose not to dwell too long on them. It was only in later life that they would understood the full intensity of their experiences.

In late December, those men from 139 Squadron who had formed the original nucleus of 627 Squadron were bolstered by the arrival of three new crews: six men who had just finished at 1665 Mosquito Training Unit, a month-long course that introduced experienced bomber pilots and navigators to their new aircraft. Approximately half the flying time was spent in the Airspeed Oxford and the rest in Mosquitos. The course consisted of a total of fifty flying hours, of which as few as ten hours were at night. It was assumed that pilots already had ample experience of night flying; an examination of their logbooks revealed hundreds of hours amassed on heavier bombers. For the bomber pilots, the Airspeed Oxford was a throw-back to their training days, many of them spent in Canada, and their first encounter with a twin-engined aircraft – a machine many of them had struggled to master. Others on the course had flown fighters and, as well as acclimatizing themselves to more than one engine, also had to get used to the presence of a fellow crew member in the cockpit.

It had been little over six weeks since the formation of 627 Squadron, but already the old hands felt established. The new aircrew brought with them a sense of unease. In the experience of all fighting forces, recent arrivals were statistically more likely to suffer losses than those who were longer established. In airman's terms, this might be the result of unfamiliarity with an aircraft or airfield, but also with the type of operation they were called to carry out. Some losses were inexplicable and written down to bad luck. Within a superstitious and – at times – highly strung group of men, omens good and bad, however strange and inconsequential they might appear, played an important part in their mental state. Within the first week of operations in January, malignant fate would bring its influence to bear on the fortunes of three of the six new members of 627 Squadron.

Flying Officer Francis Fahey hailed from the small town of Wiluna, in a remote part of Western Australia. Wiluna was gold-mining territory, and had originated as a small cluster of huts whose occupants tried to eke a living from the red dust of the Central Desert. Amid the huge open spaces of this bleak and arid region, populated by millions of bushes stretching to a distant horizon, the promise of buried treasure was the only conceivable draw for its beleaguered denizens. Theirs was a harsh life of hard work and even harder drinking – with scores often settled on the spot with fists. The Fahey family were of Irish extraction, one of thousands of such families to be found in every corner of the world where hard manual work was the order of the day. Wiluna had grown from nothing to a peak of 9,000 people in the 1930s, each of its inhabitants hoping for regular work and a share of the elusive metal. The weather varied from hot to very hot, the sun beating down mercilessly on the white tin roofs of the houses. Wiluna had one saving grace, however: the town had access to fresh water from nearby Lake Violet, which allowed humans to survive but also provided support for the mining industry. An article in the *Perth Mirror* of September 1934 described the town's growth from the arrival of prospectors by camel to a bustling centre of industry. It had seen great hopes raised and dashed, 'some of them so acute that only a man with supreme courage, initiative and resource would have attempted to carry on'.

Francis Fahey's journey with the Royal Australian Air Force had led him from the Western Australian desert to the green – but freezing – fields of eastern England. At thirty-one years old he was older than many airmen; he was married to Laurel, who had remained in Wiluna, although its wartime shrinkage had reduced it to a near ghost town. He had finished his first tour on bombers and, prior to his training on Mosquitos and arrival at 627 Squadron, had been instructing at a Heavy Conversion Unit at RAF Lindholme in the West Riding of Yorkshire. Francis had an uncompromisingly straightforward approach, perhaps a toughness born from desert living. He was already decorated with the Air Force Medal. He teamed up with fellow Australian navigator Flying Officer Stan Hicks, a thirty-four-year-old from Melbourne. Stan had been born in Wood Green, Middlesex (now a district of north London), the son of a tram conductor who decided, like many others, that Australia provided a new world of opportunity.

Fahey's and Hicks's term with 627 Squadron was short and tragic. Their first operation to Berlin on 4 January 1944 was abortive, and they returned to Oakington within forty-five minutes owing to a fuel problem. Next day, tasked to fly to Berlin in Mosquito DZ616, Fahey and Hicks took off at 01.28 hours but crashed at Dry Drayton, northwest of Cambridge, less than two minutes later. Both men were killed. Fortunately for the nearby village, the four 500lb bombs carried by the

Mosquito did not explode on impact, but characteristically, the wooden aircraft, brim-full of fuel, burned intensely. Since the incident took place in the small hours and little evidence survived, conclusions as to the cause of the crash were hard to reach. Engine failure or loss of power was the primary suspect in accidents of this sort, but there was also the possibility that unfamiliarity with the fully laden Mosquito may have played its part. The two men were buried three days later at Cambridge City Cemetery in a growing plot of Allied airmen who had lost their lives on the airfields around the city. 'Benny' Goodman and 'Bill' Hickox counted the tragedy a lucky escape. They had test-flown Mosquito DZ616 that very morning in preparation for the raid, and had found everything satisfactory. Later, they were stood down from the raid to allow Fahey and Hicks to take their place as 'makey learns'. This Mosquito had flown its fair share of operations, and had had a number of near misses: in November 1943 it had carried Lockhart and de Boos

The funeral of Flying Officer Francis Fahey, Cambridge City Cemetery, 8 January 1944.

through their twisting ordeal above the searchlights of Cologne; it had brought Grey and Boyle safely home from the hail of flak over Berlin in December; but finally, on 6 January 1944, DZ616's luck had run out.

Frankfurt, 8 January 1944

On the same day as Fahey's and Hicks's funerals, four Mosquitos took off for Frankfurt. It was a gloomy night of unbroken cloud over the target area; in such conditions, bombing would be conducted by estimation rather than precise aiming. Of the four aircraft to embark, two were lost, making this one of the most miserable weeks in the Squadron's history. Between 6 and 14 January, Bomber Command stepped down operations for their heavy bombers because of the strong moon and unreliable weather conditions in this period. Air Marshal Bennett, determined not to give the German defenders any rest, deployed his Mosquito squadrons every night. Duisburg, Dortmund, Frankfurt, Solingen, Aachen, Essen and Koblenz were all subject to the Mosquitos' attention in a series of nuisance raids involving around twenty aircraft each night.

Squadron Leader Edward 'Dinger' Bell, 627's Flight Commander, squeezed into Mosquito DK293 with navigator Flying Officer John Battle. Bell had only flown one previous raid with the squadron on 25 November to Berlin. In the cadre of those coming from 139 Squadron, Bell had spent much of his time at Oakington on administrative matters relating to the new squadron, but he was an accomplished pilot and a holder of the Distinguished Flying Cross. That night's raid should have been relatively simple; they had little company in the skies to worry about, and since they would be flying above 20,000 feet at speed, they would have been able to shake off night fighters. The day and early evening had been bitterly cold, the small glimpses of sun doing nothing to lift temperatures. By the time they had climbed the small ladder into the cockpit they could feel the frost on the rungs. They carried four 500lb general-purpose bombs in the bomb bay – in the wider scheme of things, this was an insignificant punch compared with the weight of ordnance carried by fleets of massed Lancasters. But their task, together with the other nineteen Mosquitos dispatched from other squadrons, was to keep as many German defenders awake as possible.

Their flight was initially uneventful. As they broke into the clear moonlit night they saw beneath them a thick blanket of cloud over northern Europe. Frankfurt lay on the River Main less than 20 miles from its confluence with the Rhine – when night-time conditions were good they were easy signposts for navigation. From Flying Officer John Battle's aiming position in the Perspex nose, there was nothing to see of the city far below them. Disconcertingly, flak was rising towards them, exploding in sharp flashes at their altitude. When the hit came, both men knew the damage was serious; the report of the shell was too close, and the Mosquito shook from nose to tail. Sensing that his flying controls were not responding as they should, Bell gave Battle the order to bail out.

Leaving an aircraft travelling at several hundred miles an hour at high altitude was a dangerous undertaking. A dark night and hostile weather conditions – not to mention the hazards of an angry German population – narrowed their odds of survival.* Bell and Battle were fortunate to land safely, but their chances of evading capture were slim; almost inevitably, they were captured and became prisoners of war. After interrogation, both men were sent to Stalag Luft III, arriving two months

---

* Encouraged by Joseph Goebbels, mobs frequently killed air crew members, with *Fliegermorde*, 'flyer murder', going unpunished.

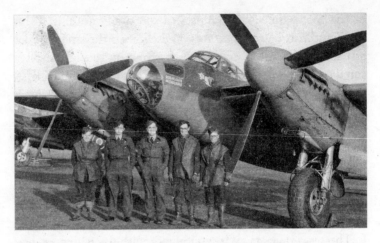

627 Squadron aircrew and ground crew at RAF Oakington: Leading Aircraftman Harding, F/Sgt Ranshaw, F/Sgt Marshallsay, Leading Aircraftmen Wookey and Kinscote.

before the 'Great Escape' of March 1944.* In a squadron full of experienced men, the loss of their Flight Commander was felt more keenly than those of the new arrivals. This was not out of a lack of compassion for the others, but simply because the recent additions to the Squadron were relative unknowns. Squadron Leader Bell was a proven leader at a time when the new squadron was still finding its feet, and he had rapidly made his presence felt. Edward Inkerman Jordan Bell† came from a family with strong military traditions. He bore exactly the same name as his father, who had been a professional footballer with Southampton before serving as a Captain in the 17th Battalion

---

* Stalag Luft III was a POW camp in Lower Silesia, run by the Luftwaffe and holding captured Allied airmen. After the 'Great Escape' of 24/25 March 1944, fifty of seventy-six men who had tunnelled out of the camp were murdered by the Gestapo.

† His middle name, Inkerman, reflected his grandfather's service as a Major with the Royal Fusiliers during the Crimean War. The Battle of Inkerman was fought on 5 November 1854.

of the Middlesex Regiment (the 'Footballers' Battalion') in the First World War. Edward Bell senior was killed in action at Delville Wood in March 1918, but twenty years later his son would pass out of Sandhurst as an officer. Transferring to the RAF in 1940 to train as a pilot, Edward later served with distinction on Vickers Wellingtons and Avro Lancasters with 12 Squadron, but not before he had enjoyed a first spell of wartime captivity in nationalist Spain. Ferrying a Wellington to the Middle East via Gibraltar on 20 June 1941, he was forced to ditch in the sea near Águilas, in southeastern Spain, after losing his way in an electrical storm. The crew were safe but were interned by the Spanish until March 1942.

The second casualties of the night of 8 January were new arrivals, Flight Lieutenant Ian Hanlon and Flying Officer Francis Evans. Flying Mosquito W4072, they attacked the diversionary target of Aachen, but suffered an engine failure on the return leg. Struggling to maintain height in the Southern Bight of the North Sea, they made a call requesting help on the 'Darky' channel, the emergency radio frequency. Hanlon was instructed to land at RAF Bradwell Bay, an airfield on the Essex coast, not far from their location. They successfully navigated themselves onto the final approach, only to discover the runway lights remained off, which made the descent very difficult. Whether the Mosquito lacked the power to continue flying or their approach was too low is unclear, but W4072 struck the sea and skipped before crashing into the water. Despite being stunned by the impact, Evans, realizing Hanlon was injured, pulled him clear through the top hatch of the sinking Mosquito. In the freezing darkness, Hanlon was subsequently found by rescuers and pulled unconscious from the waves, but Evans – the Good Samaritan who had saved his comrade's life – was drowned. Francis Evans was from Ealing, had studied journalism at King's College London before the war and had already been awarded the Distinguished Flying Medal for his service with 57 Squadron in August 1942. Writing an account of his son's loss to King's College in September 1946, his father, Albert, observed sadly that it was Francis's thirty-third operation. Hanlon, a New Zealander, would continue flying with 627 Squadron after a period of recuperation, thankful for the second chance offered him by the selfless courage of his navigator.

After the uncertain start to 1944, 627 Squadron continued its relentless assault on Berlin* and Germany's industrial cities, with the loss of only one other Mosquito in the first quarter of the year. Once again, the crew involved – Pilot Officers Tony Wilmott and John Hughes – were newcomers to the Squadron, and were on an operation to Berlin when they were shot down over Hanover on 1 February. Having begun operations on 28 January, their career with 627 Squadron had lasted only a matter of days. Despite this fresh tragedy, the mood was buoyant within the Squadron. The practice of flying at high altitude at night seemed to be paying dividends. Despite weathering numerous flak barrages, the Mosquitos were generally returning safely to base. There had been no reports of Mosquitos being engaged by enemy fighters. Furthermore, a reduction in the number of mechanical failures meant more aircraft were reaching their targets and releasing their bombs in the right places, and fewer aircraft were returning early from operations. In March 1944 the squadron flew 137 sorties without suffering any losses. For the first time in many months, Berlin began to be omitted from the list of targets. 627 Squadron was into its stride and growing in confidence. The coming of

* As well as attacking other targets such as Cologne, Stuttgart and Duisburg, 627 Squadron flew on twenty separate occasions against Berlin from November 1943 to February 1944.

spring brought lighter nights and better flying, and rumours of the forthcoming invasion of Europe began to circulate. With the Red Army advancing in the east and Allied forces inching their way inexorably up the Italian peninsula, few now doubted that the Allies were going to win the war. The only shadow to darken this optimistic outlook was the airmen's daily personal battle for survival.

Guy Lockhart, the man with the deepest well of night-flying experience, was promoted to Wing Commander in January 1944, and left 627 Squadron to take the helm of the newly formed 692 Squadron flying Mosquitos at RAF Graveley. Despite being part of Air Vice Marshal Don Bennett's continual expansion of his Mosquito force, Lockhart's tenure at 692 Squadron was surprisingly brief. He returned to RAF Oakington in March 1944 to command 7 Squadron on Avro Lancasters, an appointment that seems somewhat contrary to his experience on lighter aircraft. However, this most resourceful of airmen, who had overcome the most difficult flying challenges in his career, was increasingly weighed down by troubles in his personal life. He was still emotionally crushed by the loss of his son, Sauvan, to meningitis, and flew with the little boy's booties around his neck. It was clear to his colleagues that he was amassing gambling debts and that his mental health was becoming more fragile. Lockhart had remained an inspiration to the young men of 627 Squadron, but he was a maverick who lived on the adrenalin of operations.

Lockhart's move to the Lancasters of 7 Squadron was to be of tragically short duration. On the evening of 27 April, at 22.26, he took off from Oakington in Lancaster JB676 as part of a force of 322 bombers tasked with bombing factories in Friedrichshafen in southern Germany. The force arrived safely over the target area, but were soon attacked by German night fighters. For all his skill in night flying, on this occasion

Lockhart was unable to evade the hunters: Lancaster JB676 was shot down by Hauptmann Ernst Wallner of II./NJG 6, flying a Junkers Ju 88 – his first kill* – and crashed near the town of Lahr on the edge of the Black Forest, killing Lockhart and all six members of his crew. It was Lockhart's misfortune to be flying a Lancaster at a time when the electronic war waged by the German defenders was beginning to catch up with the RAF's heavy bombers. Bomber Command used every means at its disposal, such as offloading chaff near the target and attempting to block communications, but the Germans were quick to respond to such countermeasures. Much of the Luftwaffe's stalking was coordinated by ground radar, radio direction and the improved *Lichtenstein SN2* radar sets aboard larger aircraft like the Junkers 88 and Messerschmitt 110. Had Lockhart remained with the Mosquitos of 627 Squadron, his chances of survival would have been greatly increased, since the *Lichtenstein*-equipped fighters were much too slow to catch the 'wooden wonder'.†

The new squadron's foundation phase was drawing to a close. 627 Squadron was about to enter the most dangerous, but thrilling, stage of its brief existence – and a chapter in its history that would be seen as its defining hour. It had been the practice of Bomber Command to fly its aircraft at high altitude at night, but a new way of thinking about marking techniques would shortly emerge that would place 627 Squadron at a lower altitude than they had dared to imagine. It was a development that would drag them away from No.8 Group – the creation of Don Bennett, the founding father of Mosquito pathfinding – and for a time, cause the Squadron considerable apprehension.

---

* Ernst Wallner would go on to command 6./NJG 6 but was lost in combat on 4/5 December 1944.
† The Junkers 88 and Messerschmitt 110 were already slower than the Mosquito, and the Lichtenstein SN2's nose-mounted aerials dragged their speed down a further 30mph.

6

A CHANGE IN DIRECTION

Crawford Priory, the once fine Gothic house near the village of Springfield in Fife, formerly contained all the essential elements of an aristocratic residence, but now lies in ruins. The fine vaulted ceilings, towers and grand staircase have collapsed or been demolished. The grounds, whose manicured gardens were once the setting for tea parties and gentle strolls around the neatly trimmed shrubbery, are grazed by cows. There is no roof, and the walls that remain are overgrown with ivy, while tree trunks poke through the shattered floors. First built by the 21st Earl of Crawford in 1758, Crawford Priory suffered the ignominy of several periods of desertion before its final demise. The Gothic rebuilding of 1809 brought halcyon days of fine living, supporting a full complement of servants and groundskeepers. The occupant, Lady Mary Lindsay Crawford, remained unmarried, devoting her attention to the upkeep of animals and making Crawford Priory's future far from certain. After Lady Mary's death, the estate passed into the hands of the Earls of Glasgow.

When, in 1880, Thomas Cochrane married Gertrude Boyle,

Air Vice Marshal Ralph Cochrane, 1943.

the daughter of the 6th Earl of Glasgow and the heir of Lady Mary, he might have been forgiven for thinking that the adoption of his father-in-law's property and the resources of the estate was a perfect start to married life. Thomas, the Eton- and Cheltenham College-educated second son of the 11th Earl of Dundonald, came from a long line of distinguished Scots aristocrats. In keeping with a long and illustrious family tradition, he had pursued a military career, and was later to enter politics, becoming Under Secretary of State for the Home Department in 1902. Neither the Army nor the pay of a politician would sustain an estate, and it must have been a considerable disappointment to find after his marriage that the 6th Earl had few resources. Indeed, the owner of Crawford Priory, whom Cochrane was to dub 'the old rogue', was in debt, and soon extracted a loan from his new son-in-law, a not inconsiderable amount that the couple took years to recover.

Ralph Cochrane was born in 1895, the youngest son of the large family at Crawford Priory. With his father away in London on parliamentary business, his early life was spent in the nursery with his beloved nanny 'Ata'. Ralph loved exploring the gardens and the many acres of land belonging to the estate, where he was fascinated by the activities of the gamekeeper. His earliest memories were of the freezing house, ill-heated owing to financial constraints, and the gradual realization that he would need to leave home to pursue the path in life set out for him. After being sent to boarding school at Ardvreck in Perthshire, he entered the Royal Naval College at Osborne on the Isle of Wight* when he was thirteen years old. Prince Edward (later King Edward VIII) was two terms above Ralph, and Prince Albert (later King George VI) two terms beneath him, so there was no question that entry into the Royal Navy served as a significant introduction into society for the young man.

By the outbreak of the First World War, Cochrane was serving aboard the battleship HMS *Colossus* but found the poor weather and daily duties at the primary naval anchorage at Scapa Flow tedious. In 1915 he volunteered to join the Royal Naval Air Service and trained to fly to the new airships that were to be used as submarine hunters. His proficiency was such that by the end of the war he was serving as a test pilot on airships and found himself merged into the newly formed Royal Air Force in 1919. Although commentators have tended to place the later tensions between Bennett and Cochrane in the frame of New World Australian versus aristocratic member of the British establishment, Cochrane's elevation was as practical and experience-led as Bennett's. In the inter-war years Cochrane commanded 3 and 8 Squadrons, the latter being a bomber squadron. His experience on bombers included a tour of duty in Aden, where the RAF had been deployed to suppress an insurrection by the Subaihi tribe, a background not dissimilar to the then Squadron Leader Arthur Harris. He returned to attend staff college and in 1936 was sent to New Zealand to help form the Royal New Zealand Air Force, becoming Chief of the Air Staff in 1937.

By 1939 he was nearly forty-five years of age, had served

---

* The Royal Naval College was established in part of Queen Victoria's former residence, Osborne House.

in a world war and several smaller conflicts, and could look forward to further senior positions after his time in New Zealand. Taking command of 5 Group in February 1943, Cochrane was invited to assemble a squadron to undertake a special raid on dams in Germany's Ruhr and Eder valleys, in which highly modified Lancasters carried 'bouncing bombs' invented by the engineer Barnes Wallis. In this single galvanising raid in May of that year, the reputation of 617 Squadron under Cochrane's supervision created an enduring legacy. Rarely had a single raid dominated the front pages of Britain's newspapers for so long; reports followed day after day, accompanied – as they became available – by dramatic pictures showing breaches in the dam walls and flooded valleys and villages. 'Operation Chastise' – better known as the 'Dam Busters raid' – made heroes of the bomber crews and turned the raid's leader, Wing Commander Guy Gibson, commander of 617 Squadron, into a household name. Barnes Wallis had other spectacular weapons planned that required pinpoint accuracy, and 617 Squadron was retained as a specialist unit concentrating on targets such as docks, power stations and battleships. In effect, precision bombing began to follow a twin-route course: the high-accuracy raids on individual targets were Cochrane's responsibility, while Don Bennett's Pathfinders handled the larger city attacks.

It would be unfair, however, to portray these strategic changes as arising purely out of a conflict of personalities at Group level. Much ink has been spilled over the Bennett–Cochrane clash – and there is no doubt that it spawned a rivalry between 5 Group and 8 Group Pathfinders – but it is important to consider the wider picture. Ultimately, it was new technological developments, leading to a ratcheting-up of the sophistication of the electronic war, that made the new strategies possible. Although Harris still held to the belief that pathfinding would be best dispersed throughout his squadrons, he had bowed to the Air Ministry's directive in forming the Pathfinder Force (PFF). And when it came to establishing the PFF, Harris had not done so half-heartedly, for in Bennett he had found a man who would energetically expand the PFF, and tenaciously defend the principle of maintaining separate target-marking squadrons. However, in a raid such as Operation Chastise, Cochrane had shown that a heavy bomber could fly independently and still find its target. It was a revolutionary concept that went against the understood logic of mass attacks. Armies had always attacked together, navies in fleets and aircraft in waves. The prevailing belief that 'the bomber will always get through' was predicated on putting enough aircraft into the air to overwhelm defences. A unit that flew too far ahead of the bomber stream and became isolated ran the risk of being decimated, while an aircraft that flew on its own at low level was also placing itself in severe danger.

H2S radar was first introduced in February 1943, just as Cochrane took the helm of 5 Group, and proved to be a huge technological leap. Ground-scanning radar enabled the bomb aimer to 'see' features through cloud cover, and released the navigator from having to make pinpoint calculations as to where the target was. The image produced by early versions of H2S took a lot of deciphering – the small, round screen seemed to contain a huge amount of green fuzziness. By the autumn, however, improved models showed that, in time, it would be possible to identify a target blindly.

By late 1943 Ralph Cochrane had a significant problem. 617 Squadron was in the doldrums, having lost much of its impetus after the Dam Busters raid; crew casualties had been high (five aircraft and their crews were lost in a failed raid on the Dortmund–Ems canal in September). It was clear that the squadron would benefit from new leadership. But Cochrane had more to consider than his flagship squadron; there were eleven other squadrons in 5 Group, and Cochrane faced the

Wing Commander Leonard Cheshire, January 1943.

challenge of keeping morale high through another hard-fought winter. The answer to 617's problems came in the form of a quiet but confident twenty-six-year-old who had already completed three full tours of bombing operations, but was desperate to return to active duties. The youngest Group Captain in the Royal Air Force, Leonard Cheshire had been retired to ground duties and was in command of RAF Marston Moor in North Yorkshire, the centre of 1652 Heavy Conversion Unit (HCU).* In theory, this posting would allow Cheshire to share his wealth of hard-won experience with new bomber crews. He had already demonstrated his compassionate approach in his previous commands, rejecting authoritarianism in favour of steady encouragement. However, he felt ill-suited to the position of station commander, and his unhappiness turned into a constant chafing to return to operations. He had enjoyed the patronage of Air Officer Commanding 4 Group, Roderick Carr, who had garnered support for Cheshire's promotion. Carr, a New Zealander who had flown as a spotter during the Battle of Loos in 1915, had the square jawline and serious demeanour of a leader who was not to be trifled with. Cheshire knew he could not ask Carr

---

* The HCU was the final stage of a bomber crewman's training before he entered a front-line squadron.

for a new command, as it would mean a voluntary demotion to Wing Commander, which might suggest ingratitude on his part for Carr's patronage.

Air Vice Marshal Don Bennett visited RAF Marston Moor in the summer of 1943 and Leonard Cheshire seized the opportunity to ask him if there was an opening in the Path-finders. Bennett was uncharacteristically cool, saying there were no vacances. To add insult to injury, Bennett suggested that Cheshire would need to be assessed to see if he was proficient enough to fly with the force – an idea even the normally mild-mannered Cheshire bridled at. It was not the first time Bennett had rejected Cheshire. As Group Captain Hamish Mahaddie,* Bennett's primary recruiter, recalled, 'Chesh was the only person I selected for training with the Pathfinder Force that Bennett vetoed. I was never able to establish why.' Ralph Cochrane of 5 Group proved far more receptive, and Cheshire found a new command with 617 Squadron in October 1943 at RAF Woodhall Spa.

Although the concept of individual bombers being able to navigate and accurately to drop their own bombs on a target was established, in practice there was still some way to travel before it could be perfected. The Pathfinder was still necessary, but it was not enough to place the markers within dozens of yards of an intended target. 617 Squadron were by this time operating specially adapted Lancaster bombers carrying the 12,000lb 'Tallboy' bomb, another brainchild of Barnes Wallis. The bomb bay doors were bulged to allow carriage of the enormous weapon – a sleek single bomb that would bury itself deep into the target before exploding. Wallis calculated that the 'earthquake bombs' would require dropping from 16,000 feet within 15 yards of their target for maximum effectiveness.

* Mahaddie commanded 7 Squadron at RAF Oakington and was pro-moted by Bennett to 'Group Training Inspector' in March 1943.

This level of accuracy was difficult to achieve, and results prior to Cheshire's arrival had not been good. 617 Squadron placed all ten of their bombs close to their marker on a raid on a V-1 site at Abbeville on 16 December 1943. It was an outcome that should have resulted in celebratory drinks at the Petwood Hotel* that night, but after-raid photographs showed the knot of hits 350 yards from their intended target. Depressingly, the target marker had not hit home accurately. Faced with the shocking wastage of Tallboys, Cheshire knew he had to remedy the matter with urgency. Wallis challenged Cheshire by saying, 'If you're going to scatter my bombs all over northern France, what's the point of me building them?' Since the target marker was proving difficult to place accurately from high altitude – a problem whose effects were exacerbated by the marker's tendency to skip on landing – the only solution seemed to be to drop it from a lower level.

In February 1944 Air Marshal Harris convened a meeting at High Wycombe to discuss the threat of the V-3, a long-distance German gun capable of firing shells at London. Given the need to destroy the V-3 launch sites using the Tallboy bomb, the issue of accuracy was at the forefront of his mind. Air Vice Marshal Robert Saundby, deputy air officer commanding-in-chief, chaired the meeting with Air Vice Marshal Bennett, commander of the No.8 Group Pathfinder Force and Air Vice Marshal Cochrane commanding 5 Group in attendance. Cochrane brought Cheshire to the meeting, a somewhat daunting undertaking for Cheshire as 'a humble Wing Commander', as he later recalled.

Air Vice Marshal Bennett had achieved much with No.8 Group Pathfinders to improve the accuracy of bombing raids;

* The Petwood, a fine palatial mock-Tudor building created by Baroness Grace van Eckhardstein in 1905, served as the officers' mess for RAF Woodhall Spa.

for its advocates low-level marking seemed a natural progression in the present circumstance. On learning of the level of accuracy that was being suggested Bennett was dismissive, saying it could not be done. There were certain principles on which Bennett was immovable, including the unshakable conviction that lower-level marking was unworkable and too costly in terms of aircraft and aircrew. Affected by his own experience of low-level attacks, he believed his bombers should operate as far from flak batteries as possible. With regard to the Mosquito, perhaps the natural contender for low-level operations, Bennett was very protective. The low loss rate of Mosquitos through 1943 led him to believe that they were an essential component in high-level pathfinding – and a resource he would not allow to be wasted. Although the meeting was constructive and amiable, Bennett's uncompromising position did little to help 5 Group identify a way to achieve more accurate pathfinding. The task of finding a solution to the problem was handed back to 5 Group and Cheshire in particular – a challenge he did not find unwelcome, but a difficult and demanding one nonetheless.

Bennett's appointment to lead the Pathfinder force in July 1942 had created ripples within the command of the RAF. At thirty-three years of age, he was the youngest Air Vice Marshal to be promoted, but he also proved to be one of the most outspoken. The uneasy peace between Bennett and Cochrane was well known to Arthur Harris. There was no question that Bennett's bullishness had garnered him professional enemies, but he always maintained that he bore them no personal animosity. This perception was not always shared by those with whom he came into conflict. Bennett's intransigence at the February 1944 meeting set in play a series of events that was to lead to the fracturing of his Group and a loss of some of his squadrons to 5 Group.

To try to solve the marking issue, Cheshire had the benefit

of working with low-flying expert Squadron Leader H. B. 'Mickey' Martin. Part of 617 Squadron's old guard and one of the few 'Dam Buster' pilots who was still flying operations, Martin was an ideal companion. After test flights trying to place a marker from 5,000 feet, Cheshire came to the conclusion that the best method of ensuring accuracy was to dive to a low level and place the marker visually. Initially, a nervous Cochrane instructed them that they were not to allow the attack to fall below 5,000 feet, but Martin and Cheshire found that the manoeuvre worked best when they flew in at 3,000 feet and performed a shallow dive onto the target – sometimes as low as 500 feet – before recovering altitude. When he was presented with conclusive evidence from practice dives on the Wainfleet ranges (on the Lincolnshire coast of the Wash), Cochrane eased his objections – while observing that he still regarded it as a highly unorthodox method of target aiming.

Cochrane and Cheshire put forward their findings to Harris, and Cheshire was granted permission to attack the Gnome & Rhône engine plant at Limoges using his new technique on 8 February 1944, on the condition that there were no casualties among the French workforce.* Concerned that the air-raid sirens could not be relied on to empty the buildings before the main bomber force arrived, Cheshire decided on an unusual method of early warning. Diving his loaded Lancaster bomber as low as he dared, he roared across the steel-peaked roofs of the factory, leaving the workers in no doubt that an attack was imminent. After three passes, which gave the workers enough time to flee, Cheshire returned to deposit his flares squarely on the factory, producing an explosion of blinding light.

The ensuing attack by the bombers of 617 Squadron was an outstanding success – the Gnome & Rhône factory sustained

---

* The raid on Limoges was taken to the War Cabinet before approval was granted.

serious damage, but there were no French casualties.* However, it was clear to Cheshire that the Lancaster was not ideal for this kind of task. Gnome & Rhône had been lightly defended – it would be essential for the attacker of a more substantial and better-defended target to have greater speed and agility.

A sterner test lay ahead in the attack on the Anthéor railway viaduct in southern France along the coast between Saint-Raphaël and Nice on the night of 12/13 February. The viaduct lay on a key supply route to the German army in Italy; although the railway line had been cut before, it had been quickly repaired. Cheshire and Martin intended to mark the railway line leading to the viaduct by bringing their Lancasters in low over the valley. Since the viaduct presented such a clear target, the Germans had increased their light-flak units on either side of the valley. When they saw Cheshire and Martin's Lancasters approaching, they produced a hail of fire, driving them away. The bombers made successive attempts at marking, during which Martin suffered an injury, one of his crewman was killed,† and his Lancaster was badly damaged. He limped to an American airfield in Sardinia on two engines after placing a marker, but not in the best position. Cheshire failed to drop his marker and ordered his eight remaining 617 Squadron aircraft to bomb, but all missed the viaduct. It was a depressing failure, further compounded by the loss of Squadron Leader Suggitt in Lancaster DV382, which flew into a hill east of Chichester on the return leg. It seemed Air Vice Marshal Bennett's assessment of the hazards of low-level flying might have been correct.

Despite the difficulties at Anthéor, Cheshire pressed on and, in March 1944, made a series of successful and highly accurate attacks on targets at Albert, St Etienne, Clermont-Ferrand,

---

* One worker was slightly injured.
† The bomb aimer, Flight Lieutenant Hays.

Angoulême and Lyon. He was by now convinced that the future of low-level marking lay with the Mosquito, and after some chivvying, he was given Mosquito ML976 for trials, first flying it on 30 March. He found it was possible to aim the marker by eye in the Mosquito as the target began to loom large in the small windscreen. By doing away with the bombsight, and marking an X on the windscreen with a chinagraph pencil, he was able to place the marker within the prescribed 15 yards of the target. Convinced of the method, his goal was to have his own Mosquito squadron of highly experienced crews with him at RAF Woodhall Spa. Obtaining Mosquitos off the production line would take time, and assembling experienced men for the task even longer. There was only one quick way of getting the men and material he wanted, and that was to fish in 8 Group's plentifully stocked pond of Mosquito squadrons. In addition, 5 Group would need experienced Lancaster Pathfinders to provide support marking to the higher force of bombers.

The proposition threatened to be explosively divisive within Arthur Harris's command, and a key meeting was called in early April with senior command at RAF High Wycombe. Leonard Cheshire was invited once again into its hallowed headquarters to explain his theories. He found that his ideas were given a thoughtful and constructive reception, not at all hostile to the possibility of low-level marking. However, communicating subsequently with Air Marshal Harris, Don Bennett was vociferous in his objections, stating that the Mosquitos would be lost quickly and for no gain. It was apparent that Bennett rejected all opinions on methods of pathfinding other than his own; what was less clear was the extent to which he had alienated his peers. When he received a curt letter in reply, Bennett understood that he had stated his opinion too strongly. On 13 April he was ordered to relinquish two Lancaster squadrons to 5 Group, 97 and 83 and a precious Mosquito squadron, 627.

★

For the men of 627 Squadron, flying high in their Mosquitos through the autumn and winter of 1943/44 over the glowing cities of Hitler's Reich, life had taken on a regular pattern. They had served their time in the bombers that flew 10,000 feet below them, knowing the uncertainties and terrors that the heavy bomber crews faced. They were happy with their lot, and it appeared that Bennett's strategies were paying dividends. Night after night bombs fell on Berlin, and when the large streams of bombers were restricted by weather or phase of the moon, 627 Squadron still ventured out to harry the enemy. The crews of 627 Squadron knew from Don Bennett's visits to RAF Oakington that he could be a prickly character. Talk in the mess sometimes touched on rumours of rivalries at high command level, but they caused Squadron members little concern; it was surely inconceivable that 627 could be wrenched away from its founder.

Late in the evening of 13 April 1944 the Squadron received unexpected orders to transfer to RAF Woodhall Spa in Lincolnshire. In keeping with re-assignments of this kind, the time allocated to complete the move was forty-eight hours; all elements of the transfer were to be complete by 23.39 hours on 15 April. This very precise requirement caused a good deal of flutter. When news of the move arrived, eight Mosquitos were still airborne, returning from a raid on Berlin; the work required to get all equipment and stores together for a road move would take all night. The next morning Don Bennett arrived at RAF Oakington to address the bleary-eyed crews. As beams of morning sunshine lit the briefing room, cutting through the fine haze of cigarette smoke, Bill de Boos remembers the Air Vice Marshal was 'visibly upset', and informed the crews that they were being transferred to 5 Group. The crews gained from the briefing the impression that, in Bennett's view, their new posting might be difficult, and that it might not produce the desired result. It was sombre news. 'We all listened in silence, and a feeling of grim foreboding settled on the Squadron like a patch of low stratus,' de Boos recalled.

Flight Lieutenant Rutherford had snatched the briefest of sleeps after his return from Berlin before the frenetic activity caught up with him. After the briefing, he was ordered to fly that same day, 14 April, to RAF Woodhall Spa to lead the advance party arranging accommodation for the men. An Avro Anson had been summoned and was waiting for the men, who loaded their personal kit bags onto the aircraft, knowing this would be their last day at Oakington. On arrival at Woodhall Spa, Rutherford's first impression was that he was very glad they were not arriving in the dead of winter. Instead of substantial barrack blocks, they were to be housed once again in a village of Nissen huts with half-cylindrical skins of corrugated iron and concrete floors. Their hutted sleeping quarters lay a mile south of their dispersals. On their first day, the newly arrived officers ate at the comfortable Petwood Hotel, which served as the officers' mess. Any hopes they may have harboured that this arrangement would be extended were soon dashed, however; kitchens and mess facilities for the men of 627 Squadron were to be based on their own site in a low wooden hut located closer to the village of Tattershall Thorpe than Woodhall Spa. They also had to be up and running the following day. The transfer had been as much of a surprise to the occupants of Woodhall Spa as it had to the men of 627 Squadron; the day was therefore filled with an exhausting round of impromptu meetings and discussions about practicalities, accompanied by heavy sighs and many a raised eyebrow.

The majority of the men had to travel by road, and the snaking convoy took several hours to make the 85-mile trip north across Cambridgeshire and Lincolnshire. The fifteenth of April was a Saturday, a day when an airman might hope to escape to a dance in Cambridge or meet up with a sweetheart. There were a good number of glum faces that day as the realization dawned that what few roots the young men had put down in their six-month sojourn at Oakington were about to be ripped up. And there were days of hard work ahead of them before they would get everything in place in their new home. With more aircrews than aeroplanes to fly, Jim Marshallsay and Johnny Upton piled into Nick Ranshaw's old Morris 10 and embarked on a more leisurely journey, which included a short visit to Ranshaw's home en route. The group also had time to call in for 'essential maintenance' at the Royal Oak at Revesby, an establishment for which Upton had handled leasing arrangements before the war – which earned them a round of free drinks.

The ground elements of the Squadron had not been long at Woodhall Spa before the welcome growl of Rolls-Royce Merlins filled the air. The Mosquitos arrived by 16.00 hours and taxied around to find their new dispersals, engines chuntering and producing short puffs of exhaust smoke. Four aircraft had been sent to RAF Upwood, as 627 Squadron would no longer need the adapted Mosquitos that carried 4,000lb bombs; in exchange they received the standard 2,000lb bomb load version of the aircraft.

Woodhall Spa had been built in 1941 as a satellite base to nearby RAF Coningsby. As such it had none of the brick-built fineries of airfields constructed before the war. But the fame and effectiveness of 617 Squadron had turned Woodhall Spa into a primary airfield in a way unintended by its designers. As new residents, it was clear that 627 Squadron would be playing second fiddle to their illustrious neighbours. They would have to make do with their modest quarters, tucked away on the other side of the airfield. As it turned out, this location had the advantage of being far enough away from the airfield's hub for them to avoid unwanted scrutiny by higher command.

Ground crew at work on a 627 Squadron Mosquito,
RAF Woodhall Spa.

The officers' mess for 627 Squadron initially did not have an adequate bar, an oversight corrected sometime later by one of the crew who had some bricklaying experience, although the facilities still lacked the finesse of other messes. Some comfort was to be found at the Blue Bell Inn at nearby Tattershall Thorpe, a small pub with low ceilings, ancient timbers and open firesides that became a haven for men of all the local squadrons. In reality, Woodhall Spa was simply an extension of RAF Coningsby, an inconvenient 2½ miles away. The crews spent a good deal of time shuttling back and forth in Hillman flight vans,* as the briefings for major raids were held at Coningsby. There were advantages in having one's own vehicle

* The ubiquitous 'Tilly' came in a number of guises, from staff car to small bus. Most airfield transports were of the 'pickup' variety, with bench seats and a canvas-covered rear.

but, as a general rule, a private car was an unaffordable luxury for those on aircrew wages, and ownership was restricted to those of private means. Even then, drivers faced the perennial wartime problem of shortage of petrol – which was not the easiest problem to overcome.

In the late afternoon of their arrival day, 15 April 1944, the Squadron paraded for a visit by 5 Group commander Ralph Cochrane and Base Commander Alfred Sharpe. Such a degree of formality was unusual, and lent the occasion a certain air of foreboding. An Air Vice Marshal might be expected to address the crews in the briefing room, but gathering everyone together from Wing Commander to 'Erk'* – suggested something serious was afoot. Cochrane walked along the rows of airmen, talking to some and shaking hands with officers. Then, addressing the men in a serious tone, he emphasized not only the importance of the work ahead, but also the cost and sacrifice it might entail. For a group of crews that counted many thousands of flying hours, it was not a message they had hoped to hear, but nonetheless, the apprehension they felt was tinged with excitement. It was clear they were to perform a special task, one which, they would later discover, was unique in the Royal Air Force. The precise details of the new marking technique would be revealed through many hours of practice at the ranges. Only when Leonard Cheshire was confident in their abilities would they be allowed to mark targets, but with men of such calibre in its ranks, 627 Squadron was more than capable of meeting the challenges ahead.

---

* Derived from the WWI expression 'airk' (short for aircraftman), it came to mean any low- or basic-ranked man.

7

THE SHALLOW DIVE

RAF Woodhall Spa, 16 April 1944

On an April Sunday, as spring was still making its mind up about arriving, a chilly breeze blew unhindered across Lincolnshire from the North Sea. Airfields were always windy places, the sites chosen not only for flatness, but also to provide good wind conditions for take-offs and landings. Grey clouds had scudded across the early morning sun, but in the last few hours they had lifted enough to provide a reasonable day for flying. That day's flight weather had been easier for Met Officers to predict because, unusually, the planned activities would all take place over the aerodrome. The officers had breakfasted for the first time at their mess on the south side of the airfield and, joined by the Sergeants in the briefing room, they listened intently to instructions on the new marking strategy based on Wing Commander Cheshire's experiences. The diving technique, essential for successful marking, needed to be mastered before operational flying could begin.

At the dispersals, all available Mosquitos were being prepared. Fuel bowsers were threading their way round the perimeter tracks like bumblebees, topping up tanks before moving on to the next waiting aeroplane. Engine side panels had been removed on some aircraft as oil and coolant was checked in the Rolls-Royce Merlin engines. Chiefies,* or Chief Technicians, were on call to inspect odd drips, a worn part or an unexplained problem. Men balanced on tall stepladders, peering into engine cowlings with torches. Others sat in cockpits, checking controls, making small adjustments and noting their progress on pads. The gentle whine of a starter motor would announce an engine test, and with rapid coughs the exhaust stubs would splutter for a second before the Merlin would fire. As the technician gradually opened the throttles the sound would increase in intensity and pitch. After a few minutes full power would be applied, propellers invisible as they blasted huge quantities of air rearwards. With a swirling drone, the propellers wound down as the test was completed – the comparative silence intense as ears became accustomed once again to the breeze and the sound of distant skylarks.

There was no question who the aircraft belonged to – it was clearly the ground crews' and not the pilots and navigators. When pilots signed the Form 700 confirming they accepted the aircraft as detailed in the maintenance log before flying, it served as the handing-over agreement, but implicitly understood as a 'lease' document. Mosquito crews were always referred to by both names, as if introducing a music hall double act. 'Goodman and Hickox', 'Marshallsay and Ranshaw', 'Parlato and Thomas' tripped off the tongues of those who worked on the aeroplanes, drove the crews to different destinations or served them meals. By the time the aircrews arrived from briefing and kitting out, the work on the Mosquitos was finished and they were ready to fly. There was something potent about the look of the de Havilland design, even on the ground. Some aircraft looked

---

* 'Chiefies' were older men who had years of experience on aircraft and were expected to know everything about their charges.

clumsy sitting on the ground – perhaps the most ungainly being the giant Short Stirling bomber, the undercarriage of which pitched its cockpit to an improbable height. But the Mosquito looked sleek from every angle, and nothing, even the chunky rubber tyres and stout supporting oleo struts, could diminish its aura of power and speed.

Today the crews were uncharacteristically subdued, wearing the sort of anxious expressions normally displayed before a potentially difficult operation. When the briefing revealed the tactic they would be expected to employ in future raids, they were deeply disturbed by what they heard. Instead of the familiar cruising altitude of 30,000 feet, they were to fly at 10,000 feet, then close in on their target from 5,000 feet, dive to place their marker and recover from 500 feet. Their thoughts turned to the ground defences that would be arrayed against them – guns, fighters and barrage balloons – not to mention the arriving force of bombers high above them dropping incendiaries and bombs. As Bill de Boos recalls, 'Not one of us wanted to be a posthumous hero, and we returned to our messes in a mood of deep gloom.' But this was not a time to waste on brooding – there was flying practice to be undertaken. Sombre reflection on the dangers ahead would have to wait until later.

It was always a stirring sight, seeing the Mosquitos start up and taxi out. Ten squadron aircraft moved carefully out of the dispersals and onto the perimeter tracks, their propellers singing to the beat of the Merlin engines. At last there was time for the ground crews to grab a cup of tea from the NAAFI* van and watch the spectacle of the take-off, each ground crew eager to see their aircraft fly, just as a trainer might watch a thoroughbred horse on the starting line.

---

* NAAFI stood for the Navy, Army, and Air Force Institutes, a body responsible for providing canteens and shops for servicemen.

Forming a wide orbit around Woodhall Spa, the Mosquitos faded away against the leaden sky before reappearing over the airfield one by one. After making their approach at 5,000 feet, the Mosquitos would suddenly pitch down into a thirty-degree dive, their camouflaged upper sides and roundels fully visible as the aircraft descended rapidly. The change in sound of the engines took a few seconds to reach the watchers; by the time the shrillness of tone was audible the Mosquito was already flattening out of its dive as the aircraft behind positioned itself in preparation for the next attempt. Waiting for the attackers to pull out of their dive was slightly unnerving, but they all did so smartly, time after time. Some – whether out of skill, bravado or miscalculation – dropped lower than the 500 feet stipulated, whistling past the ground crews, their manoeuvre producing exclamations and sharp intakes of breath from the watchers. Most of the afternoon was spent in continuous practice, each Mosquito making over thirty passes.

At the end of the day, not feeling greatly encouraged by their proximity to the ground during their flying exercise, the officers repaired to a small pub at Horncastle to lift their spirits. Here the atmosphere was oppressively quiet, however, so someone turned on the pub radio, perhaps hoping for some swing and a touch of Glenn Miller. After waiting a few seconds for the glowing orange valves at the back of the radio to warm up, accompanied by the characteristic aroma of burning dust, they heard the strains of a classical concert emerging from the speaker. But the emotionally heightened mood of a concerto was too disheartening, and 'Benny' Goodman called across the room, 'Dread music! Switch it off.' Hoping to break what was now a stony silence, Bill de Boos sat down at the piano and began beating out a popular tune of the day. After a couple of minutes the publican emerged from behind the bar and forcefully closed the lid. That kind of music, he announced, was not fitting for his establishment on the Sabbath. Bill de

Boos confessed that the morale amongst the drinkers was at its lowest point that evening.

The next day, 17 April, would be dedicated to dive bombing proper on the ranges at Wainfleet, 20 miles from them on the Lincolnshire coast south of Skegness. The Mosquito crews were concerned to see that the latest technology lent to them for the task consisted of a cross drawn on their windscreen with a chinagraph pencil – in the same manner as Cheshire's first experiments. In previous bombing missions, the navigator had left his seat and entered the Perspex nose in order to aim and release the bombs, but this time it was the pilot who would press the trigger – a task that secretly pleased many of them. For the navigators, the experience took a little getting used to, but they had every confidence in their pilots. Many of them had disliked having to squeeze into the nose of the Mosquito, where they felt exposed and vulnerable to the flak rising towards them. The navigator's main task was to ensure that the aircraft travelled to and from the target accurately and in good time; during the dive over the target they became mere onlookers. A shrewd navigator would keep watch on the flying instruments in these fast and furious seconds and call out the altitude. Their usual observation at the base of the dive was 'watch your height', a recommendation made as much for reasons of self-preservation as for operational ones. It was here that the established bond between pilot and navigator was essential, since the one was entrusting his life to the skills of the other.

The flights of 17 April would prove whether the pilots were quite as accurate as their 'dry' dives over Woodhall Spa might suggest. The Mosquitos were loaded with 11½lb practice bombs, miniature devices in comparison to the 500lb versions they normally carried into action. These would produce a puff of marker smoke on impact, which allowed range observers to see their position. The mudflats at Wainfleet served as the principal range for most Lincolnshire-based bombers, and were in constant use as a result. During the day 627 Squadron would complete thirty sorties against the targets in the sands followed by a further nine at night using marker flares. This proved to be far more daunting than daytime dive-bombing, since – other than the flare-lit ground – there were no other visible external reference points in the dive.

The sound of Mosquitos was not the only thing heard in the skies of south Lincolnshire that April Monday. Throughout the day the air reverberated with the rumble of more than forty Avro Lancasters. The men and aircraft of 97 and 83 Squadrons had arrived at RAF Coningsby to fulfil their posting to 5 Group. It was a return home for 97 Squadron, who had served at Coningsby from February 1941 and Woodhall Spa from March 1942 before their transfer to 8 Group as Pathfinders in April 1943 at RAF Bourn in Cambridgeshire. Many of the men were more recent additions to the squadron and didn't remember Coningsby, and certainly none of the aircrew had served in that period. However, there was a quiet contentment within the command of 5 Group that both squadrons had returned to their fold – not to mention a mischievous satisfaction in poaching 627 Squadron from Bennett.

The crews of 627 Squadron assembled outside to wait for buses to take them the short distance from RAF Woodhall Spa to the metal-sheeted cinema at RAF Coningsby for a briefing. There was a good deal of small talk and joking as the men puffed at cigarettes, subconsciously checking their black polished shoes for any speck of dirt – senior officers would be on the prowl, and it wouldn't do to appear untidy. The Australians in the pack had done their best, but were still identifiable by a jaunty hat angle or loose button. They were engaged in a quiet but constant rebellion over what they saw as an obsession with spit and polish; they considered such activities a distraction from the real business of getting on with the war. As the buses arrived, the men's sense of anticipation was mixed with apprehension, some of them quietly hoping the task presented to them would be easier than had appeared in these first days of practice.

Among the crowd of airmen who shuffled into the station cinema, the men of 627 were very much in the minority – there were around thirty of them, compared with more than 200 from 97 and 83 Squadrons. Having seven men per crew, the Lancaster squadrons were much larger in number, and they were all trying to sit together. As the base commander, Group Captain Alfred Sharp, stood to address the men, it was apparent that there was a lot of gold braid and 'fruit salad'* in attendance. Sharp's bearing was decidedly frosty; his intention, it appeared, was to deliver to the new arrivals not words of welcome and encouragement but a warning shot across their bows. It was made clear that 5 Group were required to display the utmost discipline, and that any laxness – the implication here being that 8 Group were too free and easy – would not be tolerated. Training for their new task would begin immediately, an instruction that would later be challenged by 97 Squadron. To the further agitation of Sharp and Cochrane, they expressed the view that the burden of recent operations and their move to Coningsby was justification for their being given more time in preparation.

Wing Commander Leonard Cheshire then took to the platform to lecture the group in his new pathfinding technique. The crews could immediately sense from his more softly spoken manner that he was an authoritative leader, but one who had their welfare at heart. The crews of 627 Squadron knew something of Cheshire's methods, having spent the last couple

* RAF slang for medal ribbons.

of days rehearsing the new flying technique, but they were interested to hear him outline the wider strategic picture, and the roles played by other squadrons. Illuminating heavy bombers would arrive first and drop bright parachute flares over the target, lighting up the ground beneath. Mosquitos would then dive-bomb the target from low level, dropping marker flares in a more precise way than they had been accustomed to – and by eye. A 'Marker Leader' in a Mosquito would communicate with an experienced 'Master Bomber' above on a VHF frequency, and he in turn would speak to the arriving bombers directly. The Master Bomber would give commands at every point of the raid and, when necessary, drop his own markers. When he was satisfied the markers were in the right place and sufficiently visible, he would ask other higher-level Pathfinders to support him by dropping bombs, and would drop further indicators himself to consolidate the target. If he felt things were becoming unclear, the Master Bomber could call for fresh marking to be carried out and, in extreme circumstances, even call the raid off. To the men listening, the notion of a central voice of command amid the chaos of a raid was a highly attractive one. Having a 'ringmaster' to direct events in the circus of heavy bombers was surely a good idea; the experience of free-for-all bombing of targets had hardly proved satisfactory, after all.

RAF Coningsby, known as Base 54, would be the home to the Master Bombers. If 627 Squadron had its share of mavericks, the pilots of 54 Base Flight – as they were known – displayed a similar mix of eccentricity and exceptional airmanship. Cheshire was assembling his own dedicated group of aeroplanes for the Master Bombers – Mosquitos, a couple of twin-seat P-38 Lightnings and a P-51 Mustang for his own use. 627 Squadron would sometimes be asked to furnish a Mosquito for the leaders of a raid by 5 Group. On such occasions they hoped that their counterparts from '54 Base' would look after their precious aeroplane.

*A P-38J 'Droop Snoop' Lightning, supplied to
Leonard Cheshire by the Americans.*

As the 627 crews left the briefing, some harboured doubts
as to whether this new enterprise would work; in many minds
there lurked the lingering thought that they might be guinea
pigs in a dangerous experiment. However, they had come this
far and, buoyed by youthful enthusiasm and an underlying,
if misguided, belief in their indestructability, they were determined to 'give it a go'. The following days were filled with more
training sorties to Wainfleet, ground lectures and navigational
flights. Their first operation with 5 Group, when it came, was
something of an anti-climax.

Porte de la Chapelle, 20 April 1944

The residents of Paris drew strength from the continuing, un-
damaged beauty of their city. Even when their national pride
was at its lowest ebb, when strange uniforms and goose-stepping
parades filled their streets, the architecture of *la ville lumière*
remained intact – a statement of belief in an enduring France.
The Arc de Triomphe, little over 100 years old and originally
built to commemorate those who fell in the Revolutionary

and Napoleonic wars, was a reminder of French greatness, of a time when a victorious, seemingly unstoppable nation held sway in Europe. That permanence of symbols reassured Parisians that France would rise once again one day – the city would not allow anything less. The older men with Gauloises-stained moustaches had fought the Germans at the Marne, the Aisne and Verdun, and dozens of places in between. Their Teutonic neighbours would not stop them playing pétanque and murmuring their displeasure at the current state of affairs. Many of the young men of the city had gone – some had fled abroad, the majority pressed into working for the German war effort through forced labour programmes.* But the city of Paris itself remained materially in place, its beautiful buildings spared while destruction rained down on London and Berlin. When an attack on the city came, not from Nazi Germany but from the RAF, it caused considerable distress; Parisians did not trust the Germans, but they had assumed the Allies would show due consideration for their historic city.

As thousands of men trained for D-Day in the south of England,† the task of crippling the French rail network and transport infrastructure was moving towards the top of the list of Allied bombing priorities. Despite sustaining terrible losses in his bomber force, Air Marshal Arthur Harris had not yet vanquished Berlin, nor had he seen the collapse of the Nazi state he had hoped saturation bombing would bring about. The time when he was free to conduct his vast and brutal experiment in area bombing had expired, and he was now forced to follow the agenda of the coming invasion. He was not alone in his disappointment; many commanders who had seen the

---

* Between June 1942 and July 1944, 600,000 to 650,000 French workers were sent to Germany.
† Two days later Operation Tiger, an invasion practice, was carried out on Slapton Sands in Devon, involving 30,000 men.

Senior 627 Squadron NCOs, Ken Flatt, Doug Garton and Vic Atter, with their own motorcycles in front of Leonard Cheshire's Mk VI Mosquito NS993 at RAF Woodhall Spa.

carnage of the Great War feared a future of bloody stalemate on the continent. The railway marshalling yards at Porte de la Chapelle on the northern edge of Paris were an important rail hub for lines stretching north into Normandy, but they nestled uncomfortably close to residential streets. Since 627 Squadron were still in training for the low-level marking technique, it was Leonard Cheshire who led the diving attack with three other Mosquitos on charge at 617 Squadron. Twelve aircraft of 627 Squadron were instructed to scatter 'Window' at 16,000 feet before bombing conventionally with 500lb bombs. Perhaps it was irksome for men who had amassed thousands of flying hours to be given such a menial task, but Cheshire was already under a lot of pressure to make sure his raids were accurate – and perhaps no other target was as sensitive as Paris itself.

But in terms of bombing precision, the attack on La Chapelle was nothing like as successful as the Gnome & Rhône raid. On this warm April evening, things did not go according to plan, as bombs strayed off target and fell onto houses nearby. A local French worker wrote in his diary:

> During 2 hours and 15 minutes, a mind-boggling racket. Everything was shaking in the apartment (located in the 7th arrondissement in the very heart of Paris). At last I went down the stairs and tried to cheer up Mrs Dantin (the famously bad-tempered doorkeeper, an awful drunkard old lady) who was stricken with panic. The night sky was lighted with flares and fires, and you could see as in broad daylight. I called our warehouse right away, but there was no dial tone. I immediately thought of the worst.

The debriefing report of Squadron Leader Les Munro, a veteran of the Dam Busters raids flying Lancaster LM482, highlights the patchy nature of the raid: 'Bombs fell across the spotfires. Bombing seemed concentrated at time of own bombing, but was later scattered.' Although the initial markers had landed close to the desired target point, the bombs dropped subsequently hit places some distance away from them; such inaccuracies proved once again that, even using the Pathfinder strategy, success was far from certain. The Mosquito markers had levelled out after their dive at 1,200 feet, an altitude 627 Squadron pilots would later feel was a little high. But the nub of the problem was that the second wave of bombers, at 15,000 feet, struggled to find the precise aiming points in the conflagration below.

The raid had, in fact, gone horribly wrong. Six hundred and forty-one civilians were killed and 377 injured, causing an uproar in Paris,* which was communicated to the Free French government in London, who felt they had not been

---

* The Vichy leader, Marshal Pétain, visited Paris a few days after the bombing and received a triumphal welcome.

properly consulted about the raid. It was a blow to the Allied commanders, who relied on Free French Army support for their plans but also knew they had to maintain morale in the resistance networks throughout France. Air Marshal Harris called Cochrane and told him that, under the circumstances, Cheshire could only retain his increased resources, particularly the Mosquitos, if his next major raid was successful. There was no doubt left in Leonard Cheshire's mind that failure was not an option if he was to be able to continue to put his ideas about close marking of targets into practice.

Two days after La Chapelle, on 22 April, a smaller raid targeted Braunschweig in north-central Germany – a relatively simple flight for 627 Squadron over the North Sea, across Holland and quickly out again once the bombs were dropped. Arriving over the target at around 20,000 feet, they dropped 'Window' and 500lb bombs on the clearly marked target and set course for home relatively untroubled by the searchlights and flak. 'Benny' Goodman and 'Bill' Hickox, flying DZ484, were tasked to arrive 30 minutes after the main force to take reconnaissance photos and drop their bomb load. Goodman automatically flew to Braunschweig at 25,000 feet, an altitude he was accustomed to and considered safe, staying out of the way of flak and fighters. Landing at 04.39, the men made their way to debriefing to report what they thought had been a fairly successful, if unremarkable, night's work. Goodman, perhaps because he was one of the last to arrive, drew the attention of Air Vice Marshal Cochrane and Group Captain Sharp, who were attending the debriefing to see how their new men were performing.

'What height did you come down to?' quizzed Sharp.

'25,000 feet sir,' replied Goodman confidently.

To his surprise, Sharp's face flushed with fury. Goodman and Hickox waited nervously as the Group Captain appeared to be approaching a state of apoplexy. '25,000 feet!' he spluttered.

'Tomorrow night you'll do the same thing again, and you won't go above 1,000 feet all the way there and back.' Goodman, duly reprimanded, henceforth ensured that, in keeping with 5 Group's practices, he descended to 1,000 feet on reconnaissance flights – an altitude that would prove far more dangerous than the higher level. Sharp's public dressing-down was hardly fair to Flying Officer Goodman; he had chosen to fly at exactly the same altitude as he would have done with 8 Group, and the briefing had included no specific instructions regarding low-level flying for those flying reconnaissance missions. However, Goodman's departure to Braunschweig from Woodhall Spa in DZ484 had taken place an hour after his 627 colleagues – he had been a lone aircraft in the dark skies of Europe. By definition of 'late reconnaissance' (as written in the Operation Record Book), Sharp must have felt it should have occurred to Goodman that the mission was perilous and demanded greater caution. The misunderstanding – and Sharp's reaction – also seems to stem from his perception that the former 8 Group men had a *laissez-faire* attitude. A certain tension would remain for some weeks between Sharp and the newly arrived squadrons.

Munich, 24 April 1944

The choice of a German city as the target for Wing Commander Cheshire's next mission lowered the bar in terms of bombing accuracy. There would be no outcry if bombs went astray, but the raid would be scrutinized using photographs obtained by photoflash* over the target. It was somehow fitting that

---

* Photoflash was a small device released causing a 1/5th-of-a-second flash to allow an on-board camera to photograph the point at which a bomb had dropped. On every raid a certain percentage of bombers would have cameras installed.

Cheshire's make-or-break raid would be against a city considered the home of the Nazi movement. Although Nazism was a young movement (the National Socialist German Workers' Party, or Nazi Party, had been founded as recently as 1920), one of its successes lay in its appropriation of German folk culture, which allowed National Socialists to portray themselves as standard bearers and guardians of national tradition. Germany itself had existed formally as a nation-state only since 1871, its unification masterminded by Chancellor Otto von Bismarck. But Adolf Hitler was striving to create an empire that embraced all of the 'German-speaking peoples', a far broader interpretation of the political map of Europe than Germany's founding statesman had ever envisaged. It was in Munich that Hitler had made his first attempt to seize power in the failed 'Beer Hall Putsch' of 1923, which led to his being imprisoned for eight months in nearby Landsberg jail. Suitably embroidered, the events of 1923 soon became key elements in National Socialist mythology, and Munich its Holy City. Nazi parades and rallies held here exuded a quasi-religious aura, thereby creating a mystique around the swastika and the perched eagle – a symbol that re-appeared not only on German tanks and aeroplanes, but in every arena of German life, from newspapers to furniture.

With the political stakes high, Leonard Cheshire decided to lead the attack on Munich himself, in a Mosquito FB Mk IV,* accompanied by his regular navigator, Flying Officer Pat Kelly. He would fly to and from the target at low level, while his massive main force of 234 Lancasters made their way to the city via a much longer route. Cheshire stationed four Mosquitos with 617 Squadron† for his markers, since it was

---

* Cheshire's Mosquitos at Woodhall Spa were the FB Mk VI model, which, as the fighter variant, had a solid nose and guns compared to 627 Squadron's Perspex-nosed Mk IVs.
† It appears they were 'loaned' from 571 Squadron, and were not formally part of 617 Squadron.

too early to consider his trainees at 627 Squadron for such an important task. They would adopt their previous role in higher-level bombing, but once again would drop 'Window'.

The main bomber force took off at 20.30 hours for a flight that would be one of the longest the Lancaster bomber would undertake during the war. Owing to the lengthy route chosen for the approach to Munich, most of the aircraft were in the air for nearly ten hours. Even for the swifter Mosquitos, the flying time would be nearly five hours. Twelve 627 Squadron aircraft made the long journey, Squadron Leader Mackenzie taking the lead in Mosquito DZ547. Earlier in the day, waves of B-17 bombers of the American 8th Air Force, escorted by large numbers of fighters, had smashed into Munich's defences. The Americans attacked factories and defensive airfields in daylight, triggering fierce aerial battles on their outbound leg across France and Germany and the return through Holland. The Luftwaffe had lost forty-three aircraft, the majority of them Me 109s, to the guns of a combined force of 800 British and American fighters. Out of 700 US bombers deployed, the force lost twenty-seven B-17s, including several seeking refuge in neutral Switzerland after being damaged. The unfortunate crew of one stricken B-17, captained by First Lieutenant Everett L. Bailey, were shot down over the Greifensee, near Zürich, by Swiss fighters after a misunderstanding as to their flight course. The B-17 had been intercepted by Swiss fighters, which directed the American aircraft to make a landing. However, the B-17 turned away from the landing ground after being unable to retract its ball turret* – a move interpreted by the escorting Swiss fighters as an attempt to escape. Three American airmen, including Bailey, were killed in the attack.

It therefore was no surprise to the Germans that Munich

---

* A machine-gun turret consisting of a rotatable compartment projecting below (and retractable into) the fuselage.

came under attack that night, but in order to try to restrict their ability to anticipate the strike, the Allies' air forces chose a circuitous route for their bombers. The Mosquitos of 627 Squadron followed the same course as the Lancasters, clipping the Ardennes and then flying over eastern France before crossing the snow-peaked crests of the Alps. The Lancasters skirted neutral Switzerland and the twinkling lights of a land at peace, before splitting their force in two: some of them headed south to launch a diversionary attack on Milan, while the main force turned towards Munich, where they knew the searchlights and flak were as stern a test as any German city could mount.

By the time 627 Squadron arrived over Munich the initial work of marking by Leonard Cheshire had been done and 617 Squadron as first supporters had 'backed up', dropping high-explosive bombs into the centre. The city was already well alight, with huge fires merging into an inferno. Ian Hanlon and Johnny Upton in Mosquito DZ525 arrived at 01.55 hours and noted an 'Enormous area of blazing fires with smoke up to 12,000 feet. Fires could be seen 80 miles away.' Norman Rutherford and Fred Stanbury in DZ521 reported half an hour later that the smoke had reached 20,000 feet. They suffered a hair-raising four minutes when they were 'coned' by several German searchlights, but managed to escape their clutches, later reporting that the flak was heavy and intense. Goodman and Hickox's report said that they dropped their 'Window' material at 23,000 feet 'as ordered', perhaps keen to emphasize to a waiting Group Captain Sharp that procedure had been carried out to the letter.

Whatever its overall effect, it is clear that the scattering of 'Window' benefitted one bomber crew at least. The Hamilton crew flying Lancaster ME155 of 617 Squadron entered, 'Search-lights seemed to be affected by window'. The raid itself appeared to have been a great success; crews later described the attacks on the city as among the most concentrated attacks they had seen. The effects remained visible for a long time on the return leg; the crew of Pilot Officer Edwards, flying a Lancaster of 97 Squadron, reported seeing a huge explosion at 02.41 which lit up the cockpit from 160 miles away.

Munich was devasted by the attack. Reconnaissance photographs taken the following day showed not only smoking piles of rubble, but long trails of refugees fleeing the city. The casualties resulting from the raid –139 killed and 4,185 wounded – were in fact lighter than was the case with other massed attacks on German cities, in part because Munich had a greater number of stone buildings compared with other largely wooden-built historic German cities, which meant that the city avoided the horror of a firestorm.* Nonetheless, 50 per cent of the city lay in ruins, roughly 81,500 houses were destroyed or damaged, and 300,000 people were made homeless. This 'de-housing' of large numbers of civilians chimed perfectly with the ruthless bombing strategy proposed to the War Cabinet in March 1942 by Professor Frederick Lindemann, Churchill's Chief Scientific Adviser.

The Munich raid created a flood of refugees, many of them convinced that their city was no longer safe. Large numbers of people on the move from the Bavarian capital created problems for communities in towns and villages beyond Munich, rendering the necessary relief efforts undertaken by the German authorities yet more complex and yet more intractable. As preparations for D-Day gathered pace, it was precisely the result Air Marshal Harris and the Supreme Headquarters Allied Expeditionary Force (SHAEF) had hoped for. Cheshire's gambit had paid off – at least for now.

---

* Munich was to lose 6,632 people through the seventy-four air raids that hit the city throughout the war. Hamburg lost 37,000 killed in the seven days of the July 1943 attacks.

Lancaster JO-Q Queenie (ME580/G) of 463 Squadron, RAAF, about to touch down at RAF Waddington after the Munich raid, 24 April 1944.

Schweinfurt, 26 April 1944

The town of Schweinfurt, in the north Bavarian region of Lower Franconia, was a centre of the German metal industry and a world leader in the production of ball bearings – the friction-reducing elements of any machine with moving parts. Ball bearings had made Schweinfurt an economically thriving place, crucial to the German war effort, but they also made the town a vulnerable target for an enemy determined on disrupting their production. As the Allies prepared for D-Day, they knew that the beach landings would be only the beginning of a long struggle. Eventual victory would be as much a matter of starving the German armies of weapons and fuel as of fighting on the ground.

The invention of a humble bicycle hub, the 'Freewheeler', allowed twenty-seven-year-old Ernst Sachs to set up his own business with fellow entrepreneur Karl Fichtel in 1895. A keen cyclist, he trained hard and won many races, but as an engineer who had begun his apprenticeship in Stuttgart, he was dissatisfied with the rudimentary wheel bearings fitted to bicycles. Starting with a handful of employees, his company, Schweinfurter Präcisions-Kugellager-Werke Fichtel & Sachs, would grow into a giant of ball-bearing manufacturing, its expansion greatly assisted by the extension of Bavaria's railway network, which allowed industries to grow exponentially during Germany's era of high industrialization in the latter part of the nineteenth century. Huge profits accrued to Fichtel & Sachs during the First World War. Fichtel had died in 1911, but by the war's end the business employed as many as 8,000 workers in its Schweinfurt factory, which would successfully weather the global economic recession of the early 1930s. When Sachs died in 1932, aged sixty-four, such was his wealth and philanthropy that his funeral resembled a state event. Starting with a simple brick-built single-storey factory with a small chimney, he left behind an enormous complex of milling and assembly buildings that dominated employment in the town.

This was not a location that could be hidden from the Allies; its importance in making bearings for tanks, trains and aircraft made it a powerhouse of Reich industry. As the source of as much as half of all ball bearings used in Germany, Schweinfurt was attacked twenty-two times during the Second World War. Each raid hobbled production, but the town's factories were not rendered wholly inoperative until American forces overran Schweinfurt in April 1945.

In anticipation of the targeting of large production centres such as Schweinfurt, the Reich Minister for Armaments and War Production, Albert Speer, had ordered the dispersal of key Axis industries more widely across the country. Certain of the numerous Allied raids on Schweinfurt, notably those of August and October 1943, had been significantly well-defended, and the resulting heavy losses of US airmen and planes had shaken the United States Eighth Air Force badly. Within the Allied air forces, Schweinfurt was the epitome of a high-value target – but it had also become synonymous with grievously high casualty levels for the attackers. Part of the problem lay with the size and complexity of the factory sites. The vast profits that Ernst Sachs had made in the First World War had been re-invested in the business to create modern factory blocks, roads and other elements of infrastructure. By the time war came, at least four production areas and administrative sites were spread across the western area of the town, with signifi- cant distances between them. A successful strike on such a complex required bombing of exceptional accuracy and potency, so as to destroy completely the production floors and the machinery they contained. But earlier Allied raids had struggled to achieve this.

The USAAF and RAF had found the Germans well-prepared – they used special devices* that poured out plumes of smoke as the raiders approached. These covered the area in haze and provided false targets for the bomb aimers above. In the spring of 1944, the RAF would once again return to Schweinfurt by night, but this time with a determination to maximize the accuracy of their bombing.

Given the anxieties that members of 627 Squadron felt about their new role, the revealing of Schweinfurt as the target at the briefing of 26 April felt like a vice closing in on them. Their initial three raids from Woodhall Spa, on Porte de la Chapelle, Munich and Braunschweig, had still been carried out at higher levels, albeit down amongst the waves of heavy bombers, and not from the lofty heights they had enjoyed with 8 Group. The Schweinfurt raid would be the first time 627 were tasked

---

* Machines introduced chlorosulfuric acid into the air, which attracted moisture and created an artificial fog.

with placing markers at low level; although they would not be the very first in, they would provide early back-up marking. Four of their Mosquitos would launch diving attacks, while the other three would be required to provide early and late reconnaissance, and would carry a standard bomb load. The raid would involve 215 Lancasters and 11 Mosquitos, but it was not the evening's main event, this being a strike by as many as 834 Allied aircraft on Essen in the Ruhr Valley. But no German fighters would be diverted north from Bavaria that night. The entire defence infrastructure of Schweinfurt and its surrounding region would be intact and waiting for the arriving bombers.

At Woodhall Spa on 26 April, all the Mosquitos had taxied out and were ready for take-off by midnight. The weather in these last days of April had turned fine and warm, covering the aircraft with a misty dew that was soon dispersed by the propellers. Wing Commander Roy Elliot would lead 627 Squadron in the company of Squadron Leader Bill de Boos, and their intention was to reach Schweinfurt ahead of the others. As the final drops of moisture were blown from the cockpit canopy, Alex Hindshaw and John Daly in DZ415 were first to leave, clearing the runway at 23.59 and tasked for 'early windows' dropping, but the first marker-laden Mosquito, flown by Edward Nelles and Arthur Richards, left only three minutes later. Elliot and de Boos followed hard on their heels as the first six aircraft departed in close order, the unmistakable song of the Merlin engines reverberating through the darkness. Drawing the short straw that evening were Sidney Parlato and David Thomas in DZ521; they had to kick their heels for another hour and forty minutes as late reconnaissance. They would arrive, as their title suggested, last in the stream of bombers, drop their bombs and take photographs, hoping that they could dodge the alert German defences.

The Mosquitos chose a more direct route than the heavy bombers, averaging over 300mph in their cruise. They knew any element of surprise would be lost by the time they caught up with the Lancasters – the Germans would have seen the raid's final turn for Schweinfurt. Within two hours they were above the town and found the weather clear; they spotted the telltale bend in the River Main, but the town itself was heavily obscured by a smokescreen. Even in these early days of low-level marking, the underlying competition to reach and mark the target first was apparent. Devigne and Lewis in DZ518 arrived first at 02.02 and descended to 7,000 feet, ready for their diving attack. Despite seeing other markers and incendiaries dropping, they were uncertain whether they were in the right position, and therefore held off, hoping the scene would become clearer. Seven minutes later, Nelles and Richards dived from 5,000 feet to 400 feet to drop their red target indicator where they believed the town centre was. A church steeple protruding high into the smoke-swathed atmosphere acted as a lone finger of guidance for the Mosquito. Heavy flak was rising, but had to be ignored as Nelles banked and climbed free of the area. Content with his choice, he saw other green flares descend close to his red marker. Wing Commander Elliot and Squadron Leader de Boos dived from 5,000 feet to 1,000 feet nine minutes later, but the honour of the first low-level marking attack by 627 Squadron had gone to Squadron Leader Edward Nelles and Flying Officer Arthur Richards.

Wing Commander Carter of 97 Squadron, the Master Bomber, watching the scene unfold from high above, was not altogether satisfied with the first marking of the target. Wing Commander Cheshire was not on operations that night, and there was a feeling that the raid could have done with his reassuring presence. Trying to contact the Mosquitos, Carter had found that the pre-selected VHF channel B was jammed. He moved to channel C and managed to contact the markers before instructing his following bombing force to change channels. The first flares had dropped too far to the southwest – partly owing to a change in wind direction from what had been anticipated. Calling in his Reserve Marker Force, Carter hoped they would be able to provide the correction needed. As flak bursts peppered the sky, the tracks of burning bombers could already be seen plunging earthwards. The fighters that night were very active, and Carter was concerned that everyone was sharp as a pin in looking out for attackers, particularly since his Lancaster had loitered in the target area far longer than was prudent. Picked out both by on-board night-fighter radar and visually from above against the flares and fire below, their course was as hazardous as any that night. The Germans had also developed a device to home in on the bombers' H2S radar sets: Naxos Z, which was carried by night fighters, forcing RAF crews to limit their use of H2S. Carter found that maintaining the accuracy of the raid was proving troublesome. With the thick smokescreen obscuring the coloured markers almost as soon as they were dropped, he called in more only to encounter exactly the same problem. Eventually he dropped a cluster of his own green markers to re-mark the target, but found they were 1,500 yards short. Calling the main bomber force by radio, he instructed them to re-calibrate their bombing to overshoot his markers by 1,000 yards.

Although casualties for the night's main raids were considered acceptable, Schweinfurt once again lived up to its fearful reputation. Twenty-one Lancasters were lost in the intense flak and fighter defences, but all the Mosquitos of 627 Squadron returned home. The failure in effectiveness of the raid was attributed to the unexpectedly strong winds and smokescreen, but it was clear that mastering the diving technique would be essential for future success. Amongst the many problems faced by the crews that night, seeing the target with the human eye remained the principal issue in accuracy.

*

The town of Clermont-Ferrand, in the central French region of the Auvergne, was home to two facilities – the Michelin tyre factory and the Bréguet aircraft manufacturing works – that bore eloquent witness to the leading role France had played in the transport revolution of the early twentieth century. Two sons of the town, Edouard and André Michelin, had formed their tyre company here in 1889, and they soon captured a global market with their pneumatic tyres, targeted initially at the hugely profitable bicycle industry but later adapted for use in a new, four-wheeled vehicle, the motor car. The Michelin brothers also noted the status and potential of another new technology, the aeroplane. In 1911 they decided to stage their own air race, to draw not only the best aviators of the day, but the eyes of the entire world, to their tyre factory in Clermont-Ferrand. A prize of 100,000 francs would be awarded to the first aviators to fly from Paris to the summit of Puy de Dôme and circle Clermont-Ferrand Cathedral in less than six hours. The aircraft would need to carry two people – an early hint of the idea of passenger air travel.

The Michelin plant, Clermont-Ferrand, 1929.

One of the those who chose to take part was another energetic and resourceful French transport pioneer, named Eugène Renaux, successively a champion of bicycle, motorcycle and motor car races, who had moved into automobile production. After selling his business in 1910, Renaux turned his attention to aviation. Taught to fly a Farman III biplane by Maurice Farman, a Parisian aviator and aircraft builder of British parentage, Eugène was soon awarded his pilot's licence, and just twenty days later he participated in his first air race, at Caen. Soon his thoughts were turning towards the Michelin prize.

On 7 March 1911, after four days of waiting for the weather to be suitable for the long flight, Renaux and his passenger, Albert Senouque, an astronomer and physicist, took off in their Farman from an airfield at Buc near the Palace of Versailles. The official starting point was the park used by the Aero-Club de France, which they passed overhead at 09.25 hours. Stopping to refuel just once, they completed their task at Clermont-Ferrand in five hours, ten minutes. As they flew over the city the cathedral bells rang out and the klaxon on the Michelin factory sounded. Messages of congratulation for Renaux, Senouque and the Michelin brothers flooded in from all corners of France.

Three years later, on the outbreak of hostilities in 1914, Michelin offered to build France's first bomber. In 1916 the company built the world's first concrete runway in Clermont-Ferrand, the site becoming the home of the Bréguet aircraft company, which built some 2,000 aircraft here during the First World War. The industrial lead built by the Michelin company during the inter-war period guaranteed that it would fall under the intense scrutiny of the Nazis after the fall of France in 1940. Clermont-Ferrand lay in the region (the 'zone libre') administered by the Vichy government, rather than directly by the Nazis (as was the case in the northern 'zone occupée'), but the Vichy regime was essentially collaborationist. Michelin signed a contract to provide the Reich with tyres, and although notable members of the Michelin family did resist,* the management took the view that the survival of the company depended on fulfilling their promises to the Nazis.

Any pretence of autonomy vanished in November 1942 as the Germans took control of the unoccupied southern zone of France in response to the Allied invasion of northwest Africa (Operation Torch). When they took over the Bréguet works, the Germans found more than 200 French aircraft undergoing maintenance and repair as part of the Vichy air force. Along with output from the nearby Michelin works, production at the aircraft factory would henceforth be geared to fulfilling German military needs. Not only had Germany taken possession of France physically, they had access to the technical knowledge of its industries, which were expected to cooperate. Any businesses that showed signs of failing to do so were threatened with closure. Given the huge transport requirements of their overstretched armies, the Michelin factory was a particular prize for the Germans. The company's management believed they had little alternative but to bow to the demands of their new overlords; having weathered the economic storms of the early 1930s, they felt they had a duty to continue to offer steady employment to its large workforce. The new rules and regulations imposed by the occupiers were undoubtedly oppressive, but for Michelin the overriding priority was to make sure their workers still had money in their pockets to feed their families.

But the French resistance also had their eyes on the factory. Throughout the early weeks of 1944 furtive contacts were made with the management of the Michelin works. The proposal by the local resistance movement (organized by Britain's Special Operations Executive, or SOE), was that sabotage should take

---

* Philippe and Hubert Michelin, grandsons of founder André, fled France and became pilots in the RAF.

place to disable the factory. Perhaps fearful of German reprisals and equally troubled by disturbing their hard-won industrial relations with the workers, Michelin's management declined to help. On 16 March 1944 Wing Commander Leonard Cheshire's 617 Squadron hit the Michelin works with ten 12,000lb 'Tallboy' bombs, causing fires and widespread destruction. The raiders noted that defences around the city were negligible. It was a success Cheshire felt he could build on, particularly with the advent of his new Mosquito force.

Clermont-Ferrand, 30 April 1944

Night flying had become a normal way of life for Mosquito crews before any of them joined 627 Squadron. If anything, their nocturnal pattern of operations had moved even deeper into the hours of darkness, with flights taking off around midnight. Such was the speed of the Mosquitos that they could take off around two hours later than the Lancasters and still be over the target before them. For marking targets with 5 Group, they were also flying as smaller units. Leonard Cheshire had used four 617 Squadron Mosquitos per target, and now this practice would be mimicked by 627 Squadron: on this night eight Mosquitos would fly to two targets. The first group would leave for Clermont-Ferrand at around 23.15 hours, the second at 23.58 for an explosives factory at Saint-Médard-en-Jalles on the outskirts of Bordeaux. Using four aircraft erred on the side of caution; sometimes one Mosquito would be enough to lay the markers on a smaller target. With a city raid, the weight of bombs would sometimes obliterate the flares, and the position would need to be re-marked on several occasions. The smaller the raid, the less chance there was for the need for repeated marking and, statistically, the more accurate the bombing.

The first group would hit the airfield of which Clermont-Ferrand was so proud, primarily attacking the manufacturing hangars. The raiders were not expecting the flak to be particularly strong, although undoubtedly those defending the airfield would have lighter guns ready to fire at the Mosquitos if they caught sight of them. This prospect did not weigh too heavily on the crews' minds – indeed, it really only entered their thinking in the dive, as flashes of light rose towards them.

All four Mosquitos left RAF Woodhall Spa's runway within a span of less than two minutes, climbing into the clear air and dim light of a waxing moon. As the ground disappeared from view, Goodman and Hickox noticed a slight tremble in DZ422. The fact that it was affecting not only the control column but the whole cockpit gave both men a feeling of unease. Something was not quite right. With nagging memories of open fuel flaps on his Wellington bomber, Goodman was already thinking of his pre-flight checks, but everything had seemed secure, and he couldn't believe he had missed anything obvious. As the vibration increased the two men wondered if it might be an engine problem – something was definitely out of balance, although the Mosquito was still pulling strongly. The control surfaces were working and Goodman vainly hoped the shaking would cease, allowing them to continue their climb and get to the target. It was not in either man's nature to give up easily, so they decided to persist, but after flying for over thirty minutes, the problem seemed to be getting worse. The prospect of their successfully completing the mission was dwindling, and the disappointment of an aborted operation loomed. As the vibrations became more severe, the thudding around the aeroplane increased not only the noise, but the anxieties of Goodman and Hickox.

With no other sensible options remaining, Goodman turned DZ422 for home, radioing his intention to ground control. Still carrying their four 'spotfires',* they landed back at Woodhall Spa, more than a little dejected, at oo.45 hours. It transpired that an exhaust stub in the starboard engine had come loose and eventually sheared off. Whether the fault lay with under-tightened bolts or threads stripped by over-zealous tightening was of little concern now – they were firmly back on the ground.

Thirty minutes later the remaining Mosquitos were approaching Clermont-Ferrand, waiting for the supporting Lancasters above to release their illuminating flares. As the runway of the airfield appeared, lit up brightly in the neon light, Rutherford and Stanbury in DZ521 were the first to identify the factory buildings nearby. Thirty-year-old Flight Lieutenant Norman Rutherford was an Australian but had married and settled in London before the war, living in Half Moon Lane, Herne Hill, in 1939. He was serving as an RAF officer rather than with the Royal Australian Air Force, but he spoke in an unmistakable Antipodean accent. At his side, Warrant Officer Fred Stanbury hailed from Eccles and, like Rutherford, was married and had a son. Common to most married aircrew was a certain cautiousness of approach, instilled by the additional domestic responsibilities they faced, but as Rutherford saw his target, all other thoughts were obliterated by his concentration on a single focus – the placing of his marker where he wanted it. As he dived from 5,000 feet the sheds below looked unmissable, and when the roofs began to fill his windscreen, he pressed his release toggle. Unlike a bomb, the marker generated no loud percussion behind them as they swooped across the target at 200 feet. Climbing and banking, they could see the glow of the flare, but not on the roof – it had penetrated the interior of the factory and was now illuminating the whole building, each skylight shining as a bright red window onto the sky.

* A flare that burned more intensely in a singular area rather than dispersing sub-flares.

Mosquito DZ525, flown by Parlato and Thomas to
Clermont-Ferrand, 30 April 1944.

Rutherford had dropped his marker with admirable accuracy, but would the flare be bright enough to be visible to the approaching bombers at 15,000 feet? Fifteen minutes later, Parlato and Thomas in DZ525 dropped further markers on the factory close to the site of Rutherford's attack, before coming back to drop four 500lb bombs. The delay between target-marking and bomb release was deliberate – like Leonard Cheshire at Gnome & Rhône they were giving French workers plenty of time to escape. As the bombs began falling it was obvious to the bombers that they were on target. The hangars and sheds erupted in flames as explosions detonated across the entire site. All fifteen Lancasters furnished by 97 Squadron from RAF Coningsby reported highly accurate bombing. No fighters were seen in the area, and only a single light gun fired plaintively from the factory site. Not only was the area more lightly defended than more northerly areas of France, other Allied raids had drawn away the Luftwaffe fighter cover.

At daybreak, the fires were still burning. The factory's funeral pyre sent smoke and fumes high into the spring morning sky, where it drifted on the wind to hang over the city centre of Clermont-Ferrand, only three miles away. As the inhabitants had taken shelter through the night, they had heard and felt the enormous percussions of the bombs shaking their cellars with thunderous reports. Thankfully, the airfield was to the east of the city, and not as close to residential areas as the Michelin works. Nevertheless, the bomb blasts had left many windows cracked; closer to the airfield, the task of sweeping debris from the streets had begun. The sense of terror engendered by the raid had been temporarily replaced with sadness – many of the workers had been children when Eugène Renaux flew across the city in what now seemed like a happier, more optimistic age. Michelin and the city had prospered greatly in the intervening years, but now, in the space of barely six weeks the industrial hub of their entire region had twice been severely damaged. 'C'est la guerre',* an expression of weary resignation used as a catch-all summary of all the pain, unpleasantness and inconvenience of the last few years, was taking on a new and more immediate relevance.

Any feelings of relief that the worst might be over were cut short mid-morning, as the sirens once again wailed across the streets of the city. In the village of Lussat, four miles north of the airfield, the view towards the city across the rolling fields was obscured by thick clouds of smoke, but all had been silent for hours. And then, the deep murmur of aircraft engines began to build. At first it had been a gentle rumble over the horizon, but the unmistakable shake of hundreds of aircraft engines now echoed over the countryside. High above, in the clear blue sky, a mass of new vapour began to appear – the pure white contrails of American bombers streaking their way towards Clermont-Ferrand. Together with hundreds of accompanying fighters in their midst, visible only as tiny dots, the bombers formed a

---

* Literally, 'That's war', implying that 'it can't be helped'.

huge and terrifying theatre of sound and movement above the roofs of Lussat. The sirens of the city could still be heard in the distance as some villagers scurried to safety, while others stood and watched, transfixed by the advancing aerial armada. The air raid warning had come late; bombs were already beginning to fall in the area attacked the previous night. The whistles of falling projectiles echoed across the fields before the cracks and rumbles of their impact reached the village.

The USAAF raid of 1 May targeted the runways and the infrastructure of the airfield. The attack by 118 B-17 'Flying Fortresses' caught the defenders unawares, and some of the Focke-Wulf 190 fighters on the airfield were hit on the ground and destroyed. Other German fighters were caught by American P-51s as they attempted to climb to reach the bombers, and a twisting air battle commenced. Nine B-17s sustained damage, but the raid, together with attacks on the airfields at Lyon and Tours, was considered a success. In an open daylight battle, the Allied aircraft were much better placed to take on the Luftwaffe defenders than they were in the context of night fighting. Equipped with the latest Mustang P-51s, whose engines were a huge improvement on earlier versions and had transformed the fighter's abilities at high altitudes, the USAAF now had the height and the performance to dismantle their German opponents – a key goal in keeping the skies clear for D-Day.

From late April 1944, the pace of operations launched from RAF Woodhall Spa was remorseless. Nearly every day, elements of 627 Squadron flew against targets in France, the primary focus being airfields, factories and railways. One effect of the relentless night-time assault on German cities by RAF Bomber Command was that it forced Hitler to strengthen the air defence system along the borders of the Reich. The focus of defence was a string of radar sites stretching through Holland and Belgium to the south of Paris known as the Kammhuber Line, named after Josef Kammhuber, the career Luftwaffe officer who established it in 1940. This home defence system used Freya radar, which had first been tested in 1937 and had a range of 100 kilometres. Approaching aircraft could be detected and plotted into a defensive sector – a box that contained fighters and a radar-controlled searchlight – as well as several manually controlled searchlights. In a sub-war of countermeasures, the RAF employed Boulton Paul Defiant aircraft equipped with Moonshine, a device that amplified the return signal from the Freya to the extent that eight aircraft could appear as a hundred aircraft to the radar operators.

With the aim of overwhelming defences in a Kammhuber 'box', the RAF developed the saturation tactic of the 'bomber stream', a long tight formation of bombers which flew straight down the middle of the 'box'. The bomber stream was deployed for the first time on the thousand-bomber raid on Cologne on the night of 30/31 May 1942 and was able to overwhelm the defences over a narrower front than had previously been flown. In turn, the Germans installed shorter-range Würzburg radars – with a range of 30 kilometres – between the Freya radars, to increase accuracy of identification of incoming enemy aircraft. A radar-jamming device known as Mandrel was used by 515 Squadron (part of 100 Group, Bomber Command) to block sections of Freya and Würzburg boxes, allowing bombers to pass through the belt. The electronic war ebbed and flowed, advantage passing from attacking to defending forces and back again.

German night fighters like the Junkers Ju 88 and the Messerschmitt Me 110 had carried on-board radar since 1942, and by 1944 had been fitted with FuG 220 Lichtenstein SN2, the third – and greatly improved – version of the technology.*

---

* The Lichtenstein SN2 set proved hard for the Allies to counter until a set was captured in July 1944.

These sets proved more difficult to block, and were a key factor in the substantial losses suffered by RAF Bomber Command in the winter of 1943/44. The Mosquito NF Mk XXIII came into service in late 1943 for deployment against the German night fighters. On this more powerful variant of the Mosquito night fighter – with a 'solid' rather than a Perspex nose – the four .303 Browning guns were removed to make space for Mk VIII Airborne Interception radar, but the aircraft still possessed ample firepower in the form of four 20mm cannons.

Although losses in the German fighter force were significant, they were still able to supply a steady quantity of new aircraft to their front-line squadrons. A report published by the British Air Ministry in 1948, *The Rise and Fall of the German Air Force 1933–1945*, concluded that the Luftwaffe continued to increase in size throughout the first six months of 1944. Despite continued attacks on German aircraft production and losses in the air, the Luftwaffe increased their number of twin-engined night fighters from 550 in July 1943 to 775 twelve months later. The struggle to control the skies lay not only with the grit and determination of aircrews, but in the vast resources expended in the manufacture of war materials. Arguably, Germany was able to build more aircraft than it could provide adequately trained pilots for, but the scales were evenly balanced when it came to technological breakthroughs. Each Allied advance in new airborne electronic measures quickly fell into the hands of the Germans; thus was the course of the battle dictated as much by scientists as by the men in the air. As the Soviet advance on the Reich was to prove, technological superiority alone could not hold back mass attacks. Sooner or later the numerical advantage of the Allies would overwhelm Germany's defences.

627 Squadron's command of the new low-flying strategy and experience of the conditions in which it was to be put into practice revealed Germany's Achilles heel – their night defences were attuned to higher-level attackers. Not only were

the Mosquitos ducking under the expected altitude of attack, they were now fishing in a less well-defended pond. The technological sophistication with which the Germans policed their own aerial borders did not extend into the broad expanses of France. Furthermore, wherever they went, the speed and agility of the Mosquitos proved more than a match for the defensive measures employed to repel them. The Germans were investing in *Vergeltungswaffen* ('reprisal weapons') such as the V-1 or 'doodlebug', and also in jet aircraft technology, but for sheer effectiveness they had no aircraft to compare with the comparatively cheap and quickly made de Havilland Mosquito. The primary concern for the men of 627 Squadron was the blizzard of fire from the lighter flak guns dotted around airfields and factories; while not necessarily accurately aimed, they could throw up a protective – and potentially dangerous – curtain around their targets.

627 Squadron's operations from Woodhall Spa were almost becoming routine. Night after night the Mosquitos would land unscathed and turn off the Flare Path to taxi round the peri-track* to their dispersal point. Here they would shut down their engines and enjoy the silence for a few moments. The navigator would reach down to open the crew door, which would invariably reveal the friendly faces of the ground crews, eager to learn about their adventure. The question 'Everything alright, sir?' was generally answered in the affirmative. Torches playing across the surfaces of the Mosquito would normally find no damage; indeed, apart from the heat of the engines and the ticking of their cooling, there would be little to suggest the rigours of the raid in which they had just taken part. A WAAF driver would arrive in a car or small bus and, with the faintest of glimmers sneaking through the headlight protectors, drive

* The peri-tracks – perimeter tracks – were connecting 'roads' from the runways to other areas of the airfield.

them cautiously back to deposit their equipment and attend the debriefing. Even here there were hazards. On at least one occasion at Woodhall Spa, a WAAF driver suddenly found herself confronted by a Mosquito taxiing towards her out of the gloom. For the young men returning from one of the most exhilarating but also dangerous experiences of their lives, the sight of a WAAF rapidly transported them back to normality, a psychological shift from the dark world of combat to everyday life. Unsurprisingly, the dashing and confident aircrew were at the head of the pack when it came to attracting the romantic attentions of the WAAFs.

The welcome sight of other returning crews at the debrief, and the chatter around the events of the raid, temporarily lifted their tiredness. These early successes over France were proving that the low-level diving technique was not only working in terms of destruction of their target, but that their fears that the strategy could lead to the early obliteration of the Squadron had been unfounded. In less than three weeks the dire sense of foreboding they had felt in the pub in Horncastle had lifted. They were confident in their ability to carry out the tasks required of them, and also in the likelihood of their survival. Unlike their raids with 8 Group, not only could they see their target clearly, they got close enough to it almost to be able to touch it. Some aircrew undoubtedly flew much lower than the recommended recovery altitude. Flying Officers Saint-Smith and Heath returned from a raid on the Gnome & Rhône plant near Paris on 3 May with bricks from a chimney implanted in their wingtip. Their flying report quotes them as saying the descent was from 5,800 feet to 1,000 feet – but it was clearly much lower than that. The discovery was received with delight by the two Australians, who took the fragments of brick as souvenirs, leaving the ground crew to replace the wing tip.

While they knew of the potential dangers and were well aware that some of them would become casualties, the spirit of the Squadron would not allow them to dwell long on their mortality. Undoubtedly, some were having the time of their lives flying the Mosquito and spending nights off in unrestrained intemperance with good company. Their enemy was enjoying life far less. Night after night German pilots were called to their cockpits to fly against Allied bombers, which came in their hundreds in unrelenting waves. Despite the frequency of their 'kills', it seemed to make no difference to the massive size of the waves of Allied bombers hurled against them. As daylight raids increased, even their resting hours were interrupted by air raid warnings. And when they went home on leave, Germans pilots often faced the shock of encountering the catastrophic levels of devastation wrought by RAF Bomber Command on towns and cities throughout the Reich. Luftwaffe pilot Ernest Merian summed up the feelings of many German aircrew during this period of bitterly contested air fighting:

We knew we were beaten and deserved to be beaten. We knew that we could re-build cities – that was not the point, we fought to protect our family and friends below from the bombing – a lot of which was indiscriminate. We weren't fighting for political aims – we didn't understand them.

8

THE BREAKING STORM

There was nothing remarkable about the small village of Trouans, a settlement that had lived off the land for centuries. The single-storied farm buildings huddled close to the road, their red-tiled roofs and cream-rendered walls typical of a thousand communities dotted throughout rural France. Some families had experienced relative prosperity over the last century and had expanded their barns, created yards and built second stories on their houses. Others could not afford repairs other than an occasional splash of limewash over crumbling masonry; for poorer folk, their dwelling was simply a place that provided shelter after long days working in the fields. The village church was unpretentious and didn't have much of a spire, but the priests encouraged their congregation to give what they could. Trouans was not a rich place, but neither was it unhappy.

Fate had placed the village close to the route of medieval pilgrimages between the great cathedrals east of Paris – Reims to the north and Troyes to the south. Kings and marching armies had passed close by, some choosing to buy their wares, others considering it their right to loot from them. The French Empire and, to their west, the glories of Paris instilled a sense of pride, but to the east the burgeoning of national feeling in Germany was a cause of deep disquiet. The Prussians had passed through here on their way to besiege Paris in 1870, thousands of men in long columns marching across the quiet rural département of the Aube. Ensuing events – the swift sequence of Prussian victories in eastern France, the lengthy siege of Paris, the proclamation by the victors of a united Germany in the Hall of Mirrors at Versailles, and the annexation of large parts of the eastern French territories of Alsace and Lorraine – left the humiliated French in a belligerent mood, desperate for revenge.

In 1902 the French Army acquired a large parcel of land close to the village and created a training ground. The loss of their fields was at first deeply resented by the Trouannais, but the realization that nearby Mailly was now home to large numbers of soldiers and horses – all of whom who would need feeding – provided some economic consolation.

Mailly-le-Camp, as it was now named, became one of France's key centres of military training. It was home to the Russian Expeditionary Force during the First World War, a conflict in which France paid a brutal price in human lives for recovery of its lost eastern provinces. As use of the internal combustion engine became widespread immediately after the First World War, the growling of distant engines was increasingly heard in Trouans. One item of military technology in particular, the tank – still in its infancy in the 1920s – sparked the curiosity of the locals. In the newly extended rail yard at Mailly, trains would disgorge these new miracle machines, rattling on their metal tracks, from flatbed trucks down specially created ramps. Through the mounting tensions of the 1930s, Mailly-le-Camp increased in importance as the race to perfect new weapons gathered pace. The close-ranked, wooden-built barrack blocks of 1914 had been laid down in the horse-drawn age and were populated by men from all over France. Unlike the regimental headquarters in large cities where troops were mustered, there were no grandiose buildings or statues here, only simple structures suited to training men for the rigours of the field. But in this organized knot of buildings, little or no consideration had been given to the threat of attack from the air.

The shock of the German advance in 1940 and the fall of Sedan 75 miles away opened the way for the fall of Paris and the defeat of France. The Somua S35 tanks* that had once torn around the training grounds at Mailly had fought well and had inflicted heavy losses on the German Panzers, but they too were now vanquished. Within months the Germans had moved into Mailly-le-Camp and, as the roads around Trouans filled with trucks and motorcycles passing in and out, the locals could only reflect on how far their nation had fallen.

3 May 1944, Mailly-le-Camp

If gaining an advanced training camp was a godsend to the Wehrmacht in their fortification of France, they faced one distinct disadvantage in its defence. Despite the size of the site, the flat landscape ensured it was impossible to hide the movement of armoured units in and out of the camp. As the troop trains rumbled through the French countryside, producing plumes of steam signposting their progress, the eyes of the Allies were watching from the air; but, just as importantly, so were the men of the resistance, who merged seamlessly into the local farming community. By the spring of 1944, the great German tank strategist General Erwin Rommel was in charge

---

* The Somua S35 was a light cavalry tank that proved equal to German models. Captured S35 tanks were used by the Germans on the Eastern Front.

of the defence of northern France against an Allied invasion. By the end of April he had re-trained and re-equipped, at Mailly-le-Camp, 12 SS Panzer Division 'Hitlerjugend', a group of young men whose zeal would prove particularly trouble-some after D-Day.* News of the departure north of this unit was transmitted to London by the resistance. When another large motorized Panzer Division, the 21st, arrived at Mailly-le-Camp from the Eastern Front to train and re-equip, it was clear that Rommel's tank strategy needed to be disrupted.

Since there were French civilians living in close proximity, the task of destroying the barracks and maintenance site at Mailly-le-Camp was passed to 5 Group RAF as specialists in low-level target marking and precision bombing, but as so often happened during this period, planners were given only a few days to prepare. The attack would be led by Wing Commander Leonard Cheshire as 'Marker Leader'. Four Mosquitos were to mark the barrack blocks at low level at 00.01, one minute after lights out – in the confidence that the enemy would be in their beds.† The main force of 173 Lancaster bombers, 'Rat 1', would be held briefly 15 miles away, circling a yellow marker close to the small town of Châlons-sur-Marne. They would be called in by VHF radio by the Main Force Controller, Wing Commander Laurence Deane of 83 Squadron, once he received news that Cheshire's marking was successful. A second wave of 140 Lancasters, 'Rat 2',‡ would arrive shortly afterwards to follow the same procedure.

627 Squadron would provide ten Mosquitos, three to keep the yellow datum point flares active for the bombers' holding position, and the other seven to attack flak batteries in the

---

* The division was not formally assembled until 1 June 1944, days before the invasion.
† Ensuring lights out at midnight was standard practice throughout the Wehrmacht.
‡ 'Rat 1' were bombers of 5 Group, 'Rat 2' came from 1 Group.

vicinity of Mailly-le-Camp. On paper, it looked like a simple raid, even a 'milk run', but there were some anxieties among the following bomber crews. Sergeant Ron Eeles from Birmingham, a rear gunner in 49 Squadron, remembered that the altitudes for the holding pattern caused his crew considerable concern. Each aircraft was given an altitude to adhere to with 100-foot vertical separation, a precision in flying that Ron felt risked collisions.* The crews were also worried by the presence that night of a strong moon; while this would help prevent collisions, it also increased the possibility of their being caught by German fighters, who would provide them with a stern test.

Flying Officer James Alexander 'Alec' Saint-Smith of 627 Squadron had the task of dropping the first yellow markers at the assembly point. The twenty-seven-year-old Australian from Earlwood, New South Wales, was a popular and lively member of 627 Squadron. Alec had been a teacher in the Sydney suburb before the war but had joined the Royal Australian Air Force in January 1941. He was no doubt influenced by the pilot training being carried out at 4 Elementary Flying Training School (EFTS) in nearby Mascot,† where every day the sky was filled with the glint of silver Tiger Moth trainers. Despite the proximity of this local training facility, Saint-Smith would gain his wings in Canada, and was eventually posted to 460 Squadron flying Wellington and, later, Lancaster bombers. Completing his tour of duty in May 1943, he was awarded the Distinguished Flying Medal (DFM) together with his navigator, Geoffrey Heath. Saint-Smith was one of the first pilots of the newly formed 627 Squadron, and was determined to fly again with Heath, who hailed from Croydon, New South Wales – a stone's throw from Earlwood. The bond between the two men,

---

* In modern flying the Reduced Vertical Specification Minimum (RVSM) is specified as 1,000 feet.
† Now Sydney International Airport.

whose birthdays in December 1917 were just two days apart, was an extremely close one. Despite their being separated after their first tour of duty on Wellingtons, Saint-Smith managed to engineer Heath's posting to join him in 627 Squadron.

Although 627 Squadron were tasked with marking and support bombing, the central task of dropping red flares on the barracks at Mailly-le-Camp would fall to Leonard Cheshire, with his small contingent of 617 Squadron Mosquitos. In the event, because two of the latter were not serviceable, Cheshire would borrow two aircraft from 627 Squadron for his crews. Taking off from Woodhall Spa with Flying Officer Kelly as navigator at 22.04, Cheshire was keen not to be late. But, in the event, he found himself approaching the target too early, so he decided to buzz the night-fighter base at Saint-Dizier, some miles to the east, to give the impression he was a lone intruder, rather than circling the Mailly-le-Camp area and alerting its defenders. Having done this, he arrived at Mailly-le-Camp at exactly the moment the first Pathfinders from 97 and 83 Squadrons dropped their higher-level illumination flares over the barracks at 00.01. Seeing the close pattern of the low-roofed buildings below him, he swooped immediately, depositing his neon-red flare at the east end of the run of barrack blocks. Five minutes later, Squadron Leader Shannon of 617 Squadron pushed down the nose of Mosquito MS993 and deposited his markers. Shannon was disappointed to see his flares fall a little west of the desired point; since he pulled out of the dive at 1,500 feet, it may be that he was slightly too high in his attack. Nonetheless, as the bombs began to rain down from the accompanying Lancasters above, the initial stage of the raid seemed to be going well.

Of the seven 627 Squadron Mosquitos despatched to attack the flak batteries around the camp, one, DZ615, with Gribbin and Griffiths, had returned to Woodhall Spa after an exhaust stub had broken free. The remaining six approached

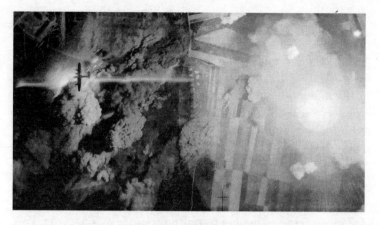

A Lancaster bomber silhouetted by flares and
exploding bombs over Mailly-le-Camp.

Mailly-le-Camp on time and waited for the order to attack. Most of the defensive positions dotted around the encampment were mobile 20mm guns, known as 'Flak 30'. Although not as potent as the larger German 88 calibre gun, the 20mm were often fitted with quadruple barrels and their rate of fire could therefore be very troublesome, particularly for the Mosquitos. The Flak 30 and improved Flak 38 models had an effective hitting altitude of more than 7,000 feet – almost the exact level at which the raiders were flying.

At five minutes to zero hour, 627 Squadron's Mosquitos began a wide circle of the camp at 7,000 feet. As they were called in after Cheshire's marking attacks, they looked out for the circular sand-bagged emplacements of the guns picked out as curves in the long-cast shadows of the illuminating flares overhead. As the Mosquitos approached and the flak guns began firing, their muzzle flash produced a spurt of tracer rounds curving up into the sky. In Mosquito DZ426 Thomson and Harris selected a single bomb on their switches from the four 500lb bombs they were carrying, and picked their target.

The blink of the gun confirmed its position, and at 00.12 they dived on the emplacement and pulled away as the bomb left the Mosquito. Lightened by the sudden loss of 500lb, the aircraft surged powerfully out of its dive. A pilot dropping a target marker might hold his Mosquito in the dive for a couple of seconds after the flare had departed; when releasing a bomb, however, the wise pilot made sure he did not get too close to the ground.

Circling and climbing, Harris kept his eye on the target and saw once again the unmistakable flash from the German gun muzzle. 'Still firing,' he said to his pilot. Thomson brought DZ426 round and made a second attack four minutes later. This time there was no further report from the gun. But there was no time to contemplate whatever unpleasant fate had befallen its operators. Of more immediate concern to the Mosquito crews was the spectacle of burning Lancasters falling like glowing balls above them. It was clear there were numerous German fighters stalking the area, and the fear of being bounced began to fray the nerves of the Mosquito men. Like Thomson and Harris, Boyden and Fenwick in DZ482 took two attacks to dispatch the flak gun they were targeting, but Marshallsay and Ranshaw in DZ415 did the job in one.

Fifteen miles to the north of Mailly-le-Camp, close to Châlons-sur-Marne, Saint-Smith and Heath arrived at the bombers' holding position on time and saw the illuminating flares begin to light up the sky in the distance. In the soft moonlight the brightness of the marking was unmistakable – the two Australians knew that the Pathfinders had found their target. Saint-Smith and Heath's target-marking task was far less precise than that undertaken by the Mosquitos over Mailly-le Camp; all they were required to do was deposit the markers in a field, where they would be undisturbed by the effects of bombing. The two waves of Lancasters, 'Rat 1' and 'Rat 2', were to circle these markers briefly, within a fifteen-minute time frame. After

Cheshire had dropped his red indicator flares, he had called up Laurence Deane of 83 Squadron, the raid leader, to inform him that he was satisfied with the initial placement of markers. Circling at 5,000 feet above the burning barracks, Deane had taken a further twenty minutes to tighten up the bombing and secondary marking by the Pathfinder Squadrons at Mailly-le-Camp. When Deane tried to call his first wave of bombers, 'Rat 1', he found to his consternation that his VHF channel was playing American big band music – a concert broadcast for American forces was blocking his line of communication to the main force. The Lancaster squadrons had already detected the problem as they listened for the order to begin their bombing run, only for the jaunty strains of 'Deep in the Heart of Texas' to fill the radio operators' ears. It was the beginning of a night fraught with communication problems, caused in part by there having been insufficient time to double-check all the preparations. Squadrons not carrying VHF radio made use of morse code, but Deane made an incorrect assumption about the radio frequency used for transmitting messages, which would also cause immense frustration as the attack developed.

With no command to proceed, the majority of the main stream of approaching bombers, still more than 150 aircraft, began to circle the yellow marking point. Devigne and Lewis had dropped a further four yellow markers between 00.05 and 00.20 hours to keep the area illuminated as planned. Realizing there was a delay, Rutherford and Stanbury took over, dropping their last flare at 00.32. The result was a large stack of circling bombers, dark vultures clearly visible to the other Lancaster crews and frighteningly exposed to arriving German fighters. The Luftwaffe, having fielded sixty fighters in boxes ahead of the incoming raid, were astonished to find such a huge force of bombers congregating, stacked from low to high altitude. At close quarters, there was enough light to see the dark shapes of the four-engined bombers drawn like moths to the yellow flares below. In a matter of minutes, Lancasters began to fall, the dreadful spectacle evident to all crews as multiple balls of flame dropped into the darkened countryside below. Realizing the danger, some pilots decided to fly a triangular course bringing them out of the immediate area, an action they later believed saved them from the twisting air battle.

On the ground at Mailly-le-Camp the raid had come as a complete surprise. The deep rumbling of heavy bombers high above was often heard here late at night, and there was nothing to suggest that it was not just another raid heading towards Germany. As the British had anticipated, the troops in their barracks were just turning in when Leonard Cheshire's Mosquito shook them in their bunks. Low-flying aircraft were not that uncommon, and some might have assumed that a Luftwaffe fighter had flown over. But the wail of hand-wound air-raid sirens echoing throughout the camp told a very different story; the men rushed out in their underwear and dropped into air-raid trenches dug nearby. The red magnesium glow of the first markers shone from behind the wooden buildings 100 yards away, silhouetting the roofs and filling the sky with an eerie light. Despite attempts to contain them, each marker had exploded into numerous fizzing shards of different shapes. Water was no use; the only way to put out these small fragments was with sand buckets, of which there were clearly not enough. As the flak batteries defending the camp began firing, the men crouched down, pulling their steel helmets down with both hands. Within minutes the whistling of bombs, shrieking down close to the trenches, added to the deafening confusion; the enormous blast waves that followed jarred men's bodies in shock after shock. The wooden barrack buildings disintegrated, sending lethal splinters flying in all directions as they erupted in flame. They heard the whistle of more Mosquitos diving, saw more red flares plummeting to earth. It was a hellish scene: the only human noises that punctuated the booming maelstrom of sound produced by the bombs of the Allied raiders and the flak guns of the camp's German defenders were the cries of the injured and the dying.

The men of 21st Panzer Division were being subjected to a raid of a ferocity hardly known outside a major city. Unlike Berlin, Mailly-le-Camp had no deep air-raid shelters or bunkers where, even amid the terror, the air was filtered and wardens could instruct and reassure. These men had known bombardments on the Eastern Front as the Russians had tried to push them back – but they were as nothing compared to this onslaught. Belatedly, the main force of Lancasters had been released from their cage* and now, keen to complete their bombing run before German fighters could catch them, they pounded every area of the camp. The garages, stores and tank-parking areas erupted in explosions. Fuel tanks sent plumes of black smoke high into the air, and the acrid smell of burning wood and oil choked the men in their trenches. For a time the whistle of bombs stopped and the rumble of bombers overhead seemed to subside. The voices of the *Stabsfeldwebel*† could be heard barking orders, and soon the surviving men were out of the trenches and forming chains to carry buckets of water and man hoses against the burning barrack blocks. Unknown to them, the second wave of Lancasters – 'Rat 2' – were about to start the final bombing run; many Germans were caught in the open during this second stage of the attack.

In Mosquito DZ421 Goodman and Hickox had also engaged in picking off the German gun positions one by one. Despite their thousands of hours of flying experience, there was something about this night that they found deeply unsettling. Goodman described his experience as offering him a

---

* It is still not fully known how the message to bomb was finally received.
† Sergeant Majors.

'worm's-eye view', a reversal of their role with 8 Group, when they flew well above the main bomber stream. Instead, they were perilously close to the ground. The flicker of the light flak from below and of the burning Lancasters falling from above induced a feeling of anxiety that clouded logical thinking.[*] With all four bombs gone, they called in on their VHF channel, which was on a different frequency from the main force and free from interference. Leonard Cheshire, the Marker Leader, instructed them to turn for home, but it was at this point that Goodman took a decision that came close to ending in disaster for him and his navigator. As he later wrote, 'I made a grave tactical miscalculation which might easily have killed us – or alternatively might have sent 'Bill' Hickox on another long hike home from an enemy target with me in tow.'[†] Instead of climbing to a safe return altitude of 25,000 feet, Goodman decided to maintain his flight home at low level. In retrospect it was an irrational fear of climbing towards perceived dangers when, as he was to discover, the real threat lay much closer at hand. Plotting a direct course towards the coast placed DZ421 directly in the path of the string of flak defences to the east of the gap between Beauvais and Amiens, a favoured course for bomber streams and reconnaissance aircraft. To add to the dangers they faced by taking this route, coastal defences had been strengthened in preparation for an Allied seaborne assault.

When he left the target area, Goodman was confident enough to open the throttles further; with enough fuel in the tanks, he had no concerns about the additional consumption. Even with the moon shining brightly, there wasn't enough

---

[*] Goodman later said that, despite the fact that the risk of collision with a crashing Lancaster was slim, it still seemed as though each one was falling towards them.

[†] *FlyPast* magazine, August 1984.

light to identify the ground features that rushed towards them in the darkness. At first, Goodman's and Hickox's journey home seemed to be going well as they followed a route that took them across the open countryside northeast of Paris. Then, from nowhere, a searchlight shone directly on them and, within seconds, two or three more swung together to cone their Mosquito. Light flak guns opened up, creating red, blue and green flickers of tracer that poured towards them, the shells zipping close by. Goodman immediately wanted to pull the nose of DZ421 up, but at 500 feet he instinctively knew this would be a death sentence, as it would make him easier for the searchlights to follow. Going lower was also not an option, as the glare from the searchlights made the ground – which was already shrouded in darkness – impossible to make out. Banking into a 30-degree port turn, Goodman levelled out before jinking the Mosquito into a similar starboard manoeuvre, while 'Bill' Hickox called out, 'watch your instruments'. For the next few anxious minutes both men fell silent, determined to concentrate on shaking off the searchlights and flak guns. The zigzagging appeared to have worked; as they weaved their way towards the coast they continued to be fired on, but not accurately.

Breasting a low hill, they could see the sea and, below them, the course of a river, the Bresle, flowing towards its estuary at Le Tréport. Searchlights swung towards them from the nearby wooded slope, but by now Goodman, guided by the shining water beneath him, was skimming the surface. The searchlights above them helpfully illuminated their course as flak batteries pounded away on each side – the bands of tracer passing harmlessly over the cockpit in a frenzy of patterns. The harbour burst into view in front of them and, within seconds, they had cleared it and made it into the peace of open water. 'Did you see that bloody lighthouse?' Hickox exclaimed after seeing the low conical structure zip past them. They had been flying level with the breakwater and, in his haste, it was clear Goodman had not seen the structure.

As they approached the comforting sight of Beachy Head, they became aware of the chill of perspiration in their clothing – there was no doubt this had been a near miss. The journey home would be a time of relief and talking. Landing at Woodhall Spa at the same time as others from their squadron, they found, remarkably, that DZ421 was unscathed by their flight through the flak batteries. Their lightning tour of Le Tréport was a salutary lesson in how an early error of judgement could lead to dire consequences. All of 627 Squadron's Mosquitos had returned safely, despite the depth of defence thrown against them. For the Lancaster force, however, it had been a night of cruel losses: 42 aircraft failed to return and 258 aircrew perished. Undoubtedly the problems in communication had greatly increased the losses, but in the planning, not enough thought had been given to the proximity of night-fighter air-fields. The loss of 11.8 per cent of the bombers sent on the raid was a shattering blow in itself, and made Mailly-le-Camp the most costly Allied raid of the French campaign. In comparison with attacks on Berlin, Hamburg or Dresden, the operation has received little public attention, and remains largely unknown, but it was indelibly imprinted on the minds of the crews who flew it on 3/4 May 1944.

Had the operation been completely ineffective, arguably 5 Group's diving pathfinding technique and raid supervision by radio might have been consigned to history. However, the target had been devastated; 21st Panzer Division suffered 102 vehicles lost, including 37 battle tanks. In addition, 218 men had been killed, 156 wounded and 114 barrack buildings destroyed. Sadly, owing to the proximity of the pre-camp French village of Mailly, 100 French civilians also died, a toll that weighed heavily on the consciences of some of the aircrew after the war. Strategically, this was the first time a Panzer Division in France had been so directly and effectively attacked, a fact not lost on Allied commanders. The inexorable march towards D-Day meant that there was no time to dwell at length on a single operation; plans for 627 Squadron to attack their next target proceeded without pause.

The war had come slowly to the ancient villages and small towns of the southwest of England. With troubling news from Poland, families crowded around their radio sets at home to listen to the unfolding drama. The declaration of war in 1939 was greeted with the firm belief that Germany would be defeated, just as they had been twenty-one years previously. The reaction of the men who had fought in the Great War was rather more muted; they feared that the horrors they had witnessed might be visited on this next generation.

In the first year of the war, little changed in the rural idyll of the West Country, the narrow winding roads seeing little extra traffic. Occasionally the wail of air-raid sirens could be heard drifting from larger towns, but in the period of the 'Phoney War' nothing seemed to come of such alarms. A single raider dropped a stick of bombs on Exeter in August 1940 and, shortly afterwards, child evacuees from the larger cities began arriving in the area to be accommodated by local families. Even this sudden influx did little to alter the pace of life in the villages; while there were more young mouths to feed and numbers at the village schools surged, the area adapted. Exeter was bombed heavily in April and May 1942 as part of the Baedeker Raids;* villagers watched the spectacle from a safe distance as the skies lit up with the glow of burning buildings in the city.

---

* Hitler's revenge for effective RAF raids on German cities was to adopt the Baedeker tourist guide as a method of choosing historic towns and cities in Britain as targets for bombing.

Throughout the area the British Army was setting up training camps, but by mid-1943 these were beginning to be filled
with a new kind of soldier. Their uniforms were better tailored,
their pockets appeared to carry an endless supply of chewing
gum and there seemed no shortage of money available to
these teenage recruits. The US Army had arrived in Britain,
and the GIs based in the camps soon began to make their
friendly presence felt. Dances were arranged and new festivals
observed – on the Fourth of July the troops offered the locals
freshly made donuts and rides in military vehicles. The nature
of dating changed as the young women of the village met men
with 'Hollywood' accents for the first time. Whether the recruits
came from Alabama, Arkansas or Arizona, few of them had
ever seen such old houses or narrow streets – or roofs made
from 'grass'. Army life kept most of the men fully occupied,
with little time for relaxation – or 'trouble', as the authorities
tended to see it. Their days were filled with endless drills and
exercises, often carried out in cold, sodden weather as they
prepared for fighting in the European winter. Every soldier
knew that their ultimate aim was the invasion of Europe. In
preparation for the challenge ahead, the Allies were building
their strength up to thirty-nine divisions – 2 million men –
stationed in the south of England. They would be required to
land on beaches in the most hostile conditions, and thereafter to
continue their advance for hundreds of miles across northwest
Europe, creating a support network that would need to provide not only food, weaponry and ammunition, but every item
necessary to sustain a vast army.* A further 4 million people
were involved in the preparations for D-Day, the supply chain
stretching all the way across the Atlantic.

In August 1942 the Allies had launched an amphibious raid

---

* The *Red Ball Express* was a post-D-Day transport system that, at its
peak, employed 5,958 vehicles carrying 12,500 tons of supplies per day.

by 6,000 mainly Canadian troops on the northern French port town of Dieppe, intended to test the viability of an invasion. The raid was a costly disaster, leading to more than half of the men landed becoming casualties or prisoners of war and the loss of 106 aircraft. Dieppe taught the Allies the salutary lesson that unless every detail of an invasion was thought through, its chances of success were greatly reduced. Hitler's preparations for a German invasion of Britain in 1940, code-named Operation Sea Lion, were miniscule in comparison to the Allied build-up for D-Day. A number of the pilots of 627 Squadron, including Jack Goodman, had cut their teeth flying against German invasion barges in Holland, and knew first-hand how important such targets were. The cost in lost aircrew had at times been high, but the constant erosion of Germany's naval and aerial capability – most notably through the defeat of the Luftwaffe by the RAF in the Battle of Britain – would ultimately lead Hitler to cancel Sea Lion.

It was critical for the Allies to prevent the Germans from destroying any of their matériel before D-Day; Allied fighters and light bombers therefore swept the German coastal defences, attacking airfields from the Pas de Calais to the Cherbourg Peninsula. The heavy bombing strategy of night and day raids across France and the Low Countries, many of them with many hundreds of aircraft, tested German air defences to their limit.

The few German reconnaissance photographs taken of the south coast of England showed the extent of preparations for an invasion of Europe. On 28 April, E-boats* had attacked

---

* 749 American troops were killed when German torpedo boats operated by the Kriegsmarine caught Allied tank landing ships waiting in Lyme Bay. A further 197 deaths had occurred the day before through friendly fire on beach landings. The casualties of Operation Tiger, as the Allied exercise was known, were not revealed until August 1944, and the incident was not widely reported at the time.

Allied vessels preparing to land troops in an invasion rehearsal at Slapton Sands in South Devon. It was clear to German commanders that preparations for the invasion of France were in their final stages. The two key unknown elements in defending against the invasion were where it would fall and when. Most, including General Erwin Rommel, believed the Allies would attempt to land in the Pas de Calais at high tide – a misconception on both counts. The Atlantic Wall, the huge string of concrete defences stretching over 3,000 miles of the western and northern European coastline – whose strengthening had been Rommel's responsibility as General Inspector of the Western Defences – had cost 3.7 billion Deutschmarks, but he knew that the proof of its efficacy would come in the first twenty-four hours after an invasion. Either the wall would hold the attackers and allow the German defenders to pin them down on the beaches, or all would be lost. Rommel did not underestimate the task before him: 'The war will be won or lost on the beaches,' he said. 'We'll have only one chance to stop the enemy and that's while he's in the water.' In terms of heavy armour, Rommel could, potentially, have ten Panzer Divisions at his disposal, but only three, the 2nd, 21st and 116th Panzer, were under his direct command. To move the other seven – three of which were based in the south of France – would require Hitler's direct permission. The immense task of entraining a division would take time, but Rommel optimistically believed he could bring a southern unit to the field in five days. What he failed to anticipate was the rate of Allied destruction of rail yards, bridges and rolling stock in the four weeks prior to the invasion.

In their corner of the airfield at RAF Woodhall Spa, 627 Squadron were adapting to the intense rate of operations. The weather in the early part of May was dismal and wet, although the latter part of the month would provide a blistering heat-wave. To the men who spent much of their time working outside, the welcome warmth of spring lifted their spirits – despite their still having to work with waterproofs on to protect them from the inevitable English rain.

Two aspects of life particularly cheered the Squadron. The first was that more of their aircraft were returning safely from raids, disproving early predictions that they were being asked to undertake suicide dives onto heavily defended targets. It was reassuring that Goodman and Hickox had successfully navigated a hail of fire on the Mailly-le-Camp operation without sustaining even a scratch to their Mosquito's paintwork. On another occasion, a Mosquito had tangled with barrage balloons around Ipswich and returned with the whole of the leading edge of its starboard wing torn off, but still landed safely. The second element was that, despite Woodhall Spa being under the watchful eye of senior officers like Cochrane, Sharpe and Cheshire, whose reputation for strictness could not be doubted, 627 Squadron were largely left to their own devices. Many of the airmen testified later that it was the happiest squadron they had served on – a state of affairs that resulted from Wing Commander Roy Elliot's practice of keeping junior ranks informed of everything that was happening. This universal feeling of camaraderie raised spirits and created strong feelings of loyalty that would carry the men of the Squadron through harder times.

The ground crews were finding their feet and discovering ways of lightening their load through a very busy period. Courtesy of an inconspicuous path by which a cyclist could leave the airfield unobserved, they were able to make a daily run to the bakery in Woodhall Spa town and bring back buns for the mid-morning break. The speed with which new airfields were being built meant that surprisingly few of them had wholly secure perimeter fences. Immensely pleased with themselves for finding such a conveniently placed escape route, the men assumed they had succeeded in keeping the 'Chiefies' in the dark about their activities. They were disconcerted, therefore, to discover that their clandestine 'bun run' was in fact common knowledge. Later that summer, when a Chiefie was summoned to supervise work on a troublesome engine, and found that the job had overrun the normal break period, he inquired casually, 'No buns this morning, lads? I'm starving.'

Morale was good, but with four Lancaster squadrons in the locality – 83 and 97 Squadrons at Coningsby, 106 Squadron at Metheringham and 617 Squadron at Woodhall Spa – the mood could change after a single night of losses. Leading 54 Base,* Air Commodore Sharp ceaselessly urged his men to set their aim high, both in the accuracy of their target marking and in expanding their leisure time interests. The cadre of Master Bombers and Marker Leaders would meet for separate briefings which, owing to the importance of their work, were also attended by pilots from 627 Squadron. As junior ranks in a room full of experienced, high-ranking officers, the men of 627 Squadron tended to remain quiet, but they remembered the insistent nature of the instructions they were given: 'If you don't get this target tonight, we will go tomorrow and every day after that until you get it.' Such was the importance of pre-D-Day targets that no compromise was suggested – a strategy uncomfortably close to that of the First World War, where objectives were frequently assigned 'at all costs'.

Unlike the United States Army Air Force (USAAF), which seemed to have the ability to finance leisure facilities of all types on their bases – including clubs, bars, gyms and cinemas – Air Commodore Sharp had to watch his budget carefully, and found himself dealing with the minutiae of balancing the

* 54 Base, RAF Coningsby was the designation given to the group of airfields led by Sharp, encompassing more than 5,000 men and women.

station books. An instruction on the matter of the quantity of sweet rations allowed, issued in May 1944, read:

> The choice of aircrew rations taken into the air come under the following scale:
>> Barley Sugar 3x 3d packets, packets per aircrew per week
>>
>> Chocolate 4x 2oz bars per aircrew per week
>>
>> Glocodine Tablets 2x 2d packets per aircrew per week
>>
>> Raisins 6oz per aircrew per week
>
> It must be clearly understood that rations taken into the air commonly comprise some of the above articles and aircrew are asked to state their preference through the Squadron Adjutant

The entry went on to specify that only operations and training lasting more than four hours qualified for the weekly budget of one shilling for the items listed. For operations cancelled within one hour of take-off the budget was reduced to 6d. In effect, rations would be denied to those flying 627 Squadron operations lasting less than four hours – a time period not uncommon for the rapid Mosquito. It is not known whether the crews managed to negotiate their own scale, or whether crews delayed landing for a few minutes to prevent consumed items from being charged to their mess bill. Given that the men were preparing for the largest invasion in military history, and that the cost of an entire month's sweet rations for all Squadron 627 crews was likely to be less than the cost of a single bomb fuse, it seems curious that the issue of barley sugars should warrant an instruction from a commanding officer. The level of sweet rations was probably the responsibility of a junior clerk in the Air Ministry, and the instruction issued by Sharp no doubt a general order distributed to all Bomber Command bases for their expected compliance. Precisely how the number of raisins a crewman might consume was calculated is not reported. It is a moot point whether such directives are evidence of a cheese-paring obsession with pettifogging detail on the part of the wartime civil service at a time of national rationing, or an illustration of the labyrinthine complexity of invasion planning.

Football, cricket and hockey competitions continued throughout the period, and were perhaps considered by some to be only slightly less important than airborne operations. Attempts to interest servicemen with more artistic endeavours were a little less enthusiastically received – although Sharp was keen to promote entertainment on the airfields. The 'Rupert Ballet' had performed at Coningsby in March, and were greeted politely but with understandable reticence by men who had never seen anything like it before – although they found the sight of a young woman dancing in tights stirring enough. A travelling concert party organized by the Entertainments National Service Association (ENSA) arrived on 4 May and were received with more warmth, although the title of their show, 'The wind and the rain', mirrored the local weather a little too closely.

Other entertainments came from sources much closer to the base, and it appears that RAF support staff were also encouraged to pursue their talents for the delectation of the airmen. On one occasion, as crews from 627 Squadron were preparing at their dispersals after midnight, following the departure of the Lancasters, they saw a three-ton lorry approaching them out of the gloom. Strapped to the back of the flatbed vehicle was a piano, whose player promptly struck up a popular tune of the day, accompanying a female soprano who proceeded to sing to the surprised airmen. Jack Goodman remembers the singer as being very good, but also that it was an awkward situation and incongruous being sung to while they were fully kitted up ready for flight and about to face dangers that attended any operation. The performers received a small and somewhat embarrassed round of applause before the blushing singer and accompanist disappeared into the darkness on their temporary 'stage' to repeat their performance at the next dispersal. Had the light been better it is possible the men might have recognized the piano player as 'Jock' Stares, the RAF dental officer from Woodhall Spa who filled and pulled their teeth. His abilities on the piano were undiminished by his consumption of alcohol on the late-night route.

Tours Airfield, 7 May 1944

Postings in France were greatly coveted by Luftwaffe pilots, and Tours, in the Loire Valley, had much to recommend it. Training grounds in Germany were becoming dangerous places, but here – amid the vineyards and soft sunshine of the département of Indre-et-Loire – there was a distinct impression of safety. Wheeling a Junkers 88 or Heinkel 111 around the airfield circuit at Tours felt more like a pleasure flight than a preparation for war. The city lay invitingly below under a spring haze, the fine bridges and tree-lined avenues unblemished by battle. The bomber pilots here were under the instruction of seasoned flyers who had flown against Britain in the summer of 1940, but more recently had known the privations of the Eastern Front. They too counted the posting to Tours as a blessing: the city itself, a bustling metropolis offering the pleasures of plentiful bars and cafes, was just a short bus ride away from the airfield. It was not difficult to find female company. With so many young French men pressed into labour programmes further afield, a Luftwaffe officer, dashing in his uniform, could easily catch the eye of a mademoiselle. Luftwaffe personnel were accommodated at the Château des Belles Ruries, an attractive mansion 7 kilometres from the airfield, while officers enjoyed the comforts of a hotel closer to the city. Fifty kilometres to the north, in a railway carriage at Montoire-sur-le-Loir in October 1940, a meeting had taken place between Hitler and Marshal Pétain that marked the start of collaboration between Vichy France and Nazi Germany.

The era of peaceful flying from Tours in 1943 came to an abrupt end on 31 December, when a daylight raid by American B-17 bombers left five German aircraft destroyed. Three other heavy daylight raids in January, February and March 1944 left the Luftwaffe in no doubt that Tours was no secret, as the Allies searched far and wide for German bombers and aircraft factories. On 5 January, seventy-eight B-17s of the USAAF 1st Bombardment Group hit the airfield; the raid of 5 February, again by B-17s, destroyed or damaged sixty-five aircraft, hangars and workshops. The February action was part of 'Operation Argument' or, as it became known, 'Big Week', a concentrated attack on German aircraft building and maintenance sites. The Germans remained obsessed with defending the coastline of occupied Europe, but the Allies were already thinking beyond the moment of invasion, and planning for a deep advance to which even an airfield as distant as the Loire Valley could pose a threat.

On 7 May 1944, Woodhall Spa was bustling, as it always was on an operational day. With the sun rising earlier and the coming of warmer weather, the business of getting out of bed and starting the day in the Nissen hut encampment was much less unpleasant than it had been during the colder months. Just as they had been days earlier at Mailly-le-Camp, the dive-bombing Mosquitos were being called on to suppress flak guns around the airfield at Tours. Owing to the nature of the target area, which under illumination would be difficult to miss, the marking was to be more conventional. Unlike some of the less defended industrial targets in France, the airfield had been reinforced with one heavy flak battery position and eight searchlights. The main bomber force was to attack at

8,000 feet – a level they were far from happy with, but the command was clear: there could be no scattering of bombs so near to the city. Eight Mosquitos of 627 Squadron would attack the flak positions at Tours, while a further four would mark the ammunition dump at Salbris, 60 miles to the east.

After the formal briefings, the crews gathered around wooden tables to examine photographs of Tours. Taken using a twin lens camera, target photographs could be examined using a viewer that gave the impression of a 3-D image. As time wore on, the air grew progressively denser with cigarette smoke. The airfield buildings were easy to see – ten large hangars, some already scarred by the previous raids. The headquarters building and numerous offices and workshops were also clear, but what interested the men of 627 Squadron most was the position of the circular gun emplacements. The photographs were detailed, and the airmen could see the shadow of the gun barrels and the ammunition stores around the revetment, which allowed for rapid loading. Landing a bomb in the middle of one of these circular defences would be perfect, but they knew that just getting a 500lb bomb close would trigger the ammunition and cause a cataclysmic chain reaction that would destroy the gun. Each of them knew the destructive power of the flak guns; they had risked their lives against them on numerous occasions and all too often seen their effects on other aircraft. Some of the Mosquito men had lost crewmen on their previous tour on 'heavies'. The sight of injured men and blood-spattered bomber turrets would linger long in their memories. There was no sympathy for the German gunners or, come to that, anyone who threatened the lives of Allied servicemen.

With these images fresh in their minds, they headed out to the dispersals to see their camouflaged wooden steeds. The air test was a chance to check every part of their aeroplane and set their minds at ease by satisfying themselves that all was in order. While aircrew carried out dozens of flights and air tests each day, ground crews continued to work away undisturbed. Afternoons on an operational day were always busy – other than when their aircraft was taken out, there were few chances for a break. They hoped that the crew would not return from their test flight with long lists of matters requiring attention – the pressure would then be on to get the aircraft serviceable for the night's mission. That day had been no different, Mosquitos toing and froing above the base and the air humming with the constant drone of engines. When a sudden, thunderous noise boomed and echoed across the airfield, for a few seconds no one paid much attention to it. The men in the Watch Office witnessed a Mosquito approaching on one engine before falling suddenly into a spin and crashing near the bomb dump, half a mile south of 627 Squadron's dispersals. An ominous plume of black smoke rose from the area – a chilling portent to the fate of the crew. Already a corporal had picked up the phone, and as alarm bells chimed, firemen scattered to their vehicles.

At the dispersals, the distant pillar of smoke was greeted with astonishment as word quickly spread. Men walked out from under their aircraft, some with tools still in hand, and stared blankly towards the angry cloud still billowing into the sky. The older hands had seen this kind of thing before – air accidents were not uncommon on an airfield – but they instinctively knew that such a sudden and ferocious fire normally spelled disaster. For a few minutes the men stood in vigil watching the commotion, overcome by a numb feeling of powerlessness. Naturally, their eyes scanned the dispersals for gaps in the parked line of Mosquitos, for it was here that evidence as to the identity of the crashed aircraft would probably be found. Twenty minutes before, Flight Lieutenants Thomas Hogg and Ronald Woodhouse had signalled 'chocks away' at their dispersal and departed for their test flight in DZ422. There was a gap where their aircraft should have been, and as time ticked by, the waiting men became more anxious. When word finally came that the crashed Mosquito was indeed DZ422, it was a bitter blow to the ground crew. Some wanted to talk, going through each stage of the aircraft's preparation that day, while others silently took in the disaster. Each was gripped with anxiety that it was an error on their part or a failure to notice a mechanical problem that had caused the crash. A brief questioning of eyewitnesses by Warrant Officer Palmer (always known as 'Peddler') revealed a split in testimony, some seeing the port propeller stopped, others the starboard.

As official records all too frequently show, the Mosquito flew beautifully but could quickly become uncontrollable if it lost an engine – particularly on landings and take-offs. This tendency to be so unforgiving is borne out by statistics that show that nearly as many Mosquitos were lost to accidents as to enemy activity. Flight Lieutenant Thomas Hogg, a twenty-nine-year-old Manxman, was a highly experienced pilot who already held the Distinguished Flying Cross from his service with 11 Squadron in 1942 flying Bristol Blenheims. Flight Lieutenant Ronald Woodhouse, a married man of thirty from Bicester in Oxfordshire was equally accomplished. The crew had arrived little over a month earlier, and had flown seven operations with 627 Squadron before the tragedy. Whatever problem DZ422 had manifested during its final flight was obliterated by the fierce fire that broke out on impact. The Court of Enquiry was comparatively brief in such circumstances, concluding that technical failure was the most likely cause of the incident.

In the manner of all Second World War RAF stations, no incident, no matter how catastrophic, was allowed to delay the fulfilment of the day's orders. Although their Mosquitos were already loaded and fuelled, crews still faced a long wait before take-off that day. The four Mosquitos tasked to attack Salbris would leave at 22.30 hours, but the remaining eight would have to wait a further two and a half hours. Throughout the day the Allies had begun an onslaught against Luftwaffe airfields and other targets associated with D-Day. Some attacks were made in daylight, as in the low-level attack on Gael airfield near Saint-Malo by Mosquitos of 21 Squadron – others only as night began to fall. The defenders' radar screens were peppered with the fuzzy dots of approaching Allied raiders, spanning many hundreds of miles. Luftwaffe interceptors barely had time to refuel and re-arm in an exhausting day of incursions. As the attacks on airfields and supply dumps continued for hours unabated, the defenders of the French sector of the Atlantic Wall watched the horizon anxiously from their concrete bunkers. Despite the intensity of the attacks, it became clear that the invasion was not imminent, and the depressing reality that the Allies had so much air power to throw against them in preparation for a future sea-borne attack struck home.

Four miles away from Woodhall Spa, at around 22.00 hours, the nightly procession of Lancasters began to take off from RAF Coningsby. 83 Squadron left first for Salbris, followed by 97 Squadron to Tours at 00.30. The final wait at the dispersals was sometimes the longest period of the day for the 627 crews. While they busied themselves with pre-flight checks there was always the sense that the unnatural quietness masked something more profound. Because of the need to fly in darkness, the timing of operations had slipped later and later into the evening, but even by 01.15, the dying embers of the day could still be seen on the western horizon at 10,000 feet. By the time the Tours-bound Lancasters returned – confident that they would encounter no enemy ambush close to home – the sun had already risen. Compared to the grim winter nights of 1943/44, when German night fighters would infiltrate the bomber stream and launch head-on attacks on the approach to the airfields, life was now far safer.

Thirty minutes before 627's departure from Woodhall Spa, their colleagues at 83 Squadron had begun marking the ammunition dump at Salbris. Some carried 4,000lb 'Cookies' that created huge blast waves over the site. At 4,000 feet, this low-level raid produced immediate results, and within minutes the target was enveloped in thick smoke rising thousands of feet to their flight level. Other squadrons were now bombing the smoke, and as flashes and rumbles filled the air it was clear that the destruction was extensive. Such was the turbulence caused by the explosions that Flying Officer Kennedy in Lancaster ND854 of 83 Squadron did not realize his bombs had failed to drop:

> We were bumping so much as a result of explosions from target we did not realise this until we checked over the Channel and found bomb(s) had not gone. 1x 4000 HC, 6 x 500MC & photoflash hung up.

The flaming mass at Salbris served as an eastern reference point for the raid heading for Tours. At 01.02, 'A' Flight commander Squadron Leader Nelles released the brakes on Mosquito 'K' DX477 and began his thunderous take-off run from Woodhall with two red 'spot fire' flares and two 500lb bombs. The rumble of the tyres ceased halfway down the runway as he selected the undercarriage lever, and with a gentle whirring, the wheels clunked back into the engine nacelles. The familiar sound of the rushing wind on the windscreen and tiny whistles around the canopy told him that all was well. Behind him, the remaining Mosquitos of his command took off at two-minute intervals. Two hours later, after an uneventful flight through the dead blackness of northern France, the concrete runways of Tours appeared, starkly illuminated by dropping parachute flares. To Nelles's port side a glowing mark stood out of the darkness – the furiously burning dump at Salbris. Feeling his way around the perimeter of the target, he picked out two gun emplacements and made diving attacks from 2,500 feet. The airfield was now under intense attack, and the raid controller advised Nelles that his flares would not be needed, and to return home.

Of the force of eight Mosquitos, six would successfully attack. Marshallsay and Ranshaw repeated their Mailly-le-Camp performance by rapidly silencing their gun position, as did five others, although they reported the results were hard to see due to the rising smoke. The squadron should have returned satisfied and triumphant, but in the end the day had not been kind to them. On landing they discovered that one of their force, Mosquito DZ644, crewed by Pilot Officer Percy Turnor and Warrant Officer John Hewson, was late returning. This was not unusual in itself, and at first there were few worries as to the men's whereabouts. As time passed, however, and they received no word, it soon became clear that Turnor and Hewson were in all likelihood lost.* The words of the squadron Operations Record Book – 'This aircraft failed to return; nothing heard of it after take-off' – which are standard under such circumstances, shed no light on the mystery. In the course of operations most aircrew confessed they spent little time speculating on what might have befallen a lost crew. News was slow and often suppressed, particularly if the men had entered a French escape network. Even after the war, few details were available about Turnor and Hewson, other than that they were buried in the Pont-du-Cens Communal Cemetery near Nantes. Their crash north of Tours might suggest that they were hit by the flak guns they sought to disable at the airfield, but little is known about the circumstances of their loss.

A second Mosquito, DZ525, flown by Flying Officers Alexander Hindshaw and John Daly, returned early to Woodhall

---

* Many records list Turnor and Hewson lost in DZ478, a Mosquito not apparently on charge with 627 Squadron at the time. In a mystery of identification, DZ644 is later identified as lost with 139 Squadron.

Spa. Hindshaw appears to have lost control of the Mosquito in an inexplicable event off the south coast of England. 627 Squadron records are unusually candid on this point, reporting:

> Mission abandoned 15 miles south of Portsmouth owing to indisposition of pilot who found himself going into a steep dive for no apparent reason and found great difficulty in flying the a.c. No defect in a.c. suspected.

Hindshaw was removed from flying duties, the suspicion being that events earlier in the day may have unsettled him. Squadron commanders often removed men from duty quickly if any lack of nerve was suspected. The stigma of 'LMF', Lack of Moral Fibre, could affect an airman's career significantly. In the case of Hindshaw, the evidence may point to a medical issue, such as a problem with an inner ear, but it was clear that, despite his experience and a number of successful operations flown with 627 in the past, no risks were to be taken.* John Daly was to fly again on one other occasion, to Braunschweig with Squadron Leader Nelles two weeks later, but the two-man crews were well established by now – and this was also the case with the new crews arriving at Woodhall Spa – so there was little room for a spare navigator.

All in all, it had been a sobering day for 627 Squadron. There was consolation to be found, perhaps, in the knowledge that the events of the last twenty-four hours were exceptional, a rare departure from the normal run of things. But the loss of two crews and the disabling of a third nonetheless made this a troubling time for this small and closely knit group of men.

*

---

* Hindshaw was awarded the Distinguished Flying Cross for his service a month later in June 1944.

Throughout May 1944 the list of targets continued to grow as 627 Squadron was tasked to support raids throughout France and into Holland and Germany. Rail yards, factories and military installations, including gun batteries on the Normandy coast, were all recipients of their attentions. The weather improved dramatically through the latter half of the month, turning into a record-breaking heatwave. Men who a couple of weeks earlier had been swaddled in waterproofs and fighting the cold now found themselves stripped to the waist in fine summer weather. The wind, so often biting and able to penetrate layers of clothing, had turned into a warm blast. The tents for the ground crew were now sun shields – but there were few complaints. The aircrew were a little less enthusiastic about the increased temperatures, which during the daytime turned their cockpits into sweaty greenhouses as they ran through pre-flight checks. For fliers wearing not only heavy RAF uniforms but also leather flying helmets with built-in headphones for radio transmissions, it was a relief to climb to higher altitudes and reach cooler air.

As losses remained low, the confidence of the Squadron continued to rise, although not all raids went according to plan, despite the calming voice of the controller on the VHF channel. On 11 May, all eight 627 Mosquitos returned without having dropped either marker flares or bomb load after a raid on Bourg-Leopold military camp east of Antwerp. The main bomber force arrived too early, and began bombing a single red marker, making 627 Squadron's task of backing it up correctly too hazardous. Since they were at risk of being struck by bombs from above, the Squadron were told to return home. As they moved from operation to operation, the crews of 627 Squadron still had no inkling where the coming invasion might fall, but they had noticed that one of their priorities seemed to be attacks on German batteries in Normandy. Had any members of 627 Squadron fallen into

German hands, the defenders might have had the opportunity to quiz them about why an elite pathfinding squadron was being deployed so relentlessly against coastal batteries in Normandy. But 627 Squadron's losses were negligible, and the situation never arose. A small number of 83 and 97 Squadron aircraft had been shot down, but not over coastal targets. Those RAF crew who were captured knew that with the Allied invasion coming, it was all the more important to remain tight-lipped.

Saint-Martin-de-Varreville, 28 May 1944

Nestling in the flat farmland of the Cherbourg Peninsula, Oberleutnant* Erben, the commander of Coastal Artillery Regiment 1261, was well aware that his guns might be targeted by the Allies. Daily attacks in the region and low-flying reconnaissance flights gave him little feeling of security. All too frequently his days were disturbed by the crackling of four-barrel flak guns as a Spitfire roared over the hedgerows not far from his command post. For all the ammunition expended, there was little to show for his gunners' efforts – the aircraft appeared and departed so quickly that there was not enough time to get an accurate aim on them. What concerned him most were his principal charges, two 122mm guns set a mile back from the coast. His priority was to keep them well camouflaged, using nets covered in khaki cloth pulled tightly around each gun position, with only a small amount of muzzle poking out. He spent his days ensuring that his battery was kept supplied with food and essentials. Discipline was good, but he chided men who failed to move on quickly enough any vehicle or cart that stopped outside their position, or to

* First Lieutenant.

make sure air raid precautions were observed. His men were generally older than front-line infantrymen, and were drawn from a wide range of backgrounds. There was a smattering of Poles and Ukrainians among their number – their German could be hard to understand, but perhaps no less intelligible than the Bavarians'.

The warm evening of 27 May passed without incident, his men sitting outside chatting and playing cards on the canteen tables until the light faded. As normal, everyone other than the night guards had turned in by midnight, heading into the concrete bunkers that served as accommodation and shelters. An hour had passed before the commander was alerted by the sentries and the mournful sound of hand-cranked air-raid sirens. The doorway leading out from the bunker was illuminated by an eerie light, and the rumble of bombers shook the sky above his emplacement. Flares drifted slowly down from high above, filling the landscape with bright white light as he ordered all but three of his men to the shelters. The roar of low-flying aircraft was followed shortly afterwards by the shriek of falling bombs, signalling the start of a raid of unimaginable intensity.

Four 627 Squadron Mosquitos led the raid of sixty-four Lancaster bombers on a target that had no obvious distinctive features in the flat coastal plain. Freed from the risk of colliding with buildings, Flight Lieutenants Bartley and Mitchell in DZ421 brought their Mosquito down in the dive from 3,000 feet to 300 feet, observing the terrain illuminated by the spot flare they had dropped as they circled. In keeping with a pattern of marking that was proving highly effective, the marker was dropped 60 yards to one side of the main target. The others then followed in short succession, dropping their markers 200 yards to each side, forming a ring around the area they wished the Lancasters to bomb. Thompson and Harris in DZ601 finished the task by dropping green target indicators in the red circle to show that the marking had been completed to their satisfaction. The bombing force streamed in as planned, and with little flak opposition, concentrated their efforts on the small area clearly picked out below.

When the light of early morning revealed the carnage left behind, the smell of explosives and concrete dust still hung heavily in the damp air. The ammunition dump was on fire, presenting an extreme hazard to those nearby. The battery commander found one of his gun emplacements completely destroyed, but the other one, some 50 yards away, was untouched under its camouflage netting. Later that day he wrote a detailed report to his command headquarters, itemizing his losses. Of the three sentries left outside, two had disappeared without trace and were, he assumed, buried under the rubble. *Unteroffizier** Klauke and *Obergefreiter†* Wenal had been at the entrance of the main shelter when it had been hit, as had *Oberkanonier‡* Majrowski, who was dug out alive. Another smaller shelter, housing *Unteroffizier* Herreman and *Obergefreiter* Huesmann, had 'burst open and collapsed'; no attempt had been made to rescue the two men, as the pile of rubble lay too close to the burning ammunition store. Six men had been injured and, of the six horses on site, three had fled and had yet to be found. Of the buildings close by, the battery had lost an equipment hut, armoury, artillery and signals equipment. The commander's report noted that they had all received direct hits, and 'only a few twisted girders remained'. In all he had lost 900 rounds of ammunition, and he was forced to move the surviving gun crews to farms in the area.

Perhaps the most telling part of the commander's report was

---

* Non-commissioned officer, Sergeant.
† Acting Corporal.
‡ Senior Private, artillery.

the statement that 'The position has been hit with uncanny accuracy by the Enemy Air Force.' A week later, 21,000 men of the American 4th Division stormed ashore a little over a mile away on Utah beach. They encountered little opposition there (they suffered just 197 casualties), and soon secured the immediate area, whereas at neighbouring Omaha beach, where German heavy artillery continued to fire for some time, two US infantry divisions achieved only a tenuous foothold, and at a far heavier cost. Pushing inland, American troops found the battered site of the guns of Saint-Martin-de-Varreville, with the surviving artillery position empty.

Although it is possible with hindsight to say that the raid on Saint Martin-de-Varreville was a strong indication of a landing point, many other raids on batteries along the northern French coast were diversionary in nature. 627 Squadron had been operating at full strength that day, despatching fourteen Mosquitos on four separate raids. The gun battery at Morsalines further north on the Cherbourg Peninsula was attacked, as was a railway repair yard at Nantes. Further along the coast, to the northeast and closer to the Pas de Calais, the gun battery at Saint-Valery-sur-Somme was attacked, with the marking completed by three 627 Mosquitos. Tellingly, the flak defences were much stronger here, and Flying Officers Foxcroft and Acworth in DZ468 were hit and failed to return. They were still in radio contact over the target, but their aircraft was later seen in flames, plunging towards the sea. Both men, who were highly experienced DFC holders, were lost without trace.*

★

* Flying Officer Phillip Spencer Foxcroft and Flying Officer Dennis Herbert Acworth are remembered on the Runnymede Memorial to the missing.

*The rail yard at Saumur before the attack of 1 June 1944 (above)
and the aftermath of the raid (below).*

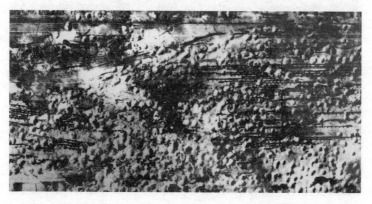

'Benny' Goodman and 'Bill' Hickox had completed a successful
raid on the Saumur rail yard on 1 June. Circling to provide
reserve marking, they had placed their marker on the east
side of the tracks leading into the main marshalling yard. The
other three Mosquitos of 627 Squadron had laid markers at
the other end of the tracks, revealing a target that was hard to
miss. The broad sweep of the Loire River with the Château de
Saumur perched on an incline on its southern bank provided
an unmistakable landmark. Despite this, the raid controller

halted bombing at one point when it began to stray away from the area and had new markers placed where the flares had been obscured.

After loitering for over thirty minutes watching the concentrated destruction of the rail hub, Goodman and Hickox had been ordered home, as no further marking was necessary. Despite this textbook performance, the men were surprised to be asked to step into Wing Commander Elliot's office. The news was surprising. They were both to be stood down from operations, as they were deemed to be at the end of their tour – they had done enough. Goodman had flown seventy-eight operations in his combat career, and though it was the eve of the largest invasion in history, he was informed that his services would no longer be required.

Leaving the office, Goodman and Hickox felt the rush of relief, an exhilaration that after all the dangers they had faced, they were going to survive this war. Although training postings had been comparatively dull and, at times, tedious, they had little idea how much the burden of operations had affected them until it was lifted. The news was sudden, but there was time to pack and share a drink with their colleagues before departing on leave to take up a position at a training establishment. Goodman and Hickox would both be posted to 1655 MTU (Mosquito Training Unit) at RAF Warboys to pass on their hard-won knowledge to other pilots and navigators. Amid the relief, they experienced some feelings of sadness, because 627 Squadron had been the happiest and most fulfilling posting of their long and hazardous careers. The fact that two experienced and gifted aircrew were able to end their tour at this most crucial point in the war proved how prepared the Royal Air Force was for the task ahead. Another highly experienced crew would fill their cockpit at a time when the Luftwaffe could only release a pilot in the event of injury or death. At the other end of the supply chain, after the grievous

Group Captain J. R. Goodman DFC, AFC, with a painting depicting his final operation on the Saumur rail yard.

losses of the winter campaign, Bomber Command now had a surfeit of available competent men – enough to supply crews to the hundreds of new aircraft rolling off the production lines, with trained airmen to spare.

9

DOUGHBOYS

Ken Oatley finished his evening meal and, in the regular pattern of life for a baker's son, went to help his father prepare dough for the next morning at the small bakery in Frome, Somerset. The familiar smell of yeasty dough proving had been part of his life from his earliest childhood. Ken was thirteen years old, and he was on the eve of leaving school – a touch early even by the standards of 1935. He seemed to spend a lot of time in detention, perhaps displaying a spark of individuality that was not always appreciated by his teachers. To the casual observer, Ken seemed destined to work in the family business, rising early and making his way through the dimly lit streets to the baker's shop. By the time the first customers arrived to savour the aroma of freshly baked bread and cakes, the equivalent of a whole day's work had been crammed into the hours before dawn. His father was a man who believed in hard work. While Ken was not a highly academic student, he was musically gifted, and his father had hopes that he might one day become a concert violinist. Ken had been given his first violin at three years of age; by the time

*Ken Oatley wearing his
navigator's brevet.*

he was five he had won second place in the Bristol Eisteddfod* for the under sixes. He practised for one and a half hours each day, and on Saturdays he made the train journey to Bristol for lessons.

Ken's great-uncle, William Oatley, had opened the first all-electric bakery in Frome in the early years of the new century. It was a bold step into modern technology, revealing a family fascination for science that would flower most brilliantly in his son Charles, who was born in 1904. The investment revolutionized William's bakery and, as the business grew, William became increasingly aware that he needed trustworthy help. Charles was still too young to play an active role in the business, and he seemed to be academic in temperament, rather than practical. It was clear he was destined for greater challenges in life than a sleepy Somerset town could offer.

The solution to the expansion of the bakery lay within the family – but far away, in the vast prairies of Illinois in the midwestern United States, where William's nephew James worked as a cowboy on the farm of his adoptive parents, Silas and Annie Dickinson. Born in 1893, James and his brother had lost their parents, James and Mary, who had emigrated

* Founded by William Ernest Fowler in 1903, the Bristol Eisteddfod has run continuously ever since, and is now called 'The Bristol Festival of Music, Speech and Drama'.

from England looking for a new life but had both died young. The boys were sent to an orphanage in St Louis before Bessie Dickinson, a young nurse at the establishment, persuaded her parents to take James in. This display of compassion may have contained an element of practicality, since the Dickinsons had five daughters but only one son. Life was tough; the two boys lived in a cellar dug out by the original pioneers before a house was built on top of it.

James Oatley as a cowboy, c. 1910.

James rode to school each day on horseback. The main highway headed east–west and, like most roads in the area, was dead straight, disappearing into a hazy horizon. Although James had known nothing else but life on the prairie, he was intrigued by his English relatives, with whom he maintained contact by letter. But England lay an unimaginable distance away.

In 1912 James Oatley received a life-changing invitation. His Uncle William in Frome asked him to come over to England and learn to be a baker, with the implication that this would be at least a partnership. At nineteen years old he knew the world was far bigger than the distance he could ride in a day, and that his roots in the 'old country' had presented him with an opportunity that was not to be missed. The Dickinsons were supportive, but to make up for the loss of James's work on the farm, they requested that his uncle refund the price of his passage to England with the purchase of a wagon and horses – a condition that William agreed to.

James found that his new occupation in Frome suited him well, but it was very different from the life he had known. He had to work long hours indoors, and the town felt quaint and strange, even if its inhabitants were welcoming. When the First World War broke out, however, he noticed a change in the locals' attitude to him; he was a foreigner in a country that was now at war, and they treated him with some suspicion. It didn't help that he was of fighting age but remained working in the bakery while the rest of the town's young men marched off to war. James ignored the whisperings and decided to stay put; after all, he was an American citizen trying to master a new trade, and it could be detrimental to his career prospects if he gave it up and volunteered for the British Army.

When America entered the war in 1917, however, James was ready to enlist. After assuring William he would return to his old job in the bakery, he sailed from Liverpool to New York on the SS *Orduna* to join the American Expeditionary Forces bound for the Western Front. Appropriately, he was to serve with the 316th Bakery Company in France, supplying thousands of loaves of bread to ever-hungry regiments – making him a 'doughboy'* in more ways than one. He kept his promise to return to Frome after his army service, and in 1921 he was joined by his fiancée, Marie Geller, from Nashville, Tennessee, whom he had met during his time in the States. His brother had married her older sister Gertrude, but their father

---

* The name given to American soldiers in the First World War.

had stipulated that any marriage to James should be on condition that he rent a house in England first. James and Marie did not wait to reach Frome, and were married in Liverpool by special licence on her disembarkation. The years up to 1912 had been a remarkable period in James's life, during which he had found the strength and resilience to better himself in the teeth of a veritable blizzard of challenges.

Kenneth Roy Oatley would be born in 1922 at a time when the memories of the Great War were still fresh and painful, but into a society that was regaining its optimism for life.

James Oatley as a 'doughboy' in the First World War.

Having soloed on a Tiger Moth, Ken Oatley was feeling confident in his abilities. Nearing the end of his Elementary Flying Training at RAF Sealand in Flintshire, he was within touching distance of the next stage of his training and the promise of flying Spitfires. On his second flight of the day, Ken decided to go out over the River Dee with another Tiger Moth to practise dogfighting. It was supposed to be a forty-five-minute exercise, but time passed quickly as the aircraft twisted and turned, their bright yellow undersides flashing in the evening sunshine. As he broke away to return home, Ken noticed his partner was nowhere to be seen; in the thrill of the aerobatics he had lost all sense of where he was. The Dee estuary, the great navigational signpost to RAF Sealand, had disappeared, and he found himself over unfamiliar countryside with a stretch of anonymous coastline ahead. He knew that to dally would consume fuel and, given the risk of losing the light, decided to set the Tiger Moth down in a field and ask for directions. Choosing what appeared to be a long stretch of unbroken grass, he descended carefully, a hedge passing under his wheels, and then set the biplane down gingerly. But a few seconds later he saw a ditch running across the field, and to avoid disaster he had to twitch the aircraft's nose back up so as to clear it before touching down again and braking gently

The navigator's position in a Stirling bomber – with much more space than the cramped Mosquito.

to stop on the far side of the field. Satisfied with his landing, he got out, only to see that the Tiger Moth had demolished a small row of wooden stakes that lay in his path.

By now Ken's landing had attracted a small group of curious onlookers. A man on a bicycle explained he was 5 miles from Blackpool. They located his exact position by consulting Ken's flying map, spread across the cyclist's handlebars. With little time to lose, Ken picked a diagonal course across the field to avoid a small wood and took off again. Circling around, he made a low pass over the crowd and gave a wave before heading south in the gathering gloom. It was nearly dark when he arrived back at RAF Sealand, but other than comments that they were about to send for a search party, all seemed well as he retired to bed.

The next morning Ken was summoned to see the commanding officer, who told him that his actions the previous evening were close to being a court martial offence. He was informed that he should not have taken off again, as the aircraft could have sustained damage. Ken had never been made aware of the existence of such a rule, but in the way of military life, he was nonetheless expected to obey it. The Tiger Moth episode was Ken's first close call with a senior officer, and it seems to have affected his flying career. He escaped further censure, but instead of being posted north to fly Miles Masters* in preparation for Spitfires, Ken was posted to Canada and put into a course that would train him to fly heavier aircraft. The twenty-day journey in October 1941 took Ken across the Atlantic by convoy and then onwards for hundreds of miles by train to the small town of North Battleford in Saskatchewan. Now he could see for himself the sort of American landscape his father had described to him: the flat, featureless Canadian fields were broken only by dead-straight roads lined by telegraph poles disappearing into infinity. The sky was vast, but already in autumn the sun did little to warm the ground, temperatures every day remaining below zero. Ken's twelve-week course took place in the coldest months of the Canadian winter; by December, temperatures were dropping to minus 20 degrees Celsius. Their workhorses were the Avro Anson and Airspeed Oxford trainers – both twin-engined aeroplanes with a level of sophistication far beyond the humble Tiger Moth. Ken confesses to not getting on well with the Oxfords, particularly the need to make a three-point landing,† the correct technique for which he felt was never explained adequately to him. Every

* Introduced in 1939, the Miles Master was a two-seat monoplane employed for training aircrew for service with front-line fighter squadrons.
† In an aircraft with a tail wheel – often referred to as a 'tail dragger' – the preferred method of landing is to try to get all three wheels to touch down simultaneously.

time he touched down his aircraft would veer to one side or the other. He was unable to make much improvement to his flying; by the end of the course it was clear he would progress no further as a pilot, and that he would be offered a place in navigator training.

Alongside this bitter disappointment, there were consolations. That Christmas, he had the opportunity to entertain Canadian families with his violin playing, reviving memories of what might have been a promising musical career. When he was sixteen years old Ken had been offered a place at the Royal College of Music in London, but before the days of state aid, he was unable to take it up. Even in pre-war London, and however much his father might try to help, rents for rooms were beyond the means of a baker's son. Ken's Canadian adventure also yielded an engagement to a local girl with whom he had spent only a little time. He didn't get to 'marry in haste and repent at leisure', as his posting back to England meant a long-term relationship by letter – but one that eventually fizzled out.

Despite having joined the Royal Air Force in January 1941, it would be April 1944 before Ken arrived at RAF Metheringham, near Lincoln, to fly as a navigator on Lancasters with 106 Squadron. Among its former commanders, the squadron boasted the now famous Wing Commander Guy Gibson, who had flown Lancasters from RAF Coningsby and then Syerston before the Dam Busters raid – a man whose fate would become entangled with Ken's in an unexpected way later that year. Before his posting to Metheringham, Ken had spent long periods being moved about in an RAF training system that seemed to lose him frequently in the vast machinery of aircrew production. His navigator training had taken him from Eastbourne to Cape Town in South Africa before he joined an Operational Conversion Unit on Vickers Wellington bombers at RAF Upper Heyford in Oxfordshire. Here he was 'crewed up'* but, despite being ready for operations, the crew was sent next for conversion to Short Stirlings – before yet another conversion course to fly on Lancasters. But now, having travelled the longest of roads in training, he had arrived at 106 Squadron, and would at last have the chance to fly in action.

On 22 April 1944, Lancaster JB567 took off from RAF Metheringham carrying Ken Oatley's captain, Pilot Officer John Tucker, on a first raid to Braunschweig. It was an operation supported by the newly formed 627 Squadron, together with other 5 Group bombers. As was common practice, Tucker was to fly a first operation as a second pilot with an experienced crew before taking his own. He was placed with Flight Lieutenant James Lee's crew, who were about to finish their tour of duty. They did not return. It later transpired that they had sustained flak over Braunschweig before being finished off by a night fighter. JB567 crashed near Berge, east of their target; as was common with many high-altitude incidents, there were no survivors. The loss of JB567 created a significant problem for the remaining men of Tucker's crew and, much to Ken Oatley's chagrin, they were sent to RAF Scampton to be re-assigned. In the machinations of RAF governance, rather than simply sourcing a new pilot for the surviving crew members, they were split up and went their separate ways. After 'crewing up', Ken concluded that his new partners were satisfactory, but when he compared them to the previous group of men, who had bonded together over seven months, he could not help but be somewhat dissatisfied. Not for the first time, he was back at the beginning of what seemed an interminable process.

---

* A process where men were placed in a room with the appropriate number of airmen to make up bomber crews and were asked to form crews by self-selection.

Ken returned to training on the large and airy Short Stirlings, in which his navigator's position was further rearwards in the fuselage than the Lancaster, meaning he was more remote from his pilot. When the crew transferred to Lancaster finishing school at RAF Sywell in Northamptonshire, Ken encountered a significant problem. Seated directly behind the pilot, he was exposed to the pilot's most peculiar and overwhelming body odour. He confesses that it was so bad that he could not imagine sitting in such proximity to the pilot for as long as eight hours. If this had been the only problem he encountered, Ken would have simply had to grin and bear it, but it was becoming clear that quite apart from the pungency of his personal aroma, their captain did not inspire confidence in the other crew members. The breaking point came as an instructor was leaving the Lancaster and patted Ken on the shoulder: 'Good luck with that one,' he said.

Mutinous actions are often born of desperation, and after a frank discussion amongst themselves, the crew asked to see the commander. In what must have been a difficult meeting they informed him of their misgivings about their present pilot, and that they wished to be assigned to a new one. They reassured the commander that they remained entirely prepared to fly on operations; their actions were prompted not by a lack of stamina or moral fibre but by the pilot's intolerable character and unsuitedness for his role.

The commander, however, was far from sympathetic; his response was to threaten them with a brace of court martials. For the second time in his RAF career, Ken faced the prospect of official retribution of the severest kind. But the crew stood firm. The irate commander, after promising that they would be scattered to the four winds, dismissed them from his presence to be transported unceremoniously off the course.

D-Day came and went, and by July 1944, as Allied forces continued to fight tooth and nail to break out from their

Normandy beachheads, it looked as if Ken Oatley would never fly on operations. After the contretemps with his commanding officer at Sywell, Ken had returned to RAF Scampton, where his frustration and boredom knew no bounds. Lying disconsolately on his bunk a few days after his return, he was surprised to be approached by a Scots pilot. 'Are you Oatley?' he asked. 'You're going to be my navigator; we're going to fly Mosquitos.'

Forêt de l'Isle-Adam, 18 August 1944

The brief weeks of training on the Mosquito had been a delight. Despite the small size of the space he had to squeeze into, Ken felt entirely at home in the 'wooden wonder'; he felt no regret whatsoever at leaving behind the rumbling interior of the Lancaster, despite it being so much more spacious than the Mosquito.

In the hands of James Walker, it seemed the Mosquito would do everything asked of it, and Ken Oatley quickly developed great respect for his pilot. Walker had served a full tour on Wellington bombers, survived many scrapes and was a highly accomplished airman. He was congenial and easy to get on with – perhaps a little moody at times, but no less approachable for that; to Ken's relief in such a confined cockpit, his new partner presented no problems of personal hygiene. Before the war, James Walker, inevitably nicknamed 'Jock', had worked in the building trade with his father in Aberdeen. In Walker, Ken encountered a man whose working-class background was not dissimilar to his own. The ranks of the RAF were filled with such men – uncomplicated, straightforward and possessed of a deep well of practical common sense. Many of them flew as non-commissioned officers, but some of them achieved promotion to the rank of officer. This could perhaps be seen as a sign of growing social mobility in a class-conscious service,

James Walker as a Sergeant Pilot prior to his service with 627 Squadron.

but, as happened in the First World War, the armed forces were obliged to promote men owing to heavy losses in the perceived 'officer class'.

After completing their Mosquito orientation course with 1655 Mosquito Training Unit at RAF Warboys in Cambridgeshire in early August 1944, Walker and Oatley were posted to 627 Squadron at RAF Woodhall Spa. It came as no surprise that they would be serving in Lincolnshire, a county already familiar to them and home to the majority of Bomber Command's resources. Arriving as new men in a well-established and bustling squadron was always a challenge, and the living accommodation did little to impress them, but there was no chance of a transfer out.

Their first operation together was a raid on a V-1 storage facility in a forest 25 kilometres north of Paris; to their surprise, it was to be a daytime attack. Nearly all of Ken Oatley's training had been geared to night attacks, and all of Jock Walker's previous operations had been flown during the hours of darkness. That Bomber Command felt it could use its black-and camouflage-painted heavy bombers in broad daylight was testament to the effectiveness of the Allies' air-to-ground hunting at this stage of the war. The impact of the D-Day operations had been disastrous on the Luftwaffe in France, with squadrons caught on the ground by waves of Allied ground-attack aircraft. In the face of these losses, it became yet more imperative for the Germans to conceal the location of supplies and weaponry – notably their newly developed *Vergeltungswaffen* ('vengeance weapons'). Far more advanced in their thinking on storing and protecting their assets than the Allies, they had built bunkers and requisitioned caves, tunnels and woods throughout occupied Europe. In response, the development of 'bunker-busting' bombs in high-accuracy air attacks by 617 Squadron had a crucial part to play, but the role of less specialized Lancaster and Halifax squadrons within 5 Group was important too. Their payload of 500, 1,000 and 4,000lb bombs was particularly effective in destroying key installations above ground, and accurate marking by 627 Squadron was essential in helping concentrate this devastating firepower.

Long a hunting ground favoured by French royalty, by the time war broke out in 1939 the Forêt de l'Isle-Adam had been repurposed as a public park. After their invasion of May 1940, however, the Germans turned the forest over to military use without any consultation – as they did vast swathes of land all over France. The Forêt de l'Isle-Adam now became the site of a storage depot for Hitler's 'V' weapons project. However, even under the forest canopy, Allied photo reconnaissance was able to identify the concrete access roads and paths built by the Germans. And before the depot's completion, the French resistance had discovered that forced labour was being used on the site, and passed the information on to the Allies. Despite the Germans' best efforts, this was no secret establishment.

One week after D-Day, on 13 June 1944, the first V-1s were fired towards southern England from a launch site in the Pas-de-Calais in northern France. Most of these early cruise missiles fell short of their target, but one V-1 reached Mile End in East London, where it killed six people. Between June and October

1944, when the V-1 launch ramps were finally overrun, as many as 9,521 V-1s would be launched at London and the southeast of England, killing 6,184, injuring a further 17,981 and consuming large amounts of resources in civil defence. Destruction of the V-1 launch sites therefore became an urgent priority for RAF Bomber Command.

It was 12.30 hours as the four Mosquitos tasked to mark Forêt de l'Isle-Adam took off from RAF Woodhall Spa on a clear, bright day. On such a beautiful day, it seemed incongruous that they were going to war; it felt more like a practice flight than an operational mission. The flight would be a quick one, no more than a dart over the Channel, the waters of which were streaked white with the wakes of Allied ships supplying Normandy. At 5,000 feet the coast of France slipped beneath them as they turned towards Paris. A course change at night could be almost imperceptible, but today the brilliance of the light cast small shadows through the cockpit frame, creating a moving sundial. There was no sign of enemy aircraft, or even a single puff of flak smoke – it was as if the war was on holiday. As they sped south, they saw the windows of houses in towns and villages glinting beneath them in the sunlight. The dark shape of the forest was not difficult to identify. Ahead lay the grey mass of Paris. As peaceful as their journey had been, they knew that if they strayed too close to the city they would certainly provoke a response from the anti-aircraft guns stationed on the outskirts. The principle of the attack was simple. The Mosquitos would mark the corners of the forest and the bombers would attack within the space, pounding the area intensively where the storage bunkers and access roads had been built.

Walker and Oatley in DZ635 were tasked with marking a crossroads on the western edge of the forest. As they approached, they expected to see signs of the other markers. The Mosquitos were also carrying smoke bombs to back up their flares should the need arise – but nothing was visible. This led them to believe they were first on the scene, so in order to be certain of their location they circled the area. Once they had spotted the crossroads, they agreed they were in the right position, and Walker pushed the nose of DZ635 down into a shallow dive. At this point, Oatley became an observer, as his pilot concentrated on the target in the front windscreen. As the ground came closer Ken noticed a man on a bicycle pedalling furiously towards where their marker would land. What became of the man and how close the exploding flare got to him, Ken would never know – but those few seconds and the image of the cyclist remained with him, a curious spectacle of misfortune frozen in time. Most men of Bomber Command would, if they survived, pass through their whole career without seeing a soul below them. Their world was one of flickering lights and thunderous rumbles in the intense darkness.

Releasing their 'spot fire' at 500 feet, Walker climbed again, although still at low level, and assessed how accurate the marking had been. He estimated it was lying 75 yards from where he intended and, as he heard the other markers radio in their attacks, he continued to wonder whether they were in the right location. From his altitude, the other markers were still not visible. But the answer came as the heavy force above began to drop their bombs. Shockwaves shimmered through the trees, and soon huge walls of vertical smoke were rising hundreds of feet in the still August air. There was no need for further marking, as it was clear the bombers had found their target, and the raid leader called off the Mosquitos. Looking back, Ken could see the clouds of smoke for many miles on the homeward leg. It had been a memorable first operation – and not at all as he had imagined.

The war on the V-1 sites had already inflicted a sad and unusual loss on 627 Squadron. On 29 June 1944, a few weeks before Jock Walker's and Ken Oatley's arrival, Wing Commander

Ken Oatley photographed with a Mosquito, RAF Woodhall Spa.

George Curry* led three other Mosquitos in a daylight attack on a V-1 construction site at Beauvoir† in the Pas de Calais. Pressing home their diving attacks, the raid was successful, with all the Mosquitos performing admirably. But only two aircraft returned, those flown by Curry and Wing Commander Simpson, who had acted as raid controller. It transpired that DZ482, flown by Flying Officers Platts and Thompson, had been hit by flak in the target area. Climbing to 3,000 fleet, they abandoned their aircraft near the village of Boubers-sur-Canche, west of Abbeville, when it was clear the aircraft would not make it back to England. Julian Platts was captured and became a prisoner of war, but the Canadian George Thompson escaped and was

* Curry took over command of 627 Squadron from Elliot on 3 June 1944.
† The commune of Beauvoir-Wavans.

given shelter by the French. He remained hidden on the same farm until the Allies liberated the area.

The second Mosquito, DZ516, flown by the immensely popular Australian duo of Flying Officers Alex Saint-Smith and Geoffrey Heath, was less fortunate. Returning at low level from the raid, they were caught in the premature explosion of a V-1 close to Beauvoir. Whether their Mosquito collided with the recently launched weapon, or by mischance flew close to it, upsetting the gyro-control and tipping the V-1 into the ground, is unclear. Whatever the sequence of events, the explosion of the 850kg warhead instantaneously enveloped the Mosquito, leaving its crew no prospect of survival. The incident, which took place within the confines of the First World War battle-field north of Bapaume, was another sad reminder for nearby villagers of the immense tragedy of war. The loss of Saint-Smith and Heath was keenly felt within the Squadron – a sentiment remaining with those who recount the incident decades later.

The arrival of 'Jock' Walker and Ken Oatley at RAF Woodhall Spa coincided with the appointment of a more famous charac-ter to command 54 Base. Wing Commander Guy Gibson arrived at RAF Coningsby in early August 1944 to coordinate the operation of a group of Lincolnshire airfields, with which he had become very familiar earlier in his career. Woodhall Spa was especially significant for him, in that 617 Squadron was in residence – although it was now quite different from the unit he had led on the Dam Busters raid from RAF Scampton in May 1943. Gibson's remit at Coningsby – which included the planning of raids – would, in theory, not involve him in any operational flying. The role of Base Air Staff Officer (BASO) was clearly defined, and he would be under the watchful eye of 5 Group commander Ralph Cochrane and Base Commander Alfred Sharp. But Gibson was itching to be allowed to return to flying duties. Gibson's status within the RAF, on account of the central role he had played in the Dam Busters raids, was close to legendary; as a consequence, there was a widespread belief that he must not be placed in any situation that carried a risk of his falling into German hands. Besides, Gibson had not been involved in operational flying for twelve months and, by virtue of his absence, he was considered likely to be a little rusty. Although he had arguably been a pioneer in low-level night raiding with 617 Squadron, more experienced men than Gibson had now risen through the ranks to become Master Bombers. This elite group operated in the shadows at RAF Coningsby, flying Leonard Cheshire's 'private' collection of fast aeroplanes, but they also used 627 Squadron Mosquitos whenever the need arose. One of Gibson's close friends, Charles Owen, had completed his Lancaster tour with 97 Squadron, and had moved seamlessly over to 54 Base Flight to continue his duties in raid controlling. But it was undoubtedly difficult for an individual of Gibson's headstrong type to watch those close to him continuing to fly while he was tied to a desk.

While it was the raid of May 1943 that elevated Guy Gibson to public adulation, his rise to prominence within the Royal Air Force had begun rather earlier, during his time with 106 Squadron, which he joined as its commanding officer in the spring of 1942, at the age of just twenty-three. The fact that, on 16 January 1943, he flew the BBC's war correspondent, Major Richard Dimbleby, to Berlin in a Lancaster suggests that he was already regarded as a natural ambassador for Bomber Command. Once his tour with 106 Squadron had ended, in March 1943, he was posted to the Headquarters of 5 Group. His commanders clearly considered Gibson – who had amassed 172 bombing and night-fighter sorties, plus a DSO and bar – to be an outstanding leader, but he was also a very lucky man to have survived for so long.

On 18 March, Air Vice Marshal Ralph Cochrane, AOC of

Guy Gibson, 1943.

5 Group, asked Gibson if he would be prepared to fly one last operation as commander of a new squadron – 617 – tasked with destroying the Ruhr dams. The successful attack of 16/17 May 1943, carried out by nineteen Lancasters flying from RAF Scampton, became the most famous British air raid of the Second World War, launching the legend of the 'Dam Busters' and ensuring celebrity status for both the Lancaster and the young man who led the raid. In June 1943, Gibson's name and photograph were splashed across every national newspaper when he attended an investiture at Buckingham Place to receive the Victoria Cross. Further prizes included an invitation to lunch with Winston Churchill at Chequers in July, followed by an extensive tour of Canada and the United States in the late summer and autumn. By the time he appeared on *Desert Island Discs* with Roy Plomley on 19 February 1944, Gibson had been ordered to write a book about his experiences, and was busy writing it. Completed in September 1944, *Enemy Coast Ahead*

was serialized in the *Sunday Express* in December, but it was not published in book form until 1946, after its author's death. Although it was strongly supportive of Bomber Command and the strategic air offensive, certain elements of *Enemy Coast Ahead* – notably its revelation of a level of disorganization, particularly in the early months of the war – were a cause of some disquiet in the RAF, even after the censors had removed some questionable passages.

His rise to stardom appears to have done little to enhance Gibson's personality. Still only twenty-five years of age, he did not display the warm confidence depicted by Richard Todd in his portrayal of Gibson in the 1955 film *The Dam Busters*. His contemporaries agreed that he possessed outstanding qualities as an airman; as a person, however, he was rather more complex than the *Boys' Own* depiction of Gibson the war hero might suggest. Air Marshal Harris was to confide in Cochrane that 'the Americans have spoiled Gibson', but it would appear senior commanders were late in reading Gibson's character. Despite his many fine qualities, Gibson was far from popular with the rank and file of the squadrons he served with. His indifference – and sometimes outright hostility – towards junior ranks particularly rankled. He also had a reputation as being a stickler for rules and regulations – some felt he had 'little man syndrome',* and did not appreciate his presence. These unfortunate traits were in evidence long before he achieved national celebrity in May 1943. As early as 1937, when he was a member of the Advanced Training Squadron, his behaviour as a companion had been marked down because of his rude and condescending behaviour towards ground crews. During his first posting to 83 Squadron he gained the epitaph 'Bumptious Bastard', while 106 Squadron later nicknamed him 'The Boy Emperor' and 'Arch Bastard'.

---

* Gibson was five feet six inches in height.

Such were the complexities of the man who arrived at the gates of RAF Coningsby on 4 August 1944 to take up his position – a posting which, in theory, would not allow him to fly operationally. During his staff preparation period at RAF East Kirby, Gibson had already slipped into a 630 Squadron Lancaster for a raid in July on a V-1 facility. It was clear that the progress of the Allies subsequent to the D-Day landings had a profound effect on Gibson's mood. With combat flying so deeply entrenched in his psyche, his impatience to return, however unreasonable a proposition, was to prove his downfall. Sergeant Ernie Groeger of 97 Squadron remembers Gibson walking into the Blue Bell Inn at Tattershall and declaring that from henceforth, it was an officers-only pub, and ordering all the non-commissioned men to leave. As well as causing a great deal of offence, not least to the airmen who served valiantly as Sergeants alongside fellow officers as equals, the incident was entirely outside Gibson's remit. What the publican thought of Gibson's intervention is unrecorded, but he is hardly likely to have looked favourably on the banishment of half of his customers, or to have allowed such a situation to continue.

Squadron Leader Frank Boyle, an Australian navigator who had already amassed over seventy operations, had stayed on with 627 Squadron. Part of his reasoning was to support Leo Devigne, whose regular navigator, Norman Lewis, had left after 100 operations. He understood the conflict of emotions between the draw of adrenalin-fuelled days of combat flying and the wish to retire and simply live. Boyle remembers encountering Gibson on a number of occasions, describing him as a 'lost soul'. On his final meeting in 627 Squadron's mess, it was clear Gibson was upset about the awarding of the Victoria Cross to Leonard Cheshire. Unlike his own award, Cheshire's had been given on the basis of a number of raids and longstanding service rather than a single action. Boyle recalled that Gibson expressed his dissatisfaction too forcibly, complaining that in the circumstances he should be given a bar to his VC. For fear that Gibson would create a scene in front of some of the junior officers, Boyle suggested that Gibson leave – which he did, to the relief of those present.

The 627 Squadron officers' mess at Woodhall Spa was a rustic affair compared to others, having none of the palatial splendour of the Petwood Hotel used by 617 Squadron. Because of the small size of the Squadron, the mess was often quiet, and Guy Gibson's unannounced visit one evening found Jock Walker and two Canadians propping up the bar. What was said is uncertain, but it appears Gibson tried to tear a strip off the men for not acknowledging his arrival in the room. Under the influence of a number of whiskies, the men took exception to being upbraided, and Gibson was unceremoniously bundled out and 'de-bagged' – the RAF tradition of removing a person's trousers. Jock Walker subsequently received fourteen days' detention on base for his actions, but the others escaped without further action, since Gibson was unable to identify them. Walker was known as a sensible and meticulous pilot rather than a hothead, but the incident demonstrates again Gibson's ability to rile others – to such an extent in this case that junior officers actually turned on him physically. A line had been drawn in the sand, and Gibson did not casually visit 627 Squadron's mess again.

Mönchengladbach, 19 September 1944

Four days before Walker and Oatley began operations together, they had made a training flight with a recently acquired Mosquito from Woodhall Spa to RAF Ford in West Sussex. During this simple daylight flight – one of a number of mostly unmemorable trips to prepare them for action – KB267 behaved as they expected. Painted in green and grey camouflage, the

Mosquito's fuselage and wings were adorned with black-and-white stripes to enable her to be recognized as an Allied aircraft.* Shortly after KB267 had arrived at Woodhall Spa, her squadron code letters 'AZ' were applied in dark red, to identify her as 627 Squadron, and 'E' to designate her individual place in the flight. On 15 August, the day after her flight with Walker and Oatley, Flight Lieutenant Oakley and Pilot Officer Crombie took KB267 on her first operational flight, to attack Deelen airfield in the Netherlands. Other than a slight problem with a target indicator failing to drop, which obliged them to make a second pass, the daylight operation proceeded smoothly. She would make frequent flights against the enemy, becoming a reliable and familiar workhorse. At this point, no one could have imagined that KB267 would become the Squadron's most famous aircraft – but for all the wrong reasons.

Tuesday 19 September 1944 dawned somewhat overcast over Lincolnshire; the airmen had to dodge the occasional light shower as they left their quarters to check the notice boards for the day's operation. In the planning office, all preparations since the early hours had been focused on attacking Bremen, with the more southerly targets of Mönchengladbach and its neighbouring borough of Rheydt as reserve targets. Throughout the day, however, meteorological reconnaissance aircraft reported that the weather in the north and east was poor. The low pressure currently affecting northern Europe was deepening, rendering a night-time raid on Bremen unviable. At 16.45 the target was changed; the men attending the briefing for the raid leaders and target markers were surprised to hear that Wing Commander Guy Gibson was to act as raid leader. Although Gibson had arguably been the first Master Bomber in his actions during the Dam Busters raid, he had

---

* Most Allied aircraft were hastily painted with stripes on the eve of D-Day, 5 June 1944.

not completed the rigorous training and assessment that others had undertaken before promotion to the role. He was *not* a Master Bomber in the strict sense, but in the way of seniority, no one could challenge his presence.

The raid plan presented seemed unusually complex; the target area was divided into three zones – red, yellow and green – with different aircraft assigned to each. It was difficult enough to orientate oneself when the boundary of the target area was indicated using a single colour – and communicating with the main bomber force was always a challenge – but this multi-coloured arrangement was more than a little perplexing. As the briefing commenced, it was emphasized that Gibson would be on hand to supervise progress and iron out any problems; in fact, the crews were beginning to suspect Gibson's influence behind what seemed to be an unhelpfully convoluted scheme. Although the division of the target area into different zones was only a moderate expansion of existing practice, those who had their doubts about Gibson felt things were being arranged so he could be seen as orchestrator-in-chief of a complex target-marking procedure – and thereby enjoy another moment of glory. They also knew that the base commander, Sharp, was away for the day; had Gibson perhaps taken advantage of his absence to insert himself into the raid plan at the last minute? There were no doubts as to his airmanship; he had recently flown one of 54 Base's Lockheed Lightings to observe a raid, but had not actively taken part in it. As a concession to Gibson's constant agitation for action, senior commanders prescribed that any flight Gibson made should avoid German-occupied areas as much as possible, but it was unclear whether they had actually forbidden him from flying in combat altogether. This restriction meant that rather than cutting across the lowlands of Holland, Gibson would have to take a longer flight route, taking him over north-eastern France, which was now in Allied hands.

627 Squadron would field nine Mosquitos, three per zone, loaded with the coloured markers designated. Gibson would take a tenth 627 Squadron Mosquito, KB213, to command the raid. At RAF Woodhall Spa news of the change of target came late in the day, setting ground crews working feverishly to prepare the aircraft, in particular to make sure the correct coloured indicators were in place. Although the flares were not as dangerous as standard bombs, the job of winching them up into the Mosquito's bomb bay required just as much care and attention to detail. Securings and switches had to be checked, fuel loads balanced and batteries charged. Gibson's aircraft would carry a mix of colours to allow him to re-mark any area of concern. The ground crews were proud of their work, and in the tradition of the Squadron, were kept informed of the night's plans.

Gibson arrived at Woodhall Spa at 16.30 in the company of Squadron Leader Jim Warwick to act as navigator. Warwick was a squadron navigational officer; he had completed his operational tours, and this was, in effect, a ground position. He not had not been expecting to fly. It appears word had circulated around RAF Coningsby that Gibson was looking for a navigator, and other Base 54 crew had made themselves scarce.* Gibson's friend Charles Owen, who had served two tours with 97 Squadron and now resided at Coningsby as a Master Bomber, had driven the pair over to 627 Squadron. On arrival, Gibson rejected the Mosquito allocated to him, KB213, and commandeered KB267, much to the irritation of its scheduled crew, Flight Lieutenants Mallender and Gaunt, who were 'bumped' off their prepared Mosquito and onto the rejected KB213. Superstitions played a significant role in the morale of aircrew, and a late change such as this could be interpreted

---

* Charles Owen's regular navigator, Don Bowes, was tipped off directly by Owen to avoid the mess that afternoon.

as a bad omen. On a practical level it was disappointing for Mallender and Gaunt because they had air-tested KB267 earlier in the day, and were comfortable in their minds that she was airworthy. Nor did the episode do much for Gibson's popularity with the ground crew, since they were required to rearrange the marker load to his precise requirements with little over an hour left before take-off.

What caused Gibson to reject KB213 remains a mystery, but it appears his mood was far from good immediately prior to take-off. Both aircraft were very similar, they were the same Mark of Mosquito, Mk BXX, and came from the same production run. Perhaps what made Gibson's ill-humoured manner stand out that day was that it clashed with 627 Squadron's *esprit de corps*. A pilot, even one occupying a position of seniority within the Squadron, would not normally reject an aircraft out of hand without explaining his reasoning. Gibson had flown only nine hours in a Mosquito, so it is possible he became distracted by an unfamiliar detail that turned his mind against KB213. It may be that Gibson's bad mood was occasioned by the stress of having to find a navigator, or by the atmosphere of palpable scepticism that attended the raid briefing. We will never know for certain, but it is possible that, deep down, Gibson knew he was about to overstep the mark in the conditions laid out for him by his senior officers. Charles Owen was next to feel Gibson's displeasure, as he tried to advise him on the best route out of the target. Owen had flown a similar route recently, as controller on a raid to Mönchengladbach on 10 September, but Gibson was adamant to the point of rudeness that he would fly the shortest route home at low level, despite this being in contravention of a key condition of his permission to fly. The conversation was still ongoing as Owen leant into the open door of the Mosquito while Gibson and Warwick strapped into Mosquito KB267. The argument with Owen, one of his best friends, was a further indication of Gibson's state of mind that evening.

As the late afternoon September light faded away, the shapes of the Mosquitos were still clearly visible at their dispersals at RAF Woodhall Spa when they started their engines. Each group of three aircraft, Green, Yellow and Red Force, would take off individually and strike the target within a few minutes of each other. Jock Walker and Ken Oatley, in the Yellow section, completed their final checks under the shielded orange cockpit bulbs. Their engines were already running, and the unmistakable smell of the warming aircraft mingled with the distinctive odour of heated dust emanating from the valves as the radio set was turned on. It was just one month since they had made their first operational flight, yet already the proximity of the propeller tips whirring at high speed within inches of the cockpit wall seemed normal rather than unnerving. The squadron members prided themselves on taking off on time – not only did it help set a positive pattern for the success of a raid, but just as importantly for the crews, it settled them into their routine.

With Mosquito KB345 fully primed, the ground crew bade Walker and Oatley good luck and slammed the crew door shut, making sure the handle was pressed home. They hoped that they would be the first ones to touch the door again on the aircraft's safe return. There were a few minutes for Walker and Oatley to lift their heads from their instruments and watch the other aircraft waiting for the signal to move forward. Gibson and the three other Mosquitos that made up Red Force were the first to be marshalled out onto the perimeter track to taxi round to the runway threshold. The Red Force was led by Squadron Leader Ronnie Churcher,* who would act as deputy raid controller. A former 619 Squadron Lancaster pilot who had joined 627 in July 1944, Churcher's broad smile and pencil-thin RAF moustache had become a familiar sight

---

* Churcher would later become a highly trusted pilot on the Queen's Flight in the 1950s.

around the Squadron. His navigator, Pilot Officer Harry Willis, would also bear significant responsibility that night, since he was tasked with correctly identifying the railway marshalling yard at Rheydt. Churcher and Willis's Mosquito, DZ640, left Woodhall Spa precisely on time at 19.52.

The remaining six Mosquitos left in short order in a mixture of Green and Yellow Force. Walker and Oatley were airborne at 20.04 and quickly broke through the massed darkness of the grey clouds that had processed slowly across Lincolnshire all that day. The last remnants of the fading day greeted them as the deep-blue clarity of the air above came into sight. Stars were already glittering as the Mosquitos struck out towards Germany at 10,000 feet. Gradually, as the light receded, the accompanying aircraft – spaced out to avoid collisions – began to disappear into the blackness. Ahead, the main force of bombers were making their lumbering progress towards the target. While Walker and Oatley might glimpse some of the bombing force during the raid, ostensibly, they were alone in their own world of charts and stopwatch.

At around 21.35 the Avro Lancasters from 83 Squadron, part of the Pathfinders, began their run into Mönchengladbach. They had shaken off the undercast some time before, and deep in the darkness, 15,000 feet below, the city waited to see if the approaching raiders would attack or fly over. To this end, the searchlights remained switched off, making it necessary for the bombers to identify their target with H2S radar. 83 Squadron were covering the Green and Yellow Sectors over Mönchengladbach, and 97 Squadron the Red sector over Rheydt. Both squadrons began to drop their white illuminating flares; as dozens of glaring stars appeared, the city appeared naked under their ephemeral light. The first inkling of a problem was the very weak VHF radio contact with Gibson as raid controller. Some did not hear him at all, and those who managed to catch the orders given did so only with some difficulty.

Within five minutes of the first flares beginning to descend, the high Pathfinder force heard the Mosquito markers radio in their 'Tally Ho' announcement of their diving attack. Squadron Leader Hatcher of 83 Squadron saw the Green and Yellow markers down by 20.42, but still no Red. Walker and Oatley had dived on the target from 2,000 feet, recovering at 600 feet after following down Devigne and Boyle, who had marked first. When the main force arrived and bombs began to drop there were still no Red markers showing, and as the Pathfinders circled to see if further flares would be required, Gibson's communications continued to be very quiet and crackly. 97 Squadron heard Gibson's command to re-illuminate the Red sector – clearly this order had not been followed. Ironically, two of the Red-marking Mosquitos had been circling since 20.30, but were following strict protocol in allowing the Red Force leader, Churcher, to mark first, as had been planned. In other raids the markers would dive on their target as soon as they were sure of its location – competing to be the first to mark the target. The obsessive orderliness and inexperience of Gibson was becoming apparent; rather than sticking pedantically to the planned order of events, he should have commanded his available Red markers to drop as soon as it became clear there had been a delay. By now, nearly fifteen minutes had elapsed since the Red sector should have been marked, and the main bombing force had arrived. In the absence of markers and with a lack of any communication, they began their attack of their own volition. But it soon became clear to Gibson that some of this bombing was inaccurate, and was threatening to derail the entire course of the raid.

By this point in its development, aerial warfare had become extraordinarily complex. With hundreds of men and machines above the target, the number of component parts involved in a large operation could run into millions. Any operation was a risky and potentially fragile undertaking, which could

– conceivably – be compromised by the malfunctioning of a single, apparently insignificant, component. This was certainly the case with the Mönchengladbach raid of 19 September. Not for the first time, an exhaust manifold stud had sheared from a 627 Squadron Mosquito engine, causing the short pipe of the exhaust stub to blow off and take with it the anti-glare shield that covered the bank of exhausts. That it had happened to the DZ640 carrying Churcher and Willis as Deputy Controlling Mosquito and lead Red marker was immensely inconvenient. Churcher, blinded by the light from the unshielded exhausts on the port side and deafened by the noise and vibration of the errant engine, was forced to shut it down and feather the prop. Determined to press his attack home, he reached Gibson on the VHF radio and called in his problem, while assuring Gibson he would make it to the target area. His first marking dive was, by his own admission, unsatisfactory, and he repeated the manoeuvre five minutes later. Marker No.3, KB122 with Brown and Cowan, powered in next to back up the Red marking, but Gibson was unhappy. In his mind the location was still not right and, rather than risk the third marking Mosquito reinforcing the error, he declared that he was going in to mark the target himself. He ordered 627 Squadron's Hanlon and Tice in DZ650, who had been circling the target the longest, to return home. But it appears that Gibson's marker failed to drop; although his voice remained calm as he gave instructions to the bombing force, it was evident that the multi-colour marking plan had sown confusion.

Precisely which of Gibson's radio calls was the last to be heard from him is uncertain. Ken Oatley did not hear anything further beyond Gibson's message that he was going to place his marker. Later, a crew from 61 Squadron claimed they had heard Gibson say he had a damaged engine. However, as the quality of the VHF channel was poor that night, it may be that this call came from Churcher, the Deputy Controller. The raid was complete by 21.58; it is assumed Gibson remained in the area until that time.

Residents of the city of Steenbergen in the southern Netherlands observed an aircraft circling at around 22.30 with the cockpit apparently illuminated. Shortly afterwards the engines cut out and the sound of an impact was heard. The plane debris was located at first light. With little left of Mosquito KB267 and few human remains, the Germans initially believed only one person had been present in the Mosquito at the time of the crash, leading them to conclude that the other crew member had bailed out. Jim Warwick was identified by his dog tag, but Gibson was only identified by a sock tag after the gruesome discovery of a third hand had prompted further investigation. The local deputy mayor, Mr Herbers, insisted that the men be given a proper funeral, and a horse-drawn hearse was hired from nearby Halsteren. A cross was erected over the grave with Jim Warwick's full rank and name. At this point, they did not know the rank of the other man, simply inscribing the name 'Guy Gibson' underneath. Later, when Gibson's identity was confirmed, a new cross was erected detailing his rank and decorations.

Had the pilot not been a national hero, his loss would have been consigned to history with little examination of the circumstances. Ken Oatley and the cadre of 627 Squadron later came to the conclusion that as both Gibson and Warwick had little experience on the Mosquito (indeed, Warwick had never flown in one until that night), they had been unable to locate the fuel cocks located behind the pilot's seat. This meant that the critical switch-over to their reserve tanks – necessary at this advanced stage in their flight – was not completed in time, causing the engines to become starved of fuel. Perhaps the only problem with this arresting theory was that by 22.30 Gibson was 70 miles*

* Steenbergen is less than 100 miles from Mönchengladbach.

behind where he should have been at the time, which suggests he had experienced mechanical problems prior to the crash. In 2011 reports circulated that rear gunner Sergeant Bernard McCormack of 61 Squadron believed he had accidentally shot down Gibson over Steenbergen when he was approached by what he believed was a Ju 88. Although McCormack had died in 1992, his confession to his wife seems at first to tally with records of the time, including that of another Lancaster crew, who witnessed the action and saw a red flare burning at the crash site. Even in the clarity of this account, some doubts remain. Gibson had declared his intention to fly the return leg at low level, which makes his appearance at the Lancaster's altitude of 11,000 feet puzzling. The absence of any mention of the action in the crew report of Lancaster LM729 that night also casts doubt on McCormack's later memory. The third possibility is that KB267 was damaged either in the diving attack at Mönchengladbach or subsequently as Gibson circled the target – which would account for his late arrival at Steenbergen.

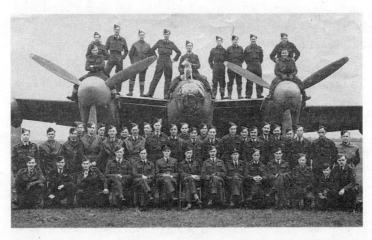

'Mosquito Men' of 627 Squadron. Ken Oatley is front row, far left.

Whatever misfortune had befallen Gibson and Warwick, the feeling in 627 Squadron was that Gibson had lost them a perfectly good aeroplane – a brutally clinical reflection of his unpopularity within the Squadron. It had become clear that he had not followed instructions to fly home across France, and that the crash that killed him and the unfortunate Warwick was ultimately down to his headstrong nature. Of course, the outcome of his actions could have been very different. Had the Mönchengladbach raid been successful and he had returned home safely, it might have been hailed as the birth of a groundbreaking new technique. Nevertheless, Gibson's superiors would still have insisted that his operational flying days were numbered. The drama and mystery of Gibson's last flight has had the unfortunate effect of obscuring the significant role played by 627 Squadron as target-marking Pathfinders; all too often, 627 is remembered for being the squadron from which Guy Gibson borrowed his Mosquito.

The strength of a Mosquito crew was their ability to work together, honing their skills to understand their aeroplane and bring out the best facets of its performance. It was an element that Gibson and Warwick lacked on their ill-fated flight – and a critical factor in their loss. Ken Oatley was still learning about Jock Walker and his single-minded attitude to flying. When they were over the target, he seemed to be oblivious to all other distractions; while Oatley noticed rising flak or the drift of searchlights, Walker's attention would be entirely focused on the target – a characteristic that earned him the nickname 'Mad' Jock Walker. Once he was certain of the target, it seemed he would happily tip the aircraft into the dive without any consideration of the attendant risks. However, the epithet was not recognized by his family, who remember him as diligent and meticulous – essential qualities for his pre-war trade as an apprentice plasterer. Walker was a believer in good planning and preparation – a man disinclined to be distracted in the pursuit of perfection.

It was noticeable too that even on those occasions when Ken was unsure of their position – a situation that, he confesses, arose on a number of occasions – Jock Walker seemed to know where to go. It was not a case of his having an innate 'homing pigeon' instinct, but rather was down to the punctiliousness of his preparation. Walker had good reason to be cautious, since navigational problems were all too common during operations, and he knew that in combat he might even lose his navigator to enemy fire. It wasn't that Walker didn't trust Oatley; his extreme wariness was born of an incident that took place during his first operational sortie on 26 February 1941, and which nearly cost him his life.

At the time, Walker was stationed at RAF Dishforth in North Yorkshire, one of the most northerly of the rapidly expanding group of airfields that dotted the length of the eastern side of England, from Northumberland to Suffolk. He was posted with his crew to 51 Squadron flying the Armstrong Whitworth Whitley, a twin-engined medium bomber that shared some design characteristics with the later Avro Lancaster, but was smaller and more cramped than the heavy bomber. Walker was tasked to fly his first operation with an experienced crew as second pilot, and took off from Dishforth bound for Cologne at 19.01 hours. After forty-five minutes, while over the North Sea, the captain, Sergeant Tom Wall, decided to abort the mission and turn for home because of a generator failure. In the absence of navigational aids like H2S, which was not introduced until 1943, it was far from straightforward to calculate their exact position in the darkness of a February night. As they passed the Yorkshire coast and drew closer to Dishforth, the weather below them was poor – a common problem in this part of northern England. When Whitley T4148 lost height and descended into a bank of cloud, they hoped they would break free from it and would be able to identify the Vale of York below and see a clear path home to their airfield. Unfortunately, the navigator had miscalculated their position and flown 20 miles off course. They had overshot all three of the airfields where they could have landed – RAF Topcliffe, Leeming and Dishforth – and were headed towards the high ground of the Yorkshire Dales to the west.

In the gloom, an expanse of snow-capped moorland loomed up to meet them. Whether Tom Wall had time to react is unknown, but the Whitley struck the ground heavily and slid to a halt on Scrafton Moor. The deep snow had saved the crew from the worst effects of the impact, but some of the incendiaries in the bomb bay ignited. Their first instinct was to pile snow on them to prevent further fire, which they successfully accomplished. It was perhaps a pointless exercise, though, because the Whitley was damaged beyond repair, her underside ripped away and her back broken.

The shock of the crash had been huge; the blazing incendiaries had temporarily illuminated their immediate surroundings, but once the fire died down they found themselves marooned in the blackness of the moorland night, with no map and no idea where they should go. The crew worried that despite the protection of their flying kit, the cold could finish them off if they didn't walk in the right direction. There was little hope that their accident had been seen or heard; their rescue was very much in their own hands. The silence of the vast moor around them closed in, making their isolation seem even more acute. The landscape was immensely beautiful but also terrifying. They stumbled through the deep snow for some time in a disoriented fashion before descending the long slope of the moor in the hope that it would yield some sign of civilization. Eventually, thanks to the faintest glimmer of light escaping a black-out curtain, they found a farmhouse, whose occupants took them in. The operations room at RAF Dishforth did not learn of the accident until 07.52 the next morning, and it would be 17.00 hours before the crew arrived at Masham police station for transportation back to base. They had learnt a hard lesson, but the accident had not been as costly as it could have been. Navigational miscalculation led many a crew to their deaths in the high ground of the north of England.

Jock Walker relished the precision of 627's attacks, which the Squadron was becoming highly proficient at. Even in the scanty descriptions of operations made by crews on their return, it is possible to detect that note of pride in a job well done. In the operation against Bremen on the night of 6 October 1944, the target was marked by five Mosquitos – all of which dropped their indicators within four minutes of each other. In the rapidity of the action, some crews saw that their markers were off target and communicated this to their colleagues. When Bartley and Mitchell radioed that their indicator was off-centre, Walker and Oatley in 'Marker No.6' were able to remedy the problem with more accurate marking.

Completing a 2,000-foot shallow dive above the target, Walker and Oatley were confident they had hit the 'pickle barrel'. The squadron intelligence officer recorded Jock Walker's account of the raid as follows:

Backed up Marker No.2 whose markers dropped 100 yards S of M/P. My markers fell on A/P. [Aiming Point]

The raid on Bremen was a textbook lesson in how low-level marking was meant to work. By keeping the bombers within the bounds of the marked area, the attackers ensured that they inflicted the intended level of damage to the installations, and that it was a concentrated devastation that would make repair difficult. One of the myths that attaches to Bomber Command operations is that bombs were scattered on parts of German cities that lay outside the target area, without regard for the human consequences; in reality, it was not uncommon for bombers to be ordered to cease their attack once the controller was satisfied the target was covered.

While much of the docks and the old city centre of Bremen were destroyed in this raid, the targeting was still limited. Aerial strategy had moved on from Arthur Harris's thinking ten months before. Harris's hope had been that a relentless campaign of saturation bombing would break German civilian morale, but he had underestimated the degree to which Nazi ideology and totalitarian methods of control had permeated and brainwashed German society. After D-Day, Allied strategy focused on causing maximum disruption to the enemy's supply chains. This could only be achieved via a gradual process of strangulation rather than through some sudden, decisive military breakthrough. A small town on a transport route could be disabled in a single raid by blowing up a bridge or tunnel, but crippling the entire infrastructure of a large city was a much harder proposition.

After a significant attack, Bremen and other similar urban centres would be down for a while, but materials would then begin to move into and out of the city again and, once the Allies saw this happening, the bombers would need to return.

The bakery in Frome continued serving the quiet Somerset community throughout the war. Ken Oatley's father, James, knew only a little of his son's life in the Royal Air Force, but enough to know he was in danger. The high rate of casualties within Bomber Command was not publicly known until the end of the war, but as a Doughboy in the First World War, James knew the cost of conflict. For the baker's son to have risen from modest roots to serve as a navigator in an elite RAF Pathfinder squadron was remarkable enough, but Ken was not the only noteworthy product of the Oatley family business. His second cousin Charles would achieve distinction in a rather different field, but one that also allowed him to make a significant contribution to Britain's war effort.

Radar technology evolved from the work of a number of great scientists. Equations developed by the Scottish physicist James Clerk Maxwell in 1862–64 provided the basis for the theory of electromagnetic radiation, and twenty-two years later the German physicist Heinrich Hertz conducted groundbreaking experiments with electromagnetic waves. In 1899, Guglielmo Marconi, who had studied Hertz's work and later developed the world's first working radio, noticed that his radio waves were bouncing back towards his transmitter when they struck hard objects. This intriguing phenomenon became the subject of much research; by the 1930s, eight countries, including all the combatants in the coming war, had their own secret radar programmes. In Britain, scientists from Cambridge University played a key role in designing Chain Home radar, a network whose first five masts, covering the Thames Estuary, were set up in 1937. Following an initial grant of £60,000 in government funding in 1935, the expansion of radar research and invention continued apace. By the time war broke out the number of Chain Home radar stations had risen to twenty-one.

William Oatley was correct in his assessment of his son's abilities, and in his conviction that Charles's future did not lie in the bakery. But Charles would nonetheless benefit from the profitability of the family business, which made it possible for him to receive his secondary education at Bedford Modern School, from where he went on to study at St John's College, Cambridge. He worked as a lecturer in physics and electronic engineering at King's College, London, for twelve years before the war. Given the secrecy surrounding radar research and development, the men hired for such sensitive work were recruited discreetly from trusted sources. John Cockcroft was a contemporary of Charles's at St John's, and had pioneered experiments in nuclear fission in 1932* before becoming Assistant Director of Scientific Research in the Ministry of Supply. In 1939 he wrote to Oatley inviting him to join a group of scientists to assist with the war effort.

Working at the Air Defence Research and Development Establishment (ADRDE), Charles created test equipment that improved the functioning of the Home Chain radar system, sat on many influential technical committees and served as Deputy to Cockcroft. In 1943, he took over the leadership of ADRDE and its 4,000 staff when Cockcroft moved to the Canadian Chalk River Nuclear Project. Despite the huge responsibilities he bore, Charles remained at heart an academic rather than an industrial manager. He loved university life and tended to downplay his wartime achievements. But men like Oatley, while choosing to stay out of the limelight, worked with quiet dedication and brilliance to create the radar equipment that thousands of servicemen used and to which many of them owed their lives.

Although Charles Oatley did not contribute directly to the Mosquito story, his work in the development of radar had an immeasurable impact on the war effort. Home defence radar enabled the outgoing and incoming bomber streams to be plotted and, where necessary, provided them with navigational assistance. Although radio silence was requisite, the emergency radio channel 'Darky' enabled direct contact with lost or damaged aircraft, saving many lives in the process. H2S radar sets incorporated in the bombers enabled a view of the terrain below and introduced a level of autonomy and accuracy in their bombing that greatly increased their potency. Tellingly,

* In 1951 Cockcroft was awarded the joint Nobel Prize in Physics for his work in nuclear fission.

at the end of hostilities Charles returned to academia, where his wartime service became only a footnote to his life's work. He was professor of electrical engineering at Cambridge from 1960 to 1971. Knighted in 1974, Sir Charles Oatley is remembered as the man who, with his research department, invented the electron microscope, and was feted by the scientific community until his passing at the age of ninety-two in 1996. When Ken Oatley met Charles after the war, the scientist was characteristically reserved about his achievements – but both men owed much to the bakery in Frome.

10

TRIUMPH AND TRAGEDY

As the nights drew in and the evenings became cooler in the autumn of 1944, RAF airmen could sense that once again a winter at war would be soon upon them. An ambitious Allied operation, Market Garden, involving combined British and US airborne forces, had failed in its objective of securing a bridge-head over the River Rhine in the German-held Netherlands – one that would allow a rapid advance into northern Germany. Allied forces had swept north across Holland, liberating Eindhoven and Nijmegen, but their advance was halted by fierce German resistance at Arnhem in late September. Field Marshal Bernard Montgomery's hopes of fully liberating the Netherlands and ending the war by Christmas had been cruelly crushed. The realization that the Allies would have to push into Germany at a slower rate raised fears of getting bogged down in a war of attrition that could lead to an unsatisfactory peace agreement. For Bomber Command it would be yet another seasonal trial, for although the night had become their friend, the winters – with their potentially lethal mix of wind, snow and freezing temperatures – were the very devil.

By the autumn, whatever doubts that had been expressed in the diving marking technique had been dispelled. Their record through this period was exemplary, but as in all operational units, it came at a cost – even if casualties were less than had been anticipated. Unlike their brethren on Lancasters, losses among Mosquito crews were infrequent, but nonetheless pain-

John Herriman at the controls of a Mosquito.

ful. The Australians Eric Arthur and his pilot John Herriman had arrived at RAF Woodhall Spa on 6 October. Unlike some of their colleagues in the squadron, they were not seasoned veterans who had beaten the odds to make second or even third tours with Bomber Command, but had stepped into their roles directly from training.

Making the long sea journey from Australia began their adventure of a lifetime, but the reality of a war-gripped Britain soon tempered any overenthusiasm.

They had served their time at 1655 Mosquito Training Unit* at RAF Warboys in Huntingdonshire, but still had more specific training to do at Woodhall Spa before they would be ready for operational flying. They flew every day, carrying out hour after hour of dive-bombing practice on the Wainfleet ranges, until the Mosquito began to feel like an extension of their very selves.

Eric was left in no doubt as to the risks of flying when he was called from his duties on 23 October to act as a pall bearer at the funeral of one of his colleagues. He had completed the morning

---

* 1655 MTU was part of 8 Group but also served 5 Group in preparing Mosquito crews for pathfinding.

round of dive-bombing at Wainfleet and found it a strange way to finish the day. He made sure his uniform was pristine and applied an extra rub of polish to his shoes; once his colleagues had inspected him and told him he would pass muster, he took a deep breath and stepped out into the autumn afternoon. There was some brief pre-funeral instruction on his duties, but all too soon he found himself standing by the graveside staring at the casket of Flying Officer Cornell. He might have expected to have

Eric Arthur braving the cold in a sheepskin waistcoat, winter of 1944–45.

served alongside this airman in the coming months, shared debriefings and perhaps a drink at the bar, but instead he was overcome by an overwhelming feeling of disconnection.

A few weeks earlier, on the Mosquito training course, a decision had needed to be made as to which pilot to fly with. Two pilots, John Herriman and Flying Officer Stan Reeder, a twenty-three-year-old from East Ham, were looking for navigators. Eric had become firm friends with fellow navigator and Aussie Bob Bolton, so the two men tossed a coin to decide which navigator would go with which pilot. As it turned out, Eric joined John Herriman, while Bolton went with Reeder. On 12 October, only six days after Eric had arrived at Woodhall Spa, Reeder and Bolton failed to return from Berlin with 608 Squadron Mosquito KB348: thus did a flipped coin have the power of life and death for the young men of Bomber Command.*

---

* Reeder and Bolton are buried at the CWGC Berlin 1939–45 cemetery.

The circumstances that had led to the latest untimely loss to 627 Squadron were, sadly, not uncommon to all units, both training and operational. Flight Lieutenant Bland and Flying Officer Cornell had left Woodhall Spa for a practice-bombing sortie to Wainfleet on 19 October. They were both experienced men who had flown together operationally, but 627's successes were obtained only by persistent training flights. Their Mosquito, KB215, had just entered the shallow diving attack on the range, but as the drop button was pressed the aircraft was shaken by an explosion. The cockpit filled with noxious smoke, and it was immediately clear that the practice bomb had detonated in the bomb bay, in all probability detonating other ordnance carried on board. Instinctively, Bland pulled back on his joystick – the first priority in such an emergency was to gain height. KB215 began a desperate climb, but its power seemed to be seeping away – the result of the failure of the spluttering starboard engine. The Mosquito hung in the air before the wing dropped and it went into a slow spiral dive. It was time to leave the crippled aeroplane. Escape drills had revealed that the Mosquito was a difficult aeroplane to leave quickly, with many attempts taking as long as thirty seconds. Jettisoning the crew door, Cornell tried to push himself out, but his thickset build amplified his struggle with his flying suit and the small cockpit opening. Deciding that there was no time to wait for Cornell to get free, Bland pushed out the top escape hatch and forced himself upwards into the slipstream. Falling free, he pulled his ripcord and was relieved to feel the yank of the parachute lines.

Reginald Cornell never escaped from the hatch, and his body was thrown free only by the impact of KB215 with the ground. The thirty-three-year-old from Forest Hill in London had been only two days away from taking leave, when he would have seen his wife and five-month-old baby daughter. Instead he joined others in a special plot in Coningsby's cemetery, which is within touching distance of the airfield perimeter. For the young men of the funeral party, once they had shown their respects to the deceased, it was important to shake themselves free of the shadow of loss that was all too close a companion in their daily lives. For this reason, when the opportunity arose, they would celebrate wildly, letting off steam in a series of antics that in peacetime would have been seen as irresponsible.

All those who survived their service with 627 Squadron had stories to tell of near misses where they too might have joined the silent lines of white headstones – but also of the times of carefree inebriation that punctuated their lives of extreme danger.

Air Vice Marshal Don Bennett's dire warnings that low-level marking attacks would be suicidal may have been overstated but, as time went by, there was evidence that the Germans were finding ways of countering the threat posed by the Pathfinder Mosquitos. Of particular concern to 627 Squadron was the intensity of the Germans' light flak gunfire; although the majority of shells fired were wide of their mark, the Squadron was still suffering damage – and some losses. In September 1944, four aircraft* had failed to return, and with a complement of sixteen aircraft in the Squadron, this was a proportionately high figure. Among this unfortunate few were Flight Lieutenants Harry 'Buzz' Brown and Hugh Cowan, who were shot down directly over their target on 28 September. Targeting a rail workshop near Kaiserslautern, Brown and Cowan, flying KB366, called in 'Tally Ho' to begin their dive seconds before Devigne and Boyle, who were designated as the 'Number 1' markers, began theirs. It was all part of the friendly rivalry between crews to be the first to mark the target. Boyle was later to recount that it was this change of position that ensured Brown and Cowan were shot down, rather than him and Devigne. Watching as the Mosquito

---

* A figure that includes Guy Gibson's flight of 19 September.

headed into the mêlée of tracer shells ahead of them, Devigne and Boyle had a clear view of the end of KB366: 'He was hit by the flak cross-fire and we saw him crash – ploughing along the ground with an awesome display of exploding coloured TIs; we followed him down and marked the target as he exploded,' Boyle wrote in *At First Sight* in 1991. There was no doubt in the crew's mind that the crash was not survivable; knowing the area would be obliterated by bombs within minutes, they had no hesitation in pressing on with their attack.

That night would also see the loss of Flying Officers Matherson and Fitzpatrick in Mosquito KB512. Part of a second flight of six Mosquitos heading for Karlsruhe, they came down near King's Lynn on the outbound journey only twenty-four minutes after take-off. Fortunately, as with many similar incidents, the aircraft crashed without inflicting any civilian casualties in a field at Tilney All Saints. Bob Burrows, a schoolboy who had already witnessed the flaming destruction of a Halifax bomber close by with the loss of all on board, went into the field with a friend after the salvage crew had departed and collected pieces of Perspex.* Mosquitos had the reputation of being hard to fly after a technical failure and, once again, this seems to have played a part in the incident.

Unlike earlier periods in the war, when good news was in short supply, the closing weeks of 1944 brought significant victories to cheer the British public, even if progress on the Western Front had slowed. On 13 November, the Lancasters of 617 Squadron dropped 'Tallboy' bombs on the battleship *Tirpitz*, scoring two direct hits and causing the ship to capsize. The destruction of Germany's most powerful warship was the culmination of four years of repeated British attempts to put the *Tirpitz* out of action. It would take three attacks

---

* Perspex from the aircraft glazing was collected by children, who found it could be melted down to make rings and other trinkets.

by 9 and 617 Squadrons with the 'Tallboy' bomb to finally destroy the battleship.

The first, on 15 September, involved ferrying Lancasters to Yagodnik airfield near Archangel in the northern USSR, which was to be used as a temporary base for the latest raid on the *Tirpitz* – then at anchor in Kaafjord in the far north of German-occupied Norway. The attack itself produced only one notable hit to the German battleship's bows, but the damage was sufficient for the Kriegsmarine to move *Tirpitz* south from Kaafjord to Tromsø for repairs, and put the battleship within reach of raiders from Scotland. A second attack by 9 and 617 Squadron on 29 October produced no hits, but finally on 12 November all the conditions were perfect for an effective attack on *Tirpitz* at its anchorage near Tromsø, and the 'Beast' was finally vanquished.

One of the 617 Squadron pilots who took part in the *Tirpitz* raid of 29 October was another Australian, Bill Carey, who had been at Woodhall Spa since April 1944. Shortly before the *Tirpitz* raid, Eric Arthur of 627 Squadron, who had arrived at the base only in September, experienced something of a surprise one evening when he wandered into the bar of the nearby Abbey Lodge Hotel – a place frequented by crews of both 617 and 627 Squadrons. There, drinking at the bar, was a familiar face from home. Bill Carey's family were in the hotel trade and lived just a few hundred metres from Eric's home at Mount Gambier in South Australia. Bill was a little startled to see Eric, and joked, 'What are you doing here? Are you following me around?' By the time *Tirpitz* was sunk, Bill Carey and his crew were no longer around to celebrate – but their story has a happier ending than many.

On the second *Tirpitz* raid on 29 October Carey's Lancaster, carrying a single precious 'Tallboy' bomb, was hit by flak, which disabled a starboard engine and punctured his fuel tanks. Bill was determined not to give up; he brought the Lancaster

Eric Arthur (second from right) with his ground crew.

around on six runs before dropping his bomb. Seeing that he had no hope of reaching home in a damaged aircraft with a diminishing fuel supply, Carey turned his Lancaster towards neutral Sweden. The aircraft was hit again by Swedish flak, which put out the hydraulics and caused the undercarriage to drop. Carey had no choice but to put the stricken aeroplane down on two engines on a frozen bog near Porjus in Swedish Lapland. Bill suffered a knee injury during the crash-landing. The remaining members of the crew were safe, although their hopes of a swift return to Britain were dashed as they had to serve a period of internment with their Swedish hosts.

The capsizing of the *Tirpitz* was an event for 617 Squadron to celebrate. Since 627 Squadron resided in close proximity at Woodhall Spa, they were included in the festivities. The celebration involved a chicken dinner, and relied in no small part on the men 'scavenging' the main course. In a rural location, the requisite fowl were not difficult to find – all that was required was a quick hop over Woodhall Spa's fence onto the neighbouring farmland. The birds they took were probably older, egg-laying hens, and their meat was probably a bit tough – although this was unlikely to have occurred to the chicken-snatching airmen, many of whom were city boys and unaccustomed to farming life.

A short time after the celebration dinner had taken place, some of the local farmers approached 617 Squadron's commanding officer, Wing Commander James Tait, and expressed concern that 'foxes' seemed to be 'a bit more active than usual'. The C/O made clear to the men that the missing chickens had to be replaced. Thanks to the combined efforts of Arthur, Herriman and others, more than enough chickens were found and returned to the farmers around Woodhall Spa. Certain farmers further afield were less than happy to find that 'foxes' had been active on their land as well.

Cycling through the busy streets of Oslo, the young man looked like hundreds of others commuting back and forth from work. He wore a flat cap with a tweed jacket and trousers and, when the weather demanded, a long woollen overcoat with scarf tucked into the collar. On his bicycle, its chain clicking gently in time with his pedalling, Gunnar Sønsteby was able to negotiate the smallest side streets and back lanes just as quickly as in a motor car.

With 100,000 German troops occupying his country, backed up by a force of Nazi-inspired Norwegian police, checkpoints were frequent, but he passed through each unmolested. His demeanour gave nothing away – no widening of the eyes or nervous shuffle – he was a master at playing the 'grey man'. Sønsteby's cool, emotionless manner had enabled him to evade capture for four years. He was a man with no name – or to be precise, a man with more than thirty names. He was adept at forging the signature of Karl Marthinsen (the hated police minister in Vidkun Quisling's puppet government), and could adopt multiple identities. He rarely slept in the same place for two nights, passing through a complex network of helpers and moving constantly to keep his pursuers guessing.

Agent 24, as he was known to the Special Operations Executive (SOE), was a man of extraordinary abilities who led a significant part of the resistance movement, Norwegian Independent Company 1. As a unit formed for sabotage, it was one of the most successful such entities of the Second World War, completing numerous operations with cold efficiency.* But such actions inevitably provoked severe responses from the occupying Germans, and the constant stream of arrests and executions weighed heavily on the consciences of members of the resistance. Gunnar's father was held as a hostage for nearly two years by the Gestapo, although ironically they were unaware of the level of activities Sønsteby was involved in until late in the war, or that he was the shadowy figure behind so much resistance activity. Despite the shock of the raid on the Victoria Terrasse in 1942,† the building had continued to be used as a Gestapo interrogation and torture facility. By December 1944, Sønsteby was carrying a grenade with him at all times – he was determined that in the event of his capture he would commit suicide rather than risk betraying his comrades. Some of those taken by the Gestapo had been his close friends, known to him from his high school years, and had formed the backbone of a close-knit resistance group. They did not fear

* These operations included the assassination of Karl Marthinsen on 8 February 1945.
† See Chapter 1. The Mosquito raid of 25 September 1942 by 105 Squadron led by Squadron Leader George Parry.

death, but were anxious that they might break under torture. Sønsteby and the SOE were convinced that the time was right for another strike at the building at the heart of the Gestapo's operations in Oslo.

Despite the mixed fortunes of the first attack on the Victoria Terrasse, there were reasons to believe the RAF and their force of Mosquitos were now more experienced in the capabilities of their aircraft and the lethal firepower it could deliver. On 18 February 1944 an attack on the prison at Amiens in northern France by Mosquitos from two squadrons, 464 and 487, had destroyed the guard quarters and breached the walls, allowing 255 prisoners – including many men condemned to be executed – to escape. More than 100 prisoners died in the raid, and many of those who escaped were recaptured, but the raid had shown the potency of the Mosquito at low level.

On 31 October Mosquitos from 140 Wing attacked a barrack block close to Aarhus University in Denmark with pinpoint accuracy. The Danish resistance estimated 150–200 German troops, including Gestapo staff, were killed. Although the figure produced later by the German authorities was only 59 killed, with casualties including 39 Gestapo personnel, it was still a large enough number to have a negative impact on the German operation in the city. The role of the Mosquito in weakening the grip of Nazi administrations in occupied countries was ongoing. Although a single raid might not achieve huge results, the effect on the resistance movements was to instil them with confidence that they were not alone in their efforts.

Oslo, 31 December 1944

As the Christmas period approached, the airmen of 627 Squadron sensed that a special operation was being planned. Day-bombing practice in formation had started as early as

28 November, and after weeks of rehearsal it seemed certain 'a show' was in the offing. On 16 December the Germans mounted a surprise counter-attack through the deeply forested Belgian and Luxembourg Ardennes, taking advantage of atrocious weather conditions that carpeted most of Europe in deep snow and grounded the Allies' superior air forces. 627 Squadron knew that they were unlikely to be called on – even once the weather improved – since they were not an army close-support unit. But it was a period of uncertainty, and all that daytime bombing practice made them wonder nevertheless whether their target might have some close connection with what was to be called the 'Battle of the Bulge'.

Ken Oatley remembers the days of preparation and their certainty that something unusual was coming. Although an operation seemed only days away, he and Jock Walker were sent on leave, as was one of the lead marking crews, Bill Topper and Vic Davies. This fuelled speculation that the secrecy of the mission – whatever it might be – had been compromised, and that the sudden granting of furlough to four squadron members was all part of a ploy to put watchers off the scent.

Ken Oatley was happy with his fourteen days' leave, not least because he had a wedding to prepare for. The wedding was his own, for he was engaged to Irene Browning, an eighteen-year-old WAAF whom he had met in September. Ken's father, James, was very much against the union, feeling that Irene was not of the right social standing for his son. A single photograph and the fact that the young parachute packer had been brought up on a council estate were sufficient evidence for him to conclude that Irene was not good enough for Ken.

It was ironic that James took this attitude; this was a man, after all, who had once been a Kansas cowboy and lived in a sod-covered cellar, but the success of the Frome bakery had instilled in him a strong sense that he had enhanced his social standing, and he was anxious that his son should not throw this away. Such was the rift between them that James declared he would sell the bakery – something he held true to, although the two were later reconciled and set up a very successful bakery business in Northampton after the war.

Those remaining at Woodhall Spa flew many operations over the Christmas and New Year period. There was no seasonal holiday for them – nor, in the wider infantry war, was there any let-up in the intensity of the fighting. The Wehrmacht had already made their intentions clear in throwing 406,000 men into Belgium in the intense counter-attack of the 'Battle of the Bulge'. In northern Italy, where the Germans were desperate to hold the Gothic Line – the major line of defence that stretched from the Tuscan coast south of La Spezia to Pesaro on the Adriatic – a joint Italian and German force attacked the American 5th Army near Lucca in the Battle of Garfagnana of 26–28 December. They made initial gains, but Major-General Dudley Russell's Indian Division arrived to reinforce the Americans and turn the advance.

On 30 December, as the German 5th Panzer Army renewed its attacks on Bastogne in western Belgium, the crews of 627 Squadron finally learned what was to be the target of the long-expected operation. They were to attack Gestapo headquarters in the Victoria Terrasse in Oslo – and they were to take off in less than twenty-four hours' time. The camp was locked down, with no one attached to the operation allowed to leave the site. Secrecy was important in all operations, but the level applied to this most delicate mission was higher than usual. The plan involved two waves of six Mosquitos, the first led by Wing Commander Curry and the second by Flight Lieutenant Mallender. It was essential for the attackers to have a clear view of the target – the second wave were not to attack if the target was obscured by the first. The risk of civilian casualties was known to be high, but the war often threw up high-stakes targets. What the briefing failed to mention was that the Kriegsmarine had ships anchored in the waters close to Oslo during the Christmas period – a force that had ample defensive armament. They were to approach at an altitude of 28,000 feet, dropping to 7,000 feet as they neared Oslo and then to 3,000 feet to acquire the target. They would level out the diving attack at 1,000 feet and escape over the city at low level before breaking for the return leg.

The heavy snow that had hampered the Allies' defensive efforts in Belgium had now spread up the east coast of Britain. Venturing out into the freezing snowscape of the base, the airmen's breath formed plumes of cloud as they chatted and tried not to slip on paths and steps. Their mood was one of controlled apprehension. There was a time for anxiety, but that time had not yet come; they were to fly to northeast Scotland and spend the night at Peterhead before setting out on their mission to Oslo. They had to take things one step at a time. Like many others, they were confident that within the next year the war in Europe would be won, but nobody wanted to die on New Year's Eve – despite the planners making life difficult for them.

Tractors cleared the frozen taxiways and runway. As the Mosquitos moved slowly forward they created their own mini-blizzards of blown snow, spraying the watching ground crew, who shielded their eyes from this sudden icy spatter. The growl of the Merlin engines was strangely muted, its sound seemingly deadened by the thick blanket of snow. A few short years previous, most of the young men would have been enjoying prolonged snowball fights and sledging in the glorious white landscape – but now they were at war. One by one the Mosquitos began their take-off runs, picking up what remained of the powdery surface and flinging it into a swirling mist behind them. The flight north was made at low level to avoid their having to negotiate thick cloud. Flying in daylight allowed the crews a clear view over the snow-bound countryside; it looked very peaceful – the very image of a traditional Christmas. The dark ribbon of the main east-coast railway line helped keep them on course, long plumes of steam marking where engines hauling freight or carriages were plying the route. The snow seemed even thicker below them as they passed Newcastle and then Edinburgh on their port side. There was time to chat and take in the spectacle of the Mosquitos around them thundering effortlessly northwards through the calm and chilly skies.

Peterhead hove into view, perched unmistakably on its headland but somehow rendered insignificant by the surrounding expanse of the North Sea. Landing at RAF Peterhead was relatively simple, as the runways had been cleared, leaving black marks in the whiteness. As they taxied, waving arms directed them to the dispersals, where they discovered that their final parking positions formed more of a straight line than they were used to. This far north, German raids were uncommon, and a more relaxed routine seemed to be in place. A contingent of American B-17s – an aircraft mainly employed in daylight bombing of German targets – was parked nearby; each of these 'Flying Fortresses' was about the size of a Lancaster, and dwarfed the Mosquitos. A couple of the Mosquito crews had been shown around the B-17s in the past and came away with the feeling that they were 'flying coffins'. Their nimble machines could carry the same bomb load at twice the speed with a quarter of the crew. Flying in a heavy bomber with a full complement of crew and bombs was taxing enough at night, but the thought of formation flying in broad daylight over Germany was perplexing.

The Americans were welcoming but wondered what tom-foolery had brought this group so far north at this time. Although curious to know what operation the Mosquitos were engaged in, they sensed from the crews' silence on the matter that it would not be appropriate to probe further. Wing Commander Jack Curry no doubt shared a glass or two of malt with the Americans that night – he wanted to make a good impression. The following day he instructed that the Mosquitos' take-off and departure should be in formation. This raised a few eyebrows, since the aircraft would be fully laden, each carrying a 2,000lb bomb load. The Americans were, of necessity, masters of close formation flying, but 627 Squadron had done very little – and certainly not when departing for an operation. Curry was a little more prone to 'shows' than his predecessor, and on at least one occasion held the order to mark back until he had completed his attack, despite the arrival of other 627 Squadron Mosquitos before him. However, he remained a man very well thought of as a leader in the Squadron, and was always spoken about with respect.

The Mosquitos departed safely from RAF Peterhead at around 09.30 hours on Sunday 31 December and split into their two sections of six – climbing gently to their cruising altitude of 28,000 feet. This was unusual for them, not only in terms of height but also because they were flying in daylight. The Canadian pilot Bob Boyden confesses he had flown only two other daylight operations. The freezing whiteness of the previous day had disappeared, replaced by the solid grey mass of the North Sea below them. Topped with a thin mist, the water had a beauty that belied its treacherous nature – any airman unfortunate enough to find himself in this wintry sea had three minutes at best to clamber into a dinghy before hypothermia took him. The mood of the men varied from cockpit to cockpit: in KB122 Herriman and Arthur chatted freely, taking in the splendour of the approaching Norwegian peaks; ahead of them, in the first wave, Boyden and Willis in DZ611 spoke very little – their state of mind more reflective, knowing the raid ahead carried tremendous risks. Writing for the Alberta Aviation Museum Society in the 1990s, Bob Boyden recalls, 'F/O Willis and I did not talk much, if at all. Each of us absorbed in his own thoughts, thinking of what could happen and Willis no doubt wondering what this bastard was going to do next.'

Some of these differences of cockpit mood were down to the relationship between pilot and navigator. All Mosquito crews had to work well together, and to a degree bond into a close unit. Those who failed to gel were weeded out in the selection and training process. While the crews of the larger bombers were more able to accommodate disparate characters – owing to the larger amount of space in the plane and the different roles carried out therein – the Mosquito men flew elbow to elbow. This did not mean they had to be close personal friends, but they did need to build a cooperative professional relationship – to develop the trust and openness with each other that would enable them to successfully complete all necessary tasks.

John Herriman and Eric Arthur had clearly forged a closer companionship than some other crews. Their decision to spend most of their spare time together bore testament to that. Shared experiences as two Aussies a long way from home must have played a part in their friendship. They chose to spend their leave together, and found a bolthole in Carlisle, north of the Lake District and close to the Scottish border. A Mrs Higgins, who allocated men on leave to households that had volunteered to take them in, sent John and Eric to the Brown family on Kingmoor Road, with whom they developed a lasting friendship. Gilbert and Mary Brown were in their fifties, and had a son and a daughter not far in age from the two Australians. Gilbert was a commercial traveller in drapery, whose supply of additional petrol coupons was a great help in exploring the beautiful scenery around them. Carefree days on which the war seemed very distant did much to lighten the men's spirits, but the precarious reality of their lives was never far away.

As the Mosquitos approached Oslo up the Oslofjord, Wing Commander Curry and the first wave began their descent, and within minutes found an intense flak barrage had opened up on them. The ships of the Kriegsmarine lying at anchor had no intention of allowing the aircraft to approach unchallenged, no doubt believing they were the targets of the attack. Bob Boyden remembers the first puffs of smoke around Curry's aircraft and almost immediately finding they too were framed by the sudden explosions. It was the first time that Boyden had heard, felt and smelled flak, and the combination was a most uncomfortable experience. Fortunately, it did not last long, as Curry called 'Tally Ho' and began his diving descent. Following, Boyden in the No.3 position heard Curry call for No.2 to close up, and after a second call realized Curry had mistaken them for No.2, DZ461, crewed by Yeadell and West. The Mosquitos jostled for position. By now, things were happening very quickly, and as the Victoria Terrasse loomed ahead through a blanket of pale chimney smoke in the still Oslo air, the first wave deposited their bombs.

Pushing their noses down farther, the aircraft levelled out over the rooftops and Boyden, seeing No.4 descending on top of him, had to break radio silence to shout a warning. The dive had, as they had hoped, shaken off the flak barrage, but at this very low level they still faced the hazards of lighter guns and even hand-held weapons. Following behind, Flight Lieutenant Mallender led the second wave in for their attack, but by now the whole area of the target was filled with a dense cloud of debris and smoke. With no chance of being able to bomb accurately, Mallender called off the attack and closed his bomb doors to follow the first wave over the rooftops. Two Mosquitos of the second wave did complete their attack, and dropped bombs despite Mallender's instruction, the pilots believing in the heat of the dive that they could see the target sufficiently well.

Overshooting his target without bombing, John Herriman had time to crack a joke about not having time to window shop as he passed down a busy street before the wide-open vista of Maridalsvannet (Lake Maridal) opened up before them. Although the resistance had been asked to encourage people to go to church, hundreds of people were out skating on the frozen lake, enjoying their New Year's Eve. Instinctively, many of them began waving frantically in greeting, still not aware that an attack had taken place. However, not all the people they saw on the lake were pleased to see them; some of the skaters were armed, and as the Mosquitos thundered over the lake, their crews could see figures with armbands lifting their rifles to shoot at them. John Herriman, flying at 50 feet, said simply, 'Just watch them go', and eased his joystick forward until the aircraft was almost skimming the frozen surface of Maridalsvannet. The men below, having been intent on firing a few seconds before, now flung themselves onto the ice in a desperate act of escape.

Boyden and Willis were now free of the city and climbing back to altitude for the return leg, but Herriman and Arthur noticed some damage to their Mosquito. Still at low level, they saw glycol coolant leaking into the cockpit. On the port wing, only a couple of feet away from the cockpit, a large hole was visible where the radiator was housed. Herriman had no choice but to close the engine down, nurse the slowing Mosquito over the mountain ahead and jettison the bombs. Their return flight on one engine was slower and lower than planned, but with no fighters in attendance, they continued on their way unmolested. Their landing at Peterhead – on one engine – had to be done with the greatest care, as there was no excess power to attempt a go-around, but Herriman touched down sweetly and, with a little squeak from the tyres, the crew could breathe a sigh of relief. Nearly every Mosquito had been hit by flak, but all had returned – a testament to their robust manufacture.

Despite the failure of most of the aircraft in the second wave to bomb, the operation was initially thought to have been a success, but troubling news began to emanate from Oslo. Although the crews believed they had hit the northeast corner of the Victoria Terrasse, it appeared few bombs had actually hit their target. As in the 1942 raid, the problem of skipping bombs was significant. Owing to the lower angle of attack, the steel casings of the bombs were touching down first rather than triggering the delayed-action fuse, causing the weapons to skid on for many metres. The raid had caused a tragically high number of civilian casualties; as many as seventy-nine were killed, including forty-four passengers on a tram that was destroyed in a bomb blast.

There were a few near misses. A bomb sailed through the front and back walls of 60 Ruselokkveien, a flat just around the corner from the Victoria Terrasse, exploding in the courtyard behind. The Carlstrand family were left homeless but were otherwise unscathed.

Although the Germans did suffer some casualties, the attack was not as decisive as the raid on the barracks at Aarhus in October. The aim of the Oslo operation had been to aid the Norwegian resistance by liberating – or silencing – those of their members who were held under torture, but in this respect the raid had failed. Nevertheless, the Gestapo were unnerved to the extent that they moved out of Victoria Terrasse, a significant disruption to their operations, which made the raid – albeit belatedly – a partial success for the RAF. Even if the building had been razed to the ground, the Gestapo would have re-established themselves elsewhere. In retrospect, the second Oslo raid could have been carried out by other Mosquito squadrons, a number of which, like 464 Squadron RAAF, were carrying out regular low-level daylight raids on targets in France in support of the Allied advance. But there were intense dangers attached to such raids, and allocating them more evenly across the entire Mosquito force eased the burden on crews. Squadron Leader Sydney Claydon, who had flown in the Aarhus raid, summed up the bravery of the men involved: 'It was frightening to be on low-level raids – anybody who says it wasn't, is lying.'

A later report on 627 Squadron's action on 31 December concluded that the attack would have been better executed in a single larger wave rather than split into two. The second wave were greatly hampered by the rising smoke and dust from the first. In fairness to the crews, their precision flying was exemplary, but the attack was let down by the strategy employed and the weaponry supplied to them – both of which were beyond their control.

Twelve men of 627 Squadron awoke on the first day of 1945 with clear heads owing to the absence of celebratory drinks the night before. Most crews from the Oslo raid were rested and able to spend time around an ingenious tri-cornered chimney in the officers' mess, which allowed them to sit by the fire on three sides. Designed and built by pilot and former bricklayer Wilf Yeadell in early December, it had proved a godsend during the freezing weather. But there was no immediate rest for Flight Lieutenant Yeadell and Pilot Officer West, who had been No.2 in the first wave at Oslo – they had drawn the short straw, and were required to fly again on 1 January. Two inland waterways were to be marked in daylight, the Dortmund–Ems Canal near Ladbergen and the Mittelland Canal at Gravenhorst. The first two Mosquitos left early for the Dortmund–Ems Canal, lifting away from Woodhall Spa at 8.43 hours on what turned out to be a dazzlingly clear morning. Leading, Squadron Leader Rupert Oakley reported that there was 'No cloud, visibility unlimited' over the target. He was able to mark the canal using a 1,000lb target indicator, much larger than earlier versions and capable of burning longer – a great advantage in daylight. Oakley observed that the following bombers were a little less fastidious in their accuracy, with a tendency to overshoot.

The conditions Oakley encountered on 1 January 1945 were perfect for the Luftwaffe to mount extensive attacks on Allied airfields in the Low Countries. German commanders knew that the arrival of clearer weather would also allow the Allies' numerically superior air forces to resume their attacks on their positions and supply lines; so it was now or never for the Luftwaffe – they had to throw everything they had at the enemy to try to knock out Allied air power in northern Europe and recapture lost momentum in the 'Battle of the Bulge'. The German assaults of 1 January – designated *Operation Bodenplatte* ('Operation Baseplate') – destroyed many aircraft on the ground, inflicting on Allied aerial capability the worst setback it had suffered since D-Day. Controversy rages as to the exact numbers of aircraft lost on either side, but it seems likely that the Luftwaffe destroyed 305 RAF and USAAF aircraft and damaged a further 190 on New Year's Day. The price they paid in men and machines was heavy, however; they lost 280 aircraft, with 143 pilots killed.* Despite these losses, the overall strength of the Allied air forces remained unassailable: they had 1,000 light and medium bombers and 1,700 fighters – many of them ground-attack P-47 Thunderbolts – at their disposal. The deployment of such air power rapidly made movement on clear roads during the day almost impossible, and Gerd von Rundstedt's leading echelons soon ran out of fuel and supplies. By 4 January the tide had turned decisively in favour of the Allies; by the middle of the month the Germans were in retreat in the Ardennes.

---

* The figures quoted here are from authors John Manrho and Ronald Pütz, quoted in *Bodenplatte: The Luftwaffe's Last Hope* – Stackpole Military History 2010.

Like many other Allied units at this time, 627 Squadron had more crews in its ranks than it had aircraft for them to fly in. In practical terms this meant fewer operations per flyer than was the norm; Ken Oatley, having joined the Squadron in the summer of 1944, would fly only twenty-two operations before the end of the war in Europe, considerably short of a full tour.

Although the heavy bombers were still enduring the extreme hazards of night-time raids over Hitler's Reich, the terrible losses of the winter of 1943–44 were a thing of the past. That 627 could allow men to depart on leave, launch a significant raid at long distance to Oslo and still be able to field six aircraft in a raid on two targets the next day was symptomatic of the victory coming. The Commonwealth training grounds of Canada and South Africa were producing prodigious numbers of airmen, many of them gaining daily battle experience in operations. By the start of 1945 the average Allied pilot had flown 300 hours, as opposed to the Germans' 170. At this stage of the war, with the likelihood of their being harried by enemy aircraft so vastly reduced, RAF fliers could spend countless hours honing their skills on bombing ranges, flying cross-country exercises and testing their aeroplanes after servicing. It was this luxury – as much as the innate qualities of the crews – that ensured the success of 627 Squadron and, indeed, all the RAF squadrons in the United Kingdom between D-Day and the war's end. Not only was the ground war shrinking Hitler's empire daily, his air force were, by the end of the Ardennes offensive, on the brink of collapse. Although Nazi underground factories were still producing impressive numbers of aircraft, the shortage of fully trained pilots was becoming acute. *Bodenplatte* had been a last desperate throw of the dice.

★

The New Year dawned with the promise of peace, but for Londoners, the quiet of the streets and the smoke from thousands of chimneys hanging in the chill air could not hide the fact that Britain's capital was still under attack. The Luftwaffe may have lacked air crews, but Hitler had been using pilotless technology to terrorize southern England since the first V-1 attack in June 1944. As the Allies advanced through France, the number of V-1 weapons fired reduced as their launch sites were overrun, but not before 10,482 had been launched. Britain responded by siting banks of anti-aircraft guns on the south coast to produce a curtain of fire, causing a large number of V-1s to blow up before significant landfall was made.

Fighters, if positioned correctly, could catch a V-1, and the Mosquito made an outstanding contribution in shooting them down. Wing Commander Russell Bannock and his navigator Pilot Officer Robert Bruce of 418 Squadron (RCAF) developed an interception technique that reduced the risk of the attacking aircraft being hit by debris from an exploding V-1. Bannock's squadron had been deployed shortly after D-Day to strike targets at low level in support of troop movements, and had observed flying V-1s at close range. Re-allocated to 'Diver Patrols', searching for V-1s as they raced across the English Channel, Bannock realized that the 390–400mph of the V-1 was still above their Mosquito's cruising speed. To counter this, Bannock placed his Mosquitos at 10,000 feet, allowing them to dive on a flying bomb when it was seen. Using their excess speed, they caught up with it and drew alongside before allowing the V1 to pull gently away. Positioning themselves to the rear, they were able to aim more accurately before firing their nose-mounted cannon.* Invariably, the 1,000lb warhead

---

* The intercepting Mosquitos were the FB Mk VI versions, which had forward-firing guns, as opposed to the Perspex observation position of 627 Squadron's aircraft.

exploded, producing a cloud of debris that was very hazardous for the Mosquito – but not as dangerous as engaging the V-1 directly in the dive, where the attacker was still approaching the V-1 at speed as it blew up. Bannock was to claim nineteen V1s destroyed – a fine personal total of the 628 V-1s destroyed by the Mosquito.

On 8 September 1944 a new and potentially more deadly weapon was unleashed on Britain – *Vergeltungswaffe* 2. The first V-2 rocket, fired from the Netherlands, fell on a suburban street in Chiswick, West London, killing three people and obliterating eleven houses. The government initially claimed the deadly blast had been caused by a gas explosion. Unlike its predecessor, the V-2 gave no warning of its arrival; even more troublingly, once the rocket had left its launch pad, it was impossible to intercept – the Allies simply did not have the technology in their arsenal to do so. This, the world's first long-range guided ballistic missile, was more advanced than any weapon previously deployed; it was difficult to conceal that, for all the recent Allied territorial gains, Germany appeared to have the lead in weapons technology. Scores more Londoners were killed in V-2 attacks on London during the autumn. Only on 10 November 1944 did Churchill inform Parliament that Britain had been under rocket attack for the past few weeks. The worst attack came on the twenty-fifth of that month, when a V-2 demolished a branch of Woolworth's in New Cross, in southeast London, at 12.26 in the afternoon. One hundred and sixty-eight people were killed or injured in the crowded shop.

The Allied response was a two-pronged assault on the V-2. First, they continued to strike any target of opportunity, mostly railheads and transport links that moved components or whole rockets to their mobile launch sites. The existence of the V weapons had been known many months before their first launch, and in November 1943, the Allies had set up Operation Crossbow to strike at the manufacturing and distribution of

German long-range weapons, but it proved relatively unsuc-
cessful and consumed a huge amount of resources.

Flying home from a daylight raid, 627 Squadron's Ken Oatley
remembers seeing the white plume of a V-2 streaking into the
sky close by. Jock Walker and he were over Holland, and he
confesses to not knowing precisely where they were at the time.
Jock was operating on his own navigational sense – something
he could perform with unerring accuracy – and Ken's arms
were temporarily over his chart on his lap. As a result, when it
came to debriefing, Ken could not give the intelligence officer
a location. This did not seem to trouble the officer, who knew
that, as V-2s were transported on lorries, their launch site was
vacated as soon as the rocket was sent on its 50-mile curving
climb into the stratosphere.

As the Second World War in Europe wound its way inex-
tricably towards its painful end, 627 Squadron were to find
themselves at the forefront of a number of controversial raids.
With war leaders beginning to consider the world order after
the conflict, it is arguable that some attacks had political overtones rather than being purely strategic operations.

Royan, 5 January 1945

Perched just above the northern shore of the Gironde estuary,
on France's southwestern coast, Royan had been a thriving
seaside resort since the first half of the nineteenth century, its
palatial casino, built in 1895, inviting visitors to spend time
and money in a place blessed by sunshine and warm breezes.
By the time war broke out, the sand dunes and beaches of this
attractive stretch of coast had acquired the touristic name of
'Côte de Beauté'. After 1940, however, the occupying Germans
fortified the coast of Charente-Maritime with a line of massive
concrete defensive positions, erected by an army of slave

labourers, as part of Hitler's Atlantic Wall. Two eighteenth-century forts were reinforced at the mouth of the Gironde estuary: *Gironde Mündung Nord*, Fort du Chay on its northern side at Royan, and *Gironde Mündung Süd*, Fort du Verdon at La Pointe de Grave. In the seventeenth century Royan had been a Huguenot (Protestant) enclave, and endured a siege by the forces of King Louis XIII in 1622; some 320 years later, in January 1944, Hitler designated the town as one of a number of strongholds (*Atlantikfestungen*) along the Atlantic Wall that were to be defended for as long as possible in the event of an Allied invasion of western Europe.

The aftermath of the bombardment of Royan, January 1945.

After D-Day, as the Allies pushed south and east, Royan's forces and its echelons became entirely detached from the rest of the German forces. The advance of the Americans and Free French from the south cut off any prospect of escape in that direction, and to the north, La Rochelle was surrounded. Supply problems meant that the German troops garrisoned in Royan faced a daily struggle to keep themselves adequately fed.

Beleaguered though this German garrison undoubtedly already was, two factors persuaded the Allies to attack Royan. The first was that the *Atlantikfestungen* constituted the only parts of France that remained in German hands, and the liberated French were anxious for their country to be completely rid of the hated occupiers. The second factor was that the Germans were sending out parties of soldiers from the forts to seize food, often from local farmers.

The dissatisfaction at this state of affairs was communicated to a senior USAAF officer by French army officers on 10 December 1944 in the town of Cognac. After a meal where some sources report that a significant amount of alcohol had been consumed, the question of the continued resistance of the Germans in Royan was broached. When the suggestion was made that the garrison should be 'softened up' by bombing, the American officer asked about the civilian population and was told, quite erroneously, that 'the only civilians remaining in Royan are collaborators'.

Royan was, in fact, still fully populated with civilians. Whether the resistance considered them to be collaborators because they were selling supplies to the German garrison, or whether they harboured a more subtle distrust of the Royannais because of their tradition of religious non-conformism, is debateable. Nevertheless, the decision was made to launch a substantial raid of 340 Lancaster bombers supported by six Mosquitos of 627 Squadron. Flight Lieutenant Devigne and Squadron Leader Boyle in Mosquito DZ461 led the raid, taking off at 02.23 hours. Of the raids 627 Squadron was asked to carry out, this appeared to be one of the simplest. Flying over a country now largely free of its German occupiers, they did not worry about meeting enemy aircraft; the extent of French liberation meant they were unlikely to encounter much opposition during their flight southwestwards. Royan lay under a thick frost, its inhabitants tucked up in bed as the temperature dropped to negative 10 degrees. For the German guards on the Fort de Chay, that night was another cold, dark watch; they stamped their feet and clapped their hands to keep warm, trying not to slip on the large paving stones that formed their path along the sea wall. Despite the apparent calm and quiet, the resistance frequently caused trouble here; at times they could hear shots being fired, echoing in the quiet streets outside their defences, so there was no room to be complacent. The waves lapped the base of the walls as the town, enveloped in a freezing mist, continued to sleep.

The sounds of the sea seemed to shift a little, and above the sound of the shore, a deep hum began to develop. Within the space of a minute the noise had become the unmistakable rumble of approaching aircraft engines. A bell ringing, and the shouts and the noise of footsteps, broke the silence as men made for the flak guns within the fort enclosure. Most of the garrison – made up of the very young and the very old, in soldiering terms – had never experienced an air raid. Young boys of seventeen with wire-rimmed spectacles who should have been in college were serving alongside men with greying hair who wished they were back tending their cattle in Bavarian pastures. There was a scattering of 'true soldiers' who had seen action on the Eastern Front and bore the scars to prove it. Trapped in their enclave and surrounded by hostile forces, they knew they faced an uncertain fate and greeted any talk of relief with quiet disbelief; but they retained their pride in the Wehrmacht – they would always do their duty, however hopeless the situation.

After making sure his family had left the town for their own safety, Pastor Samuel Besançon had remained behind in Royan. He was far from a collaborator, but was rather a man of compassion who believed he should remain with his congregation, many of whom were not in a position to flee. The night of 5 January 1945 would stay with him for many years, and he would meet and talk with other survivors, eventually seeing his testimony published in 2000. Besançon is one of the few eyewitnesses of the marking of 627 Squadron and subsequent bombing to commit his memories to paper. In the confusion of the raid, and still in his nightclothes, he was not able to understand fully what was happening, but his description provides a vivid evocation of the terror visited upon Royan that winter's evening:

> The noise of the engines increased sharply and became unbearable; then light flooded the room and immediately the clash of the anti-aircraft fire began. Finally, fully awake and a little worried, I jumped to the window and it was a completely new sight that I had before my eyes. Parachutes slowly descended through the pale and crisscrossing beams of searchlights highlighted by the flashes of the shells. They supported large flares; some of a bright red, most of a dazzling white.

Usually, the Lancaster Pathfinders would drop their flares over the target before 627 Squadron marked, but on this occasion four of the 627 Mosquitos also carried these illuminators. Because of the prevailing weather conditions, they used the sky-marking method known as Wanganui, which was followed in conditions of minimal visibility and involved dropping parachute flares to highlight the clouds above the target area. Devigne and Boyle dropped their target indicators at 03.54 hours; two minutes later, after swift circling the area, they called 'Tally Ho' and dived on Royan.

To their consternation, their primary red indicator did not fall and, suspecting a hang-up, they climbed again, only to find that their two 1,000lb red target indicators had detached themselves when they had dropped their illuminating parachute flare, threatening to widen the target area. Devigne used the VHF radio channel to inform the raid controller, Wing Commander Smith, of the mishap and he, in turn, instructed the approaching main force to alter their aiming to offset the problem.

As the other Mosquitos began their dives, Pastor Besançon became aware of a sudden increase in engine noise. It is likely that the sound Besançon heard was 'Marker No.4' – Mosquito DZ643, crewed by Flying Officer Nash and Flight Sergeant Wetherall – diving to back up at 04.02.

'The anti-aircraft gun slowed down their fire a little because the signalling planes, missions ended – they were moving away in a south-westerly direction, it seemed,' recalled Besançon. Standing transfixed at his window, he realized he was in a perilous position: 'A heavy, terrifying noise already filled the sky, constantly increasing in intensity; it sounded a hundred times louder than the roars of the raging ocean or a thousand freight trains travelling together on parallel tracks.'

The main force of bombers was arriving over Royan; Besançon threw his clothes on, forgetting his braces (something he says he later regretted), and fled from the house without shoes. He ran to the bottom of his garden and threw himself against a low wall, only 30cm high, pulling down his beret and turning up the collar of his overcoat. For a time he forgot about the numbing cold, instead remembering the stories of Verdun told to him by men of his generation who knew the tricks to surviving close explosions. He shuddered at the idea of going to a cellar because of the danger of being entombed; he much preferred lying in the open, pressing his body close to the freezing earth. He knew that a direct hit or a bomb exploding close by would finish him off, but at least if he kept low he was less likely to be caught by flying shards of metal or debris. The sky above began to fill with the shrieking and whistling of bombs:

> The first bombs fell towards Fort du Chay and instantly Villa Lucie was a mass of ruins and flames. First thought: They are having it because of their height, but watch out for us because we are under that trajectory. Then the blows multiplied and came dangerously close. No one who has experienced this first interlude in the open air can forget the sound of this apocalyptic rhapsody. The enormous, collective roar of three hundred or three hundred and fifty planes circling very low in the light of the bombs, one could sometimes make out a fuselage, a wing or the stabilizer. The tempo increased again by the furious volume of the engines which propelled the aircraft unloaded from their heavy and dangerous packages towards altitude.

The pounding of bombs grew closer to Besançon, the explosions too numerous to count, causing the earth to shake, and his body to involuntarily spasm at each impact: 'And we say to ourselves: "That one is still far away, that one too. Oh! Here are two, three, four! It's getting closer! Oh! This one is mine! How close it is!" Indeed the central point of the crater was four meters from my feet. Fortunately, it was only two hundred and fifty kilos!'

He describes the feeling of being shaken 'like a salad in a basket', but was still able to watch the results of the raid. An aircraft passed low overhead, seemingly only a few metres above his head, silhouetted against the flaming glow of the sky. It is possible that this was Devigne and Boyle in DZ461, reconnoitring the area once again as they remained in the target area for as long as an hour. Most of the bombing force were at an altitude of between 10,000 and 15,000 feet, so it was unlikely to have been a Lancaster at such a low level.

As the bombing force departed, Besançon was left with the sounds of intermittent gun fire and the crackling of burning houses. He emerged from his 'shelter' to witness a scene of utter destruction; he described himself as: 'Blinded by dust and smoke from explosives, sprinkled and even covered with earth, tree branches, small rubble, pieces of lumber, panting, teeth clenched, kidneys aching, head bloody and with a dirty burn on the right foot … but still breathing, and alive.' The town of Royan had been virtually razed to the ground; although the defending guns had accounted for four Lancasters, no real defence had been mounted against the attack. Casualties among the French population were reported as 1,000 dead, a figure later calculated to be closer to 500, with the same number injured. Of the German occupiers, just twenty-three were killed – a fraction of the total German force in the area – and the 'Royan pocket' was to remain in German hands for some time yet.

In mid-April, French and US forces embarked on an operation to recapture the Gironde estuary and Île d'Oléron. An Allied attack on Royan from both land and sea was supported by an immense contingent of American B-17 Flying Fortresses and B-24 Liberators. On 14 and 15 April 1945, this aerial armada unleashed a savage bombardment, using napalm for the first time in an effort to reach German troops hiding in their bunkers. As well as completing the destruction of Royan begun on 5 January, the USAAF killed as many as 1,700 of its civilians.

Royan – dubbed the 'martyred city' for its sufferings so cruelly close to the war's inevitable end – can be seen as the victim of impatience on the part of politicians and military commanders to see France fully liberated. In a year that saw the making of the geopolitical boundaries of a new European order, it was, sadly, not the only town to find itself sacrificed to political interests. Nor was the raid on Royan of 5 January the last time that the men of 627 Squadron would find themselves placed in the unenviable position of participating in an action that would later be subjected to intense moral as well as strategic criticism.

Between the first and second bombardments of Royan, there took place in eastern Germany, on 13–15 February 1945, perhaps the most controversial of all Allied strategic bombing operations of the Second World War. It was code-named 'Thunderclap'.

11

DÉNOUEMENT

Dresden, 13 February 1945

As the light faded on an exceptionally mild February day at RAF Woodhall Spa, there was no inkling that the planned raid that night would be significantly different from the dozens before it. It was going to be, in RAF parlance, 'a big show', with hundreds of bombers flying against the city of Dresden, but no one sensed that the finger of history would single out this action for special attention. At 627 Squadron, the preparations for the raid followed the same daily routine. Crew names were posted on the noticeboard for operations in the morning, and then there was air testing, the raid briefing and the studying of maps and photographs before the traditional pre-raid meal of eggs and bacon. By the time the Rolls-Royce Merlin engines crackled into life that evening the crews had already spent twelve hours in preparation.

Tonight, Jock Walker and Ken Oatley were assigned DZ599 and designated as 'Marker 2', although they always hoped – but never quite managed – to sneak in to drop the first marker ahead of the appointed leader. Checks were completed and, with their engines running, they waited for the signal to move from their dispersal point. The Merlins were ticking over smoothly, filling their world with familiar vibrations that gave them the sense that they were a part of this powerful machine. Ken Oatley looked down at the piece of ply balancing on his knees that served as his navigation desk. The original flip-down table had been too small, and this replacement, although impractical in terms of security, was the best solution the Squadron could think of. Small sharpened pencils were tied to pieces of string to avoid their being lost in some dark corner of the Mosquito's cockpit. Elastic bands were used to hold the corner of the map down. Ken had a good feeling about this evening; things had gone smoothly so far, and he hoped that this augured an uneventful trip. Not all engine starts were as untroubled as night's had been. On one occasion, Oatley had been suffering with a bad stomach, and the starting vibrations of the engine had produced unforeseen consequences. Within the confines of the cockpit and the impossibility of adjusting clothing, it had been a matter of 'sitting tight' for the rest of the operation.

Jock Walker had run through the pre-flight checks with his normal punctilious efficiency; the neatness of his cockpit matched his flying – there would be no corners cut. The same principle did not always apply to his conduct off duty, and he had a robust reputation for enjoying his whisky. His tangle with Guy Gibson, which had resulted in the Wing Commander losing his trousers, had entered squadron folklore, as had the events of the night of 2 February, less than two weeks previous.

After enjoying a jovial evening in the bar of the officers' mess, Flight Lieutenant John Whitehead and friends had noticed that Jock Walker had lapsed into a happy slumber, and was quite incapable of managing the quarter-mile walk back to their Nissen huts. Finding a stretcher, they strapped Walker to it and began the journey across the darkened accommodation area somewhat unsteadily. By mischance they found themselves out in the open on the only evening that German raiders would attack RAF Woodhall Spa.* It was the sharp report of gunfire that first alerted them to a problem, and the wail of air-raid sirens added to the confusion as the inebriated party did their best to take cover. It was a cold evening, and the paths were slippery with snow. Finding a nearby ditch to shelter in, they quickly set Walker down on the lip, the stretcher being too cumbersome to bring with them. The firing and commotion lasted twenty minutes, and when they emerged, they found that Walker's stretcher had been tipped upside down, and the still-sleeping Walker was face down in the snow. As they carefully lifted him, they found, in their confused state, that righting the stretcher was beyond their capabilities, so they were obliged to carry him the remaining distance upside down. Once they got into their Nissen hut, they placed Walker face down on his bed, still strapped to his stretcher, to sleep off the effects.

The evening of 13 February would prove far more orthodox, and Jock Walker watched as Marker Leaders Bill Topper and Vic Davies began moving onto the taxiway in DZ631. In an ideal world, Walker and Oatley would have liked to have tucked in behind them. However, they were too far away, and found themselves the fifth Mosquito in the group of eight making their way to the runway threshold. In their competitiveness, they knew the three-minute head start Topper and Davies had over them would give them the edge in the race to drop the first marker on Dresden. The city lay towards the edge of the Mosquito's operating range – that night's would be a long one. Despite England enjoying a spell of mild, cloudy weather, a cold front snaking through Europe meant that – for a relatively short period of time – ideal conditions were available for the attack. All too often a crew would fly through the crispness

---

* The strafing attack did little damage at Woodhall Spa. It was, in fact, one of the Luftwaffe's final actions over England. The last bomb dropped was by a single aircraft over Hull, on 17 March 1945.

of a clear winter's night on the outbound flight only to find heavy cloud cover over the target. But on the evening in question, conditions over Dresden would be clear, a significant contributing factor in making the raid so dramatically – indeed lethally – effective.

Once they were in the air, Ken Oatley tuned in to the Gee signal to establish his course, tracing the outline of the English coast below them with his finger in the dim light over his map. They were still flying over the North Sea, and approaching Holland, when Oatley's Gee signal suddenly died. Whether it had been blocked or his set had suffered a malfunction he wasn't sure – but he knew that if they were to get to Dresden he would have to navigate by dead reckoning. He hid his concerns from Walker – it was one of those problems he would have to work around himself. At the same time, he knew that as little as a single degree of error could place them 40 or more miles adrift. In fact, Oatley was not wholly reliant on his own calculations. The aircraft was also equipped with the LORAN (Long Range Navigation) system, which used lower radio wave frequencies than Gee sets did. The round cathode ray tube produced, as Oatley recalls, 'a beautiful picture of an uncut lawn', but by picking the longest piece of 'grass' he hoped he would be able to find Dresden. The LORAN device was relatively new to the Squadron and, although it was an expensive addition to their equipment, it was not yet fully trusted by crews. Oatley continued to feed Walker small changes of course, hoping that the pilot would remain oblivious to the uncertain nature of his navigation, until eventually, 'with crossed fingers', he told Walker in a confident voice that he could make his final turn to the target.

To Oatley's immense relief, and right on time, the sky ahead lit up in a clear white light as the higher-flying Pathfinders dropped their parachute flares. Walker wasted no time in pointing the Mosquito's nose down, and rapidly descended from

15,000 to 5,000 feet before levelling out close to their aiming point. Seeing their planned target, the oval outline of the Ostragehege Stadium, clearly picked out in the sharp shadows created by the flares, Walker was about to flick his intercom switch to deliver his 'Tally Ho' message when Flight Lieutenant Bill Topper's cut-glass accent was heard to announce, 'Number One Tally Ho'. Once again, Topper had reached the target precisely as he had planned, robbing his friends of the honour of attacking first. As Topper had turned on his final approach, he had had to negotiate a bank of heavy cloud, but once he broke free of it, a broad vista of the city opened out before him. The Master Bomber above him, Wing Commander Maurice Smith, was already asking Topper what cloud conditions were like as he emerged into the clear air over the city. But for the smoke of chimneys, the visibility was near perfect, and the rooftops and spires of Dresden, lit by the white light of the Pathfinders' flares, stood gaunt and exposed in the winter night. Diving towards the stadium, Topper dropped his flare; as he released it, a photoflash that enabled the recently installed on-board camera to take a series of pictures also dropped. Alarmed by the sudden explosion of light, one of the following Mosquitos radioed that they thought Topper had been hit – but it soon became clear that DZ631 was unharmed.

The partnership of Flight Lieutenant Bill Topper and Flying Officer Vic 'Garth' Davies was one of the more improbable pairings in the Royal Air Force. Davies, a self-confessed country boy who enjoyed nothing more than bird-watching and roaming the woods and fields, was a little thrown when Topper first introduced himself as his pilot. Hailing from Pendleton in Lancashire, Topper was nonetheless clearly a 'city gent', whose tastes and privilege placed him in a different social class from the unworldly Davies, but the unlikely duo formed a strong partnership. Legend had it that Topper had bought a Bentley from a woman in Bournemouth for twenty pounds; he was often seen driving the vehicle, with his dog, Rostov, hanging out of the open-top car. Sometimes Davies accompanied Topper on his jaunts, holding on to the enthusiastic Rostov as they belted along country lanes – everyone thrilling to the speed of the vehicle. Both men were highly experienced airmen who had earned the coveted 'Number One' marking position on account of their flying skills.

Topper had served three years as a flying instructor before his posting to 627, but despite his lack of front-line service, he proved highly adaptable. In keeping with a significant number of 627 Squadron men who had previously evaded capture, Davies had been shot down near Mons in Belgium in Halifax JD368 on 28 August 1944. Successfully navigating the escape networks established by the French resistance, he had made his way across France, then walked over the Pyrenees to freedom and eventual repatriation to England.

Jock Walker and Ken Oatley had followed Topper in over the Ostragehege Stadium, dropping their bright-red flare on the pitch. Topper's flare had been green to signify it came from the lead marker. Recovering from the dive, Walker kept the Mosquito low over the rooftops, but looking up, Oatley noticed the looming twin spires, one of which belonged to the cathedral and the other to the *Hausmannsturm*, part of the castle across the road. After calling out a warning, Oatley was relieved when Walker managed to slip DZ599 safely between the twin towers – there had been precious little room to spare, but they were now free of the city centre. As they banked to circle the city, nothing seemed to happen: no furious anti-aircraft fire criss-crossed their nose; no one was visible on the streets so clearly illuminated below them. The other Mosquitos followed in a textbook performance, their flares leaving the Ostragehege Stadium lit up with the brightest of light – an unmistakable signpost for the bombers waiting to release their deadly payload. Walker decided to bring DZ599 back across the city to see what was happening, and only decided to beat a retreat when he felt the Mosquito lifted suddenly by the percussive force of a large bomb exploding underneath him.

The Lancasters of 5 Group had arrived. Using the marked stadium as an offset reference point, they began dropping their bombs 200 yards to the south before turning away to leave the area before the arrival of the main force. With VHF radio functioning smoothly, the message from the Master Bomber circling above that the Mosquitos were free to return home was heard loud and clear. Topper and Davies, briefed to loiter longer, flew in a wide, low arc over the city, just to ensure that further marking was not necessary. Bill Topper later recalled that the buildings and bridges reminded him of Shropshire; even as the bombs fell, he could appreciate their beauty. Within a few minutes, they too were cleared to return, and began the long flight home.

The runway lights at Woodhall Spa were switched on at 01.30, a time when the night was still eerily quiet. As the ground crews listened intently to the night breezes, the faint song of Merlin engines could be heard south of the airfield. Unlike other stations around Lincolnshire, where the deep pulsating sound of the bomber's return would become a cacophony before they landed, 627 Squadron's arrival would be less dramatic. Despite the frequency of these operations, they prepared themselves for any eventuality – be it damage to the aircraft or, worse, injured crew members. They had seen the last of the eight Mosquitos off by 20.07, and at 01.34 the first to sweep out of the night were Flying Officers Rolland and Holling in DZ606. Six more crews had joined them by 01.46, and the airfield was alive with purring Mosquitos making their short journey from the runway back to their dispersals. Last to arrive were Topper and Davies in DZ631 at 01.53, still carrying their 1,000lb red back-up marker. There was a collective sigh of relief that once again the weary travellers had returned safely to the fold.

Although ground crews were not party to the debriefings, they knew that returned back-up markers generally meant a successful raid.

The men of 627 Squadron had no idea that the actions of that night would come to be regarded as some of the most controversial of the Second World War. They were aware only that the raid had been a success, and that the bombing had been particularly accurate. The force that had hit Dresden was not the largest they had flown with – it consisted of some 244 Lancasters in the main contingent, code-named 'Plate Rack' – but the firestorm unleashed by the bombing of the ancient centre of the city resulted in a huge number of casualties. The second, heavier wave of 529 Lancasters arrived three hours later, and were able to bomb unopposed, finding no flak or fighter opposition around their target. Of the 796 RAF bombers that participated, only six were lost, of which three were victims of 'friendly fire', from bombs dropped from aircraft above.

The next morning, 14 February, saw another huge attack, this time by 316 American B-17 bombers; it was centred on the railway marshalling yards, but it would cruelly exacerbate the damage already done to the city the night before. Many areas were still burning uncontrollably; the approaching American bomber crews could see the pall of smoke rising from the ruined city when they were still miles away from their target. The destruction inflicted on a relatively small area of Dresden's city centre by the British and American raids of 13 and 14 February was immense; the power of the bombs and the raging fire they caused had sucked the oxygen from the atmosphere, asphyxiating anyone caught in the area. The inferno was further fuelled by the large number of timber-framed buildings in the old city, and here the death toll was tragically high. But Dresden's nightmare was not yet over. On 15 February, 210 B-17s of the USAAF returned to the city's still burning funeral pyre; they missed the city centre, but dropped bombs on its southeastern suburbs. In the four Allied raids of 13–15 February 1945, 3,000 tons of high-explosive bombs and incendiary devices dropped by the RAF and USAAF had destroyed more than 2½ square miles of Dresden's city centre and killed many thousands of its inhabitants. The heart of the Saxon capital city, a cultural centre known as 'Florence on the Elbe' for its wealth of fine baroque architecture, art collections and museums – a legacy of the patronage of Elector Augustus the Strong in the eighteenth century – lay in smoking ruins.

Dresden was to become the most emotive victim of the Allied area bombing campaign. In comparison with other German urban centres, the city had remained largely untouched until February 1945, but it was undoubtedly a hub of both military and civilian importance. Dresden was crowded with refugees and foreign labourers brought here under duress, and many have argued, with some justification, that its destruction so close to the end of the war was unnecessary. The figures for civilian deaths at Dresden have always been a topic of dispute. Early Allied estimates placed the number killed at 70,000, although in wartime conditions it was impossible to verify. In March 1945 the Nazis published a false figure of 200,000 casualties; some later writers even speculated that as many as 500,000 lives had been lost.

In his 1963 book *The Destruction of Dresden*, David Irving suggested a figure of 100,000 to 250,000 dead; this figure was widely accepted for many years, but in later editions of the work Irving adjusted it downwards. By 2010, the year Dresden city council commissioned a study of the casualties, Irving's reputation as a historian had long since been discredited by his outspoken Holocaust denial. The Dresden study was based on a more reliable estimate of bodies disposed of, and produced the figure of 25,000, which is now held to be an accurate representation of losses.

It now seems unlikely that the wilder estimations of casualties have any substance in fact. Nevertheless, the losses were so significant that even Churchill – a man who had pressed for the bombing campaign to continue unabated – became worried. This was not the first time Churchill had allowed himself to question the morality of bombing cities. Even as early as June 1943, while watching footage of an attack, he had suddenly sat bolt upright in his chair and asked, 'Are we beasts? Are we taking this too far?' On 28 March, Churchill issued a memorandum to his Chiefs of Staff that so shocked Charles Portal, Chief of the Air Staff, that he insisted it be edited before circulation. The original draft included the statement that 'the moment has come when the question of bombing German cities simply for the sake of increasing terror, though under other pretexts, should be reviewed'. The amended version read, 'It seems to me that the moment has come when the question of the so called "area bombing" of German cities should be reviewed from the point of view of our own interests.'

Debate has since raged as to whether this was the moment Churchill turned his back on Bomber Command, but this discourse divides sharply between those who like Churchill and those who do not. It is true that, post-war, Churchill prevaricated in his support for Bomber Command, a position that left many former bomber crew members feeling betrayed.

Although often picked out for special historical attention, the attack on Dresden was not an isolated effort, but part of a more extensive plan for massive aerial attacks on a number of German cities, code-named Operation Thunderclap. First proposed in the summer of 1944 as an intensive bombing assault on Berlin, the scheme was shelved, but then was revived in early 1945 with a change of emphasis. For some time, the Soviets had been pressuring the Allies to assist their advance on the Eastern Front by cutting off the flow of Hitler's resources. As the site of a significant railhead, Dresden was one of a number of key strategic locations targeted in an expansive series of raids whose aim was to weaken the German army's ability to resupply their troops.

Undoubtedly, the execution of the attack on Dresden was in no small part influenced by the meeting of Roosevelt, Churchill and Stalin at Yalta in the Crimea on 4–11 February 1945. Roosevelt was in poor health and Stalin, triumphant at the advance of the Red Army to within 80 miles of Berlin, was insistent in his demand for a Soviet sphere of influence in Eastern Europe. Caught in the middle, Churchill was in a weakened position, and Yalta saw a bargaining away of the rights of Poland to the Soviets. Since the Soviets had already occupied all of Polish territory, there was little short of war that could dislodge them.

Rositz oil refinery, 14 February 1945

The day after the Dresden raid, 14 February, 627 Squadron sent seven Mosquitos to a German oil refinery at Rositz, south of Leipzig – a target within the remit of Thunderclap. The refinery at Rositz had been hit before, including a significant daylight raid by B-17s in August 1944. Following the attack, the Germans had worked tirelessly to get production back on track, as they always did when an important plant was hit, but they knew all the while that the bombers would probably return.

There were now enough aircrew on the Squadron to rest the men from the Dresden raid and continue operations the next day with fresh crews. On this occasion, the 'Number One' markers, Flight Lieutenant Yeadell and Pilot Officer West in DZ631, could not repeat the faultless accuracy of Bill Topper and Vic 'Garth' Davies, and found themselves 25 miles adrift when the first sky markers dropped over the refinery at Rositz. They rushed to try to reach the target in time, but were four minutes late. The benefits of sending multiple Mosquitos to target mark were amply demonstrated as marker Number Two, DZ599, with Pilot Officer Pate and Flight Lieutenant Jackson, swept in to mark precisely on time – no doubt to their glee. Perhaps unluckiest in the race to mark were Flying Officer Barnett and Flight Sergeant Day in KB345, who had arrived early and had turned south to wait for the overhead flares to illuminate the target. Slightly out of position when the precise moment came, they had to satisfy themselves with being called in to back up the target. They entered their dive, but their first effort failed, as the target indicator remained firmly attached to the aircraft. The problem of 'hang-ups', ordnance failing to drop, was frequently caused by issues with the electrical relays that operated the bomb release, the catches that held the weapon within the bomb bay. Coming around for a third pass, Barnett and Day successfully deposited their markers on the mass of light that lit the chimneys and network of pipes and tanks of the refinery.*

By the time Yeadell and West reached the target, the rest of the Mosquitos had marked, backing up Pate and Jackson's original indicators. In a final ignominy, the raid controller instructed Yeadell to hold off their attack and return home – the target was now unmistakable to the arriving bombing force. Within minutes, and with the Mosquitos still circling above the refinery in preparation for leaving the area, bombs rained down, causing large explosions and fires. The Pathfinder bomber crews could see huge plumes of smoke rising thousands of feet from burning storage tanks.

*

* Target indicators burned for three to four minutes, so repeated marking prolonged the period during which markers were visible to the bombers overhead.

Even with more time on their hands owing to an excess of crews available, the men of 627 Squadron appear to have spent little time reflecting on the morality of their operations. The clear reduction in the intensity of the flak and the number of fighters they had encountered over Dresden had come as a welcome relief; it clearly demonstrated that German defences were faltering. Operational flying remained a dangerous occupation, however; squadron members knew that, despite their enemy's failing strength, they could still lose their lives. On 2 February, only two weeks before the Dresden raid, Flight Lieutenant Baker and Sergeant Betts in DZ637 failed to return from a raid on Siegen in North Rhine-Westphalia. Caught by flak over the target, the Mosquito is recorded by German sources as having crash-landed across a road, with the loss of both crew. At Woodhall Spa, colleagues could only comfort themselves that if the crew had survived, they might be hidden in an escape network. The situation in Germany was now becoming chaotic, but even in liberated areas of occupied Europe, the huge numbers of people on the move – either as refugees or attempting to get back to their homes – meant that news of downed airmen could take many weeks to reach an operational unit. Sadly, any hopes that 627 Squadron may have held out for Ronald Baker and Douglas Betts would come to nothing.

Germany now existed as an island surrounded by two vast armies: to the west and southwest the British and Americans; and to the east and southeast the Soviet Red Army. On the day of the Dresden raid, Budapest had fallen to the Soviets and the Allies had reached the Rhine. The Royal Air Force continued to decimate Hitler's war industries and transport links by night, and the American USAAF did the same by day. The rapidly changing situation on the ground was reflected in the eclectic nature of the operations undertaken by 627 Squadron during the remainder of February and through March 1945. Broadly, the targets divided into two categories – oil-producing installations and Germany's transport infrastructure. The aim was to prevent any free movement that could replenish the German armies now facing their final battle – not only to prop up the fragile Reich, but even to function as cohesive units on the battlefields.

In late February 627 Squadron were tasked to hit the German canal network; these were familiar targets – the Squadron had been used for bombing operations against them throughout the autumn of 1944. On these raids, the Mosquitos used their normal payload of target indicators to allow bombers to destroy bridges, aqueducts and locks. 627 Squadron also found themselves supporting the Lancasters of 617 Squadron carrying the 12,000lb 'Tallboy' bombs. On 24 February, four Mosquitos, led by Flight Lieutenant Armstrong and his navigator Pilot Officer Patterson in Mosquito KB345, operated as 'wind-finders' over the Dortmund–Ems Canal at Ladbergen. Given the jaunty title of 'Breeze Leaders', their services were not fully employed on this occasion, as the Lancasters returned home without dropping their cargo because of low cloud over the target. The demand for accuracy and the improving technology in the Lancasters meant that it was possible to enter wind speeds into the bombing 'computers', mechanical calculators that affected the precise moment the bomb would drop. 627 Squadron's wind-finders would operate at differing altitudes to feed back a constant stream of information over their radios to aid the Lancaster bomb aimers.

Remagen, 7 March 1945

In the history of warfare, battles and, indeed, whole conflicts can be decided on a single event: a stroke of luck, a change in the weather, a sudden decision to alter strategy. Edging their way through the wooded slopes above the German town of Remagen, on the River Rhine, the patrols of the US 9th Armored Division found the stillness eerie. When they had brought their jeeps to a halt, the maps showed a road that snaked its way down – a prime location for an ambush, particularly when the lumbering Sherman tanks attempted their clanking descent towards the town. Only a few weeks earlier, during the 'Battle of the Bulge', the division had faced some of the fiercest fighting of that bloody campaign at Saint-Vith, Echternach and Bastogne. They had been deafened by the cacophony of artillery fire in the wooded slopes of the snow-covered Ardennes, and had to dodge lethal wood splinters and sniper fire. Having held their positions, while sustaining heavy casualties, they had then seen the strength of the Wehrmacht melt away in front of them. On 28 February they left the treacherous forests behind them, moving forward into an area of flat land amid the rolling landscape of the Eifel, the low range of hills on Germany's western border with Belgium that adjoins the Ardennes. Despite having to fight frequent skirmishes after crossing the German border, it was clear to the advancing Americans that the enemy was drawing back to the Rhine. Ahead of them, the high plateau would drop suddenly to the river and the small town on its western bank. Remagen would be theirs for the taking.

As the patrols moved cautiously forward, they caught their first sight of the Rhine. Emerging from the treeline, they had a grandstand view of Remagen, nestling by the waterway that had been such a crucial transport route for Germany's war machine. But now that the Allies were pressing against the Rhine's western bank, the river had ceased to be a viable artery for the carrying of matériel; nothing could pass here. Instead, it had become a defensive line, and with the bridges blown, a moat on the Reich's border. The river was broad here, more than 400 yards across, and not easily navigable in small craft, especially under fire. Below, to their immense surprise, the soldiers could see the span of the Ludendorff railway bridge – tantalizingly close and still intact. They knew it was probably laden with explosives to blow when the American forces drew near, just as bridges further north had been. The retreating Germans had been clinical in the way they had destroyed structures well ahead of the American advance – but not in this case. The guards on the bridge could be seen clearly through binoculars; they seemed unhurried and unaware of the closeness of the patrols. Lieutenant Karl Timmermann of the 27th Armored Infantry Battalion, ordered by his battalion commander to get 'A' Company across the bridge, led his men down the steep slope. The first man over, through intense German small arms fire, was Sergeant Alexander Albert Drabik, a twenty-four-year-old butcher from Ohio whose family were originally from Poland. The bridge had been wired with explosives as predicted, but the charges were set wrongly and failed to detonate. Over the next ten days, despite every effort the Germans could muster to destroy the bridge,* the Americans poured 125,000 men over it to establish a bridgehead south of Bonn.

The American crossing surprised those Allied commanders who were preparing to cross the Rhine two weeks later at Wesel, some 90 miles to the north with the 21st Army Group under Field Marshal Bernard Montgomery. Preparations for this crossing, code-named Operation Plunder, continued apace, its prospects enhanced when – following the Remagen crossing – German units were rushed south in a desperate attempt to prevent the Americans from advancing out of their bridgehead on the eastern bank of the Rhine.

As the war in Europe moved swiftly towards its endgame, Bomber Command continued to hit German transport networks

---

* Amongst many efforts, V-2 rockets were launched tactically at the bridge but fell hundreds of yards short. The bridge finally collapsed on 17 March, ten days after the first crossing.

and the fuel refineries that supplied them. On 20 March the target for 627 Squadron was the synthetic oil plant at Böhlen, south of Leipzig, part of a network of twenty-five refineries producing fuel and oil products crucial for Germany's war effort. At their height in early 1944, these refineries had produced 124,000 barrels a day, but now, twelve months on, their production was down to 19,000 barrels.

On 21 March seven 627 Mosquitos set out on 'gardening' operations to drop mines in the River Weser. The payload, known as 'vegetables', were 'Type R' mines (where 'R' denoted river uses). In a cloak-and-dagger operation, the mines were brought into RAF Woodhall Spa in covered lorries and unloaded by a selected group of ground crew. This team installed the mines into the Mosquito bomb bays and ensured the bay doors were shut quickly afterwards to maintain secrecy of this particular design of mine. The flying crews were ordered not to open the doors again so that they would have no knowledge of the appearance of the mines in the event of their being shot down.

Streaking across Holland at low level, Flying Officers Macleod and Philips in ML935 were to mark the course into the target with yellow, green and red markers indicating the turning points for the mine-carrying Mosquitos. To their consternation, three markers out of the four they were carrying departed the bomb bay at the first marking point, leaving them with only one. They pressed on, hoping to at least deposit their remaining marker on the target, but then their H2S radar set stopped working. With little hope of locating the target in time, they were forced to abandon their mission and return home. Despite this setback of navigation, the other six Mosquitos all managed to locate the target and drop their mines.

Earlier in the day, twenty Mosquitos from RAF's No.2 group had attacked Gestapo headquarters in Copenhagen. The *Shellhus* had been used for the detention and torture of Danish citizens, as well as for storing documents. At 11.00 the

Mosquitos of 2 Group RAF attack the Shellhus,
Copenhagen, 21 March 1945.

Mosquitos attacked in three waves of six, shattering the main building and completely demolishing a large section into a flaming heap of rubble. Sadly, one of the low-flying Mosquitos clipped a lamp post, causing it to crash into the Institut Jeanne d'Arc, a French-language Roman Catholic school staffed by nuns. A number of aircraft in the second and third waves then mistook the burning school for the principal target and dropped their bombs, causing heavy casualties. Fifty-five German soldiers and forty-six Danish employees died in the attack at the *Shellhus*, but at the school, one hundred and twenty-five died, including eighty-six children. Despite the incredible success of the Mosquito throughout the war, this day was undoubtedly its darkest.

On the following evening, 22 March, the target for 627 Squadron was the River Elbe, another long transport route

*Avro Lancaster PB996, YZ-C, of 617 Squadron releases a
22,000-pound Grand Slam bomb over the railway viaduct at
Arnsberg, Germany, 19 March 1945.*

flowing southeast–northwest across Germany, through Dresden,
Magdeburg and Hamburg and passing the entrance of the Kiel
Canal before debouching into the North Sea. This time Flight
Lieutenant Armstrong and Pilot Officer Patterson in DZ451
succeeded in dropping their indicators in the correct places,
thereby providing a clear lead for the other seven Mosquitos
following. All but one Mosquito saw the markers clearly
and placed their mines in the centre of the river. The devices
dropped incorporated a heavy weight and chain that acted as
an anchor, tethering the mine to allow it to float just beneath
the surface of the water. Since it had both contact and magnetic
triggers, the mine would detonate at the close passage of a
steel-hulled barge. All the Mosquitos returned safely, and the
phrase that appeared repeatedly in the debriefing reports was
'excellent marking'. The only crew to return with their mine
still in the bomb bay was Pilot Officer Nash and Flight Sergeant
Wetherall flying Mosquito DZ599; they aborted their mission
after failing to see any markers. Nash and Wetherall were the
last to land back at RAF Woodhall Spa, raising suspicions

that they had got lost. Under the circumstances, they knew they would be subject to a ferocious amount of light-hearted ribbing by the other crews. They took it in good part, as such teasing served as encouragement to get things right the next time. As it happened, the opportunity to do just that came the following evening.

Wesel, 23 March 1945

Sitting at the confluence of the rivers Lippe and Rhine, the small city of Wesel found itself at the tip of the formation of Field Marshal Bernard Montgomery's Operation Plunder. The northern crossing of the Rhine would take place over a 35-mile front, but key to the centre of the attack was the objective of taking Wesel early on. From Wesel, roads led out into the flatlands beyond, and once they reached the city, Montgomery's forces would be able to fan out and connect with the airborne landing grounds beyond. The lessons of Market Garden, the attempt to cross the Rhine at Arnhem in September 1944, had been learned. The airborne forces landing by parachute and glider ahead of the main attack would be far more accessible, but a successful and rapid crossing at Wesel was essential.

The Allied armies waiting to rush the Rhine – comprising British, American and Canadian troops – numbered more than 1.2 million men. Bomber Command had already laid most of Wesel to waste in attacks on 16–19 February, using air-burst bombs to destroy most of the structures of the city. Knowing their probable fate, many of its inhabitants had already fled along the long, straight road that led east to Schermbeck and beyond. The smouldering ruin of what had once been a flourishing Rhineland town stood helpless in the path of the Allies.

On the morning of 23 March, as the Mosquito men of 627 Squadron were finishing breakfast, 617 Squadron were departing from RAF Woodhall Spa to attack Bremen with enormous 'Tallboy' bombs. Weighed down by these 12,000lb devices, which required specially enlarged bulbous bomb-bay doors – the heavily pregnant bombers took their time leaving the runway. As their wheels lost contact with the ground, the Lancasters' wings bowed under the weight of the bombs, almost as if they were pausing to consider whether to fly before beginning their gentle climb away. In the Watch Office (as the control tower was then known), each take-off was viewed by the nervous eyes of the ground controller; only once the shape of the departing Lancaster became clear in the sky was the next one given the go-ahead to begin rolling along the runway. The heavy bombers would be accompanied by fighters all the way to Bremen and back for this daylight raid, illustrating how confident the Allies were by now in their air supremacy.

The crews of 627 Squadron travelled over to RAF Coningsby for their briefing. This was to be an all-out effort; ten Mosquitos were tasked to mark Wesel, and the need for absolute accuracy was impressed upon them. Any creepback* in the bombing force could drop on Allied forces waiting to cross the Rhine – a danger of 'friendly fire' that did not exist when Bomber Command were attacking targets deep in enemy territory. This was the first time the Mosquitos had supported a troop movement at such close quarters. Studying the maps carefully, they chose as the marking point a clearly defined jetty formed from a strip of land precisely on the confluence of the Lippe and Rhine rivers. The night would be moonlit, so the jetty promised to be clearly visible.

627 Squadron were unlikely to have much to fear from enemy fighters over Wesel. By now, the Allies had pushed the Luftwaffe back by making their forward airfields almost impossible to fly

* Creepback describes the tendency of bombers to release their weapons early, aimed at fires rather than the target markers.

from. They still faced danger from German flak batteries; there were an estimated 114 heavy and 712 light units, but these were spaced over the entire breadth of the front (in order to prevent airborne landings) and were not concentrated around Wesel. By midday, as the Mosquitos of 627 Squadron began their air tests, the twenty Lancasters despatched to Bremen had all returned safely. Their work was complete, but the sense of busyness around Woodhall Spa was undiminished.

At 17.00 hours, as the Mosquitos were being equipped with their target indicators for that night, a huge barrage opened up on the Rhine crossing points some 300 miles to the east. Four thousand Allied guns began to pound the German defensive positions, and as the evening light began to fade, the sky was full of muzzle flashes and the rushing sound of shells fired towards the eastern bank of the Rhine. At Wesel, the guns would inflict considerable damage on the German-held side of the Rhine, thereby limiting the potency of the Wehrmacht's attacks on the fleet of small Allied boats poised to cross the river. But there would be no assumption on the part of the Allies that artillery alone would do the job. Bomber Command would strike at potential strongpoints on the eastern side of the river and further reduce the town of Wesel.

Around 20.45, ten Mosquitos of 627 Squadron took off from RAF Woodhall Spa in the darkness. Squadron Leader Mallender and Flight Lieutenant Gaunt were Marker Leaders in DZ599, with the dependable Topper and Davies in the Number Two position, Bridges and Doyle in third and Walker and Oatley in fourth – or at least this was the planned order. It would not be a long flight, and the margin for navigational error was narrow; each of them knew that Allied lives would depend on the accuracy of their marking.

Fifteen minutes later, at 21.00, the 7th Battalion, Black Watch (Royal Highland Regiment), began crossing the Rhine near the town of Rees, 12 miles north of Wesel. An hour later,

627 Squadron approached Wesel as part of the attacking force of 5 Group. Below, the crews could clearly see the Rhine, not only by the light of the moon, but from the numerous fires burning along the eastern bank caused by the artillery barrage. The shelling had stopped, and Wesel was identifiable by a broad bend in the river.

From high above, a green marker flare was dropped into the target area by a Pathfinder Lancaster using Oboe. There was to be no illumination of Wesel from above – as happened in raids such as that on Dresden on 13 February with the use of parachute flares. The thinking behind this was to avoid revealing the movement of Allied troops on the Rhine in the light cast.* 627 Squadron arrived shortly after the dropping of the green flare, using the low light of the moon to pick out the jetty. As planned, Mallender and Gaunt laid the first 1,000lb red indicator, which exploded in a mass of pyrotechnics. Following Mallender and Gaunt as Number Two, Topper and Davies called their 'Tally Ho' and backed up with their flare, only realizing later that Walker and Oatley had dived at precisely the same moment. Both crews had pushed their 'transmit' button to call in their attack simultaneously, but fortunately each was flying a different course into the target. Pulling back, the Mosquitos circled, watching the bright flashes of the falling bombs forming knots of light around the centre of the city. In the Lancasters, the bomb aimers were setting their bomb sights to drop 200 yards from the marking spot. To assist them, four of 627 Squadron's Mosquitos acted as 'windfinders', led by Flight Lieutenant Alford and Flight Sergeant Murphy in KB345, as 'Breeze Leader', coordinating a constant stream of wind reports from the other Mosquitos to the Master Bomber. In turn, he would communicate the wind conditions to the approaching Lancasters.

* Commandos had already crossed the Rhine close by.

Opposing the Allied crossing were the German 1st Parachute Army of Army Group H. Already depleted by the fierce fighting in the Reichwald Forest on the Dutch–German border in February and early March, their strength stood at 69,000 men, but these numbers were spread over a 60-mile front. With only forty-five tanks, Generals Schlemm* and Blaskowitz could have had little hope of holding out against the Allied onslaught. 5 Group's unhindered bombing of Wesel proved to be as accurate as desired, and by the time the Allies advanced through it, 97 per cent of its buildings had been destroyed. They encountered little opposition. The civilian death toll of thirty-six, while deeply regrettable, showed that Wesel was already a ghost town.

627 Squadron's crews were landed, debriefed and able to turn in by 1am. As they slept, E and C Companies of the 17th Armored Engineer Battalion, part of the US 2nd Armored Division, assembled an ambitious pontoon bridge to span the Rhine. The next morning, 24 March, saw Winston Churchill perched on a low hill overlooking the Rhine puffing on a large cigar. Served tea and coffee, his assembled group of commanders stared upwards, hardly needing the binoculars they gazed through. From this vantage point of rough grass and stones, Churchill could see a vast armada of troop transports overhead. They signalled that Operation Varsity was underway – a vast airborne operation involving 16,000 troops and thousands of aircraft, whose aim was the reinforcement of the Allied bridgehead on the eastern bank of the Rhine near Wesel.

The next day, after a meeting with Eisenhower and other generals including Montgomery in a villa overlooking the Rhine, Churchill took a boat over the river. He spent thirty minutes on the eastern bank clambering over the rubble surrounding the

---

* Schlemm was injured two days before the assault and replaced by General Blumentritt.

Churchill steps ashore at Wesel, 24 March 1945.

destroyed Wesel railway bridge and chatting to senior officers. His presence there emphasized just how far the Allies had come – and how close they were to victory.

27 March 1945

Since the 1880s the impoverished Whitechapel area of East London had been home to a large Jewish population who had fled the pogroms taking place in Tsarist Russia. Hughes Mansions in Vallance Road – three parallel blocks of flats of five storeys each – had been built as local authority housing as recently as 1928, part of an effort to improve a run-down and slum-infested district. At 07.20 on the morning of 27 March, fifteen-year-old Ben Glaizner was woken by his father telling him it was time to get up and go to work. He remembered the time as his father was pointing at his wristwatch. Seconds later, the room was illuminated by a sudden flash of blue light. Ben remembers little after this. A V-2 rocket had torn through the middle block of Hughes Mansions, its 1,000kg warhead reducing the building to rubble in a fraction of a second; as well as virtually demolishing the two other blocks, the missile strike had caused serious blast damage to a neighbouring hospital and school. The V-2 differed from its less sophisticated cousin, the V-1, in providing no audible warning of its imminent impact; nor was there any defence against it. The sonic boom of the arriving rocket would only be heard after it had exploded. The V-2 strike on Hughes Mansions killed 134 of its residents, 120 of whom were Jewish. It would have been of little consolation to the bereaved that 27 March would prove to be the final day of V-2 attacks on London; a further rocket fell in Orpington later that day, killing one person. In total, some 2,750 Londoners were killed in V-2 attacks, and more than 6,500 injured.

The day also marked the near complete collapse of the German 4th Army defending East Prussia against the Soviets. In June 1941, the 4th Army had been one of the spearhead units of Operation Barbarossa, the invasion of the Soviet Union, but now its remnants – under the command of General Friedrich Hossbach – feared complete encirclement by the Red Army and retreated, against Hitler's orders.

Significant for so many, 27 March was also the day that saw the last operational loss of a 627 Squadron Mosquito in the Second World War. The target that evening was the River Elbe, a familiar location given its mounting strategic importance and the Squadron's use of mines. The force of eight aircraft took off at 19.40 hours, successfully delivered their payload on target by 21.30 and turned for home. Flying Officer Bill Barnett of the Royal New Zealand Air Force and Flight Sergeant John Day, an Australian, were flying in DZ599, the aircraft that Jock Walker and Ken Oatley had flown on the Dresden raid. Barnett and Day had enjoyed an uneventful flight, but as they crossed the German coast on their homeward leg they were caught by light flak, which knocked out an engine and caused DZ599 to lose height. The Mosquito was capable of making it home on a single engine, but on this occasion it was clear that the loss of altitude was going to cause a very serious problem. Barnett had few options – and turning back to land was not one of them. As the needle of the altimeter continued to fall, both men prepared to ditch in the North Sea. Barnett flicked the transmit lever on his control column and sent a message on the VHS channel to the raid leader saying he had lost an engine and was ditching.

This last radio call did not give DZ599's position – it could well be that events were unfolding too quickly for Flight Sergeant Day to give a precise location to Barnett. Settling the Mosquito into the best approach that he could and watching the dark horizon of the sea fill his windscreen, Barnett waited for the touchdown. The impact was jarring, and with the rush of water and spray over the cockpit, both men feared the Mosquito would sink immediately. Once all forward momentum was lost, she wallowed, bobbing up and down; but it was clear that when she did sink, it would be nose first, owing to the weight of the engines. Using the upper escape hatch, the two men climbed out, only to find that the dinghy, which would normally deploy automatically, had failed to emerge. Instead, Barnett had to rely on his 'K' type dinghy, a small one-man inflatable that came equipped with paddles and a sail. However, Day had not managed to retrieve his 'K' type dinghy from the cockpit and, once Barnett had clambered into his, he made desperate efforts to haul Day on board – but to no avail, since the intense cold made it impossible to get a good grip. Day was left clinging to part of the floating wing, although this precarious position could not be sustained for long, and he slipped into the water.

The strong breeze and moving waves meant that Barnett soon lost contact with Day in the darkness. The twenty-year-old from the Melbourne suburb of Murrumbeena, Victoria, who had celebrated his birthday only four weeks earlier, was lost without trace. Unlike earlier members of 627 Squadron, Day did not have a tour on bombers under his belt, but had joined 627 as his first operational unit after arriving from Australia. In the ocean of missing and displaced persons in post-war Europe, his death was not formally recognized until 1949. Adrift in the North Sea, Bill Barnett must have wondered whether a similar fate awaited him. The loneliness of his situation was intense; daybreak came without any sign of rescuers, and he was to spend another two days and agonizing nights at the mercy of the waves. On the fourth day he managed to make landfall on one of the Frisian Islands, where the Germans took him into custody as a prisoner of war.

After two weeks in hospital recovering from his ordeal, and from the injuries he had sustained in the crash, Barnett was sent to Stalag X-A in Schleswig-Hesterberg, north of Hamburg – not far from where he had been found. This was not a Luftwaffe-run camp of the type that airmen were normally sent to, but a reception centre that now housed Polish, Russian and Italian soldiers – and a smattering of British airmen. By this point in the war, the Germans were having difficulties coping with prisoners of war; the normally efficient system of detaining and interrogating airmen had broken down. The camp was located in a former children's hospital in Hesterberg – an imposing three-storied building in the town. Barnett's incarceration period of five weeks was brief by the standards of most prisoners of war.

★

The disappearance of Barnett and Day had little effect on the men of 627 Squadron; it was sad, of course, but the days and weeks following were filled with activity and speculation. There was no doubt that Germany's capitulation was close. The target list for what would be 627 Squadron's seven final operations was dominated by oil-refining facilities. Missions were flown to Molbis, Lützkendorf, Pilsen and Leipzig, all of which were successfully marked and bombed. The effects of reducing German oil-refining capacity could have taken many weeks to become manifest on the battlefields. In hindsight, with the war rapidly nearing its conclusion, such raids might appear ineffectual, but there is a sense that Allied command were planning for every eventuality – including the war entering a protracted stage of guerrilla fighting. There was a fear that Hitler might flee south from Berlin with an entourage of resistance fighters – or even with significant elements of his army. The Allies believed his destination could be the Obersalzberg, high in the Bavarian Alps above Berchtesgaden, where Hitler maintained the retreat known in English as the 'Eagle's Nest'. Was Hitler's plan to make a last stand in the labyrinth of old salt mine tunnels beneath the mountain?

On 15 April the Soviets launched their last attack on Berlin, with two marshals, Zhukov and Konev, competing for the honour of being the first to enter the city. There was now no doubt that they would take the German capital, and American troops were ordered to cease their advance on the Elbe.* As the Red Army inched closer to Hitler's lair, the Allies held their breath, waiting to see which way he would run – if he chose to.

* American and Soviet troops would not formally meet and shake hands on the Elbe until 25 April 1945.

Tønsberg, 25 April 1945

The move against a potential final Nazi hiding place was one of the last acts of Bomber Command in the European theatre. On 25 April, Numbers 1, 5 and 8 Group sent 359 Avro Lancasters and twelve Mosquitos against the Obersalzberg in Bavaria. Twisting through the mountains, they found their target, but the bombing that took place during this unopposed daylight raid did more to destroy the town of Berchtesgaden than to touch assets that might have proved useful to Hitler. Surprisingly, given it was such a large raid, 627 Squadron were not involved, although their neighbours, 617 Squadron, were part of the operation.

627 Squadron's target that day, for what would be their last raid of the war, was Norway. The country that had been the scene of some of the most dramatic actions in the operational history of the Mosquito now provided its closing curtain. Even at this point, with the war's end so close, Bomber Command's machinery of planning operations was still churning out targets for bombing. Perhaps it was pressure to find fresh targets that dictated the selection of the Vallø oil plant at Tønsberg, southwest of Oslo. The purpose and effectiveness of the raid has since been questioned, but the airmen instructed to engage in the attack could only trust their superiors to have chosen an appropriate target.

The reality for the German army of occupation in Norway was that they were now cut off from the rest of Europe; given time, the collapse of the Reich would make their surrender inevitable.

Located on the western shore of the Oslofjord, the refinery was built on a spit of land jutting into the sea 3 miles from the town of Tønsberg. A small settlement of seventy wooden clapboard houses, typical of many Norwegian dwellings, sat

The oil refinery at Vallø, Norway.

uncomfortably close to the plant at Vallø. It was not a large, sprawling site, but a modest refinery with two tall chimneys and a collection of cylindrical tanks. It had escaped the attentions of the Allied bombers throughout the war, perhaps because production there was modest compared with other refineries.

Even at this very late stage of the war, the threat of anti-aircraft guns and fighters remained over Norway, so this was to be a night raid. 627 Squadron left RAF Woodhall Spa at 21.06 hours; ahead of them, 121 Lancasters were streaming out over the North Sea. Squadron Leader Bill Topper led the pack of the Mosquitos, but his regular navigator, Vic Davies, had recently left after finishing his tour. Topper regretted Davies going, they had been a steady team for some time, but in his place an equally experienced man, Flight Lieutenant Tice, had stepped into the breach. He was Squadron Navigation Officer and, with this seniority, was a man who was not shy of expressing his opinion when it mattered. On a recent raid when light flak was flicking across the sky close to them, Topper had found himself being beaten on the head and shoulders with a navigation ruler by Tice, who was urging him, 'Lower, lower!' Despite being 'encouraged' like a filly at Newmarket, Topper worked well with Tice, although he remembered thinking, 'I'm doing the best I can.'

Behind Topper and Tice the trusty duo of Walker and Oatley acted as marker Number Two, with four other marking Mosquitos behind them. The weather over the North Sea was fine, but a large cloudbank loomed over the target, climbing thousands of feet and reducing visibility significantly. However, once they descended under 6,500 feet they found perfect weather, and the rocky coastline near Tønsberg appeared with its scattering of small islands close by. In such clear conditions, the refinery was not difficult to identify. Topper and Tice swooped to launch their first Target Indicator, a 1,000lb red flare that fell 100 yards east of the target centre. The following Mosquitos roared in, settling their markers in the prescribed positions, allowing the bombers above to see a clearly defined box within which to drop their bombs.

In certain earlier raids, notably those launched against factories in France, Wing Commander Leonard Cheshire had allowed time for civilians to flee the area, but on this occasion, the bombers arrived very soon after the marker Mosquitos. Most of the inhabitants of Vallø had decided to shelter in their houses rather than venture out. The alternative would have involved running half a mile along a road that crossed a thin neck of land in the direction of Tønsberg – a distinctly unpleasant prospect when a fleet of bombers were growling angrily above them. Despite the accuracy of the raid, which was borne out by daylight photos the next day, part of the force dropped their bombs short of the marked area and onto the residential streets close by. The terrible power of the bombs split

Vallø refinery after the raid of 25 April 1945.

open the wooden framework of the houses, collapsing them
into piles of splintered timber. A crude oil tank on the refinery
site began burning, sending a telltale plume of black smoke
upwards – a further sign for the following bombers.

Despite the refinery fires, surviving residents testified later that
most of the oil tanks were empty, and that work at the site had
been all but suspended. In a forty-five minute raid, 380 tonnes of
high explosive and six tonnes of incendiaries* were launched
against the Vallø refinery, destroying it completely. Arguably,
the size of the target did not justify a raid of such intensity.

---

* Although metric tonnes are quoted, it is possible the figures are actually
imperial tons and converted by later researchers.

The little settlement of Vallø certainly paid a heavy price for Bomber Command's seizing the opportunity to wreak certain destruction on an undefended target. Fifty-three of its civilians were killed, and half of its houses demolished: a bitter blow to a tiny community so close to the end of their country's five-year occupation by the Nazis.

Landing back at Woodhall Spa at 02.28, Topper and Tice taxied to their dispersal point. Once he had applied the parking brake, Topper pulled out the slow-running cut-outs and waited for the engines to stop. As the propeller blades slowed to a halt, Topper turned the ignition switches off and closed the fuel cocks. The men loosened themselves from the grip of their Mosquito and, collecting essential items from the cockpit, stepped down the short ladder and onto terra firma once again. Although they didn't know it, theirs had been the last landing that night, marking the end of the last operational flight of 627 Squadron. It was an honour that could have fallen to the new Squadron commanding officer, Wing Commander Rollo Kingsford-Smith, who had landed only six minutes earlier, but there was something right about the last landing of a 627 Mosquito being performed by Topper and Tice, experienced squadron men both. Kingsford-Smith had taken the helm of 627 Squadron only thirteen days before; the Tønsberg raid was only his second operational outing with his new squadron. Kingsford-Smith's career at 627 Squadron may have been short, but the Australian had already led 467 and 463 Squadrons, both Royal Australian Air Force units flying Lancaster bombers. Inspired by his uncle, the aviation adventurer Sir Charles Kingsford Smith, who had taken part in the MacRobertson Trophy Air Race, Rollo had learned to fly with the Royal Australian Air Force at Cook's Point in 1938 before coming to England in 1942.

Wednesday 25 April was also the day when American and Soviet forces met on the Elbe, and the day Italians would celebrate as liberation day. In Berlin, the Red Army pressed remorselessly through the city's ruined suburbs towards the centre of the city. With artillery lowered almost to the horizontal, they pounded buildings in their path, sending men forward in waves to engage in frantic street fighting. On Thursday 26 April, French Vichy leader Philippe Pétain was arrested on the Swiss border, and on Saturday 28th, Benito Mussolini and his mistress Clara Petacci were captured attempting to flee to Switzerland and executed by partisans near Lake Como. On Monday 30 April, Hitler and his wife of twenty-four hours, Eva Braun, committed suicide in the Berlin command bunker after transferring Presidency of the Reich to Admiral Karl Dönitz. Within days, the identity of those who wielded power over large parts of Europe had changed irrevocably, while for millions the future looked deeply uncertain.

RAF Woodhall Spa waited during these days of change. No names appeared on the noticeboards for operations. 627 Squadron engaged in the normal test and training flights, but most of its airmen suspected that they would not have to fly in anger again – at least over Europe. After so many hectic days of operational flying, an eerie calm seemed to have descended over the Lincolnshire countryside. For 617 Squadron's Lancaster crews, the days followed a similar pattern; their foray to Berchtesgaden had proved to be their last action of the war. Each day men crowded around their radios to hear the news; there was so much of it that they could scarcely believe the speed with which events were unfolding. As it transpired, there was little Admiral Dönitz could do with what remained of his armed forces but negotiate surrender.

Flying Officer Bill Barnett's experience of captivity after his days adrift in the North Sea had been far from conventional. In hospital under guard he had been well looked after, but he noticed that the privations of war seemed to have affected

German food supplies far more than was the case in Britain. Once he left the hospital world of white sheets and nurses he was up against the reality of being a prisoner. When he arrived at Stalag X-A he was uncertain what he would find, and the rag-tag collection of nationalities from Russian to Czech took him by surprise. The camp swirled with rumours about the approach of the war's end; Barnett found himself surrounded with curious men wanting to know the latest news from the outside. As a lowly Pilot Officer he was also surprised to learn that he was the most senior officer in the camp – or at least the only one that the Germans would trust.

On 5 May 1945, five days after Hitler's suicide and only hours after the unconditional surrender at Lüneberg Heath of all German forces in the Netherlands and northern Germany, the Commandant of Stalag X-A retired and handed control of the camp and its 1,600 inmates to Bill Barnett. The German guards were disarmed, but, not knowing what to do, remained at their guard posts – although the prisoners had the freedom to come and go as they pleased. The next day, a unit of the RAF Regiment took control of the area, and were tasked to find the prisoner of war camp as part of their brief to keep order in what was rapidly becoming a sea of chaos. Five thousand forced labourers roamed the area, looting and looking for food. Sending a staff car, the regiment picked up Bill Barnett to discuss the position at their Headquarters, but when the vehicle was fired at on the return journey, Barnett had to take refuge at the local airfield. He was to remain in the area several weeks after being appointed by the Allied Control Commission as officer responsible for all the territory between the Danish border and the Kiel Canal. It was a heavy responsibility, which included administering over 5,000 SS troops in captivity. In addition, Barnett oversaw the surrender of 500 Luftwaffe aircraft, including many single-seat Focke-Wulf Fw 190s, which continued to arrive from the Eastern Front with up to three pilots sharing the one seat – such was their desperation not to fall into the hands of the Russians.

At Horncastle, the nearest town to RAF Woodhall Spa, the evening of 7 May 1945 was filled with excitement at the news that the following day was to be declared Victory in Europe Day. Here, and throughout Britain, lofts and cellars were raided to find boxes of union jacks and streamers left over from the coronation of George VI in May 1937. Large street parties were organized overnight, with trestle tables filling the streets the next morning. The bells of churches rang all day, with three services of thanksgiving held in Horncastle. At 3pm the familiar growling voice of Winston Churchill filled radio speakers, informing the nation of the unconditional surrender of all German forces. His stirringly patriotic speech, clouded only by mention of the continuing war with Japan, was the trigger for riotous celebrations. For the servicemen at Woodhall Spa, well versed in letting off steam, the merrymaking continued long into the night. Pilot Officer Hector Bridges appeared to be more or less coherent the next day, and was asked to ferry a VIP over to RAF Waddington in a Mosquito. It was a relatively short distance – less than 15 miles – and ordinarily a staff car would have been employed, but with the motor pool temporarily and understandably unavailable, Bridges was tasked with making the short hop by air. The atmosphere in the cockpit that morning is unrecorded, but it seems reasonable to assume that the smells of plywood and glue native to the Mosquito were supplemented by the aroma of alcohol. Hector Bridges remembered taxiing out and turning onto the runway for take-off, only to find that there were two runways, each moving disconcertingly back and forth before his eyes. Despite his delicate state of health, he completed his task successfully, but confessed himself very relieved to get the Mosquito safely back on the ground on his return to Woodhall Spa.

Later that day, Wing Commander Rollo Kingsford-Smith

persuaded 617 Squadron to allow him to fly one of their Lancasters to Rheine airfield, west of Osnabrück, in an attempt to find his brother. As part of Operation Exodus, a series of flights to repatriate British prisoners of war from Europe to Britain, the flight was authorized, but it was a little unusual

627 Squadron members enjoy a celebratory drink,
VE Day, 8 May 1945.

nonetheless. Kingsford-Smith took Pilot Officer Eric Arthur as navigator, as he had flown to the area in recent times. The remainder of the crew were 617 volunteers – Kingsford-Smith was advised to carry a full complement of crew owing to reports of sporadic German resistance, even after the official surrender. Kingsford-Smith did not succeed in locating his brother that day, and describes the scene he found as 'a bit of a shambles', but he was able to bring back a group of former prisoners. Happily, his brother found another flight, and safely made the trip back to England later that day.

After nearly six long years, the war in Europe had come to an end. Training would resume at RAF Woodhall Spa within days to prepare the Squadron for its move to the Far East, with a sense of unreality reigning over the base. The war in the east would be for another set of crews – perhaps those unwearied by years of night flying.

Epilogue

July 1944

Walking along the broad, tree-lined streets of Washington DC, Group Captain Leonard Cheshire couldn't help noticing how utterly different the city was from London, which had known such privations and suffered such grievous damage. Here there were no ruined or bomb-damaged buildings, no taped-up glass or sand-bagged revetments. There were no signs of queues outside the bustling shops and restaurants; only outside the well-patronized cinemas, which drew an excited throng of moviegoers eager to see the latest release, did he see anyone standing in line. The city was filled with people wearing well-pressed uniforms and carrying smart briefcases, a far cry from the bedraggled Australian airmen who had made up his command on airfields in Britain. However, the signs of war were not absent from Washington DC; the city had almost doubled in size over the past few years, and its skyline was altered as temporary office blocks were built to accommodate the thousands of new workers required to service a war economy. Anti-aircraft guns were visible on many roofs, guard posts housing round-helmeted men carrying P-14 rifles dotted the sidewalks, and military vehicles cruised the streets.

Cheshire's posting to America had been a safe one in the light of his warm relations with US senior officers. Even before Air Marshal Harris had granted full resources for Cheshire's marking work at 5 Group, US Eighth Air Force Commander Carl Spaatz had been a keen advocate of Cheshire's low-level marking technique. He had visited RAF Coningsby and subsequently gifted a number of aircraft for use in specialized marking. By July 1945 Leonard Cheshire was bored of his desk duties in Washington, even though his work in helping coordinate the RAF's Tiger Force – a long-range heavy bomber force intended for operations against the Japanese in the east – was at an advanced stage. The plan included squadrons close to his heart, including the Lancasters of 617 Squadron and the Mosquitos of 627, but nothing seemed to ease the tedium of paperwork.

When Cheshire was briefed in strictest secrecy on the existence of the Manhattan Project – America's development of the atomic bomb – it came as a huge surprise to him. Shortly afterwards, he was invited to Tinian, Marianas Islands, in the Western Pacific to fly as an observer on an atomic bomb dropping over Japan. The lines of bright silver B-29 Boeing Superfortresses glinting in the strong sun on Tinian's field were immediately impressive. This tiny island in the azure waters of the western Pacific Ocean lay some 5,500 miles distant from America's west coast, but it had become a veritable aircraft carrier. The B-29 Superfortress, the largest of all Second World War bombers, dwarfed the Avro Lancaster. These fully pressurized goliaths were capable of striking Japan from higher altitudes than the European theatre. The USAAF had already launched many long-distance bombing raids on Japan, but as yet, despite the absence of Germany as an ally in the west, nothing had persuaded the Japanese to negotiate an end to the war.

In the early hours of 9 August 1945, Leonard Cheshire took off from Tinian aboard B-29 *Big Stink* on the 1,570-mile flight to Japan. Along with the nuclear physicist William Penney, Cheshire was travelling as an official British observer of the nuclear bombing of a Japanese city. Flying ahead of them to the city of Kokura, B-29 *Bock's Car*, flown by Major Charles Sweeney, carried the nuclear bomb, nicknamed 'Fat Man'. When weather conditions over Kokura were found to be unfavourable, Sweeney radioed his entourage that the target city had been changed to Nagasaki. By the time the nuclear weapon was released, *Big Stink* was still 50 miles away, but close enough to see the terrible effect of the explosion. Leonard Cheshire would write: 'I was overcome, not by its size, nor by its speed of ascent, but by what appeared to me its perfect and faultless symmetry... Against me, it seemed to declare, you cannot fight. My whole being felt overwhelmed, first by a tidal wave of relief and hope – it's all over! – then by a revolt against using such a weapon.'

Although the Japanese had declared they would fight on after the first atom bomb dropped over Hiroshima on 6 August,* the reality of the power of nuclear weapons had dawned on them. The nuclear strike on Nagasaki tipped the scales, achieving in the Far East what Air Chief Marshal Harris had vainly hoped the saturation bombing of Berlin would accomplish during the winter of 1943–44. Emperor Hirohito's capitulation speech was broadcast to the Japanese nation on 15 August; after the loss of many millions of lives, the Second World War was finally over. In Britain, still preparing to deploy the Tiger Force in the lead-up to an invasion of the Japanese home islands that would not now take place, a further round of celebrations were in order; but this time, unlike on VE Day, there was no prospect of lingering war to contain their joy.

*

* A radio interception allowed the Americans to listen in on the highest Japanese government communications.

Although 627 Squadron had been practising day after day for their new Far Eastern role, the reality was that the Squadron had changed completely in the weeks after VE Day. Many of the crews had been stood down, and most had been posted away from the base in the preceding weeks. Some of the old guard remained to teach the new generation the principles of the marking dive. On 1 June 1945, all the Australians were formally posted to 54 Base, RAF Coningsby, awaiting repatriation. Twenty-one fresh crews joined 627 on 14 June, and a further eleven crews on 30 June. With these departures and new arrivals, the Squadron's wartime memory and identity had been swept aside. For those who had spent long hours in darkened skies, the elation they experienced at the war's final end in August was almost indescribable.

Australians John Herriman and Eric Arthur had already made

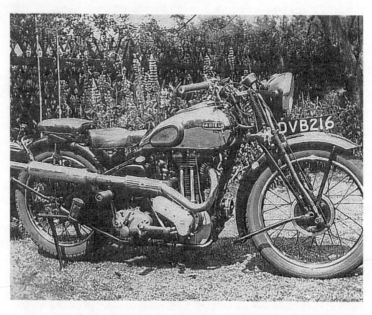

John Herriman's and Eric Arthur's Euphemia.

plans for their summer, even before hostilities had formally ended. On 1 May they had bought an Ariel Hunter motorcycle from Wests Garage in Lincoln, paying the princely sum of £80. Named *Euphemia* after a brief tryst Herriman had had with a Greek girlfriend, the motorcycle became a passage to freedom for the men. At times, they would return from flying to find the fuel tank topped up by the ground crew – petrol was a rationed commodity. Transported by train, the motorcycle enabled them to explore further afield and still conserve fuel. They continued to spend their leave in their favourite haunt – with the Brown family in Carlisle. One afternoon in July, just as Eric was returning from a picnic, he met a young woman on the driveway of the house on Kingmoor Road. Evelyn Currie lived out of town, close to the Scottish border at Blackbank and, for the first and only time in her life, had missed the bus home. Having time to wait, she decided to visit her friends the Browns. She was just leaving as John and Eric arrived back. In the briefest of exchanges, Eric had fallen hopelessly and inexplicably in love, and made arrangements to meet Evelyn again. It was not something he had planned, or even imagined could happen, but this brief encounter changed their lives forever. Evelyn would join Eric in Australia and they would marry in October 1950. In microcosm, Eric and Evelyn epitomized the generation of young people who had fought in the war, but now looked forward to a much brighter and safer life. Many thousands had met their future partners in time of war and forged what would be life-long relationships.

On 11 September 1945, an order was received at RAF Woodhall Spa and noted in the Operational Record Book: 'Instruction to disband 627 Squadron. All Mosquito flying to cease forthwith.' The Squadron officially disbanded on 30 September, ending two years of intense and skilled operational flying by men who had risked their lives in mission after mission over occupied Europe.

The aircraft themselves were transferred to other squadrons, but within weeks, as the process of shrinking Britain's vast wartime air force came into play, many were flown to holding airfields. Thousands of aeroplanes lined runways and dispersals until there was no space left and surrounding farmers' fields were used. By early 1946 three letters denoted the end of a Mosquito, 'SOC', Struck Off Charge. Unlike the aluminium aircraft, there was little to salvage when it came to scrap, and many were chopped up and burned. In a society ravaged by war there was no desire to keep the weapons that reminded them of the years of hardship.

The 'Wooden Wonder', for a brief period a technological masterpiece, had been supplanted by the latest generation of fast aeroplanes. The writing had been on the wall for some time – the jet engine changed flying for good. In January 1944 John Herriman and Eric Arthur found themselves at RAF Manston in Kent, and were taxiing out for a flight as two new Gloster Meteor jets prepared to leave. Signalling across, the pilots indicated they wanted a competition, and so Herriman and Arthur drew level with them for a race. When the brakes were released, the Mosquito bounded away ahead of the jets and its wheels seemed to leave the ground first – but the Meteors overtook them and soon disappeared into the distance. There was no doubting that jet aircraft were the future; had it not been for Hitler's preference for vengeance weapons and the constant pressure on German manufacturing, jet aircraft in the Luftwaffe such as the Messerschmitt Me 262 might have made more of an impact.

At war's end, de Havilland did not abandon the concept of wooden laminates and produced two jet fighters – the Vampire and the Venom – with timber fuselages. These highly successful designs, which replaced many of their propeller-driven cousins, would serve in the Royal Air Force until 1966 – and even later in other air forces: the Swiss finally retired their fleet of Venoms in 1983.

In the post-war years and the generation of the baby boomers, the exploits of 627 Squadron were largely forgotten. There were careers to build and new, more peaceable ventures to be explored. With the help of his father, Ken Oatley returned to the baking trade and opened new shops in Northampton. Jock Walker returned to the building trade in Scotland, garnering a reputation as a skilled plasterer. The men did not forget 627 Squadron – it had been the happiest squadron they had served with. As the years passed, there was time to recollect that, as young men, they had flown a remarkable aircraft in a noble cause, and to remember with sadness – but also with gratitude – those who had not returned to enjoy the lives that victory against Nazi tyranny made possible. There had been many outstanding Mosquito squadrons; by its nature, this was

Eric Arthur's family greet his return to Australia.

an aeroplane that enabled an average pilot to perform feats of airmanship of which he might not have thought himself capable earlier in the war, in a different aircraft.

With the passage of time, only Ken Oatley remains still living of the aircrews of 627 Squadron; at the time of writing, he is 100 years old. However, the memory of the exploits of the men of 627 Squadron lives on in the families of those who flew. They are remembered in blurred black-and-white photographs of uniformed airmen in family albums; and in old stories – ever fresh in the re-telling, whether at the dinner table or at the pub bar – of pilots and navigators in their tiny cockpit, of missions achieved or missions aborted.

Ken Oatley displays his Légion d'honneur, awarded to veterans by the French government on the seventieth Anniversary of the Liberation of France, 2014.

The airfield at RAF Woodhall Spa lies deserted, and is now a nature reserve. What remains of the runways can be clearly seen, vast concrete bands stretching for hundreds of yards. Their surface is uneven, the asphalt topping eroded as weeds squeeze through the gaps in the concrete, gradually seeking to return this sleeping giant to the fields from whence it came. Fittingly, the only part of the airfield retained by the Royal Air Force is the area once used by 627 Squadron. Among the storage sheds there is a deserted metal-clad 'hush room', once used for testing Tornado jet engines.

The whistling sound of the Mosquito has long been replaced by the calls of water birds on the lakes left by the gravel-quarrying at Woodhall Spa. Amid this oasis of tranquillity, the noise of fighter jets from nearby RAF Coningsby can be heard daily – practising for wars that hopefully will never come. But the deep music of wartime engines is not completely lost, for here, more than any former airfield in Britain, the air still reverberates to the sound of the Rolls-Royce Merlin. The Battle of Britain Memorial Flight's use of RAF Coningsby, just four miles south of here, guarantees that, although 627 Squadron is a distant memory, part of them has never left.

Notes on Sources and
Further Notes on the Text

Although the story of the de Havilland Mosquito is familiar to many, the exploits of 627 Squadron have remained relatively untold. Having seen many of their contemporaries featured in print, the veterans took matters into their own hands in 1991 and published an anthology of memories of their experiences of service in 627 Squadron under the title *At First Sight*. Since the book had only a limited print run, most copies are the treasured possessions of families, but happily, it is available to read on the internet free of charge on the website '627 Squadron in Retirement' (http://www.627squadron. co.uk). *At First Sight* was my starting point in seeking to gain greater understanding of the exploits of 627 Squadron. Fascinating as I found it to be, it did not, however, fully explain the background of each of their operations.

In writing about the Mosquito, my decision to concentrate on 627 Squadron was not a random selection from the many squadrons who flew this remarkable aircraft. I came across 627 Squadron while I was researching my previous book, *The Crew: The Story of a Lancaster Bomber Crew*, and mentioned them briefly in that volume. I was later drawn to them through the intriguing activities of the Master Bombers of 54 Base, RAF Coningsby. After ending his tour with 97 Squadron, Don

Bowes, the navigator of *The Crew*, made twelve further flights with the pilot Charles Owen – often in a de Havilland Mosquito and sometimes in a Lockheed Lightning, an unusual and intriguing combination for an RAF unit. The Master Bombers at Coningsby had a small collection of aeroplanes attached to them, but without a squadron identity, they borrowed aircraft freely from squadrons based nearby – and often from 627 Squadron. It was the dawning realization that 627 were not just a 'normal' Pathfinder Squadron, but a specialized unit, that propelled me into their story.

In turn, credit must be given to the hundreds of aviation enthusiasts who have taken some small part of a published account and commented on it online, straining out inaccuracies and focusing on single events in a way that an author writing a broader narrative often does not have time to. In this world of intricate attention to detail, forum discussions often question long-held assumptions, provide new evidence and locate sources of information otherwise hidden to a researcher. Online sources have thus proved a fruitful seam to mine, but of course not all things on the internet are accurate, and I have found numerous inconsistencies in the course of research. My approach is always to try to compare the available accounts with each other, in order to achieve as balanced a picture as possible. I apologise in advance for any cases where I have drawn the wrong conclusion or, in the process of writing, slow-wittedness has allowed a glaring error to sneak in.

Nor are official historical documents of the time consistently accurate; Operation Record Books, for instance, are illuminating, but not inerrant. In their collation of information, they too are subject to the fallibilities of human interaction. Most of the crew accounts of a raid were verbally obtained, handwritten by a briefing officer and then sent to a typing pool before being read and signed by the commanding officer at the month's end. In such a process, there is considerable scope for misunderstanding and muddling of details, which remain a challenge for researchers. Where contradictions remain unresolved, I have had to assume the most likely scenario, although in such cases I have attempted to make clear, through further explanation and footnotes, that a degree of factual uncertainty exists.

My thanks go to those who have provided personal information about their relatives, delving into family archives and relating stories told by the airmen. My conversations with Ken Oatley, the last surviving member of 627 Squadron aircrew, have been enlightening and pleasurable in equal measure. Hearing the personal testimonies of servicemen brings the dry, tersely expressed detail of the official records to vibrant life. The digital archive of the International Bomber Command Centre in Lincoln has been very useful, and their collection of recorded interviews invaluable.

PROLOGUE

My first interviews with Ken Oatley were by telephone, quite lengthy calls during which I wrote notes feverishly, trying to capture every detail of what he was telling me. By the time we met face to face, in September 2020, I was familiar with Ken's story, but we went over the ground again nonetheless. It was fascinating how at each interview new details emerged – whether nuances of emotion or facts that shed fresh light on small but significant events. There is also a kind of power in repetition: asking the same question in a different way allowed further information to reveal itself. But above all, the researcher's greatest asset is the ability to sit and listen.

There is another critical component to the process of interviewing, and that is the expressiveness of the human face. In it, we find the person behind the words; we can suddenly be transported back in time to experience the events and meet the individuals they are describing. I regret very much that the constraints of space did not allow me to include as many personal details of the participants as I might have wished.

I was very aware that Ken Oatley is one of the very few men still with us who took part in the Dresden raid. Moreover, the fact that he was part of only the second crew to drop a marker on the city places him in a unique position. His emphasis on the normality of the procedure 627 Squadron engaged in on 13 February 1945 cannot be overstated. For Ken, it was just another raid that followed many hours of training; he had no inkling that the events of this night would be remembered above the many others on which he flew operations. Owing to the notoriety of Dresden, it is tempting to try to draw veterans into discussions about the morality of the bombing war. By and large, their views are no different from the generation of Britons who lived through the events of 1939 to 1945, even though the airmen actually saw the effect of their bombs (albeit from a height of several thousand feet). While people were still dying in Britain's towns and cities – and German V-weapons went on killing British civilians up until 27 March 1945 – there would be no great sympathy for the plight of German civilians under the saturation bombing campaign of the RAF.

CHAPTER ONE – THREE FLIGHTS TO SCANDINAVIA

The production list of the de Havilland Mosquito can be viewed on the internet (http://www.airhistory.org.uk/dh/_DH98%20 prodn%20list.txt), and reveals how rapidly the aircraft was developed from the design stage to operation. W4056 was only the seventh Mosquito built, and only the second fully operational aeroplane. The activities of 1 Photo Reconnaissance Unit are well documented, Hutchinson and Allen's experience over Norway less so. One of the downsides of the internet is its transient nature – fascinating information can disappear overnight without any signpost to a new location. Some of the details of Ørland and the loss of W4056 were obtained from a Norwegian website that suddenly disappeared while I was still at the research stage. Although books go out of print and copies can be hard to find, there is some comfort that they are likely to be found *somewhere* – an assurance not possible with websites.

Ian Hutchinson's recovery at RAF hospital Uxbridge after the Battle of Britain is worthy of more detailed coverage than the constraints of space allowed. After the battle, on 6 November 1940, Archibald McIndoe and Sir Harold Gillies presented their treatment for severe burns to the Royal Society of Medicine. Their ground-breaking methods utilised saline baths and skin grafts rather than the standard burns treatment with tannic acid, which formed a hard shell over the wound and made successful reconstructive surgery difficult – as well as being very painful to remove. Ian Hutchinson was one of the last to receive tannic acid treatment; in his own words, it 'produced great scabs that covered my face and legs while the whites of my eyes turned bright red'. Given the rigour of his treatment, it is remarkable that he was able to return to operational duty so soon.

The role of the de Havilland Mosquito in the war over Norway is in itself a fascinating subject for study. The Banff Strike Wing, based in Scotland, played a particularly aggressive role in attacking Germany's maritime interests. Seven Mosquito squadrons strong, the wing attacked shipping with wing-mounted rockets off the coast of Norway with spectacular results during 1943–44. In order to avoid the narrative becoming too bulky, *Mosquito Men* makes only brief mentions of the activities of other Mosquito squadrons, but this is in no way intended to minimize the importance of their impact.

CHAPTER TWO – THE FLYING SWEETHEARTS

The development of the high-tensile lightweight woods used in the de Havilland Mosquito was in no small part influenced by air racing. The strength of public interest in air racing in the late 1920s and early 1930s allowed investment into aircraft development at a time when the industry was in the doldrums.

Publications providing details of the MacRobertson air race proved to be in short supply, but I am indebted to an online publication by the Numismatic Association of Australia that proved invaluable in its detail (https://numismatics.org.au/wp-content/uploads/2021/06/Vol-4-Article-1.pdf). Just as the Schneider Trophy air races directly influenced the development of the Spitfire, so the MacRobertson air race spurred de Havilland to push the limits of lightweight plywood design. The Comet racers were not Mosquitos, but their pilots were arguably the first 'Mosquito Men' and women. In featuring the MacRobertson air race strongly in this account, I am seeking to focus not only on the design and development of the later Mosquito, but on the part played by numerous pilots and technicians who brought their skills and experiences to bear on the air war during the Second World War. I found a concise and helpful description of the woods used for the Mosquito and their sources at https://www.heraldnet.com/life/wood-from-around-the-globe-made-the-de-havilland-mosquito/.

There are very few cases of a new aircraft being developed entirely in isolation from other designs and not borrowing from them. Although many studies concentrate their attention on the period of months or years during which a particular design emerges, I was keen to look at a longer developmental time span, one that embraced the decades beforehand. The development of the all-metal Junkers J1 in 1916 was greeted by the air arm of the imperial German army with the same incredulity that the wooden-laminated Mosquito concept provoked at Britain's Air Ministry. In retrospect, it is easy to examine the records of meetings and wonder at the lack of imagination of bureaucrats and senior military men. However, a fuller examination of this period, not possible within the bounds of this volume, would reveal the decision-makers to be both intelligent and forward-thinking. After all, although it made many mistakes, the Air Ministry did manage to re-equip the Royal Air Force and transform it into a modern fighting force.

Space did not allow me to give as full an account of the development of the Mosquito as I might have wished, but it is worth noting that in April 1940, USAAF General Hap Arnold took a complete set of Mosquito blueprints back to the United States for evaluation. Arnold is famed for his support of the RAF through the 'Arnold Scheme', a pilot training venture based in the USA, which was set in motion even before America was at war with Germany. He distributed the plans for the Mosquito to five American aircraft manufacturers for an honest appraisal. None returned positive reports, with Beechcraft's response being the most contemptuous: 'This airplane has sacrificed serviceability, structural strength, ease of construction and flying characteristics in an attempt to use construction material that is not suitable for the manufacture of efficient airplanes.'

Although drawing-board assessments such as these turned out to be wide of the mark, we should be cautious in being over-critical of the Air Ministry and the RAF officers who sat on their committees. The wealth of technical opinion available to them, including the American response quoted above, seemed to show the Mosquito required a lot of effort for the promise of only a very low return. However enthusiastic and convincing de Havilland may have appeared, the Air Ministry were mindful that the proposal, despite the demands of war, was still a commercial venture. De Havilland was a prosperous company that had excelled in the civilian market during the interwar years.

Although he finally secured orders for his aircraft, de Havilland's path to success was not trouble-free. During the development and early production of the Mosquito, de Havilland would be surprised by some of the factors that affected performance. Painting the Mosquito NF Mk II night fighter in matt black, for instance, reduced its top speed by 25 mph, while repainting it with glossier finishes created a problem of shine, particularly in searchlights. It took some time to settle on a semi-gloss dark colour that bridged the gap between speed and stealth.

CHAPTER THREE – THE MAN FROM TOOWOOMBA

The imposing figure of Don Bennett stands tall in the story of the formation of 627 Squadron, and this chapter looks in greater depth at his background. Although the introduction of Bennett further delays the start of the story of 627 Squadron, I decided that anything less than a substantial account of this key figure in the wider story of the Pathfinders and the Mosquito would leave holes in the narrative. Credit here is due to my editor, Richard Milbank, who suggested changes in my original manuscript to improve the clarity of the timeline in regard to Bennett.

Most commentators praise Bennett's decisive input into the development of the Pathfinders, but his leadership style and record of inter-personal conflict with other senior commanders has drawn criticism. In my research, I prefer to begin with first-hand accounts and, wherever possible, to seek out interviews and writings by the subject in question rather than commentary. Bennett's account of his life in his 1958 autobiography, *Pathfinder*, paints an interesting picture of his experiences, but also – probably unintentionally – sheds light on why he was neither universally liked nor accepted. The book itself is not a classic, like Paul Brickhill's *The Dam Busters*, perhaps because it is not objective enough. One is left with a feeling that Bennett is too quick to justify his own thinking above that of others; but *Pathfinder* opens a fascinating window onto Bennett's soul nonetheless. The video interview Bennett gave for the RAF Centre for Air and Space Power Studies (CASPs) in 1980 also reveals an unyielding belief in his thinking and actions during the war. It is perhaps this unrepentant tone that kept Bennett out of the inner circle of the British establishment.

Among the rank-and-file airmen who served under him, Bennett had a reputation as a strong but fair commander – albeit a somewhat humourless one. Veterans of 8 Group complained that the lack of post-war recognition for Bennett reflected upon their efforts. Given that many of his fellow senior RAF officers were awarded knighthoods, it is telling that Bennett never received this honour. His supporters see this as a case of the British establishment closing ranks against an outsider, but it has to be pointed out that his vocal criticism of the direction of Allied policy after the war made him a controversial figure. After resigning his RAF position, he ventured briefly into politics. He won a by-election in 1945 as a Liberal for Middlesbrough West, but was defeated in the 1945 General Election after only seventy-three days. Bennett became more nationalistic in his pronouncements; his open criticism of Churchill for not having a war aim beyond 'mere survival' was not a view that garnered much support.

CHAPTER FOUR – FRESH FACES

While I was researching *Mosquito Men*, it was noticeable that personal accounts of 627 Squadron in its earliest days at RAF Oakington (1943–44) were in shorter supply than those from the period after the Squadron moved to RAF Woodhall Spa in spring 1944. The term at Oakington was relatively short, and the whole operational period of the Squadron relatively brief compared to those squadrons that served through the entire duration of the war. The most obvious reason for this is that a number of years have elapsed since the passing of the early members of the Squadron. With scant official documentary evidence of the details of their service, I was reliant on stories related to me by relatives. With the passage of time, some of these accounts have become faded or fragmented, making a precise chronological narrative more difficult. Most, if not all, who gathered at RAF Oakington had flown early in the war, and by 1943 were seasoned aviators. Some, like Guy Lockhart, had flown in the pre-war RAF, while others joined on the outbreak of the war. Even within the course of a few months into 1944, a new generation of pilots and navigators arrived at 627 Squadron. These were younger men, some of whom joined direct from training rather than serving tours of operations beforehand.

I am particularly indebted to Peter Goodman, the son of Jack 'Benny' Goodman, who opened his family archive and unearthed a rich seam of stories and photographs from this earlier period. Many families testify that their relatives never spoke much about the war. Jack Goodman, however, spoke – and wrote – freely of his experiences, without exaggeration (or 'shooting a line', in RAF parlance) to leave us with a clear and detailed picture of life with 627 Squadron. Compared to the hours studying written records, it was refreshing to hear the actual voices of Jack Goodman and others on sound files recorded by the Imperial War Museum and the International Bomber Command Centre.

I also benefitted from other face-to-face interviews and meetings with veterans who served at this time. Wing Commander Ken Cook, of 97 Squadron, served at RAF Bourn, a stone's throw from RAF Oakington, and spoke of the daily life and routine of bomber crews at this time. Arthur Spencer, also a veteran of 97 Squadron – and, at the time of writing, still with us at the age of 101 – served at RAF Woodhall Spa in 1943. Although their memories regarding the airfields are not remarkable in themselves, they were helpful in that they corroborated accounts and details from other sources.

CHAPTER FIVE – AGENTS OF THE NIGHT

There remain many unanswered questions about the operational and family history of Guy Lockhart. His daughter, Tanya Bruce-Lockhart, does not remember her father, but she was able to provide me with links to material already published on the internet, and also recounted certain stories about her parents that had been told to her. Like many children of aircrew who died on operational duty, she retains a profound sense of loss and waste – a reminder that the effects of the Second World War are still keenly felt today.

I chose to devote much of the chapter to the story of Wing Commander Lockhart not only in recognition of his achievements, but also in order to focus on the experience that pilots brought to 627 Squadron. While Lockhart and Air Vice Marshal Don Bennett clearly enjoyed a close working relationship, the circumstances of, and background to, their first meeting are not known. However, it is safe to assume that Lockhart was, in the words of his daughter, something of a maverick, but had the element of free thinking that Bennett also possessed and recognized in others.

The fate of most of the British aircrews who parachuted from their aircraft over Germany is well recorded, but we have only sparse details of what befell Squadron Leader Edward 'Dinger' Bell and Flying Officer John Battle on 8 January 1944. The exact location where their Mosquito crashed is not known, and little is known of their reception on the ground, other than that they were confined in Stalag Luft III.

Airmen who bailed out over Germany were in significant peril from the German civilian population. I first became aware of these dangers when researching a previous book, *A Bomber Crew Mystery: The Forgotten Heroes of 388th Bombardment Group*. The son of a downed 388th airman recounted how his father had narrowly escaped being killed by civilians near a railway station. They were under the guard of soldiers who were escorting them to a train, but were horrified to see the bodies of three Royal Air Force aircrew hanging nearby. A hostile crowd had gathered and the lives of the prisoners were only spared when the guards fired over the heads of the mob.

In a spirit of post-war reconciliation, stories of these murderous events were downplayed by the Allies. The commission of such atrocities had been all too frequent during the years of conflict, and the process of acquiring evidence for civilian trials of those held responsible was deemed to be too complex. More recent articles on the subject, many of them available on the internet (for example, https://military-history.fandom. com/wiki/R%C3%BCsselsheim_massacre), make sobering reading. Attacks perpetrated by 'normal' Germans on airmen were commonplace, and the savagery displayed illustrates once again the hold the Nazi state had on its population. The propaganda minister, Joseph Goebbels, had encouraged the killing of Allied airmen by civilians in his speeches from early 1943. Speaking in Hamburg's old town square in May 1943, he had told his audience: 'You, the people, have beaten them [the airmen] to death or cut their throats – and similar things. We won't shed any crocodile tears over it, and whoever [among you] who has done this will not be led to the scaffold. We are not so insane [as to punish you]. We can understand this rage of the German people very well.'

CHAPTER SIX – A CHANGE
IN DIRECTION

In my previous book, *The Crew*, I dwelt at some length on the apparent conflicts between 8 and 5 Groups and on the differences of opinion regarding Pathfinder strategies. Max Hastings in his book *Bomber Command* (first published in 1979) explored the experiences of 97 Squadron in this period of conflict between senior officers like Harris, Cochrane and Bennett. Through my interviews with Wing Commander Ken Cook for *The Crew* I discovered further detail, particularly in what the move from 5 Group to 8 Group meant to ordinary airmen. In writing *Mosquito Men*, I felt it necessary – in order fully to explain why 627 Squadron was moved from high-level pathfinding to a new role in low-level marking – to cover some of the same ground. I trust those readers familiar with *The Crew* will forgive my repeating myself in the interests of narrative coherence. However, I found the addition of accounts from 'Benny' Goodman and other 627 Squadron crewmen further enhanced previously published accounts of the period.

While it is relatively simple to understand why conflict arose between Air Vice Marshals Bennett and Cochrane, both men being leaders of strong and unyielding conviction, it is harder to reconcile Bennett's rejection of Wing Commander Leonard Cheshire. In Bennett's 1980 CASPS interview he recognizes Cheshire's achievements, but in reference to his joining the Pathfinders, says that Cheshire was 'never a navigator'. Given Cheshire's undoubted abilities, not least in flying alone to observe raids in a P-51 fighter, this statement seems strangely misplaced. I can only conclude that Bennett's dislike of Cheshire was based on differences of personality rather than on a judgement of his ability.

CHAPTER SEVEN – THE SHALLOW DIVE

In order to gain a clear picture of the area where 627 Squadron were based and to get a broader sense of the geography and topography of Lincolnshire, I visited RAF Coningsby and RAF Woodhall Spa. I'm indebted to Royal Air Force staff for making me so welcome during my visits, and am grateful for their enthusiastic assistance in helping me unravel some of the minutiae of station life there during the Second World War. I'd particularly like to mention Chief Technician Andrew Copley, who has made a tireless contribution to the establishing of the RAF Coningsby Heritage Centre.

The airmen based at RAF Woodhall Spa spent a good deal of time travelling back and forth to RAF Coninsgby for meetings and briefings. Woodhall Spa was not originally intended to house two operational squadrons, and was stretched to meet the needs of 627 Squadron, who found themselves occupying less than perfect accommodation. A visit to today's Thorpe Camp Museum gives an interesting insight into the types of building used – the museum using parts of the accommodation and services site of the former Woodhall Spa airfield. Larger buildings suitable for meetings were limited in number, as in the case of the first briefing for the newly arrived squadrons in mid-April 1944. In this instance, the station cinema was used, a building that stood near the present entrance to RAF Coningsby, but has since been demolished.

In researching the role of the Master Bomber and the formation of 54 Base Flight at RAF Coningsby, I had expected to find more detailed records of their operations. The flight appears to have lacked the structure of a formalised squadron, in which an Operational Record Book (ORB) would have been maintained. This absence of detailed information on each operation represents an unusual gap in what are otherwise comprehensive RAF records. In addition to the small group of specialized aircraft granted to them, 54 Base Flight used aircraft from the squadrons based at Coningsby and Woodhall Spa. Leonard Cheshire's early acquisitions seem to be four Mosquitos, which were on charge with 617 Squadron under a loan arrangement with 571 Squadron. This in itself is unusual, in that a squadron normally operated only one type of aircraft on operations – often for ease of maintenance. With the support of General Carl Spaatz, commander of the US Strategic Air Forces in Europe, Cheshire's initiative in target marking was aided by the 'gifting' of a P-51 fighter and at least two P-38 Lightnings. However, it remains unclear whether these aircraft were 'Taken on Charge' – this being the formal acceptance of an aircraft by the RAF. However, by reference to pilots' log books and diaries, particularly that of Charles Owen, who served two tours of duty with 97 Squadron before his move to 54 Base Flight, it was possible for me to see both the variety of operations and the different aeroplanes they flew.

In using the term 'maverick' to describe the Master Bombers, I am still unsure whether these men who survived dozens of previous operations were, in their character, different from other airmen, or whether they were shaped by their experiences. The conclusion to this question is not easy to arrive at. In statistical terms, they were very lucky to have completed over forty operations – and often many more. All had lived through near-death episodes, and their ability to continue to fly competently is testament to a 'true grit' mentality.

In looking for accounts of the experiences of civilians on the ground who endured Allied air raids, finding translated testimonies is useful, but they are not always easy to attribute to an originator. The account by a French worker of the bombing at Porte de la Chapelle was translated from a French Second World War internet forum. The original source is unattributed –

the only information it provides as to its source is that it was from a letter from a French worker to his wife.

'Benny' Goodman's achievement of returning to Woodhall Spa with a sheared exhaust stub on 30 April 1944 is typical of the tenacity of the members of 627 Squadron. In conversation, Goodman's son Peter told me a story that illustrated perfectly his father's sheer doggedness. He described a car journey from London to Cornwall that they had made with a broken clutch cable. Not to be defeated, his father nursed the car homeward, trying not to stop, and gently crashing the gearbox whenever a change of gear was necessary. Such was the bloody-mindedness – and technical skill – that saw Goodman and Hickox safely home after technical difficulties forced them to abort their mission to Clermont-Ferrand.

Space constraints did not allow an analysis of the activities of other Mosquito squadrons during the spring of 1944, but in mentioning the gun-carrying NF Mk XIII, it is worth noting that the Luftwaffe greatly feared these prowling fighters. Improved from the earlier night fighter marks, this model had a greater range owing to its underwing tanks, which allowed it to fly deep into German airspace and loiter there, looking for targets. There are a number of cases of German twin-engined aircraft being lost to 'friendly fire' during this period, after being mistaken for a Mosquito.

CHAPTER EIGHT – THE BREAKING STORM

When I described the raid on Mailly-le-Camp in *The Crew*, I did so from the perspective of a Lancaster crew flying with 97 Squadron and therefore at a higher level than 627 Squadron. Goodman and Hickox's flight home and low-level escape over the harbour at Le Tréport has an interesting postscript. Jack Goodman subsequently visited the town and its harbour in the 1980s, and was astounded to see how low the lighthouse was. His survival was no doubt aided by the inability of the defending anti-aircraft guns to adjust their aim to such a low-flying aircraft.

Jack's son Peter remembers the impact on his father of the Mailly-le-Camp raid – in particular his concern at the number of French civilian casualties, which amounted to more than one hundred. In May 1987 Jack journeyed to Voué, south of the Mailly-le-Camp site, for a commemorative event. He was overwhelmed by the reception he received and particularly touched that the mayor, Louis Clément, assured him that the community had nothing but feelings of respect for the men of the RAF. When Goodman – along with other former RAF crew – returned to attend a memorial event at Mailly-le-Camp to celebrate the fiftieth anniversary of the attack on 7 May 1994, the warmth of the reception they received again far exceeded their expectations.

In researching life at RAF Woodhall Spa and other airfields, I have been surprised by the apparent lack of security at many of these bases during wartime. The assumption that military bases were protected by high security fences is commonplace, but inaccurate. The fact that ground crew were able to leave the airfield at Woodhall Spa unobserved to go to the bakery each day illustrates that even sensitive airfields were not especially secure. In the rush to build airfields in a time of war, the resources available did not stretch to anything more than low fencing around the airfield perimeter, consisting of wooden posts with pig wire stretched between them. There might be a single strand of barbed wire attached to the top, but this was more about deterring animals than preventing hostile incursion. German fighters of course attacked RAF airfields from the air, but there is no record of any land-based sabotage of an RAF air base by German agents.

I was delighted to have Jack Goodman's memories of the

arrival of the late-night piano player and soprano at Woodhall Spa corroborated by a second source. In the course of correspondence unrelated to this book, the son of Dental Officer Jock Stares wrote to me and mentioned his father playing the piano on the back of a lorry – a remarkable feat given the amount of alcohol he had apparently consumed at the time. Nor was this the most unusual sight glimpsed by the airmen of 627 Squadron. Perhaps the most bizarre occurrence was when elephants appeared out of the fog on a perimeter track. It seems that one fog-bound day the station commander gave circus owner Billy Smart permission to exercise his animals on his airfield.

'Benny' Goodman and 'Bill' Hickox's final raid on the Saumur rail yard on 1 June 1944 was spoken of by Goodman in later life. It was the inspiration for a painting by Don Breckon, currently held by the Royal Air Force Museum in Hendon, showing Goodman's Mosquito G-George, DZ484, after laying a red marker flare on the railway tracks. Intriguingly, the ORB entry for that day notes that Goodman and Hickox returned without dropping their flares. This entry appears to be inaccurate, not least because Goodman had commissioned Breckon to depict the scene of his final operation – so there seems little doubt that Goodman dropped his markers. The report attributed to another crew, Flying Officer Gribbin and Flight Lieutenant Griffiths in Mosquito DZ353, is strikingly similar to Goodman's, and it would seem that the notes made by the debriefing officer may have confused the two crews.

CHAPTER NINE – DOUGHBOYS

Ken Oatley, the last surviving member of 627 Squadron, recounted his fascinating family history during the course of phone conversations and a face-to-face meeting in his home in

Ipswich. Ken's son Rodger, who never took more than twenty-four hours to respond to my emails, was able to pass on his father's answers to some outstanding queries, including the vexed question of the location of 627 Squadron's officers' mess building, which has now long since disappeared.

James 'Jock' Walker's son Jim was able to provide a number of helpful insights into his father's life. Sadly, James did not live into old age, and said only a little about his exploits flying Mosquitos. However, it was possible to make an assessment of James's operations through the entries in Ken Oatley's log book and after-raid reports in the 627 Squadron ORB. The precise date of James Walker's 'tangle' with Guy Gibson is unknown, but from the gap in flying duties, we can assume it took place around 6 September 1944, approximately two weeks before Gibson perished on the way back from Mönchengladbach.

Over the past ten years I have met a significant number of people whose relatives had some contact, often fleetingly, with Guy Gibson. Their accounts have formed the basis of my character study of Gibson. A fascinating combination of brilliance and luck is clearly central to his life story, but for all the weight of his achievements, there were clearly many who found his personality somewhat difficult. Gibson's ill-fated final operation has been the subject of much debate and speculation over the years. In *The Crew* I leant strongly towards the view that Lancaster tail gunner Sergeant Bernard McCormack of 61 Squadron had accidentally shot at Gibson's Mosquito, damaging it and causing it to crash. In my interview with Ken Oatley, he was firmly of the opinion that Gibson ran out of fuel because his navigator, Warwick, was unable to find the fuel transfer cocks located behind the pilot's seat.

This alternative view of the causes of the crash led me to research McCormack's account further. In the light of low-level target marking and Guy Gibson's declared intention to fly the return leg at low altitude, it seemed unlikely that he would have appeared behind a Lancaster flying at 11,000 feet. I looked again at 61 Squadron's ORB, where the raid report by McCormack's fellow crew members makes no mention of an approaching aircraft. (Later, McCormack would say that he believed the aircraft was a Junkers Ju 88.) Moreover, 61 Squadron's summary of events for the night notes the following: 'fighter flares were seen but no fighters encountered'. This omission from the ORB is all the more curious, in that McCormack claimed to have shot the aircraft down – an action that would surely have merited an entry in the report. Even though the gunner came to believe that his action had brought down Gibson's Mosquito, at the time of landing and debriefing, McCormack would still have thought he had attacked a German aircraft – since Gibson's failure to return would not yet have been known. While some might argue that records were subsequently altered to maintain Gibson's heroic status, I can find no evidence of this. The loss of Gibson on 19 September occurred just eleven days before the monthly records were signed and despatched to the Air Ministry. There was, therefore, little time to make the connection with Gibson, particularly since the location of his crash only became known much later.

CHAPTER TEN – TRIUMPH AND TRAGEDY

The extent of losses to non-operational flying in the Second World War, both during airmen's training or at operational air bases, is not fully appreciated. Aircraft lost or damaged in incidents ran into the tens of thousands, with the estimate of airmen thus killed standing at around 8,000 – some 2,700 more than the total of British servicemen lost in all conflicts since. There is a depressing familiarity to the circumstances of the accident involving Flight Lieutenant Bland and Flying

Officer Cornell. Despite its glowing reputation in the air, the Mosquito's high stalling speed – the point at which the aircraft ceases to fly – was 120 mph with wheels and flaps retracted. Although it has not been possible to fully expand on the causes of the various Mosquito crashes described in this book, the aircraft's high stall speed was often the most significant contributing factor.

As a native of Cumbria, I was delighted to find that John Herriman and Eric Arthur had such close connections to Carlisle and the house on Kingmoor Road – somewhere I pass frequently. In correspondence with Eric Arthur's son, Alan, I found that Eric had made a return visit to England in June 2012 for the opening of the Bomber Command Memorial at Green Park. He had also travelled on to Woodhall Spa to visit his old haunts around the airfield. Eric passed away in June 2019, only months before research for this book began, but the freshness of his accounts is borne out in Alan Arthur's webpages about his father. It is first-hand material of this sort, often containing a wealth of small but telling personal details, that are a godsend to an author.

It is interesting to note that John Herriman's and Eric Arthur's friendship continued after the war in Australia, both men making visits to see each other. making visits to see each other. Sadly, this relationship was cut short by John's untimely death in a road accident in 1962. In the close working environment of the Mosquito cockpit, all the crews had to have a degree of closeness that often imitated friendship, but in the case of Herriman and Arthur, there is no doubt as to the strength of their bond.

I have made a number of visits to the French département of Charente-Maritime, and particularly to the Île d'Oléron, twenty miles north of Royan. For some years I was puzzled by a small war memorial at the side of the road leading to a popular beach at Le Grand-Village-Plage. This small obelisk, listing the names of just five men, is passed every year by hundreds of holidaymakers carrying beach bags and surf boards to relax on the white sands of the Atlantic coast. It commemorates those lost on 30 April 1945 in a full-scale amphibious landing there by American and Free French forces. Coming so close to the end of the war, it illustrates the impatience of the French to achieve their final liberation. The tragedy of losing men against a force of around 2,000 beleaguered and completely surrounded Germans so close to Germany's capitulation is indeed poignant.

Although the action against Royan four months earlier, in January 1945, may be seen as more strategically important, the destruction it wreaked on the city far outstripped its significance as a German defensive position. The level of civilian losses in Royan cannot escape censure, and the cavalier attitude shown by French commanders in requesting the attack is particularly inexcusable. The title of 'Martyred City' sits uncomfortably in the list of other French conurbations caught in fighting after D-Day. Accounts suggest the unnamed American intelligence officer who liaised with the French – and whose recommendations formed the substance of SHAEF's decision to strike – was later disciplined. There is some suggestion, notably from socialist writers, that the inhabitants of Royan fell victim to centuries of distrust on account of their Protestant tendencies. The siege of the Protestant stronghold of Royan by Louis XIII in 1622 was short-lived, with many of the Huguenots fleeing northwards towards La Rochelle. The king's inability to fully suppress the Huguenots lives on in the region's spirit of independent thinking – something the author has experienced first-hand. Clearly, in the context of 627 Squadron actions, no blame can be attached to the airmen, who, at all times, had to trust the judgement of Bomber Command raid planners.

The account of Pastor Samuel Besançon is particularly significant in the context of Royan. Besançon continued to live in Royan after the war, and his collection of memories gleaned from other survivors of the attack was finally published in 2000, *Croix sur Royan: Cahiers d'un resistant*.

CHAPTER ELEVEN – DÉNOUEMENT

My account of the Dresden raid of 13 February 1945 centres on Ken Oatley's experience of the event as a member of 627 Squadron, and is based on his testimony. I make no attempt to describe the wider strategic background to the raid, and the deep controversy that later attached to it owing to the appalling loss of German civilian lives. Other writers, notably Frederick Taylor, *Dresden: Tuesday, 13 February 1945* (2004) and Sinclair McKay, *Dresden: The Fire and the Darkness* (2020), have written of these matters with clarity, sensitivity and insight.

In describing the Rhine crossings at Remagen and Wesel, my intention was to illustrate, at this key point in the war, the overall strength of the Allied forces poised to cross this most important waterway. Having spent many hours on the battlefields of the First World War, I am struck by how far both Germany and the Allies had progressed in their technology in the twenty-six years intervening. The crossing of a river as wide as the Rhine in 1918 would have been a hugely costly affair, if it would have been possible at all. I am reminded of the struggle faced by my grandfather in July 1917 to cross the narrow Yser Canal at the village of Boesinghe, three miles north of the devasted city of Ypres. Getting his battery of 18lb guns over the remains of the canal and the sea of mud on both sides of it took the best part of two days.

The action at Wesel stands out as 627 Squadron's most prominent and direct attack on German ground forces in the field, but the damaging effect of its operations against transport hubs and war manufacturing sites should not be underestimated. Unlike in the First World War, in which supply lines to hundreds of thousands of German troops continued to function relatively unhindered, in 1944–45 Allied attacks on German railheads, bridges and oil refineries greatly weakened the Wehrmacht's ability to move, supply and feed its armies.

EPILOGUE

To write fully about what happened to the men of 627 Squadron in the immediate aftermath of the war would have filled several further volumes. In the Epilogue I was able to provide only a few brief lines on the generally happy and fulfilling lives these men lived after the war, most of them marrying, forging careers and having families. In their gentle passing, we are left with a paper trail of life.

My visits to RAF Woodhall Spa and RAF Coningsby have always been immensely rewarding, and have provided me with the opportunity to witness the modern RAF at work. Like many other former RAF airfields I have visited, Woodhall Spa is now in a state of decay. Each airfield deserves to be immaculately preserved in the memory of the airmen who were stationed there and gave their lives in the service of their country, but this is, of course, impossible. The sheer number of airfields that were built, and whose crumbling remains scatter our countryside, is both astonishing and rather humbling. Often hidden behind hedges and fences, they receive few visitors, yet for those who retain an interest in them, they are, in their size and impotent majesty, haunting and atmospheric places.

Bibliography

Ambrose, Stephen, *D-Day* (Simon & Schuster 1994)

Barker, Ralph, *Strike Hard, Strike Sure* (Pan 1965)

Bending, Kevin, *Achieve Your Aim* (Woodfield Publishing 2007)

Beevor, Antony, *Berlin: The Downfall, 1945* (Viking 2002)

Beevor, Antony, *Ardennes* (Viking 2015)

Bennett, Don CT, *Pathfinder* (Frederick Muller Ltd 1958)

Brickhill, Paul, *The Dam Busters* (Evans Brothers Ltd 1951)

Chorlton, Martyn, *The RAF Pathfinders* (Countryside Books 2012)

Churchill, Winston, *The Gathering Storm* (Cassell 1948)

Cooper, Alan W, *Beyond the Dams to the Tirpitz: The Later Operations of 617 Squadron* (William Kimber and Co. 1983)

Currie, Jack, *Battle Under the Moon: The RAF Raid on Mailly-le-Camp, May 1944* (Crecy 1995)

Feast, Sean, *Master Bombers* (Grubb Street 2008)

Fort, Adrian, *Prof: The Life and Times of Frederick Lindemann* (Vintage Publishing 2004)

Gibson, Guy, *Enemy Coast Ahead – Uncensored* (Crecy 2003)

Hampton, James, *Selected for Aircrew* (Air Research Publications 1993)

Harris, Arthur, *Bomber Offensive* (Collins 1947)

Hastings, Max, *Bomber Command* (Michael Joseph Ltd 1979)

Hastings, Max, *Catastrophe* (William Collins 2013)

Hinsley, Francis Harry, *British Intelligence in the Second World War* (Cambridge University Press 1979)

Johnson, Boris, *The Churchill Factor* (Hodder 2014)

Keegan, John, *Six Armies in Normandy* (Jonathan Cape 1982)

Kershaw, Ian, *The End* (Allen Lane 2011)

Lee, Michael, *Marg and Don* (Michael Lee 2018)

Levine, Joshua, *Forgotten Voices of the Blitz and the Battle for Britain* (Ebury Press 2006)

Lovell, Bernard, *Echoes of War* (CRC Press 1991)

Lowe, Keith, *Savage Continent* (Viking 2012)

Lyman, Robert, *The Jail Busters: The Secret Story of MI6, the French Resistance and Operation Jericho* (Quercus 2014)

McKay, Sinclair, *The Secret Life of Bletchley Park* (Aurum Press 2010)

McLoughlin, Roy, *Living with the Enemy* (Starlight 1995)

Mead, Richard: *Dambuster-in-Chief: The Life of Air Chief Marshal Sir Ralph Cochrane* (Pen and Sword Publishing 2020)

Middlebrook, Martin, and Everitt, Chris, *The Bomber Command War Diaries* (Midland 1996)

Middlebrook, Martin, *Mosquito Mayhem: De Havilland's Wooden Wonder in Action in WWII* (Pen and Sword 2010)

Overy, Richard, *The Bombing War* (Allen Lane 2013)

Price, David, *A Bomber Crew Mystery* (Pen & Sword 2014)

Price, David, *The Crew: The story of a Lancaster Bomber Crew* (Head of Zeus 2020)

Redmond, Ian, *Bloody Terrified: The True Story of a Pathfinder Crew* (independently published 2020)

Ross, David, *Richard Hillary: The Authorised Biography of a Second World War Fighter Pilot* (Grubb Street Publishing 2008)

Rees, Laurence, *Hitler and Stalin: The tyrants and the Second World War* (Penguin 2020)

Stokes, Raymond G, *The Oil Industry in Nazi Germany, 1936–1945* (The President and Fellows of Harvard College 1985)

The Air Ministry, *The Rise and Fall of the German Air Force* (The Air Ministry 1948)

Uhl, Matthais and Eberle, Henrikby, *The Hitler Book* (Public Affairs US 2006)

Wells, Mark K, *Courage and Air Warfare: The allied aircrew experience in the Second World War* (Routledge 1995)

Wrench, John Evelyn, *Struggle 1914–1920* (Ivor Nicholson & Watson Ltd 1935)

Wilson, Kevin, *Bomber Boys* (Cassell 2005)

Web Sources

Chapter 1

Loss of W4055 Trondheim: https://aviation-safety.net/wikibase/70524

Loss of W4056: https://aviation-safety.net/wikibase/70523

Ian Hutchinson: http://www.bbm.org.uk/airmen/HutchinsonI.htm

Bristol Blenheim: http://www.kbobm.org/blenheim_project.html

Herbert Huppertz: http://www.cieldegloire.com/_001_huppertz_h.php

Norwegian airfields : http://www.ww2.dk/Airfields%20-%20Norway.pdf

HE Bevan, Jimmy, survivor of Lancaster JB567: http://www.omclub.co.uk/news/h-e-bevan-jimmy-1911-2009-mhs-25-29

John Lovelace Tucker (casualty): https://www.cwgc.org/find-war-dead/casualty/2046538/tucker,-john-lovelace/

Casualty details – Tucker: http://www.rafcommands.com/database/wardead/details.php?qnum=46051

Loss of Oakeshott: https://aviation-safety.net/wikibase/205722

Churchill's reaction to Singapore: https://winstonchurchill.org/publications/finest-hour/finest-hour-169/churchill-and-the-fall-of-singapore/

Oslo attack: http://ww2today.com/25th-september-1942-raf-bomb-gestapo-hq-in-oslo

Interview with Parry: https://www.iwm.org.uk/collections/item/object/80014889

Ball bearing run and Shetland Bus: https://www.secret-bases.co.uk/wiki/Shetland_bus

Parry and Robson's trip to Stockholm: https://www.bbc.co.uk/history/ww2peopleswar/stories/16/a2679816.shtml

Chapter 2

MacRobertson air race: https://www.thisdayinaviation.com/tag/de-havilland-dh-88-comet/

https://web.archive.org/web/20040404081435/http://www.dc3airways.com/1934-1.html

https://terencecgannon.medium.com/the-comet-64962ce642ce

Geoffrey de Havilland: https://www.rafmuseum.org.uk/research/archive-exhibitions/de-havilland-the-man-and-the-company/captain-sir-geoffrey-de-havilland.aspx

https://www.baesystems.com/en/heritage/de-havilland-no1-biplane--1909-

Balsa wood: https://www.heraldnet.com/life/wood-from-around-the-globe-made-the-de-havilland-mosquito/

BAE description: https://www.baesystems.com/en/heritage/de-havilland-mosquito

Full production list: http://www.airhistory.org.uk/dh/_DH98%20prodn%20list.txt

Mosquito prototype: https://shortfinals.org/2013/09/10/the-start-of-it-all-w4050-the-mosquito-prototype/

Karl Richter: https://www.hertsmemories.org.uk/content/herts-history/towns-and-villages/london_colney/a_german_spy_in_london_colney#:~:text=On%2013th%20May%20

1941%2C%20during,a%20lorry%20driver%20seeking%20directions.

https://www.dehavillandmuseum.co.uk/aircraft/de-havilland-dh98-mosquito-prototype/

105 Squadron and early operations: https://thewoodenwonder.org.uk/de-havilland-mosquito-history

Mosquito NF Mk II: http://www.historyofwar.org/articles/weapons_mosquito_II.html

Bomber Command losses: https://www.awm.gov.au/wartime/25/article

Arthur Harris: https://www.rafmuseum.org.uk/documents/Research/RAF-Historical-Society-Journals/Bomber_harris.pdf

RAF kit bags: https://talesfromthesupplydepot.blog/2015/03/15/raf-kit-bag/

Issued clothing: https://rafvrtrainingwwii.wordpress.com/scale-of-issue/

HMT *River Spey*: https://drojkent.wordpress.com/2014/10/18/trawler-teapots-the-story-of-hmt-river-spey/

Lack of Moral Fibre: https://www.kcl.ac.uk/kcmhr/publications/assetfiles/historical/jones2006-lmf.pdf

Berlin raids, November 1943: https://www.berlinexperiences.com/battle-of-berlin-november-22nd-1943/

Manfred Gräber: https://www.pbs.
org/wgbh/americanexperience/
features/bombing-manfred-
graber/

Chapter 3

Career: https://www.rafweb.org/
Biographies/BennettD.htm
https://adb.anu.edu.au/biography/
bennett-donald-clifford-
don-12194
210 Squadron: https://www.
westerntelegraph.co.uk/
news/18548431.bomber-harris-
flew-pembroke-dock/

Jimmy Woods: http://www.
airwaysmuseum.com/
Lockheed%20DL-1A%20
Vega%20VH-UVK%20&%20
Jimmy%20Woods.htm
10 Squadron attack on Tirpitz:
http://www.archieraf.co.uk/
archie/1041zab.html

Chapter 4

John Hickox: http://www.
wycombeworldonline.co.uk/a-
lifetime-in-aviation-the-flying-
life-of-a-j-l-bill-hickox/

Chapter 5

Shanghai: https://foreignpolicy.
com/2012/08/13/the-rise-and-
fall-and-rise-of-new-shanghai/
SS *Plassy*: http://www.roll-
of-honour.com/Ships/
HMTroopshipPlassy.html
Service career: http://www.
conscript-heroes.com/Escaper-
Evaders.html
http://www.conscript-heroes.com/
Art48-Lockhart-960.html
http://aircrewremembered.com/
william-lockhart-dso-dfc-and-
bar.html
Norbert Fillerin: https://

translate.google.com/
translate?hl=en&sl=fr&u=
https://resistancepasdecalais.
fr/norbert-fillerin-1897-
1977/&prev=search&pto=aue
http://www.rafcommands.com/
forum/showthread.php?7073-
Lancaster-JB676-MG-K-7-Sqn-
RAF&highlight=LOCKHART&
p=40643#post40643
RAF Warmwell: https://
web.archive.org/
web/20080118155145/http://
daveg40tu.tripod.com/dorset/
war.html

RAF Lichfield: http://www.raf-lichfield.co.uk/OTUindex.htm

Bremen, 29 November: https://www.americanairmuseum.com/mission/1538

Fahey, Wiluna: https://trove.nla.gov.au/newspaper/article/75993029

1665 Mosquito Training Unit:

https://raf-pathfinders.com/training-the-mosquito-crews/

Edward Bell: https://www.saintsplayers.co.uk/player/edward-bell/

Francis Evans: https://kingscollections.org/warmemorials/kings-college/memorials/evans-francis-kent

Chapter 6

Crawford Priory: https://adcochrane.wordpress.com/2014/01/06/crawford-priory-riddle-of-a-ruin/

https://www.thecastlesofscotland.co.uk/the-best-castles/other-articles/crawford-priory/

Leonard Cheshire: https://rewind.leonardcheshire.org/spotlight/leonard-cheshires-raf-career/

https://www.lincolnshirelife.co.uk/posts/view/group-captain-leonard-cheshire-vc-om-dso-and-two-bars-dfc

Chapter 7

617 Squadron RAF 1943: http://eprints.hud.ac.uk/id/eprint/25017/1/THE...10615-PDF_.pdf

Porte de la Chappelle raid: https://ww2today.com/21-april-1944-heavy-civilian-casualties-as-the-allies-bomb-paris

https://www.skyscrapercity.com/threads/paris-under-the-bombs.830546/8th Air Force over Munich

http://www.wwiiaircraftperformance.org/24april44.html

Norman Jackson VC: http://aircrewremembered.com/mifflin-frederick-manuel.html

https://medium.com/raf-caps/one-night-in-april-1944-a-tale-of-courage-and-fortitude-sergeant-later-wo-norman-jackson-vc-c2f0dc71296f

Luftwaffe Airfields 1935–45: https://www.ww2.dk/Airfields%20-%20France.pdf

Luftwaffe doctrine and practice: https://www.tandfonline.com/doi/full/10.1080/1470243042000344803

Chapter 8

Mailly-le-Camp: https://www.
memorialflightclub.com/blog/75-
years-ago-%E2%80%93-
mailly-le-camp-raid

https://www.northlincsweb.
net/103Sqn/html/the_mailly_
raid.html

https://d-dayrevisited.co.uk/
veterans/erich-bissoir/

Memoirs: https://www.bbc.co.uk/
history/ww2peopleswar/
stories/71/a6660371.shtml

https://www.49squadron.co.uk/
assets/pdf/ron_eeles.pdf

German anti-aircraft artillery:
https://stephentaylorhistorian.
files.wordpress.com/2020/02/
german-aa-weapons.pdf

21 Panzer Division defensive:
http://www.spearhead1944.com/
gerpg/21ger_rec.htm

Preparations for D-Day: https://
www.historynet.com/pre-
invasion-madness-in-england-
the-final-days-before-d-day.htm

Exercise Tiger: https://www.
historic-uk.com/HistoryUK/
HistoryofBritain/Exercise-Tiger/

Atlantic Wall: http://www.dday.
center/d-day-technology-
atlantic-wall.html

France under occupation: https://
www.keene.edu/academics/ah/
cchgs/resources/educational-
handouts/france-under-
occupation/download/

Luftwaffe bomber development:
https://www.luftkrieg-
ueber-europa.de/en/
why-did-the-german-
luftwaffe-have-no-strategic-
bomber-fleets-at-its-disposal/

Tours airfield: https://www.ww2.
dk/Airfields%20-%20France.
pdf

https://ww2today.com/7-may-1944-
attacks-on-french-airfields-are-
stepped-up

Chapter 9

Ronnie Churcher: https://www.
independent.co.uk/news/
obituaries/group-captain-
ronnie-churcher-raf-bomber-
pilot-who-worked-with-guy-
gibson-and-served-in-the-
king-s-flight-and-queen-s-
flight-8983776.html

Armstrong Whitworth Whiley
T41418: http://www.yorkshire-
aircraft.co.uk/aircraft/planes/
dales/t4148.html

Sir Charles Oatley: http://
www-g.eng.cam.ac.uk/125/
achievements/oatley/cw01.
htm

Sir John Cockroft: https://www.
chu.cam.ac.uk/news/2017/
sep/19/celebrating-sir-john-
cockcroft/

Chapter 10

Reg Cornell: https:// internationalbcc.co.uk/about-ibcc/news/memories/flying-officer-navigator-reginald-henry-cornell/

Coningsby churchyard: http://www. aeroresource.co.uk/historic-reports/coningsby-burials-lest-we-forget/

Loss of Mosquito KB366: https://aviation-safety.net/ wikibase/168056

Bob Burrows: https://www. heroesofourtime.co.uk/tapestry-of-time.html

Eric Arthur: http://alanandric. blogspot.com/

Sinking of Tirpitz: https://www. thehistorypress.co.uk/articles/ the-sinking-of-hitler-s-battleship-tirpitz/

Aarhus and Oslo attacks: https:// ww2today.com/31-december-1944-oslo-tragedy-as-raf-mosquitos-attack-gestapo-hq

Gunnar Sønsteby: https://www. smh.com.au/national/gestapos-most-wanted-was-master-of-disguise-20120517-1ysrx.html

Attacks on Gestapo buildings: https://www.warandson.co.uk/ index.php/news/39-gestapo-hunters-mosquitoes-buzzing-and-stinging-the-nazi-ss

V-2 rocket attacks: https:// heritagecalling.com/2019/11/25/ devastating-v2-rocket-attack-on-woolworths-new-cross-london/

French at Dunkirk: https:// theconversation.com/what-happened-to-the-french-army-after-dunkirk-80854

Churchill, de Gaulle and Roosevelt: https://winstonchurchill.org/ publications/finest-hour/finest-hour-157/churchill-proceedings-how-charles-de-gaulle-saw-the-anglo-saxon-relationship/

Royan: https://www.c-royan. com/histoire/histoire-contemporaine/les-guerres/1575-le-bombardement-de-royan. html&prev=search&pto=aue

Chapter 11

1655 Mosquito Training Unit: https://wingcotomjefferson. wordpress.com/1655-mtu-raf-warboys/

Ostrahege Stadium: https:// en.wikipedia.org/wiki/ Ostragehege

Bill Topper audio account: https:// www.iwm.org.uk/collections/ item/object/80015851

Churchill and Dresden: https:// winstonchurchill.org/resources/ myths/churchill-bombed-dresden-as-payback-for-coventry/

https://1d4vws37vmp124vlehy
goxxd-wpengine.netdna-ssl.com/
wp-content/uploads/2008/08/
Harmon__Are%20We%20
Beasts___np1%5B1%5D.pdf

https://core.ac.uk/download/
pdf/44341094.pdf

Dresden: https://www.history.
com/news/dresden-bombing-
wwii-allies#:~:text=The%20
punishing%2C%20
three%2Dday%20
Allied,and%20decimated%20
the%20German%20city.

Bohlen bomb aimers briefing,
19 February 1945: https://
ibccdigitalarchive.lincoln.
ac.uk/omeka/collections/
document/7255.

Last V-2 attack on London: http://
www.westendatwar.org.uk/
page_id__248.aspx

Mosquito DZ599: https://
aviation-safety.net/
wikibase/71802

Stalag X-A: http://www.alte-
schleihalle.de/stalag-xa-
schleswig-hesterberg/

John Day: https://
aviationmuseumwa.org.
au/afcraaf-roll/day-john-
alfred-431092/

Vallø: http://www.ipernity.com/
doc/146318/41773522

Kingsford-Smith: https://www.
bchg.org.au/index.php/en/
people/individuals/g-k/148-
kingsford-smith-rollo

Epilogue

Tinian: https://www.atomicheritage.
org/location/tinian-island

Leonard Cheshire: https://www.
atomicheritage.org/profile/

leonard-cheshire

https://www.iwm.org.
uk/collections/item/
object/80009644

Acknowledgements

Special thanks are extended to:

   Ken Oatley
   Rodger Oakley
   James Walker
   Tanya Bruce-Lockhart
   Max de Boos
   Peter Goodman
   Alan Arthur
   Dave Hunter

Their assistance and attention to detail have been invaluable in the research for this book. Special thanks are also due to Andy Bird who provided additional technical editorial advice. The author also acknowledges the wealth of information provided by others, too many to name, whose contribution formed a small but essential part of this story.

The author also wishes to thank his agent, Charlie Viney (The Viney Agency), for his support through this project, his editor, Richard Milbank, and all the staff at Head of Zeus who have made this book possible.

Image Credits

Every effort has been made to credit owners of the photographs. If you are an owner and have not been credited, please contact us so that we can rectify this in later editions.

Index